SONG, DANCE AND POETRY OF
THE COURT OF SCOTLAND
UNDER KING JAMES VI

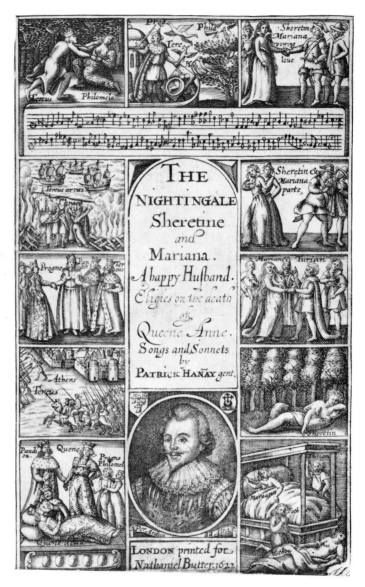

Title page of Patrick Hannay's *Philomela* (London, 1622)

SONG, DANCE AND POETRY OF THE COURT OF SCOTLAND UNDER KING JAMES VI

BY

HELENA MENNIE SHIRE

*Senior Research Fellow in Arts of the
Carnegie Trust for the Universities of Scotland, 1961-3*

*Musical illustrations of Court-song
edited by* KENNETH ELLIOTT

CAMBRIDGE
AT THE UNIVERSITY PRESS
1969

Published by the Syndics of the Cambridge University Press
Bentley House, 200 Euston Road, London N.W.1
American Branch: 32 East 57th Street, New York, N.Y.10022

Library of Congress Catalogue Card Number: 69–13793

Standard Book Number: 521 07181 x

Printed in Great Britain
at the University Printing House, Cambridge
(Brooke Crutchley, University Printer)

CONTENTS

v

CONTENTS

ILLUSTRATIONS

MUSICAL ILLUSTRATIONS

PLATES

To keep in mind
my father and mother
from whom I learned to love Scottish song,
the words—John H. Mennie
and the music—Jane E. Rae

ACKNOWLEDGEMENTS

The composition and writing of this book was made possible by the support of the Carnegie Trust for the Universities of Scotland who, with generosity and imagination, were willing to back a project of Scottish research undertaken by a Scots graduate 'furth of the realm'.

I am much in dept to certain scholars for help and advice, criticism of work in progress and inspiring exchange of ideas: Professor Thurston Dart, Professor Philip Brett, Dr John Stevens and Mr Charles Cudworth; the late Dr Harry M. Willsher; Professor Bruce Dickins and Mr Matthew P. McDiarmid, Dr George Henderson and Mr David Barrass; the Reverend Mark Dilworth and Dr Robert Bolgar. To Dr Kenneth Elliott, my colleague in research for *Music of Scotland 1500–1700*, I owe companionship of interest and his kind help and skill in editing the musical illustrations for this volume. (The foot-notes marked 'K.E.' are those for which he was responsible.) I am grateful to him, to Professor Vincent Duckles and Dr John McQuaid for permission to quote from or cite their unpublished doctoral dissertations.

Acknowledgements for songs quoted from *Music of Scotland 1500–1700* and *Musa Jocosa Mihi* are due to the Royal Musical Association and Messrs Stainer and Bell Ltd; the plates are reproduced by permission of the Public Record Office (1), the National Museum of Antiquities of Scotland (2,3 a and b), and the Library of Congress (4). Many libraries have allowed me to quote and publish from their music manuscripts or early printed books or have made available photostats in their care: the National Library of Scotland, the Bibliothèque Nationale, the libraries of the Universities of Edinburgh and Aberdeen, of Oxford and Cambridge, the British Museum, the Sandeman Public Library, Perth, the libraries of Trinity College, Dublin and of the Universities of California at Berkeley and at Los Angeles.

It is a pleasure to give formal thanks to libraries for service and permission; but it is beyond my power to express gratitude for individual acts of kindness experienced over years from individual librarians, some firm friends, some unknown and anonymous.

My warm thanks are due to the Cambridge University Press for their encouragement and assistance.

HELENA M. SHIRE

ABBREVIATIONS

B.M.	British Museum
C.N.R.S.	Centre National de la Recherche Scientifique
Cal.S.P.	Calendar of State Papers
E.E.T.S.	Early English Text Society
H.E.G.S.	*Historia Ecclesiastica Gentis Scotorum*
H.M.S.O.	Her Majesty's Stationery Office
L.H.T.A.	Lord High Treasurer's Accounts (Scotland)
J.A.M.S.	Journal of the American Musicological Society
S.T.S.	Scottish Text Society

The title of a work printed in italics refers to that work in print, either contemporary or in a subsequent edition. A title within quotation marks but not italicised refers to the work as current in manuscript, for example 'The Cherrie and the Slae', 'Rob Stene's Dream', or 'The Histoire and Life of King James the Sext'. '*The Gude and Godlie Ballatis*', though a nickname, is the title under which the Compendius Book was printed for the S.T.S. For the music manuscripts, the titles have not been placed in quotation marks.

Some minor details of Scottish spelling have been adjusted where the meaning might be unclear and where the exact transcription is available in print.

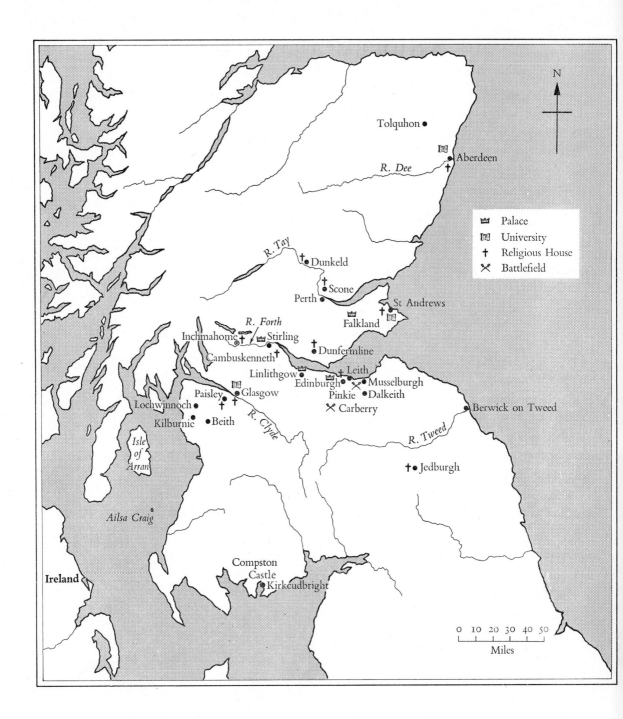

N

Tolquhon •

R. Dee

Aberdeen

👑	Palace
📖	University
†	Religious House
✕	Battlefield

† Dunkeld
R. Tay
† Scone
Perth •
St Andrews
Falkland

R. Forth
Inchmahome • Stirling
† Dunfermline
Cambuskenneth
Linlithgow † Leith
Edinburgh • Musselburgh
Paisley Glasgow Pinkie • Dalkeith
Lochwinnoch ✕ Carberry
Kilburnie • Beith
R. Clyde
Berwick on Tweed

Isle
of
Arran
R. Tweed

† • Jedburgh

Ailsa Craig

Ireland

Compston
Castle
• Kirkcudbright

0 10 20 30 40 50
Miles

Sketch map for sixteenth-century Scotland

INTRODUCTION

COURT-SONG OF SIXTEENTH-CENTURY SCOTLAND

THE SIXTEENTH century was a great one in the music of western Europe, an age distinguished in the cultivation of court-song. On the occasions when the development of music in western Europe is described, small mention if any is made of musical culture in Scotland during those hundred years—the last decades of the Middle Ages and the first of the Renaissance in a remote northern kingdom[1]. Yet during that great century of part-writing there was part-music composed and enjoyed there, part-song sacred and secular, indigenous to the country and in touch with the music of France, England and the Netherlands, even with that of far-away Italy.

As long as Scotland had a court, a repertory of art-song existed, changing and developing in its own way, somehow surviving periods of violence when court-life itself was in abeyance. The sacred part-music of the Catholic Church was succeeded by the part-music of the Reformed Kirk. As late as 1632, when King Charles was to visit his northern kingdom—a kingdom deprived of a resident court since the Union of the Crowns in 1603—a body of 'old Scotch musick' was in being; its presence on the shelves of the Chapel Royal in Scotland was noted, alongside 'all sorts of English, French, Dutch, Spaynish, Latin and Italian' music vocal and instrumental.[2] This repertory of part-music never reached print but for the issues of one late and isolated part-book. By 1701 it had passed from memory.

An anthology of this early Scottish part-music of church and court was published for the first time in the national series *Musica Britannica* as volume XV, *Music of Scotland 1500–1700*.[3] This anthology ranges from mass and motet of Latin church music to fine psalm-setting whose words are in the vernacular, from early unaccompanied dance-song to four-part song in the *chanson* style, from *air-de-cour* to regional dance-song, and it includes instrumental music for viols, for cittern and for keyboard.

---

[1] See introductory note to Bibliography.

[2] 'Information touching the Chapell-Royal of Scotland'—a letter to the King from E. Kellie, January 1631/2 printed in Dauney, Appendix IV.

[3] Edited by Kenneth Elliott, song texts edited by Helena Mennie Shire. Introduction and notes etc. by Elliott and Shire (1957); second edition (1964) gives new sources and a list of publications in this field.

Of this music only a remnant survives from what must have been a rich repertory, for years of violence and neglect had done their work of destruction. Indeed the dice of history were weighted against the very production of courtly part-music in Scotland: over the hundred years from 1503 to 1603 there were short periods only when there existed at all in Scotland the stable court culture centred on an adult monarch that would seem to provide the minimal condition of growth for court-song. Yet court-song there was, and enough of it survives to show creative vitality overcoming the severest odds. Future historians of music in western Europe must find room not only for a tribute to Scotland's treasury of 'folk-song'—music of the regional dance-song and of traditional balladry—but also for consideration of its cultivation of part-writing sacred and secular, its contribution to art-song of courtly ambience. Art-song of the court in sixteenth-century Scotland, its character, its origins and its history, is the subject of these studies.

Court-song is song enjoyed by a courtly company. It may be engendered in that company or received into it from courtly circles elsewhere or it may enter from another social milieu. Court-song is art-song, the work of a skilled musician. In the sixteenth century it was usually part-song, in three or in four parts apt for viols or voices; such song might on occasion be rendered by the single voice and lute. The Scots had a term for such song: part-writing sacred or secular, for voices or instruments, was known as *musik fyne* or *fine musick*. (The phrase appears as entitling in the music manuscripts.) Words and music of other ambience—'popular song' or 'folk-song', regional dance-air of Scotland or international dance-tune, even on occasion music of the church—might by adoption and grooming become court-song. Contrariwise, after birth or breeding as a song of the court, as *musik fyne*, a court-song might pass outwards to castle, burgh or song-school into a wide and varied currency.

Court-song of Scotland is court-song of the sixteenth century: we can study only what has happened to survive the violent courses of Stewart history, and the destructive force of the Reformation. During the Middle Ages there was courtly making of words and music round the Scottish monarch; that we know from traveller's description, from accounts of royal expenditure and from the poetry of the period. Indeed a festal song in Latin has come down to us from an occasion of state in early times, the wedding of Princess Margaret of Scotland to King Eric II of Norway, in 1290.[1] But the earliest pieces in the vernacular whose age we know come from the year 1503, from the social celebrations of the marriage of King James IV to the English Princess, Margaret Tudor. The songs are part-songs, 'Now fayre, fayrest off every fayre...Welcum of Scotland to be Quene' and '...red rosse fayre and sote of

[1] John Beveridge, 'Two Scottish Thirteenth-century Songs'.

sent'.[1] Both songs have survived in fragment only. Both songs were recorded in English manuscripts, brought back doubtless by returning wedding guests. To judge by the sense of the words, the second song may be English in origin whereas the first is patently Scottish.

Of court life under King James IV we are well informed. A detailed and perceptive account was given by a visitor from Spain, de Ayala, while a rich and humorous picture of the King and the company about him, their personalities, pastimes and celebrations, rises from the pages of the poet William Dunbar. The Treasurers' Accounts show a Household Music of some strength and a Chapel Royal set up afresh in princely style in the year 1501.[2] We know that during this king's lifetime and through the decades that followed there was fine sacred music being written in Scotland notably by Robert Carver, Canon of Scone. But from that reign and that court no trace of the music of secular song can now be found, other than the fragmentary wedding pieces.

King James IV and his court were defeated in battle and destroyed in 1513 at Flodden Field. This disaster meant an infant prince on the throne, a foreign Lord Governor in office who was for the most part *in absentia* abroad and a Queen Mother unsuited to rule who married and remarried among her subjects. The infant King was brought up in safe retirement at Stirling. To speak of court-life in the public sense we must wait ten years until his adolescence.

This prince, King James V, was musical and musically educated and he wrote verse with skill and ease. His formal education was put an end to early in his 'teens. In 1524 a powerful faction 'planted in his hand the government of all Scotland'. With the Queen Mother of their party, they or other power groups indulged and debauched the youthful King but kept him for some years 'in cure', under their control. This period has been described by David Lyndsay in verses of satiric vein. We know that the King's entourage was not without its poetry and music, 'plays' and minstrelsy. But of court-song, words and music complete, again nothing has come down to us, though some fine sacred music has survived.

A third phase of King James's life-story sees him escaped from this bondage and attaining rule in his own person. From 1528 he was head of a lively court of lords and ladies, favourites and mistresses, where royal favour was the way to 'win lands'. Here the social pleasures were actively pursued, riding and the chase, music and the dance, mummings and masquerades, games like the Italian *giuochi* and 'plays' or mimic performances. The young Stewart King was 'King of Love' in a court where

---

[1] 'Now fayre' B.M. MS Royal Appendix 58: words attributed to William Dunbar....'red rosse' : New York Public Library MS Drexel 4180. See Shire, *The Thrissil, the Rois and the Flour-de-lys*, p. 7; listed by John Stevens, *Music and Poetry in the Early Tudor Court*, Appendix B No. 273 a.

[2] Details available in Charles Rogers, *The History of the Chapel Royal of Scotland*.

épitres galantes and love-songs were in currency as well as lewd and ribald lampoon and satire.

A fourth chapter of his reign opens with his wooing journey to the Continent in 1536 and his bringing home from France as consort the Princess Madeleine. On her early death he married Marie de Lorraine, of the powerful family of Guise. The court of these years, Franco-Scottish in sympathy and in style, came to an untimely end with the King's death in 1542.

The gifts and personal taste of this Stewart monarch are important and deserve to be remembered along with his reputation for avarice and debauchery. His active participation in music-making is attested by Thomas Wode in one of his invaluable annotations to his Part-Books: 'King James was a good musician himself...but his voice was harsh.'

King James' own letters record his delight as a young man in the companionship of a visitor from Italy who provided him all one long winter with the pleasures of part-music: in a letter King James begs Maximiliam Duke of Milan, from whose court this Thomas de Averencia had come and to whom he was now returning, to allow him to visit Scotland again.[1] An early act in the King's personal reign was to restore and re-endow the Chapel Royal which had fallen on hard times during his troubled minority. Cherishing of musical culture here joins with religious enthusiasm of a Catholic prince and pious concern to maintain the Chantry Chapel of his royal ancestors, so many of them violent in their deaths. It is not surprising that the court under this music-loving monarch should have produced *fine musick* both secular and sacred.

The King's participation in the 'writing game' at court is borne witness to by Sir David Lyndsay, who had been his 'gouvernant' in infancy and was later court servitor and Lyon King at Arms. We have, indeed, Lyndsay's reply to the King's 'flyting' though we lack the royal verses of bantering invective. Lyndsay had been accused by his royal master of being 'no more valiant in Venus' works' and his reply, couched as 'advice to the prince', is a dignified rebuke. There is good reason for attributing to the court of this prince and his companions a substantial number of verse pieces of a courtly amorous nature including poems by [George] Steill royal favourite, 'Clapperton' of the Chapel Royal and Sir John Fethy, priest and musician. For several of these there was music. Sometimes kinship with Tudor England can be traced in songs of this time, which is understandable when we recall the intermittent presence at court of the Tudor Queen Mother and the attendance there from time to time of musicians from the south. A number of fine songs, however, show the

[1] Thomas de Averencia of Brescia, *The Letters of James V, 1513–42*; R. K. Hannay and Denys Hay, pp. 163, 169–70.

Franco-Scottish style in its first blossoming, from the years when King James had a French princess as queen. Song in the 'style King James V' as I call it, coming from the years between 1528 and 1542 is a prominent theme in these studies; but the full-length portrait of this reign and its music and poetry, its musicians and poets and its court pastimes is reserved for a future volume.

The death of King James V in 1542 saw once more disaster for Scotland and 'the monarch a child'. His newborn daughter was Mary, Queen of Scots. A long minority ensued with the country rent by the civil and religious strife of the years of Reformation and harried by invasion. It is hard to envisage over these years a court-life in which court-song might flourish. Some song-making is traceable, however, to circles round the French Queen Mother, Marie; some 'plays' and devisings attended ceremonial occasions under the Lord Governor. But a settled hearth for established music of the royal household and for courtly 'making' was lacking over many years.

The personal reign of Queen Mary from the time of her return to Scotland in 1562 certainly included days and nights of 'balling and dancing'. Her 'stand' of musicians and singers for part-singing gave to David Rizzio, Italian secretary with a fine singing voice, the opportunity to step into royal favour. Queen Mary's reign in Scotland was short. Little remains of the fashionable and sophisticated song, dance and devising at her court that so affronted the powers of the Reformation.

The long years of her imprisonment in England did not mean that the 'Scotch Quene' ceased to exist as a court lady. As a force in politics she was notoriously active. As a force of inspiration or patronage to poet or musician she was, although impoverished and in prison, still quite remarkably potent. Makers of court-song, poet and musician Catholic in their sympathies were, as we shall see, attendant on her 'shadow court'.

It is with the reign of her son, King James VI, that our full-length study of court-song and its making can begin, with pieces of which we know the author, the date of composition and the occasion of commission or presentation. The date and seat of our principal interest is the first decade of King James VI's personal rule and his courtly company over those years, from 1579 when he was thirteen years old and emerged from tutelage until 1590 when he married. Thereafter until the end of the story in 1603 the hazards of time, destruction and neglect have left us tantalising traces only of court-song and its making. We can read contemporary descriptions of ceremonies for a queen's coronation or a birth of a prince, devisings in which words and music played a part, but of the songs themselves only vestiges remain.

It was exactly one hundred years after the making of 'Now fayre' and 'Red rosse' that Scotland lost her royal court. In 1603 King James VI of Scotland went south to claim the throne of England. His court went with him and from that time onwards, apart from brief presence of the sovereign on state visit, in arms or in flight, Scotland lacked a court and lacked any settled focus for the making and enjoyment of court-song. Apart from the running bids for favour made by the would-be courtiers during the visits of King James in 1617 or King Charles in 1633, poets and musicians in Scotland lacked the opportunity of employment or patronage offered by a court and a courtly audience—and all chance of recognition or advancement was at an end in the north.

Not in its history only but in its geography also Scotland asks for individual consideration as a ground for the cultivation of courtly song. Remote and peripheral among countries of western Europe, it was cut off for more than half the year by impassable weather; poor in resources and undeveloped in comparison with England or France, it was yet, according to its powers, proud in princely state: torn by faction it was yet alert to foreign politics.

Scotland's remoteness in terms of Europe in general, the peripheral nature of its culture, made it retentive of old style. Its window open on the ancient Celtic culture of the far west, its turbulent history, its uneasy relations with its island neighbour, England, together with its strong ties of affinity with France—all these laid down a pattern of politico-cultural relations in which the making and development of its courtly part-song may be traced in bright threads. To do so is the pleasant task I have set myself in this book.

The book is planned as a series of linked studies rather than as a continuous exposition in chapters. Each study aims at taking new bearings on its topic. New facts are to the fore or a familiar tract of thought is renewed by cross-fertilisation with thought in another discipline. Poetry is taken with music, dance or ceremony; 'lyric' forms are examined along with song-styles or patterns of the figured dance; song in Scotland is related to song elsewhere in Europe; political history is considered pertinent to the devising of courtly entertainment.

At the same time this series of studies has a chronological basis. First, the two great manuscript collections of the 1560s, George Bannatyne's 'Ballat Buik' and Thomas Wode's Part-Books or 'Psalter', are considered as main source-books of words and music of court-song. Beside these is placed the printed volume that gives moralised versions of many court-song texts. Later source-books are then briefly enumerated with a note on their nature and provenance. An analysis follows of some ways in which words and music were combined to make court-song.

At various points in the pages that follow I review briefly what possible ways there were in sixteenth-century Scotland of combining words and music with other elements, dance, spectacle, contest, joust or ceremony, in order to make a 'devising' for courtly participation or entertainment of a simple or more complex nature—the danced song, the sung romance, the interlude or *cartel*, the wedding psalm or mourning 'mynd'. Verbal texts survive from several courtly 'plays' and many more of the court-songs, extant complete or in fragment, may indeed be residua of *fête* or ceremony, pastime or courtly celebration of seasonal rite.

The stage thus set, certain figures and phases of *Scottis Poesie* long familiar to literary critic and literary historian are brought to new account. Alexander Scott is considered as a maker of court-song, creator perhaps of music as well as words, living in courtly circles under King James V, possibly canon and organist of Inchmahome Priory under his daughter Mary, Queen of Scots, and present in old age at the court of his grandson, King James VI. Scott is revealed as an important factor for continuity in the making of court-song in Scotland.

Courtly making of *Scottis Poesie* under King James VI has often been chronicled and the story told of King James' 'Castalian band' of poets and musicians. Now the poems are discussed with the music-for-the-words in mind. The making of court-song and its live presentation are linked to the royal *puy;* this activity, in the Scottish court, begun as a boyish 'writing-game' and advancing to princely status as an academy in little, is pondered as being in itself a kind of serious 'play', *lusus regius*, 'His Majesty's recreations at vacant hours'. How far royal policy was involved with poetry in the court of King James is adumbrated in a new reading of Montgomerie's *The Cherrie and the Slae*. Montgomerie is studied as the chief maker of words for courtly part-music.

The investigation of court-song and its function in courtly society must pause at the year 1590 for paucity of surviving matter. The influence, however, of Castalian poetry and song is traced within the court to some younger writers hitherto unidentified and, without the court, to Robert Ayton. Impressed in youth by the poetry of the King's circle, Ayton shows himself heir in matter and in manner to the 'smoothly flowing' Castalian verse. This bore fruit in his light and delightful court-songs that won wide favour under King James VI and I *in aula Britannica* and under his son King Charles.

A postscript traces the currency of Scottish court-song as it continued to be enjoyed in seventeenth-century Scotland, the part-song as long as singing to four voices was taught and practised, the monophonic song as long as music for voice with instrumental accompaniment current in the north embraced courtly song of Cavalier or Covenanter poet along with the 'native airs' or indigenous folk-songs of Scotland.

Throughout these studies the master theme is court-song, its making and enjoyment, studied in the context of society. My thesis is this: Poetry, sister of Rhetoric, was in courtly society of earlier times much concerned with public celebration, was frequently related to ceremony and was for the most part enjoyed aloud. Verses might of course be made for the inner ear, *épitres galantes* for the private eye of the beloved rather than for her public praise, while narratives might be intended for silent reading as well as for enjoyment aloud in company. But where verse is found matched with music, performance is indicated. Enjoyment aloud of such a piece, where music is part-music, postulates a 'stand' or group of skilled performers, vocal or instrumental, and it postulates an audience.

Where verse is found as court-song we need to know the origin of the words and the origin of the music and also the way in which one was united with the other to form a part-song. As circumstances in which court-song was made, performed and enjoyed we look, then, for the work of the 'makar'—the Scots term for the maker of verses, the poet. We look for the presence of the 'musician', which word usually implied, over and above skill in musical performance, skill of musical composition or musical arrangement and the devising of pieces for presentation. We look also for the skilled musical personnel on the court's payment roll or in the service of near-by abbey or burgh kirk. We envisage, too, the occasion of performance and the nature of the audience and of its participation.

The makar in the Scottish court was unlikely to be supported *as* makar. (The case for Dunbar as in this sense the 'first example of a professional court-poet' has been exploded.) The poet might write for the love of it or to win fame or favour, from a niche as priest or chaplain to the Queen, Treasurer of the Chapel Royal or Keeper of the King's dogs, or as freelance courtier. The court-poet would present his work *in propyne* to King or noble as the honouring tribute-gift that looks for gracious re-compense in cash or 'lands', place or pension. The composer also, hoping for advancement, might present work of his *in propyne*. But musicians as musicians were professional and must be maintained, as members of the Chapel Royal or Music of the Household, whether they were performers with voice or instrument or composers or both. Their services were on call, their skill at command or at commission. Court-song, then, is rooted in courtly society through employment or patronage, commission or *propyne*. In matter and in manner it is keyed into the conduct of affairs, through instigation in occasion and through reaction of a courtly audience. The roots of court-song in courtly society strike deeply by way of the words and even more deeply by way of the music.

In the course of these studies here are some of the questions I am interested to ask. Who made the songs, words and music? (Many of the pieces are undated and of unknown authorship.) How were the songs made and how presented? Were they sung and listened to as in a modern concert performance, the interest being primarily musical? Or was the meaning of the words of greater pertinence, the intention of the performance of more serious import? Did the performers simply sing or did they 'act in song'—sing with gesture and significant movement? When the music was music of the dance, were the songs danced by the singers or danced by a courtly company to the singers' music? (All three modes of performance are noticed by Bacon as in use in the 1580s, the second as 'vulgar' the first and third as 'a thing of great State and Pleasure' and 'having an extreme good grace'.)

For what reason was an individual song made, for general diversion or against a specific occasion? What part did the songs play, in their making and presentation, in the life of the court that engendered them? How significantly did courtly *magnificence*, pastime or *ludus* mirror the inner life of that court—in joust or bardic contest, masque for a wedding, *cartel* for a 'joyous entry' or love-song 'feygning' the service of 'Venus Queen'? Did such 'play' on occasion voice the profound concern of the court or of its king?

In his essay 'Of Masques and Triumphs' Bacon regarded it as above all important that the 'Ditty should be fitted to the Device', the song be pertinent to the central meaning of the action. It has of recent years come to be recognised that the 'device' of courtly ceremony or pageant, *ballet de cour*, 'joyous entry' or masque, was a well-pondered shaping of a propitious *doing*: prosperity was ensured by a pageant of the fruits of the realm, a schism in the nation could be mimed in dance and thus resolved, the King's coming could be greeted as the coming of Hercules or Alexander and their strength or might would accrue to him; a masque of peace and amity might prevent the evils of civil war. A courtly 'play' or '*magnificence*' partook of the nature of a singing and dancing magic.[1]

From this point of critical interpretation I now move to investigate 'ditty' and 'device' in the court of Renaissance Scotland. This study of court-song and courtly making, of ceremony and 'play', dance and devising, has at its core the idea that such phenomena were of serious import, done for the eye of the monarch, enacted at the hub of national affairs—a 'making' for the court, the microcosm.

---

[1] Henry Prunières, *Le Ballet de Cour en France; Les Fêtes de la Renaissance* (symposium), C.N.R.S. (Paris, 1961); J. Huizinga, *Homo Ludens: A Study of the Play-Element in Culture;* John Stevens, *Music and Poetry in the Early Tudor Court*, esp. chapter 9, 'The Game of Love'.

I

THE BALLATIS PRESERVED

THE CONDITION OF POETRY AND PART-SONG IN SCOTLAND IN 1568

IN WHAT circumstances did courtly music and poetry, song and dance find themselves, when, in the year 1568, the crown of Scotland passed to the infant King James VI? In such a sorry plight after the war-torn reign of his mother and the victory of the reforming powers that two men of imagination and culture determined to record and preserve the best of Scotland's poetry and part-music, lest all knowledge of it pass from the realm 'allutterlie'. They were George Bannatyne, who 'in time of pest' collected into his 'Ballat Buik' the best that he could lay hands on of Scotland's earlier and contemporary poetry, and Thomas Wode of St Andrews, who about this time began to compile his musical anthology of part-writing, drawing in music of the past—Scots, English and Continental, sacred and some secular—and commissioning part-writing from musicians composing in Scotland at that time.

A third collection of a very different nature dates also from the infant years of King James, a printed volume, '*Ane Compendious booke of godly and spirituall songs*', popularly known as 'The Gude and Godlie Ballatis'. There among psalms and songs of the Reformed Church were presented words of courtly part-songs of earlier Scotland now 'changeit' into moral and devotional pieces for singing through which Reformed doctrine might be spread.

A consideration of these three collections will show how each in its way contributed to preserve the 'ballatis' of earlier Scotland and keep in currency the kind of music with which their words were associated. It will show also what were the forces inimical at that time to a court culture of music and poetry, dance and song. These three volumes or sets of volumes in manuscript or print are the main source-books of earlier Scottish court-song.[1] For several reasons, then, some study of these three works will make a right beginning to this book.

---

[1] One or two songs by a Scottish musician were written down in England by the mid-century (*Music of Scotland* nos. 32 and 44) but only one of the Scottish manuscripts that contain court-song dates from that epoch—the Douglas–Fischear Part-Books—and they contain but the single example of secular song, incomplete and perhaps a late inscription.

BANNATYNE'S 'BALLAT BUIK'

In the summer of 1568 Mary, Queen of Scots, was defeated at Langside: the Regent Moray and Protestant Scotland were victorious. The monarch was the infant James VI. In the autumn of that year the pest struck Edinburgh. The town emptied; business and commerce were stayed. Out of this disaster for Scotland came one thing fortunate for Scottish culture. George Bannatyne employed his enforced leisure in perfecting and having transcribed a great collection of Scottish poetry written by the best authors over the past hundred years.[1] This was achieved before the year ended.

> in time of pest
> Quhen we fra labor was compeld to rest
> In to the thre last monethis of this yeir
> frome our redimaris birth to knaw it heir
> Ane thousand is/fyve hundreth/threscoir awcht.

The actual transcription, the overseeing, the detail of arrangement and the entitling of parts and sections belong, then, to the year 1568. The work of collection is generally taken as begun some years earlier, perhaps as early as his student days at St Andrews more than ten years before. This was the decade that saw the end of medieval Catholic Scotland and the beginnings of Protestant modern Scotland.

The care with which Bannatyne marshalled his huge collection, arranging it into five Books and each Book into sections, has been taken as a sure indication that he intended his volume to be printed. With friends and relations in legal circles and a personal acquaintance with the licensed printers, Bannatyne should have found publication easy. That his five-volume collection was not printed is explained by the altered political climate. In 1563 the Reformed Church assumed the powers of control over printers that had previously belonged to the Crown. And very soon printers ran into difficulties. A volume of verses (which was in all probability an edition of 'The Gude and Godlie Ballatis' itself) was in the summer of 1568 ordered to be censored—'Ane psalme booke in the end whereof was found printed ane baudie song callit "Welcum Fortoun"', that had been printed without licence of the magistrate or 'reviseing of the Kirk'.

Bannatyne's 'Ballat Buik' as it has been handed down to us in manuscript is an index of taste and tradition in mid-century Scotland. It has not, however, been subjected to the full violence of reforming censorship of the printed word. But it was

---

[1] '*The Bannatyne Manuscript written in tyme of Pest, 1568*' (thus entitled by a later hand) edited by W. Tod Ritchie in four volumes: the main collection is in vols. II, III and IV, and in vol. I is the secondary (uncompleted) copy entitled 'Ane Ballat Buik' and the general introduction to the edition. The 'ballatis' are there numbered in roman figures here cited as, for example, B. CCX.

compiled at the time of Reformation which affected its contents and the mode of their presentation. It resembles a two-way mirror, reflecting in one direction the courtly making of the past, in another the age of change.

Bannatyne's collection, the main source of our knowledge of a hundred years of Scottish 'lyric' poetry, is justly famous. It has been drawn on time and again as one age of taste succeeded another, by Allan Ramsay, by Pinkerton, by Sir Walter Scott. Pieces from it have been edited after the fashion of these ages. Yet honest admiration for the contents has been its lot rather than critical appraisal of the repertory as a whole or scrutiny of any meaning detectable in its presentation.

First, the title: the complete collection has none in a contemporary hand, but the 'second copy', which was never completed, bears the title 'Ane Ballat Buik'. 'Ballat' is the northern counterpart of the English 'ballade/ballad', a word that has been heavily under discussion as to its origin, history and changing use, from dance-song to courtly piece in a specific metre to printed broadside.[1] We shall note what indication Bannatyne gives of its force in Scotland at the time.

George Bannatyne's 'Ballat Buik' studied as a compilation proves rewarding. His whole scheme deserves thoughtful review, but that is a project beyond the scope of this book. Here I shall look at the compilation as a whole but with an eye especially to his Fourth Book, the book of 'luve Ballatis', for it is there that are engrossed the words of the court-songs.

The collection opens with 'The Wryttar to the reidaris' which explains the scheme of his work and the spirit in which it was conceived and tells us something of the circumstances in which the poems were assembled and the texts prepared.

> Ye reverend redaris thir workis revolving richt
> gif ye get crymis, Correct thame to your micht
> And curss na clark that cunnyngly thame wrait.
> Bot blame me baldly Brocht this buik till licht
> In tenderest tyme, quhen knawledge was nocht bricht   5
> Bot lait begun to lerne and till translait.
> My copeis awld mankit and mutillait.
> Quhais trewth as standis (yit haif I, sympill wicht)
> Tryd furth Thairfoir excuse sumpairt my estait—
> Now ye haif heir this ilk buik sa provydit   10
> That in fyve pairtis It is dewly devydit
> The first concernis godis gloir and ouir salvatioun
> The nixt ar morale/grave And als besyd it
> grund on gud counsale. The thrid I will nocht hyd it

---

[1] See John Stevens, *Music and Poetry in the Early Tudor Court*, pp. 53–4, 120–5. A. B. Friedman, *The Ballad Revival*, traces the history of the word in its relation to the ballad in print, but his larger conclusions are for me invalidated by his belief (p. 47) that the tunes for the printed ballads were of folk origin.

Ar blyith and glaid Maid for ouir consollatioun.
The ferd of luve/and thair richt reformatioun.
The fyift ar tailis and storeis weill discydit
Reid as ye pleiss/I neid no moir narratioun.

These introductory verses are interesting and important but the meaning is not absolutely clear. The syntax of Bannatyne's verses is not tight-drawn and line five belongs as closely to line four as it does to the line that follows. It seems to me to mean, 'The readers giving their minds to the works he has here compiled are begged to correct according to their own abilities any mistakes—or offences—they may find there. They are not to lay the blame on the skilful writers who composed them but on the compiler-editor who boldly brought out this book in a time of religious scrupulosity when knowledge was dimmed. He has but recently set himself to study and translate his copies of the works, which were old, imperfect and mutilated. The truth—a faithful account of them as they stand—he (a simple fellow), has done his best to give.'

If the lines are syntactically linked more strongly the other way, the sense is rather this, 'Readers are to blame not the authors but the present editor and compiler, who in his youth when his knowledge was not "shining" began to learn (study) and to translate without trickery/deception (i.e. but lait) from the old copies he had, which were imperfect and mutilated.' In either case 'bot lait' has two possible meanings 'recently, only late in the day' or 'without deception'. Whether it can safely be deduced from these lines that the compilation was begun in Bannatyne's youth—say ten years earlier when he was probably at college—is seen to be in doubt. But that he is now doing his conscientious best to give the true meaning of the texts as they were available to him is in any case clear. It is just possible that Bannatyne's inscribing of introductory verses in which there are two ways of taking his meaning is due to discretion as much as to unskilled composition in verse. ('Riddling' verse was a fashion of the age.)

The poems he had collected are marshalled into five parts, each distinct but sub-servient to the whole scheme: works devotional ('of theologie'), moral, humorous, amorous and counter-amorous, and narrative. This gives a well-balanced account of the range of earlier *Scottis Poesie* with which are interwoven pieces and passages by such English poets as Chaucer and Lydgate. From full-length compositions of drama or history selected parts are given, the farcical interludes from *Ane Pleasant Satyre of the Thrie Estaitis*, the 'proheme' to Bellenden's 'Cosmographie'. The pieces presen-ted from Scottish literature are virtually complete in themselves; there are no ex-cerpts from verse chronicle or romance, from Douglas's translation of Virgil, for instance, or his 'Palace of Honour'.[1] Some of the passages from English poetry are,

[1] The Prologue to one book of his *Eneados* is, however, given deliberately without its last stanza, as we shall see.

however, excerpts from longer works. No doubt the over-all size of his collection had to be borne in mind.

Bannatyne apparently uses the word 'ballat' throughout his compilation in the general sense of verse-piece; we conclude from his address to the readers that whether current in manuscript or in print the verse-pieces were intended to be read aloud in company or silently in study. In the headings of the Five Books 'ballat' serves for all, but in the individual entitling in the contents list there is some differentiation in the terms used. For example, volume I in its first part has these items—'III the richt excellent godly and lernit werk callit the benner of peetie, IV The Proheme of the Cosmographie of Scotland [Bellenden's own title], V The prollog of the tent buik of Virgill, VI Ane ballat of the creatioun of the warld, man, his fall and redemptioun maid to the tone of the bankis of helecon, VII The lxxxiii Psalme of David, VIII A song of him lying in poynt of deth [O lord my god sen I am brocht to grit distress], ...XXVII Ane prayer for the pest and XXVIII The song of the virgin mary [The Magnificat].' The names given to the different items are specific indications of the nature of the piece; the 'songs', the 'psalm' and the 'ballat' all entitle pieces that patently were sung.

In this list the 'ballat' with the note of its music stands out from the others. It is the only one in the whole compilation where musical association is mentioned, but there may be a reason for that. It seems to me very likely that the Bannatyne contents-list records here as on some other occasions the actual entitling of the original piece which in this case was very probably a broadside; certainly the title observes broadside style, in which the naming of the tune was customary. (The name and nature of Maitland's ballat is discussed at length in chapter 2, pp. 34–37.) There is no other instance of the word 'ballat' being chosen to discriminate on any of the other points that have been subject of debate elsewhere. On the contrary, 'song' as used in section-titles points in the direction of musical association.

In the First Book the second section opens under the title 'Ballatis of the nativitie of chryste' of which there are seven. The third section-title 'finis nativitatis dei sequuntur de eius passione quidem cantilenae' shows 'cantilena' as equivalent of 'ballat'. The fourth section is of 'exortationeis of chryst to all synnaris' and its conclusion is marked 'Heir endis the first pairt of this buke/Contenand ballatis of theologie'. The Protestant cast of the book of devotional poetry is notable in contents, in certain absences and in the entitling. The ordering of the pieces within the section can be seen to be meaningful. The matter of his First Book, section one, can be 'read': God (by Bannatyne himself); the 'Banner of Piety'; a poem of advice to the Prince of Scotland (James V); poems on the creation and the created soul, its relation to God; hymns to Christ; the Magnificat.

Neither in his Second nor in his Third Book does Bannatyne's entitling show that he is using 'ballat' in a sense discriminating courtly from popular piece, or song from a piece that was not current as words for music. Yet we know that song-books were among his sources, for one part-song 'O lustie May' has obviously been transcribed from such a source where the words were engrossed with music or underlaid to a part: the scribe has by accident copied out twice one of the phrases repeated in the musical setting.[1] When Bannatyne comes to his Fourth Book, 'of ballatis of luve' and names its four sections he uses the word 'song' again implying something at least of currency as words for singing: the first section, 'songis of luve', has the ballats for which we know there was music. It is of pieces celebrating love and its value for men; the other sections give 'luve' in other aspects, again with 'use to man' as the underlying criterion.

The whole presentation of the Fourth Book repays careful attention. This book of verses about love as a power in men's hearts and lives and in society embraces work by the living poet Alexander Scott and also poems from medieval Scotland, *débat*, *pastourelle* or *ballade* from the fifteenth century or the earlier years of the reign of King James IV. Here the code of 'courtly love' still prevailed, the vaunting of what had been a code of behaviour to bring a seemliness and beauty into the conduct of life, a medium for expression of emotion and an instrument for refining it, a play-world of idealised and perfected *mœurs* that had been a primary source of 'making'. From it had sprung song and celebration in verse, praise of the beloved, of the state of being in love, of devotion and despair, analysis of the lover's joy and woe, of his and his lady's state of mind and spirit. From early in its history the celebration of this cult, this play-world in society, had had its counterpoise in realistic objection and exposure of the 'game' as vain and as grounded in lust and appetite. And it had had its serious heavenly counterpart in Christian devotion. The counter-amorous manifested itself in exhortation to Christian worship, in dignified good counsel or in merciless and zestful satire. The cult of earthly love for the worldly lady had been countered by celebration of love for God the Father, for Christ the heavenly 'leman' or for love-service of the heavenly lady, the Blessed Virgin.

To judge by what has come down to us—and this proviso is important—the makars of King James IV's reign had shown in their poetry little enthusiasm for the love-cult and little patience with it. Its idealised code of behaviour, its gestures and ceremonies in social conduct and its emotional gambits could still inform state poetry of celebration with splendid or enchanting effect, witness Dunbar's 'The Thrissil and the Rois' or the anonymous 'Quhen Tayis bank wes blumyt brycht' (no. CCLXXVIII in the Bannatyne manuscript). But Dunbar —again to judge by extant pieces—uses

[1] B. CCLXXIX.

15

it seriously only once or twice and then probably in court makar's service of Queen Margaret. He displays its values over against those of Christian devotion in the debate of the merle and the nightingale. And once he makes a fool of it grandly in his wicked overplaying of the lover's role of 'Quhone he list to feygne'—'when he was willing to play the lover-poet for fun.' On the other hand he was ever ready to the attack, wielding sarcasm or parody with savagery or with finesse. Gavin Douglas shows up the emptiness of May-time love or of the service of Venus in the course of his search for honour and he cries out against it in his Prologue 'of May or of Dido' in his *Eneados*.

All this is mirrored in Bannatyne's Fourth Book, but the mirror is held up at an angle acceptable to a Scotland now on the brink of Reformation.

> Heir followis ballatis of luve
> Devydit in four pairtis. The first
> Ar songis of luve. The secound ar
> Contemptis of luve and evill wemen
> The thrid ar contempis of evill
> fals vicius men. And the fourt
> Ar ballattis detesting of luve
> and lichery.[1]

Songs celebrating love are given with their counterpoise of 'remeid' (a remedy against it) in satire and good counsel. Lechery, misuse of love, in men or in women is exposed to scorn. To the beliefs and attitudes of the courtly love-cult and the states of mind they engender are opposed reason, mother-wit and moral and Christian values. Of the religious counterpart as devotion to the Blessed Virgin there is of course no word nor is redirection of devotion towards the love of the person of Christ specific in the book's plan though it can be traced in individual pieces. Book IV, his little 'ballat buik' then, opens with two admonitory pieces. (Later hands have written in gratuitous offerings of bawdy verses.)

> To the reidar
> Heir haif ye luvaris ballattis at your will
> How evir your natur directit is untill
> Bot wald ye luve eftir my counsalling
> Luve first your God aboif all uder thing
> Next as your self your nichtbur beir gud will
> etc.

Then comes a Sonet 'Lyke as the littil Emmet hath hir gall' to the effect that 'luve is luve in peure men as in Kingis'.[2]

---

[1] The pattern is, of course, an old one present in the Ovid moralised of the Middle Ages and kindred texts.
[2] The sonnet, the only one in the book, is English and is a late insertion.

The book begins with a 'Disputatio between Corpus and Cor,' 'O foly hairt fetterit in fantesye/Wincust with werry wardly wan plesance'. Cor speaks with high and steadfast devotion: the best of human feeling is found in 'courtly love'. The answer of Corpus is equally dignified: Cor to whom God has given direction of the body should set himself to serve Him 'idently'. The end is no surrender by Cor but a compact between Cor and Corpus, that honourable love of the lady is to be allowed. The presentation continues with one of Dunbar's rare 'straight' poems of courtly love, his advice to the lover in terms of the lover's code, 'Be secreit trew incressing of your name'. Then comes Mersar's 'advice to a son' on the good there is in the rules of love and Scott's verses on the well-known theme of love overruling disparity in class.

There are eighty of these 'ballatis of luve' and if they are read through consecutively they present a case for the cult of 'courteous love' as a force for positive good in human nature and in society. The pieces range in time from Chaucer with 'the song of Troyalus' through Henryson and Dunbar to the contemporary Scott. The majority appear to be pieces from the era that was just closing, in 'the style King James V', many of which we know had music. The section ends with a wistful ballat of impossibilities whose refrain is 'Then will my reverend lady rew on me', itself a tailpiece to this chapter of verses.

The second section could be called in modern terms poems of disillusion. These are 'remeidis of luve', 'ballatis of remedy of luve and to the reproche of evill wemen'. First among the 'remeidis of luve' is 'So prayiss me as ye think causs why' (B. cccxxi), which most fortunately has survived from the sixteenth century as a song for four voices.[1] This section gives poems for the afflicted lover on 'how to get over it', epigrams against women and satire on women in general and on female lust in especial, ending again with ballats of impossibilities, more tart here than before and, finally, laments of age. Chaucer or 'Chaucer' is again important, Dunbar is heard and poets of King James V's court, and Alexander Scott is strong. 'Courtly love' is related significantly to 'love' in the court of a sovereign of Scotland in the 'commonyng betuix the mester and the hure' with its refrain on 'when the court is in the town'. The code of courtly manners is the target from the beginning and the language of 'love talking' with it. 'Commoning' is the word for social intercourse of pleasant talking, ceremonious recreation in aristocratic circles. 'Mester' is clericus, a 'university type', the educated man. The 'mester' makes his request for 'grace' with all the eloquent terms of the love-code. The whore puts him off until such time as the court has left the town, for she is preoccupied with the real thing, 'love' among the courtiers. The procrastination cures his 'languor'; he finds 'a bonnier ane' while her

---

[1] The record of the music, which is without verbal text, is entitled 'Pryss me'.

THE BALLATIS PRESERVED

1. PRYSS ME/SO PRAYISS ME[1]

ANON   ANON

1 So prayiss me as ye think causs quhy,

so prayiss me as ye think causs quhy And lufe me as yow lyk - is

best   As pleas - is yow so ples't am I, as pleas - is yow so ples't am I

---

[1] Music: Duncan Burnett's Music-Book (*c.* 1610), Panmure MS. 10 on loan to the National Library of Scotland, fos. 164v–165r. (K.E.) Stanzas 6–8 in Bannatyne MS.

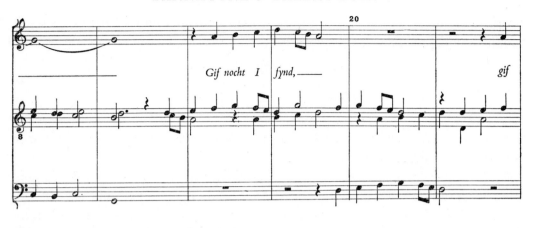

Gif nocht I fynd,—— gif

nocht I fynd of —— nocht I traist.

2 Gif ye be trew, I wil be just,
   Gif ye be fals, flattery is fre
   All tymes and houris evin as ye lust
   For me till use als weill as ye.

3 Gif ye do mok, I will bot play,
   Gif ye do lawch, I will nocht weip,
   Evin as ye list think, do or say;
   Sic law ye mak, sic law I keip.

4 Schaw fathfull lufe, lufe sall ye haif,
   Schaw dowbilness, I sal yow quyt.
   Ye can nocht use nor no ways craif
   Bot evin that same is my delyt.

5 Bot gif ye wald be trew and plane
   Ye wald me pleiss and best content
   And gif ye will nocht so remane
   As I haif said so am I lent.

Prayiss = praise; *pryss* = appraise; *till* = to; *sic* = such; *quyt* = requite; *lent* = inclined.

profit of court intercourse is the ugly end of disease; he finds her 'a plaistert up wi the glengoir [syphilis]'. The counterpoise of disillusioning satire with a burlesque of courtly 'love-talking' is here strengthened by satire on the court-men. It was this direction that the attack took of the preacher against James V 'the King of Love' and his court, for some years conspicuous for its debauchery.

The concluding piece of this section is one by Kennedy coming out of Catholic

Scotland, a lament in the role of the aged man with the refrain 'that evir I servit moith [mouth] thankless'. It begins

> An aigit man, twyss fourty yeiris
> Eftir the halydayis of Yule
> I hard him say amangis the freiris
> of ordour gray makand grit dule...

The good Christian counsel is of the destructiveness of lust's service and the message 'O brukill yowth...amend thy miss'.

'The thrid pairt of luve to the reproche of fals vicius men and prayiss of guid wemen' draws on the same authors as did the second part. The 'guid wemen' are good not in the amorous sense of Chaucer's good ladies; there is an element here of defence of innocence and modesty.

The fourth part of love is 'contempt of Blyndit Luve' ('Cupid' is not used).[1] Here verse on the suffering of the lover is mingled with angry satire on human nature *in toto* and in some pieces the service of God is urged instead of earthly passion. Here is Dunbar's 'The merle and the nychtingaill' and his carol, a Christian rejoinder to a carol of Maytime love, *Now cumis aige quhair yewth hes bene / And trew luve rysis fro the splene.*

Scott has the last word in savage laughter at the ladies' part in courtly love, couched in an admonition.

> Thir ressonis ar to raiss yow
> fra crymis undir coate
> or war ye say nocht, waiss you
> quod Allexander Scote.

> heir endis the haill four pairtis...of this
> ballat buke anno 1568.

But Bannatyne has something more to say before he moves on to his Fifth Book, of tales. In his whole compilation, the 'buke of luvaris ballatis' is bulwarked by Bishop Gavin Douglas's great condemnation of the love-cult, 'the prollog of the fourt book of virgell, Treting of the Incommoditie of luve and remeid thairof'. It ends with the penultimate stanza, the words 'Allace the quhyle thow knew the strange Enee'. (The last stanza is an explicit lead-in to the ensuing book of Virgil, the 'Book of Dido', and is in consequence omitted here.)

It may be that this piece was put as a postscript outside the little 'ballat buke' proper as being somewhat different in genre from the 'lyrical' ballats inside it. It is difficult to tell, for three folios are here missing and we cannot be sure what was engrossed before his final rubric (fo. 298 *a*) 'Heir endis the ballatis of luve...and Heir followis the fyft part of this buik'.

---

[1] Cupid, however, appears frequently in the ballats themselves.

Were a survey desired of how the later medieval view of love in society appeared to the age of Reformation, Bannatyne's could hardly be bettered. How much his choice of contents was his own and how much that choice was already narrowed by disappearance beyond his horizon of Roman Catholic devotional poetry or of certain 'love-cult' verses, we shall never know. Bannatyne's anthology itself conditions our idea of the scope of what had once existed. When we make the effort to envisage earlier *Scottis Poesie* apart from Bannatyne's choice we find there are questions to ask. Where are gone Dunbar's poems written 'in love's court', composed to answer a taste for courtly making perhaps during his younger days in the fifteenth century? Where are his tales 'of sanctis in glorie, Baithe of commoun and propir storie', the pieces in celebration of saints in general terms or written for the special keeping of their own days in the calendar?[1] For hymns to the Virgin we have to go to the earlier Asloan Manuscript and the fine 'ballatis of our ladye' by Dunbar and Dunbar's rival, Kennedy or to the later writing of covert Catholics.[2]

It is very likely that selection or pre-selection has affected the contents, and that this has made itself felt also in the texts; copies that came to Bannatyne's hands may have been 'mankit and mutillait' by forces other than wear and the passage of time. On the one hand he has missed the original version of the lines in Dunbar's, or Sir James Inglis', satire from an earlier reign (B. LXIX) 'Devorit with dreme',[3] inveighing against priests 'cled up in secular weid with blasing breistis'—priests frequenting the court in worldly garments bearing brilliant coats of arms—'Sa quhene to reid/the deirgey and the beid' ('So few to read the *Dirige* and service'); as in Maitland's manuscript, there has been substituted 'So quhene/the psalme and testament to reid'. Elsewhere Bannatyne lets through a line or two of Catholic matter—in 'the freiris of ordour gray' in the poem quoted earlier and on several occasions in his texts of Henryson's fables in his Book v. The fables in later print have at these points been 'censored' in the cause of Protestantism and the metre or sense can halt as a result.[4]

On the other hand there are points at which, on heedful reading, one can feel the blue pencil on the page. It comes in the working out of a Christian counterpart to the service of the 'King of Love' or of 'Venus Quene'. It can be seen clearly in one poem of Dunbar's 'Now of wemen this I say for me', (B. CCCLXVI) entitled (by a modern editor) 'In Prais of Wemen'. The gambit, a familiar one in medieval poetry, opens thus: Women deserve to be honoured by men for men are come of women, who

---

[1] 'Off benefice, Schir, at everie feist', stanza 3: Dunbar, ed. W. Mackay Mackenzie, no. 12. My interpretation of the poem differs from the editor's.

[2] See *Devotional Pieces in Verse and Prose*, ed. J. A. W. Bennett. In Bannatyne we have the Magnificat or 'Hymns on the Nativity of Christ'.

[3] The Maitland Folio Manuscript gives this poem to Sir James Inglis; variants in *Dunbar*, ed. Mackenzie.

[4] This point is made also by John MacQueen, 'Two Versions of Henryson's Fabillis'.

bore them and nursed them; they are 'the confort that we all haif heir'; he who will not honour them is a fool who fouls his own nest. It continues

> Chryst to his fader he had nocht ane man
> Se quhat wirschep wemen suld haif than.
> That Sone is Lord, that Sone is King of kingis
> In hevin and erth his majestie ay ringis
> Sen scho hes borne him in hir halines
> And he is well and grund of all gudnes
> All wemen of us suld haif honoring
> Service and luve, aboif all uthir thing.

This does not make sense. The deletion of the Mother of God from the argument makes a gross *non sequitur* in the poem. 'Scho' is unexplained by anything that has gone before. Plainly the poem was working towards a celebration of the Virgin Mary. Under reformed guise one of Dunbar's tales of 'saints in glory' may be here:

> Chryst to his modir he had ane woman
> Se quhat wirschep wemen suld haif than,
> That Sone is Lord, that Sone is King of kingis
> In hevin and erth his majestie ay ringis.
> Sen scho hes borne him in hir halines
> And he is well and grund of all gudnes
> All wemen of us suld haif honoring
> Service and luve aboif all othir thing.

Where Bannatyne's versions *are* 'mankit' or 'mutillait' it is probable that they were so in his originals. Perhaps Bannatyne's introduction to the readers even envisages their correcting 'according to their lights' such 'crymis' as this, such mutilations of earlier making as lie here.

Bannatyne's Fourth Book has fulfilled in content, in presentation and in detail of editing the expectations aroused by his verses introductory to that book and to the whole compilation. He has given his readers 'luvaris ballatis' at their will. What is noble and of good report in 'courtly' or 'courteous' love has been displayed and celebrated in 'songis of luve'. What was false, worthless, vile or destructive has been displayed also and countered by good counsel and the weapon of satire. This countering does not run parallel with the presentation of 'songis of luve' in *The Gude and Godlie Ballatis*, as we shall see, for there the condemnation was absolute, the counterpoise was Christian throughout and the moralisations or spiritual versions aimed at wiping out from the minds of men and women who had sung the songs of courtly love all memory of the 'Sin and harlatry' of the 'prophaine' words. Singing of love was turned right about to singing the praise and love of Christ, singing in accordance with good Reformed Christian doctrine. Cancellation and complete reorientation was aimed at, not judicious presentation that might induce a balanced estimation.

22

If the world of 1568 were to enjoy in print at all 'luvaris ballatis' of earlier making then Bannatyne's presentation was a wise one, for it went a good way towards meeting the censor's requirements. The powers of the Crown would doubtless have been satisfied. But the powers of the Kirk threw out the 'psalm-book' because of one 'baudie ballat' at the end and a failure to submit the work through the proper channels. They would hardly have let Bannatyne's 'Ballat Buik' into print. The estimation of the good there was in earthly love and, far more, the 'sin and harlatry' (however discreetly entitled) present in many of the satiric 'remeids' would both have been angrily suppressed.

What can we recover of the attitude of George Bannatyne when, perhaps as a young student of the mid-century or as an older man in the later 1560s, he gathered and set about arranging his material? A love of the song and poetry of an earlier Scotland and of poetry from England whence it drew some of its inspiration, and a profound understanding of its values—these we can clearly see, for the large scope of the undertaking, the care of detail and the even and excellent quality of the contents testify to the devotee-connoisseur. His confidence in the value of 'making' is proven by the act of compilation. The nature of his presentation of love-poetry and anti-love poetry in the Fourth Book, though conditioned by the temper of the age in which he finally put his book together reflects still, I believe, much of the values of an earlier age where there was polarity of jest and earnest, imaginative enjoyment of and participation in earthly and heavenly love over against one another yet together with one another, an all-inclusive mode of feeling where enjoyment of the play world of ideal love and its power for good went hand in hand with laughter exposing its excesses and with good sense urging its dangers, where enjoyment of 'warldis bliss' was the keener because of the opposition to it of 'hevinis bliss', where the merle and the nightingale disputed but the singing of either did not quench the other's song.

Bannatyne's 'Ballat Buik' is a testament of faith in the value of Scottish courtly making auguring well for its possible recrudescence with the opening of a new reign —in spite of the powers of an inimical Kirk.

THOMAS WODE'S PART-BOOKS, *alias* THE 'ST ANDREWS PSALTER'

The second compilation contemporary with Bannatyne's is of music, the anthology of part-song sacred and secular made over the years 1562/1566 to 1590 by Thomas Wode, one time Vicar of St Andrews.[1] Of this set of five manuscript part-books two complete copies were made; of these, two volumes are now lost. It has never been

---

[1] Details in Source List. Wode's Part-Books are studied in the Doctoral Dissertation of Kenneth Elliott. An edition was prepared by Miss Hilda S. P. Hutchison, 'The St Andrews Psalter: transcription and critical study of Thomas Wode's Psalter' (Edinburgh University Library): this I have not seen.

printed. Kenneth Elliott has suggested that Wode may have envisaged his collection of psalms being published eventually as a harmonised psalter. On one set of part-books additions were made by later hands from about the year 1620 onwards. To some degree Wode's compilation is a musical counterpart to Bannatyne's collection, for Wode says he was moved to make it from the fear lest all knowledge and skill of part-writing should disappear from the land 'allutterlie'.

Wode's care and forethought have preserved a substantial number of settings of psalms to part-music. Some from the early years of James VI's reign indicate royal or noble patronage. Some Wode commissioned from trained musicians like David Peebles. There are also

canticles, mostly set by John Angus of Dunfermline and additional motets, anthems and instrumental pieces, some from pre-Reformation times and many by Scottish composers. Among those represented are Robert Johnson, who fled to England 'lang before reformation' and went on composing there; David Peebles; Andro Kemp, who taught at the sang-schools of Dundee, St Andrews and, finally, Aberdeen; and Andro Blackhall...There were good grounds for Wode's fears, for although his anthology shows a lasting interest in the older musical heritage, psalms plain set were the order of the day.[1]

From Thomas Wode's anthology of part-music *Music of Scotland* gives these examples of sacred part-writing with Latin text: 'Descendi in hortum meum' (from 'The Song of Solomon') à 4, anonymous (no. 6); 'Deus misereatur nostri' (Psalm 67) à 4 by Robert Johnson (no. 7); 'Si quis diligit me' à 4 or à 5 by David Peebles-Francy Heagy (n. 8); 'Quam multi, Domine' (Psalm 3) à 4 by David Peebles (no. 9). As music of the Reformed Church from Wode are included: Andro Blackhall's settings of 'Blessed art thou' (Psalm 128) à 5 and 'Judge and revenge my cause' (Psalm 43) à 5 (nos. 10 and 11); Andro Kemp's Te deum 'We praise thee, O God' à 4 (no. 12); John Angus' 'Our father, whiche in Heaven art' à 4 and 'All my belief (The XII Articles of the Christian Fayth)' à 4 (nos. 13 and 14); and four settings à 4 by David Peebles of Psalms 1, 18, 113 and 124 (nos. 15, 18, 21 and 25). These give a good idea of the character and scope of Wode's anthology.

Along with the sacred music Wode engrossed several items of part-song, sometimes devotional in character; *Music of Scotland* gives 'O God abufe' by John Fethy and 'The banks of Helicon' set for four voices by John Blackhall. He also entered several pieces of instrumental music.

The survival from among Wode's volumes of one complete set of part-books is of the first importance for the recovery of earlier Scottish part-music. The Quintus Part-Book is valuable for an extra reason as in it verbal texts are included. The later additions to one set of the Part-Books, made largely by a hand of 1620–30, gives us parts for many court-songs.

[1] See Introduction, Shire and Elliott, to *Music of Scotland 1500–1700*.

For many pieces Wode carefully recorded the name of the musician and the date and circumstances of composition. From his notes the past rises up as a reality: 'King James the Fifth, who was a musician himself...had a singular good ear and could sing that he had never seen before, but his voice was "rawky and harsk"' 'Robert Johnson was a Scottish priest who fled to England "lang before Reformation"; Thomas Hudson's father that is with the King "kent him weill"', 'John Fethy first brought the new fingering of organs into Scotland'.

The transcription of music in the Part-Books is professional; but in appearance the books themselves, with their floral and formal decorations in amateur watercolour, raise only a faint echo of medieval manuscript art. Troubled times are reflected there in another way also. Wode included many drawings of scenes in castle or city street with agitated figures and cannon-fire. These may well record accurately important incidents of the time or of the recent past—at St Andrews, Stirling or Edinburgh. To my knowledge they have never been studied, though they may be the record of an eye-witness.

In his determination to preserve the past in a difficult present as in his interest in contemporary composition, Thomas Wode in his compilation did for part-music of Scotland what George Bannatyne did for Scottish poetry. His anxiety reflects the precarious circumstances of musical part-writing on whose survival the future of courtly part-song in Scotland depended.

'THE GUDE AND GODLIE BALLATIS'[1]

Ane compendius buik of godly and spirituall sangis, collectit out of sundrye partes of the Scripture, with sundrye uther Ballatis changeit out of prophaine sangis in godly sangis, for auoyding of sin and harlatry, with augmentation of syndry gude and godly ballattis not contenit in the first Edition.

Title-page 1600 / 1578

The *Compendius Buik*, commonly known as 'The Gude and Godlie Ballatis' is a major cultural phenomenon of the Reformation in Scotland. It companions the *Scottish Psalter* of 1564.[2] It has its counterpart elsewhere in Europe in the 'Psalm-books' of the sixteenth century, French Huguenot or Netherlands, German or Swiss, Danish or English. The close kinship of the Scottish 'ballat buik' to such volumes both in intention and content has been clearly demonstrated. As much as one half of the 'spirituall sangis' have been shown to be translations or adaptions from German or Scandinavian pieces. All of these volumes aimed to 'sing' the gospels and

---

[1] Edited by A. F. Mitchell.
[2] The presence, at the end of the 1567/8 copy, of a single folio, printed in the same type as the text, apparently forming the title-page of an old Scottish psalter may represent the 'advertisement' of a forthcoming psalter or may indicate that the Psalter followed. See Mitchell, pp. lxxx–lxxxi.

the reformed doctrine into the minds and hearts of men and the music they used was often music of 'prophaine' songs that had proved its power to move men's hearts to 'earthly' love. With the songs that were 'changeit' the amorous matter might be displaced completely and only the stanza-pattern and the music of the earlier song retained, or the new biblical or devotional content might follow closely the form of words of the original song as it followed the stanza-pattern that matched the music. There resulted a spiritual version or a parody.

But neither in intent nor in method was such 'conversion' an invention of the reforming powers. The preface of the Huguenot Psalter bears witness to precedent in the earlier church.[1]

Théodoret, ancien théologien, raconte au 27e chapitre du IVe de son Histoire ecclésiastique qu'environ le temps de Valentinian et de Valens...un certain Harmonius composa des chansons profanes à la musique fort douce dont plusieurs furent séduits et tirez à perdition. Mais Dieu, qui dès le commencement a tiré la lumière des ténèbres, suscita à ce même temps un excellent personnage nommé Ephraim [Syrus] lequel entre autres services notables qu'il fit à l'Eglise, y adjousta celui-ci, a sçavoir, qu'il changea la lettre meschante des chansons d'Harmonius et y appliqua un sens spirituel et à louange de Dieu, remédiant (dit Théodoret) joyeusement et utilement au mal que poète lascif avoit fait.

The preface states that a similar phenomenon had been seen of late in the songs amorous and divine of such poets as Clément Marot.

In Scotland, perhaps as early as the regency following King James V's death in 1542, a volume of psalms and verses of this nature was compiled and, apparently, reached print. This existence of the *Compendius Buik* in an 'earlier and more rudimentary form' preceding the victory of the Reformation in 1560 has been cogently argued and its composition attributed to one or more of the brothers Wedderburn.[2] Discussion, however, is of necessity based on the earliest extant edition, a unique copy, presumed to be a survivor of the censored 'Psalme-book' of 1567/8. This early printed volume was published afresh in 1897 for the Scottish Text Society by A. F. Mitchell, to whose scholarly introduction and notes I am deeply indebted. The unique copy wants the first two folios, and in consequence the title page. The edition of 1578 has a title-page which again is fragmentary but reappeared, apparently little changed, in the edition of 1600.[3]

The prologue, taken from the 1600 edition, announces

We have heir ane plane text, that the word of God increass(is) plenteouslie in us be singing of the Psalmes and hymnis and spirituall sangis and that speciallie amang young personis, and [sic] as are not exercisit in the Scriptures for thay will soner consave the trew word nor quhen thay heir

---

[1] Orentin Douen, *Clément Marot et le Psautier Huguenot.*
[2] Mitchell, Appendix III, p. cix.   [3] Edition of 1578; edited by David Laing, Edinburgh 1826.

it sung in Latine, the quhilks thay wait not quhat it is. Bot quhen thay heir it sung into thair vulgar toung or singis it thame selfis with sweit melodie, then sal thay lufe thair God with hart and minde, and cause them to put away baudrie and unclene sangis. Prays [to] God. Amen.

This is plainly a book of words for music.

But the *Compendius Buik* contained no music, to judge by the copies that have survived.[1] In this it differs from its counterparts in other European countries. These had been printed with relevant music and some of that music was for part-singing. So on one aspect the Scottish *Compendius Buik* was committed to a policy which, in its country of origin, it could not itself fully implement, the spread of the gospel by singing of the words provided. The printing of musical notation was at that time new in Scotland. The year 1564 had seen the printing of the *Scottish Psalter* with the music of the psalm tunes. But the printing of tunes, to say nothing of part-music, for all the verses in the '*Gude and Godlie Ballatis*' would have been prohibitively expensive. In some quarters among the reforming powers, moreover, opinion would appear already to be running counter to the use of elaborate music in worship.

The *Compendius Buik* confirms the declared intention of its title-page and prologue in the presentation of its contents, pointing consistently to an expected use with music. The singing of the words is implied, now in the wording of a rubric covering a group of pieces, now in the entitling of a single item. After the catechism, the commandments, the articles of faith, the Lord's Prayer and the sacraments in prose come versions 'put in metre, to be sung with the tone'. The term 'sang' is used frequently in individual entitling and 'carrall' also appears, changed in later printings to 'sang' or 'ballat'.

The 'spirituall sangis' with which the volume opens derive largely from sacred song printed furth of Scotland and include versions in Scots of such famous hymns as 'In dulci jubilo'. These sing presumably to their own tunes that could have been current in Scotland in foreign printed volumes or copies made from them. One piece, however, links a hymn in this tradition, Luther's well-known 'Vom himel hoch da kom ich her' to a tune in Scottish currency believed to be of Scottish origin —'Ane sang of the birth of Christ with the tune of Baw lula low', 'I come from hevin [heigh] to tell'. *Music of Scotland* gives the tune with both sacred and secular words (no. 69).

After the 'spirituall sangis' come 'certaine Ballatis of the Scripture' in which a cycle of Easter and Christmas song can be traced. The first three are songs of penitence leading to a love-lament on the crucified Christ. These are couched throughout in the terms of 'prophaine' love-service now redirected to this devotional use.

---

[1] But see Mitchell, pp. lxxx–lxxxi.

Originals for two of these survive and it is not surprising that the music, part-writing for four or for three voices, is as courtly as are the words. They are 'Rycht sore opprest' and 'Allace that same sweit face', published with their amorous words in *Music of Scotland* as no. 40 and no. 34.[1]

Of the 'ballatis' and 'carralls' that follow a few, but a few only, have been traced to German or Danish sources. Some may come from English broadsides;[2] but many are in all probability indigenous Scots, both the moralisation and the earlier courtly song on which it was based. An example is 'Now lat us sing with joy and myrth', printed in *Music of Scotland* with two sets of words, sacred and secular. Another song from this group, 'Quha suld my mellodie amend' is representative in that it is characteristically Scottish-courtly both in style and form. I was delighted to trace it to its amorous original when a first stanza of text and music to four voices was published recently.[3]

> 1 Who shall my malady amend
> and solace surely to me send?
> Who shall me succor or supply? (bis)
> Who shall me from the dead defend
> since that my love, my love, has lightlied me?

Compare:

> 1 Quha suld my mellodie amend
> Or solace swyftlie to me send,
> Quha suld me succour or supplie
> Quha suld me from the deide defend
> Bot God, my lufe, in hevin sa hie...   (6 stanzas)

The godly version's 'mellodie', thus in all editions, may be a mistaken spelling, but it is much more likely to mark a 'conversion' suppressing the 'malady' of courtly love and glancing at the redirection of light song to serious purpose. Besides being a close parody of matter, the godly stanza matches the other in the pattern of phrase to be repeated in the music.

The next section of the *Compendius Buik* is announced thus:

> Heir endis the Spirituall Sangis
> and beginnis the Psalmes of David
> with uther new plesand Ballatis
> as efter followis. Translatit
> out of Enchiridion Psal–
> morum to be sung.

---

[1] 'Allace that same sweit face', both versions in H. M. Shire, *The Thrissil the Rois and the Flour-de-lys.*
[2] See Mitchell, Introduction and Appendix II, p. 240, 'Notes on the Hymns and Songs'.
[3] From the Robert Taitt MS. 1676, discussed by W. H. Rubsamen: see source-list. Dr Rubsamen has not noticed the moralised version.

This, the second part of the volume, begins with psalms in stanzas characteristic of courtly Scots poetry. Authoritative linking of these psalm-versions to the music of specific psalm-settings, either in the printed *Psalter* or in manuscript record, has not yet been undertaken. Thereafter—there is no break or subtitle—the pieces to the end of the volume are predominantly godly songs 'changeit' from songs of a courtly nature, Scots, English or Continental, though now and then there appear intermingled with these a psalm-version or a satiric piece that may derive from a broadside ballad in print. Representative of courtly song from England is the moralisation of 'Grevous is my sorrow' or of 'Musing greitlie in my mynde' while 'In till ane myrthfull Maii morning' points to the Scottish courtly repertory and 'For lufe of one' to the Franco-Scottish tradition of courtly part-song, as its music is a version of the music of 'Dont vient cela' by Sermisy.[1] This last, the original words by Clément Marot, was moralised more than once and current in print in French song-books. 'Iohne, cum kis me now' is a moralisation of a very well-known piece, its tune, 'Les Bouffons', a dance-tune from the Continent.

Various though they are in origin, these 'uther new plesand ballatis' are presented not as a miscellany but rather as an ordered progression. First after the formal psalm-group comes 'For lufe of one I mak my mone', then 'Quho is at my windo, quho' leading—by way of *Deus misereatur*—'Thy face schaw us sa glorious' to 'In till ane myrthfull Maii morning', now a song of meditation in a May morning garden on Christ crucified and the angel of comfort he sent. (Gestures of love-service in May are redirected to the figure of Christ at Easter.) Songs follow of the calling of the soul to Christ, who is Light, and his glorifying—a fine group of pieces. This is linked through 'With huntis up, with huntis up / It is now perfite day' to songs of the hunting of the soul by Christ, with fierce satire on false doctrine, and the lament 'I am wo for thir wolfis sa wylde'. 'Way is the Hirdis of Israell / that feidis nocht Christis flock' brings more satire and 'The wind blawis cauld, furius and bauld / This lang and mony day', apparently an old song with traces of a refrain, is redirected to show winter weather of false doctrine at its destructive work.

There is not time to discuss the whole scheme of the collection, but one more 'changeit' sang must be mentioned as it brings a difficulty. 'Hay now the day dallis' with its refrain 'The nycht is neir gone' recalls in its first stanza a spring 'aubade' that was probably an old song. That first stanza matches in metre and reflects in content the version Montgomerie made announcing a spring morning of tournament; it would sing to the same music as would his piece.[2] But the subsequent stanzas of

[1] 'Grevous is my sorrow', see Mitchell, pp. 275–7; 'Musing greitlie', see Stevens, *Music and Poetry in the Early Tudor Court*, no. 198 in song list, pp. 124, 141. 'In till ane myrthfull': Cantus part in Robert Edwards, in Forbes and in MSS. deriving from it. Was in Straloch, but not extant. Reported in Taitt, four stanzas set for four voices. See p. 30.   [2] Discussed in chapter 6.

29

2. INTO A MIRTHFULL MAY MORNING[1]

ANON   ANON

1 In - to a mirth - full May mor - ning As Phoe - bus did up -

- spring I saw a May both fair and gay, Most good - ly for to see. I

said to her, Be kind To me that was so pynd For your love tru - ly.

2 First, therefore when I did you know
    You thirl'd my heart so low
    Unto your Grace; but now in case
    Banisht through false report:
    But I hope and I trow
    Once for to speak with you
    Which doth me comfort.

3 Wherefore I pray have mind on me
    True Love, where ever you be:
    Where ever I go, both to and fro
    You have my heart alright.
    O Lady! fair of hew
    I me commend to you
    Both the day and night.

[1] Music and text: Robert Edwards' Commonplace-Book (c. 1650), fo. 2v; Louis de France's Music-Book (c. 1680), p. 18; *Songs & Fancies* (1662–82), no. 3; John Squyer's Music-Book (1701), p. 34, which supplies the three voice-parts. The alto part is editorial. Bar 2, notes 1–2: omitted in RE, Sq. Bar 4, bass, note 2: B flat in original. Bar 5, repeat marks: LF, Sq. Bar 7, tenor, notes 1–3: dotted quaver, semiquaver, quaver; soprano, note 4: D in RE, sharp in Sq. (K.E.)

4 Since Fortune false, unkind, untrue
Hath exy'ld me from you
By sudden chance I shall advance
Your honor and your fame
Above all earthly wight
To you my truth I plight
In earnest or in game.

Sacred Song

1 Intill ane myrthfull Maii morning
Quhen Phebus did up spring
Walkand I lay in ane garding gay
Thinkand on Christ sa fre:
Quhilk meiklie for mankynde
Tholit to be pynde
On Croce Cruellie, La La.*

2 And how he hes me wrocht
And formit me of nocht
Lyke his picture, that Lord maist sure
In eird he hes me support.
Syne me to hauld in rycht
Hes send ane Angell brycht
To be my confort. La lay.

3 O Sathan, fals untrew
Quhilk cruellie dois persew
With violence and great defence
In eird to tempt mankynde
With cruell sinnis sevin
The Saule to gyde from hevin
To hell, for to be pynde. La lay.

4 Thairfoir, O Gracious Lord
Quhilk mercy hes restored
That sinfull wycht destroy his mycht
Quhilk wirkis agains thy gloir
And send thy gracious word
Thy peple may be restoird
We pray thé thairfoir. La lay.

* For 'La La', repeat the last musical phrase.

the godly song do not match the first; they launch into strong anti-papistical satire in a different and fiercer rhythm. If the old song was—like Montgomerie's version—a 'summoning daybreak song for a day of armed combat', this piece would reflect its matter; it sounds like a threatening battle-song of the early years of Reformation... 'Wo be to yow, Paip and Cardinall... *The nycht* [of papistry] *is neir gone*'. Although it may be a powerful 'changeit sang' in matter, it looks as if this song breaks the general rule in not being recognisably words-for-the-tune that is indicated in the parodic opening stanza. But the music surviving in Scotland for 'Hay nou the day dawis' is incompletely recorded as to rhythm and no firm conclusion is possible; perhaps the first stanza matched the old tune note for note and the later stanzas were to be sung to variations on it.

The fact that the pieces of the second half of the volume, psalms interwoven with 'uther new plesand ballatis' reveal a meaningful arrangement in groups and sequences is, I think, important. A 'changeit sang' where it was made as a parody on an amorous original had to match it in pattern of stanza and stress: it might reflect in devotional terms the argument of that song, but the devising of the godly version would appear to be conditioned also by consideration of the part it was to play in the ordered sequences of the *Compendius Buik*. The shaping of a parody song and its relation to its original in words and music is studied in the chapter that follows.

Much work has yet to be done before a valid judgment can be passed on '*The Gude and Godlie Ballatis*' as a book of versions intended for singing. The nature of the music to which these versions were to be sung is largely in doubt still, as is the manner of singing—to a 'tune' or single vocal line, or in parts: the prologue spoke of people hearing the true word sung or singing it themselves 'with sweit melodie'. Here and there the original was demonstrably the court-song to four voices that survives—say 'Richt soir opprest' or 'In thru the'—their music of some complexity; in such a case no 'tune' was isolable to be carried in the head. Elsewhere, for example with 'In till ane myrthfull Maii morning', we have part-song of which the cantus part survived separately and could be remembered as a tune, yet as late as the 1670s it appears set to four voices in the music-book of a song-school. Those pieces that are certainly or probably derived from broadsides would have a tune that could persist in oral currency. As to the psalm versions that are not from foreign printed books, many of them are made in stanzas characteristic of courtly Scots poetry and would not sing to well-known psalm tunes with their narrow range of metres. How these may have been matched with music can be glimpsed, however, from interesting examples written by Montgomerie, probably after 1568. These are made 'to the tune' of an amorous court-song whose words are of his own writing and their music, to four voices, has come down to us.: 'In thru the' and in all probability 'Lyk as the dum solsequium'. With the second of these the cantus part would be easily memorable but the correct transmission of the first and of both of their skilful settings would mean commission of the parts to paper.

The currency of the music taken for granted when the *Compendius Buik* was printed would appear, then, to be a currency in part of easily memorable tunes, in part of musical part-writing that would require to be committed to paper. Perhaps we can understand the Prologue as saying that for many of the pieces the 'sweit melodie' would be known and could be sung by all while some of the songs could be heard in their part-settings sung by skilled voices, whether professional or amateur.

The public for whom the *Compendius Buik* was prepared, whether kirk congregations or song-schools, families or individuals, were understood to know or to have access to the relevant music. For the 'spirituall sangis' much of this might indeed be available in printed psalm-books from abroad that gave 'the tune', or in copies made from them. (Interesting examples of words and music from such volumes are reproduced by Mitchell.) Some of the psalm versions may have been singable to tunes in the *Scottish Psalter*. For the versions certainly or apparently matching courtly part-songs a repertory is indicated vastly more extensive than the sparse surviving remnant might at first suggest. Yet currency of such a repertory can be envisaged, of songs sung now 'to the tune', now to the tune set for four voices; where the music of the original was too complex to be transmitted in a tradition that was to some extent an oral one, it can still be envisaged recorded in manuscript, copied and recopied up to that point in time (1568) and thereafter by masters of the song-schools, musicians of burgh kirk, cathedral or Chapel Royal or musical amateurs. Indeed the printing or issuing of '*The Gude and Godlie Ballatis*' *without* music may have vastly encouraged the compilation and proliferation of such music-books in manuscript.

Of explicit intent the makers of the *Compendius Buik* sought to turn the thoughts of the singers from the matter of amorous courtly song, to delete its sinful appeal and cancel its currency. To the tune of 'Solomon the King' they wrote

> Of him lat us exempill tak
> And neuer think on Cupides dart:
> Venus can nouther mar nor mak,
> Gif unto God we ioyne our hart;
> And leif this art of langing lust,
>   Allace, allace!
> And in the Lord baith hope and trust,
>   Quhilk is and was.[1]

But they needed and recommended the music as a powerful vehicle for the spread of God's word. Paradoxically enough, the use of their 'ballatis' to the music prescribed throughout the volume may well have helped to preserve courtly part-song of the earlier half of the century, including a number of songs of some complexity that might otherwise have perished, until the time of the second blossoming of court-song under King James VI. Printed anew in 1578 and again in 1600 and 1621 the volume of godly words for singing would continue to stimulate compilation and copying of the music—and in the privacy of private collection the old 'prophaine' words did not go unrecorded.

Bannatyne and Wode had been moved by a desire to rescue and record, preserve the old and cherish contemporary composition, in poetry and in music. Both may have hoped for the publication of their collections in print, the communication of their treasured matter to a wide audience. '*The Gude and Godlie Ballatis*' reached that wide audience with words that sought to displace, but may have helped to transmit and disseminate far beyond 'courtly' circles, the courtly part-song of an earlier Scotland. It may even be that the inclusion of certain earlier court-songs moralised in the *Compendius Buik* helped to determine which of such songs were to survive as words and music for the delight of later generations.

[1] Mitchell, p. 219.

2

THE MAKING OF COURT-SONG

How did a court-song come into being? Here are five 'ballatis' which were sung in courtly circles in sixteenth-century Scotland. Considering each in turn may take us some way towards an answer to the question.

MAITLAND'S BALLAT 'MAID TO THE TONE OF THE BANKIS OF HELECON'

FIRST, the ballat of the creation of the world made by Sir Richard Maitland to the tune of 'The banks of Helicon'. This ballat was made before 1568 by a courtier who was born in 1496 and lived on to a great age at the close of the sixteenth century. His ballat is a concentrated version of a passage from Sir David Lyndsay's *The Monarche* and the shortening has been done *to a tune*: the content is recast into the measure of a tune that must have been well known in Scotland of 1568—for otherwise why should its name be thus recorded?[1] The intention of the poet in so shaping his matter would apparently be—on the face of it—that the ballat would be sung to its tune. The content of the verses thus passes from printed 'literature' into a currency that could include the illiterate, for the words of a ballat thus floated with its tune were well on their way into aural and oral tradition.

Verses reproduced by Bannatyne with a rubric giving the tune to which they were made belong by this very fact to the great stream of ballats printed as broadsides where a common characteristic was the designation of the tune to which they could be sung: 'To be sung to the tune of *Lusty Gallant*' or *Crimson Velvet* or *the Cecelia pavane*, 'to its own tune' or 'to a pleasant new tune'. A ballat printed as a broadside could be enjoyed in several ways. It could be read, or read aloud, declaimed or sung, committed to memory and passed on with or without its tune.

Often the tunes thus named for ballats were dance-tunes, dance-songs for which other sets of words might already be in use. Where the rubric names the tune to

---

[1] *The Works of Sir David Lindsay*, ed. Douglas Hamer, vol. III, p. 237 and vol. IV, Appendix VI. *Ane Dialog betuix Experience and ane Courteour*, St Andrews, 1554—commonly known as 'The Monarche'. If the moralisation were made in the 1550s, from which decade the tune may derive (see ch. 6), it would be contemporary with the activities of the Wedderburns and the conjectured earliest compilation of 'The Gude and Godlie Ballatis'.

which the ballat was made or directs the ballat 'to be sung to' such and such a tune and it can be shown that the tune was in fact a dance-tune, then the words of the ballat might by implication be sung in association with the dance, by dancers as they danced or by onlookers to the dancing. Among the several ways in which a ballat could be enjoyed, then, should be included 'the dancing of it'.

The tune that was in people's ears in 1568 and went by the name of 'the banks of Helicon' has survived in Scottish music books. It can be found in *Music of Scotland* as no. 49. It was recorded as four-part music for voices and there are several sets of words known to its measure. One, 'Declair ye banks of Helicon' was recorded by Sir Richard's daughter, Mary, in her verse anthology of the 1580s. The song is studied at length in a later chapter where its form, of three self-repeating 'traces' is shown to be characteristic of the dance-song.

3. THE BANKS OF HELICON, THE CHERRIE AND THE SLAE, 'ADEU, O DESIE'
(ALIAS THE NYNE MUSES)

The content of Sir Richard's ballat is Christian and somewhat solemn. There was nothing against the singing of Christian words to a court-dance music before the Reformation—witness perhaps 'All Christen mennis' dance named in 1548. But the interesting question as to whether words of religious content could *in 1568* be 'danced to' must remain wide open. It is on the whole more likely that Maitland, knowing 'the banks of Helicon' as a ballat that was a dance-song, intended his ballat of the creation of the world as a 'moralisation', a harnessing of the dance-tune measure to godly usage, and that his ballat, recorded in Bannatyne's opening section 'of theologie', turns its back on dancing and has a place on the axis of reform. *The Monarche* was completed by 1553, which gives a first possible date of Maitland's ballat before the full severity of the Reformation hit the manners of Scotland.

The enjoying of the dance-song-ballat—words, tune and dance together—was a social pleasure in the sixteenth century. This usage is testified to in different ways and at different levels of social currency. Bacon in his essay 'Of Masques and Triumphs' says 'Dancing to song is a thing of great State and Pleasure'; that is, dancing while other people sing. His next sentence condemns dancing 'in song' as a mean and vulgar thing: that is when the dancer dances to his own singing. Both ways, then, were current. In Bacon's time and in England they were associated the one with courtly mode, the other with wider and less elevated usage.

For dancing as a social pleasure in the sixteenth century the continental authority is 'Thoinot Arbeau' whose *Orchésographie* (1588, 1596) is the main source of our information on the dances of this time, their rhythms and steps, their music and the way in which they were performed.[1] He writes of courtly practice but the dances of which he treats passed, we know, into use in circles far beyond courtly walls.

'Thoinot Arbeau' at one point gives instructions for the pavan 'Belle qui tiens ma vie' with the drum-beats and the movements for the measure and adds 'et si voulez sans la dancer, la ferez chanter ou iouer à quatre parties'. Then (fo. 32 *b*) 'La pauane cy dessus mise à quatre parties tient deux aduances et deux démarches marquées par leur caractéres ainsi...et tient trante deux mesures et battements de tambourin. Et pour prolonger fault recommencer tant de fois...parce qu'il vous pourra prendre quelque iour envie de chanter la chanson entière, la voicy par escript...' and he gives the whole text of 'Belle qui tiens ma vie'.

With such testimony from France and England we may take it that in Scotland also the dance-song was enjoyed to music 'à 4', in four parts rendered by voices or instruments. On the point of social ambience, however, we need not conclude that the distinction made by the socially conscious Francis Bacon held good earlier in the century or in a different *milieu*—that in old-style Scotland it was necessarily un-courtly to dance to one's own singing.

Of the possible ways of making a court-song we note, with Maitland's ballat, these: abbreviation of matter—a skill known in the art of rhetoric; adaptation of matter; and the matching of words 'to an ayre that was made before'—the writing of verses that correspond exactly in stanza-pattern to verses existing for the same tune and, where the tune is a dance-tune, reproduce in their rhythmic structure the 'measure' of the dance.[2] The consideration of Maitland's ballat has moreover opened up lines of thought that are to be pursued in later pages. There is the question of redirection of a song in ambience and use, when moralising or didactic words are provided for a piece that appears to have been up to that time of a courtly-amorous nature. No less important is the enquiry into the nature of dance-song, how it was enjoyed or performed. When a piece was 'danced to song', 'danced in song' or 'acted in song' what was the nature of such dancing or acting? Did it amount to gesture, mime and significant movement expressive of the meaning of the words?

---

[1] Thoinot Arbeau (pseudonym for Jean Tabourot), Lengres, 1588 and 1596; available in English as *Orchesography*, translated by C. W. Beaumont.

[2] Cf. the rubric for John Donne's 'Sweetest love' in some sources, 'Songs which were made to certain ayres which were made before'.

When the dancing was of a figured dance, say a pavan or galliard, could the performance of it have a social intention and meaning that went beyond that of recreation?

'O GOD ABUFE',
WORDS AND MUSIC BY SIR JOHN FETHY

The second example is introduced here from a source other than the ballat books though contemporary with them in compilation, Thomas Wode's part-books. From it 'O God abufe', 'Ane sang of repentance' by John Futhy (Fethy) has been chosen because it is a rare case, well documented, of words and music known to have been composed by the same hand and by a named and known personality.[1] Wode tells us in a note that it was 'composit be Shir Jhone futhy, bayth letter and note'. The 'letter' (the words) is a courtly composition, well-finished stanzas in literary Scots, and the 'note' (the music) is equally that of a skilled maker, a musician trained in the pre-Reformation Church. A priest, whose musical education was pursued abroad, he is glimpsed in the court records shortly after the death of King James V. He was the first that brought the new skill of five-fingered organ-playing to Scotland. He was later teacher and Master of the song-school in Aberdeen and in Edinburgh. (His life-records are assembled in Appendix I.)

Words of other pieces by Fethy are in the Bannatyne manuscript among the 'songis of luve'. The possibility may be mooted that Fethy made amorous court-song too, words and music both—that 'My trewth is plicht' in rhyme royal and 'Pansing in hairt with spreit opprest' may also have had their music; the second survives in fragment as part-song.[2] His song of repentance forswears the rage of youth when he 'thocht bot fantasye', which may refer to his composition of vain, amorous verse. 'O God abufe' is no. 37 in *Music of Scotland* and 'The time of youth sore I repent' which companions it there has been suggested as also coming from his pen.

We do not know what his practice was in making 'O God abufe' but it seems overwhelmingly likely that he wrote the 'letter' first and the 'note' afterwards—that he composed the verses and then set them to music. The text of two stanzas is through-composed in compact part-writing of some complexity.

As the song is a devotional piece, a recantation of 'fantasye', it belongs in a sense to the redirection of amorous court-song. Nearer than that it is not possible to come in

---

[1] *Music of Scotland*, introduction, and notes to no. 37.

[2] 'My trewth is plicht', B. CCLXXXVIII (Fethy). 'Pansing in hairt with spreit opprest', B. CCCIX (Fethe) I take to be the text indicated by the title or *incipit* 'Pansing in spreit' of the bass part in the Melvill Bassus Part-Book. See source-list.

placing it in social context. There is an overlapping of life-records of several men bearing the name of Fethy; two of them possibly styled with the priestly 'Sir'. This means that we remain in doubt as to whether this 'sang of repentance' was made within the Catholic world or in the spirit of Reformation.

'RICHT SOIR OPPREST'

'Richt soir opprest', no. 40 in *Music of Scotland*, is not among Bannatyne's ballats. It was for long known only in the form of a 'godlie ballat' among the spiritual versions in *A Compendious Book of Godlie and Spirituall Sangis*. But the courtly love-song that is without doubt its original is found several times recorded in the song manuscripts, both words and music, one stanza of the words usually underlaid to a voice part. It is a polyphonic chanson in Franco-Scottish style of the earlier half of the sixteenth century. No related text is known in French nor has the music come to light in a French source. Apparently we have here a Scottish courtly ballat set to music by a skilled musician. The refrain in the stanza is used refrain-wise in the musical form.

Phrases of the verbal text have been repeated by the musician for points of imitation in his composition, for example the first two feet of the second line in each stanza, 'Both night and day', 'Solace is caus', 'Thair is no tongue'. This raises the question: was the poem written consciously and deliberately with this careful matching of the phrase-pattern in all three stanzas because the writer had such a musical setting in view? The stanza however is one commonly found in the 'style King James V' and such matching is not uncommon. That this feature, obviously *amoene* to setting in chanson style, was fostered in courtly circles of this epoch by the prestige of the contemporary chanson from France seems on the whole likely.

The words of the spiritual version, 'Rycht sore opprest I am with panis smart' recorded in a volume as explicit in its intention as '*The Gude and Godlie Ballatis*' are clearly secondary to the amorous words. Was it made to match the words-and-music of the court-song? The stanza is the same. The refrain, 'Bot to the deid bowne, cairfull creature', reproduces the refrain of the love-song exactly in the first two stanzas—its meaning, of the creature full of care bound to death, serving the new Christian direction of the sense as well as it did the older meaning in the courtly love code. In stanzas three, four and five the refrain is adapted, 'That thow suld saif all sinfull creature', 'Than knawand it, die cairfull creature' to further the development of the new Christian argument and to clinch it at the close. In all cases the pause after the second iambic foot, present in the love-song and felt in its musical phrasing, is present also in the godly ballat. This is equally true of the phrases that are repeated in the musical setting, the first two iambs of the second line and the last two of the fourth line, 'Baith nicht and day' and 'with wo begone'. The godly ballat reproduces these two phrases exactly in the first stanza and in subsequent stanzas a phrase appears that, though different from its courtly counterpart, is similarly complete in itself and separable enough to render repetition effective as the words are sung. (The group of singers with whom we first worked on the performance of this music, 'The Saltire Singers', familiar already with the courtly love-song, sang through the spiritual version at sight without a query as to underlay of text to music. Moreover the argument of the godly ballat came through clearly and movingly, enforced and enhanced by the polyphonic music.)[1]

The godly ballat, then, 'se chante sur l'aire de' the courtly love-song.[2] From this we can go on to say that the writer of the 'parodie' knew the court-song as a part-song, words and music, and that in writing he had strongly in mind enjoyment of his new words with that music and its use in the service of God. At the same time the relationship between the sense of the sacred song and that of the secular should be noted. It is less that of a parallel in sense strictly maintained throughout than it is a parallel that becomes a divergence. Close parody in the opening stanza with retention of the phrasing becomes less close as the second poem develops. The 'godlie ballat' is in its way an overgoing of its original. The close parallel in the opening stanza effects the marrying of the new words to the known music. That done, the writer of the Christian verses is free to pursue his new line of thought. The negation of amorous values and assertion of Christian values in close parodic terms at the outset acts as a springboard for the new poem. Thereafter the writer may develop his own argument, remaining, however, sensitive to the form of the original and responding to its patterning thought.

Here we have a full documentation of the process of 'parodie' and a display of its nature as akin to 'overgoing'. While the original verses were presumably set to music, the sacred version gives evidence of having been written to match both words and part-music of the original.

'SUPPORT YOUR SERVAND PEIRLES PARAMOUR'

'Support your servand peirles paramour', no. CCLXXVII in Bannatyne's ballat book, was long enjoyed in Scotland as a polyphonic chanson. The Scots poem can now be shown to be a translation of Clément Marot's 'Secourez-moi madame par amours'.

---

[1] 'The Saltire Singers', directed by the late Hans Oppenheim: Margaret Fraser, Constance Mullay, Duncan Robertson and Frederick Westcott. To this group, with their consummate musicianship, Kenneth Elliott and I owed a great debt in the interpretation by performance of these song texts, when they were first prepared for publication.

[2] 'Se chante sur l'aire de' is the phrase found as rubric in the French *chansonniers*.

Entitled 'Chanson' and dated 1530 it is the second in the group of Chansons in the *Oevres Complètes* edited by Abel Grenier.[1] These chansons, of which there are forty-two, number among them pieces that won European favour as part-songs, 'Tant que vivray' (1524), 'Jouissance vous donneray' (1525), 'D'ou vient cela' (1525) or 'Mauldicte soit' (1525). The dates apparently indicate the issue of the song in printed song-books. 'Secourez-moi' was set many times by distinguished composers: by Claudin de Sermisy in 1528, by Gombert in 1544, Canis in 1546 and Orlando de Lassus about 1560.[2] (Later settings do not concern us here.)

The poems of Marot were printed in 1538, this piece among them. A northern makar made a version of Marot's poem in Scots in a style very close to that of courtier poets under King James V. The date of the appearance of Marot's piece whether as poetry or as song is just the time when there came an inrush of French influence in Scots courtly circles with the coming of Princess Madeleine to be his Queen.

When we read the Scots poem beside Marot's it seems that the northern poet has carried the piece back into the Middle Ages. Marot's song is an appeal for comfort to 'ma Dame par amours'. The time-honoured *Bel Acueil* is introduced but comes through less as a personification than as a precise stage in an affair of the heart; kisses are mentioned and 'l'ardent feu' is pressing on towards 'jouissance'. In the French a suit is pressed in a love-song; in Scots a gesture of courtly love is celebrated. The lover asks for comfort in recognition of his sworn devotion. His peerless paramour is his sweet daisy most 'decoir'. Of the virtues found in the lady, pity only is wanting but Dame Esperance and Lady Mercy shall engraft pity and grace in her heart. As to style, alliteration is strongly present, often alliteration by half-line, though it is absent from the refrain line. The difference in tone is to some extent a question of equivalents to hand for the remote northern makar, of unconscious acclimatisation rather than of conscious adaptation. But on the other hand the Scots poet is not tamely translating 'par lettre'; he is giving 'his way' of the song 'Secourez-moi'. The first stanza is a near-translation:

> Secourez-moy, ma Dame par amours
> Ou autrement la Mort me vient quérir.
> Autre que vous ne peult donner secours
> A mon las cueur, lequel s'en va mourir.
> Hélas, hélas! vueillez donc secourir
> Celuy qui vyt pour vous en grand' destresse
> Car de son cueur vous estes la maistresse?

---

[1] Only vol. I reached print (introduction and text). No explanatory notes are therefore available to give the evidence on which Grenier based the dates that appear with the titles of the 'Chansons'.

[2] François Lesure, 'Autour de Clément Marot et de ses Musiciens'. The music of 'Support' has not been traced to French sources by Kenneth Elliott or myself.

> Support your servand peirles paramour
> or dreidfull deth and dolour me devoir
> Sen thair is nan may schaw [me] no succour
> to my puir hairt oursett with siching soir
> Allace, allace sueit desy most decoir
> Will ye not help me of my heviness
> Sen of my hairt ye ar the cheif maistress?

The stanza-pattern is the same. The parallel is exact except for the 'desy most decoir' (which perhaps came in with the rhyme) and the telescoping of phrase in the line that follows. But now, apparently, the Scots poet begins to overgo. He takes the last line of Marot's first stanza and makes it the refrain of his song. From this new insistence on the declaration of devotion, now reiterated in the refrain, a staidness results against the forward movement in the French poet's piece. But it may be that the makar was preparing his piece for an occasion demanding a more humble and decorous service than the French poem indicated, as *propyne* perhaps for a royal or noble lady.

Whether the Scots poet was working with Marot's words alone in mind or whether he was making a version in Scots to match a French court-song, words and music, we do not know.

In 'Support your servand' we have a distinguished example of translation into an identical verse-pattern in a new tongue and at the same time of matching part-song with new words. The translation is not 'par lettre' but amounts to an 'overgoing', the second poet writing a variation on the first poet's theme. The making of his song involves both an exacting discipline and an interesting element of freedom.

'FOR LOVE OF ONE'

Our fifth example is of a poem and a musical composition that came into being independently of one another but were brought together to make a court song in Scotland. Again influence from France is seen precipitating song in the north. Again the words of a chanson by Marot are in question but this time the music is known, the four-part setting by Claudin de Sermisy. The whole song by Marot and Sermisy, 'D'ou vient cela belle je vous supply' (1525) was of all the favourite chansons of this age the most widely known and the most variously adapted, both in words and in musical use. Parodies exist for the words, 'Dont vient celas, belle' or 'D'ou vient cela mon prélat' and the music of the chanson was adapted as a *basse danse*.[1]

In Scotland the Sermisy music was current with the text 'For love of one'. It was recorded with text in Robert Edwards' song-book, without text but with title among the Scottish songs in the part-book of Mure of Rowallan and in the later

---

[1] See Lesure, *ibid*.

additions to one set of Wode's part-books.[1] It is reported in the Taitt manuscript also, three stanzas, four voices. The existence of a courtly love-song opening with this phrase had been deduced from the presence among the 'godlie ballat' parodies of a spiritual song with that *incipit*. The text of the court-song is now, I believe, printed for the first time. It is a plaint of the lover to Venus Queen.

> For love of one I mak my mone
>   rycht secretlie
> To Venus quine that ladie shein
>   for remidie
> To cause that schow grant greace to me
>   or I be gone
> For to redres my hevines
>   and al my mone
> Or I be deid send me remied anone
>   off your mercie
> For him that wrocht us all of noght
>   my faire ladie.

Here is the first stanza of the godly version.

> For lufe of one I mak my mone
> Rycht secreitlie
> To Christ Jesu that Lord maist trew
> For his mercy
> Beseiking that fre grant grace to me
> Or I be gone
> And to redres my hevynes
> And all my mone
> Or I be deide, send me remeid
> For thy pietie
> O Lord quhilk wrocht all thingis of nocht
> Grant me thy mercy.

'Fre', meaning originally 'noble one' usually implied in verse 'noble lady', but it could stand for Christ. It is corrected in later printings of the volume to 'he'. We have here the figure of Christ the heavenly beloved over against the beloved lady of courtly love.

Again as in 'Richt soir opprest' the opening stanza is a very close 'parodie' indeed in form and sense again we may assume from the presence of the godly version in the propaganda volume that it is a redirection of an earlier piece. Unfortunately Robert Edwards never wrote down any further stanzas for the love-song. The 'three stanzas' of the Taitt manuscript version are as yet unpublished. With the precedent of 'Richt soir opprest' before us we cannot conclude that the argument of the love-song and

[1] Wode (four voices) and Rowallan (cantus part).

that of the spiritual version of necessity ran parallel throughout; it may have done so, or the second may have swerved away from the first after the shared outset. In the godly ballat's second stanza God's mercy is besought for sinners. The third is an appeal 'O King of peace' to succour 'me' and keep from hell's pain by his sweet word, then shall 'I' sing his praise. The last stanza is 'Let us now sing and praise that King/For his mercy', sing 'psalmes sweit' as 'brethir deir' and pray Christ 'to mak us sure'. A plaint to Venus can easily be imagined along similar lines in amorous discourse. The lover prays to Venus that he, loving only one lady and loving her secretly, may be rewarded by her favour; Venus' mercy is promised to lovers all; if she send succour she shall be praised; let us sing praise to Venus for her mercy and live 'rycht plesandlie' as lovers all.

The single stanza salvaged from Robert Edwards' book presents some difficulty. The opening lines make very good sense as a Venus plaint, for secrecy was exacted from the lover in the code of 'Venus observance'. But the last two lines move apparently to a direct appeal to God the Creator, the power over and behind that of 'Venus genetrix', perhaps. The whole question of the mingling in of Christian values in poetry and song of the service of Venus Queen is a complicated one. In this case the simplest explanation may be the right one: that Robert Edwards knew the court-song, or a part of it, and was familiar also with the godly version and that the two merged in his mind and he introduced the godly line here by mistake.

Robert Edwards had trouble in writing out the words and music of this song. His musical text is corrupt and in underlaying words to music of the cantus part he has a word extraneous to the stanza-pattern though rhyming in with it, 'anone'. The Scots texts do not fit the French music very well; indeed this is not surprising as the stanza-patterns are different.[1] The transcriber's 'anone' may be an attempt to remedy matters. There may have been another version of the music to which both pieces in this stanza-form matched exactly. But the interest of the surviving record, unsatisfactory though it is in some ways, lies in the evidence it provides of song-making by putting together a famous piece of music from the continent and words written in a recognisable, indeed a favourite, stanza of *Scottis Poesie*. That the putting together appears to have entailed doing some violence to both makes us look back with the greater admiration at the earlier examples we have seen, abbreviation with writing to a tune, translation with 'overgoing', parody with matching of the setting, as ways of marrying words and music in the devising of court-song.

[1] The stanza-patterns are: French, 10, 10, 10, 10, 10, 11, 11 syllables against Scots 12, 12, 12, 12, 12 (+2), 12. A full discussion of the piece as words and music must await the publication of the Taitt MS. planned by Dr Rubsamen (see Appendix v).

3

ALEXANDER SCOTT (*c.* 1525–*c.* 1590) AND TRADITIONS OF COURT-SONG, DANCE AND CEREMONY

SCOTT RECONSIDERED

W E have seen the ballats and their music in the books that recorded them. We have looked into the ways in which words could be matched with music to make a part-song. Now we turn to a known makar, *the* modern poet of George Bannatyne's 'Ballat Buik' of 1568, some of whose pieces were favourite part-songs in the song collections. The music for his pieces is there anonymous. The intention here is to review afresh his work and what is known of his history in order to discover what part he and his poetry played in the cultivation of part-song in sixteenth-century Scotland.

Alexander Scott is the poet of pre-Reformation Scotland whose words are most frequently found with music. The nature of that music—courtly part-writing, sometimes polyphonic—was not understood by his earlier editors. True, the music was incompletely recorded or survived only in scattered manuscripts, and editors did not then envisage a tradition of *music fyne* in Scottish song as courtly in music as were the words of the songs in poetry.[1] Yet they gave the poet's words in as full a context as was known. Four pieces were given with their music: the 'tune' for 'How suld my febill body fure', 'Hence hairt' and 'Only to yow in warld that I loved best' and the 'tune' and 'bass part' for 'Depairte'.

In the most recent printing of Scott's poems, however, that prepared in 1952 by Mr Alexander Scott of this century for the Saltire Classics Series, all reference to the music is omitted, nor is there a hint that any pieces Scott wrote were in fact songs. Valuable proof thus disappears of one way in which the poems were enjoyed aloud

---

[1] Editions of Scott's poems: 1, ed. David Laing, Edinburgh 1821 (limited edition); 2, ed. James Cranstoun, Edinburgh 1896 (S.T.S.); 3, ed. A. K. Donald, London 1902 (E.E.T.S.); 4, ed. Alexander Scott, *The poems of Alexander Scott (c. 1530–c. 1584)*, Edinburgh 1952 (Saltire Classics). Laing printed the cantus part of 'How suld my' from Forbes and Panmure and the bass part of 'Depairte' from Wode, of whose compilation he knew only two volumes. Cranstoun gave these and added the 'tune' for 'Hence hairt' (Robert Edwards MS.) and the cantus part of 'Depairte' from Wode.

in company. A link has been broken between the poetry and its context in society. This omission must be made good if we are to read Scott's poems in the spirit of the times in which they were written or to understand them aright in terms of the society in which they were rooted. That society, as I hope to show, was the court-life under King James V in which the love-cult was still enjoyed as a courtly game. Later, when over that society had broken the storm of the Reformation, this poetry of Scott's was esteemed in a world that argued angrily against values of 'love' in that society, inveighing against the 'sin and harlatrie' of such amorous playing.

I see the language of Scott's poems as imbued with the values of 'courtly love' even when, in a particular poem, he is intent on destroying them. For example, I would gloss 'languor to leive', a key-phrase in medieval love-psychology, as 'to quit this state of debilitating love-longing' not as 'longer to live', which is Mr Scott's explanation. The wide variety of aspects of the love experience presented in his poems by Alexander Scott with apparent inconsistency I see as the apprehension by a gifted poet of the diverse and 'contrarious' nature of love as expounded in medieval poetry. Scott relishes the imbalance and non-reconcilation of contradictory and opposed values, 'code' and actuality; but he can celebrate a single attitude with deep participation and great eloquence, whether it be the 'Depairte' of the Master of Erskine or the lament 'To luve unluvit', which may be personal.

Mr Scott sees Scott as a 'lyric' poet of love in the modern or neo-romantic sense, a poet of 'sincerity' and 'self-expression' whose writing on love in its various and contradictory moods sprang primarily from his own emotional history and sexual experience. But the different aspects of love in society had been celebrated together, one in relief against another, up through the Middle Ages. Love, in all its aspects, vagaries and contradictions, was the topic. Scott the editor says 'We can find an explanation of the apparent inconsistencies of mood and attitude to be found in these poems'...in the suggestion that they were written over a period of twenty years. 'He would be an unusual man whose attitude to love was the same at seventeen as at thirty-seven.'[1]

This is to wander so far astray from Alexander Scott, courtly makar of 1547, that a fresh consideration of the poet and his work is clearly pertinent. His sparse life-records must be scrutinised. Taken together with evidence that comes in with the music for his songs they may yield something new. An approach to his poetry made through the currency of his words as song will restore his verses to their social context and may serve to redress critical balance. Scott the 'lyric' poet whose 'words sing' and

---

[1] See Mr Alexander Scott's introduction to his edition. Agnes Mure Mackenzie gives a lively appreciation of Scott's poetry in her chapter 'The Renaissance Poets (1) Scots and English', in *Scottish Poetry: A Critical Survey*, ed. James Kinsley, and also in her *An Historical Survey of Scottish Literature to 1714*, pp. 130–3; of 'My hairt is heich aboif' (B. CCLXXXV) she says, 'aut Scott aut diabolus', but I do not agree there.

whose 'metres dance' will be reconsidered as Scott the courtly makar whose words were sung and whose songs were dances, as Scott the poet 'of love matters', lively participant in the age-old debate about love; contributor to this debate in vivid pieces, song in celebration of its good, satire on its falsity or its evil.

For our knowledge of Alexander Scott's poetry we depend almost entirely on George Bannatyne's 'Ballat Buik' of 1568. For young Bannatyne, Scott was *the* established modern poet. Of his 38 pieces collected there all but a few—notably his address to the queen, his satiric *descriptio* 'Of May' and his psalm versions—are engrossed in Book IV of the 'Ballat Buik', the 'buik of luve'. Many are in the first part of the Fourth Book that is headed 'Songis of luve'. There Scott's pieces keep company with many poems for which we know there was music, songs by Steill or Fethy or the other fine court-songs whose words in Scots are of unknown authorship. His pieces on love in its varying aspects are carefully arranged in the four sections of the Ballat Buik's Book IV that present the different faces of love. The anthologist, Scott's younger contemporary, mounts his love-poetry in terms of the 'argument' about courtly love in society and its values that was highly topical in newly reformed Scotland of 1568.

Certain of the poet's verses Bannatyne thought of as songs or knew as pieces currently enjoyed with music. A move towards understanding Scott's poems in their true context was made when some of these were restored to the repertory of court-song in *Music of Scotland*. There all pieces complete enough to warrant editing and publication were printed, settings of 'Depairte, depairte' and 'How suld my febill body fure'. Several texts have since been made known as of interest even in their fragmentary form.[1] A recently discovered source-book has yielded new verbal texts and vocal parts hitherto wanting.[2] Outstanding items are included here with their music. Scott's 'Hence hairt' is given from a fresh source; the song 'Only to yow in warld that I loved best' / 'Only to you in erd' has now a third 'linked text'.

The music of these songs is for the most part of unknown authorship. Though with a famous foreign piece identity of the composer may be known and even the date of the song's circulation in print established, we still cannot be sure of the period of its currency in out-of-the-way Scotland. The music will not help us to a specific dating of the poet's words. But consideration of the words with their music allows us to take a new bearing on Scott's practice as a poet, to envisage the milieu and social intention of his writing, the traditions in song-making and in treating of matters of love on which he drew and of which he was in turn so accomplished an exponent.

An attempt to establish the life-span of Alexander Scott the poet depends on in-

---

[1] 'Hence hairt' from William Stirling's Cantus Part-Book: Cantus part, 1 stanza.

[2] Robert Taitt MS.: see source list. Publication of these lyrics as there underlaid to their music from a French *chansonnier* must await publication of the Taitt MS.

formation of two kinds, evidence from his own poems and from the verse of his contemporaries which clearly bears on the poet, and references in official documents to 'Alexander Scott' who in each and every case may or may not be the poet. Because Scott is a common surname and Alexander is a favourite Christian name liable to recur with every generation in a family, the identification of any such Alexander Scott with the poet must be made with caution; the presence or absence of the 'Schir' of priestly or knightly style or the 'Mr.' of the Master of Arts nevertheless provides a helpful clue. Consequently I separate the two kinds of evidence and consider first the information that can be gleaned from poetry.

The dating of Alexander Scott's activity as a poet and thence the fixing of the approximate year of his birth hangs on two of his own poems and their titles or colophons. His 'Welcum illustrat Ladye and oure quene', entitled 'Ane new yeir gift to the quene mary Quhen scho come first hame, 1562' (B. cLII) with its refrain 'God gif the grace aganis this guid new yeir' is dated and signed in the text of the poem 'thy sempill servand Sanderris Scott'. Here loyal and poetic service are one, but in the absence of corroboration from court records service at court cannot be deduced, though hope for such service may well have been in the poet's mind. The use here of the familiar 'Sanderris Scot' might be taken to suggest personal contact with the Queen in her service at some earlier point. But 'Sanderris' was *the* name for the Scotsman then, as 'Jock' is now; the letter of 'staitly' welcome and admonition to the prince may be signed—with a play on the poet's own name, by the simple servant of Queen Mary, Sanderris the Scot—her realm of Scotland.[1]

The second poem that helps us date his writing, 'Depairte, depairte, depairte' (B. cccx), is an eloquent and poignant celebration of the parting of a devoted lover from his lady. To judge by the text this is in all likelihood the farewell and 'gud nycht' of a lover departing on a dangerous mission but it is not explicitly the message of one on the point of death. 'My dayis ar most compleit Throw hir absence' means 'it nearly kills me to be parted from her'. The poem is subscribed in the Bannatyne manuscript 'quod Scott off the *maister* of erskyn'. The Master of Erskine of the reign of King James V, eldest son of the Earl Marischal of the kingdom, had been favourite and close friend of the king and was later, so the legend goes, the devoted lover of the widowed Queen Marie.[2] He was killed at Pinkie Cleugh in 1547. 'In that same battel was slayne the Maister of Erskin deirlie belovit of the Quein: for quhome sche maid grit Lamentatioun and bure his deythe mony dayis in mynd.'[3] The title 'The lament

---

[1] The significant use of 'Sanderris' as a precursor of 'Jock' as 'the Scotsman' was pointed out to me by Professor Bruce Dickins.

[2] The title 'Master of Erskine' was held by the eldest son of Erskine, Earl of Mar, Earl Marischal of Scotland and traditional guardian of the monarch in infancy.

[3] John Knox, *History of the Reformation*, (ed. 1732), p. 79.

of the maister of Erskyn' is late, surmounting the cantus part of the song in the additions to one set of Wode's manuscript part-books, these additions being made about 1620. How the legend grew—that Scott wrote his poem after 1547 as an elegy on the dead Master—takes some discovering.[1]

What is the force of the Bannatyne colophon? If Scott's poem celebrating a parting was written on request for the Master of Erskine—maybe for presentation to Queen Marie—it must certainly date from before the death in 1547 even if only from the eve of the battle. (The teasing question of the origin of this song as words-and-music is considered in detail at a later stage.) With these reservations the date 1547 can still be of some service. On the strength of the Bannatyne colophon the year of the poet's birth can be reckoned as about 1530 at latest, he being imagined as writing the poem, at his most precocious, in his seventeenth year. We therefore find his 'making' linked closely with court circles only a few years after the death of King James V and his activity as a poet possibly reaching back as much as ten years earlier, that is well within King James V's reign.

The third clue to the poet's life-span is the well-known reference to 'old Scot' in a sonnet of Montgomerie from the 1580s. It is Robert Hudson, court 'violar', who is addressed.

> Ye can pen out tua cuple and ye pleis
> Yourself and I, old Scot and Robert Semple
> Quhen we are deid, that all our dayis bot daffis
> Let Christian Lyndesay wryt our epitaphis.[2]

The epoch referred to, when Hudson and three poets were merry companions about the court, is 1580 to 1586. Late in Scott's life we see him in close touch with court poet and court musician and a live culture of court-song written under King James VI, grandson of King James V and Queen Marie. But we have no text associated with his name later than the Bannatyne Manuscript of 1568 (where he has a poem on the plague of that year)—nor have many been claimed for him convincingly on evidence of style from among the numerous pieces with or without music whose words remain anonymous.[3]

References in official records show an Alexander Scott in the 1580s a burgess of

---

[1] Laing believed the piece was written before the Master's death. Cranstoun (ed. *Scott*, p. xi) says 'there is every probability that the tender and pathetic lines in question were written in view of what proved to be the final parting of the lovers'.

[2] *Montgomerie*, ed. Cranstoun, p. 101, Sonnet xxv.

[3] Professor John MacQueen (British Academy Lecture 1968) holds that Scott died of plague in 1568. He takes these lines to mean that Scott and Semple, musician and poet, were dead—in contrast to Hudson and Montgomerie, musician and poet, 'that...daffis (who are merrily alive). But the sonnet is about poets as poets; and (Robert) Semple apparently lived until 1595, which is too late for the composition of the sonnet, as Hudson retired from court in 1592/3.

Edinburgh but not a merchant. A legal calling has plausibly been conjectured, but this may now be supplemented.[1]

Here I wish to revive as relevant the important suggestion made many years ago by David Laing but since belittled or neglected: that Scott the poet was the younger of two sons, John and Alexander, on whose behalf in 1549 an order of legitimation was applied for by their father, Alexander Scott, 'Prebend' of the Chapel Royal.[2] There is no way of telling how old the younger of the sons was when this was done but it might have been effected here as in other cases so that their illegitimate birth should not stand in the way of inheritance of property or of entry to or advancement in the church, should they by their father's privileged position be subject to royal favour. By 1547 the young makar had shown his skill in a piece of courtly poetry. Laing thought that the poet was the son legitimated, possibly at a mature age; I submit that the poet may have been the father.

This identification chimes well with another entry, hitherto unnoticed. An Alexander Scott (without the priestly title 'Sir') was in 1538/9 presented to a prebendcy in the Chapel Royal of Stirling.[3] If this is the poet, he was in all likelihood 'skilled in singing', trained in music of the church. Alexander Scott can easily be envisaged as himself a skilled musician in employment, brought up in day-to-day familiarity or at any rate within earshot of *music fyne*, sacred in the Chapel Royal or secular in the music of the royal household—a figure, that is, belonging to royal and Catholic Scotland in the very years of its disintegration. This makes such good sense in terms of the songs and poems he wrote that it deserves to be kept in mind. In his poetry we find celebration of an occasion in the circle of monarch or of the widowed queen; the double voice in poetry of love matters, stately celebration and zestful exposure, both themes delighted in by the 'writing' court of King James V; and a divided loyalty as he analyses the world of 1562 in his loyal greeting to the young Queen, where both sides of the religious and political strife are understood only too well. As we shall see, his work shows that he had access to courtly song in the Franco-Scottish tradition of the 'style King James V'.

Clues to the life-span of the poet both literary and documentary in nature had led to opinions on his date of birth that varied by as much as fifteen years. This might not seem of vast importance but it does matter if we hope to align phases of his life, especially his formative years, with phases of court-culture in Scotland. A careful reading of Scott's poetry convinced me that his work was more markedly of the

[1] *Register of the Privy Council of Scotland*, vol. III, pp. 396 and 696; see T. F. Henderson, *Scottish Vernacular Literature: a History*, p. 240.

[2] *Register of the Secret Seal*, 1549, no. 505, 21 November: 'The Queen grants letters of legitimation to... bastard sons of Alexander Scott, prebend of the Chapel Royal.'

[3] *Register of the Secret Seal*, 1538/9, no. 28995, 28 February.

court than had been realised and also more deeply grounded in medieval Scotland. David Laing many years ago in his introduction to Scott's poems suggested 1520 as the year of the poet's birth but he felt that Scott's poetry was not of the court courtly in the absence of verses of adulation or petition.[1] But when we think of Scott's pieces as sung by skilled voices and postulate a receptive audience we introduce another dimension into the idea of 'of the court, courtly'.

With the writing and rewriting of literary history one commentator succeeded another and Scott's date of birth moved down the years to 'about 1530'. This as we saw remains the latest credible date. To think of him as born in 1530 brings his adult life clear of 'medieval' Scotland under King James V and closer to the years of Reformation. A mean date between 1520 and 1530 gives us this picture: Alexander Scott was born perhaps in the entourage of the Scottish court, by the year 1525. The prebendcy at the age of fourteen may have been an award to a promising chorister when his voice broke. He would then be a young man of seventeen past when the last royal courtly company of medieval Scotland dispersed with the defeat at Solway Moss, the birth of Princess Mary and the death of King James V. Scott, at twenty-two perhaps already known as a poet, would devise the courtly piece for the Master of Erskine, aimed perhaps at the aristocratic company about the Queen Mother. About his twenty-fifth year would come the order of legitimation; if he is the father, the children would be young. When the young Queen Mary first came home the loyal address of welcome would be written by her loyal servant Sanders Scott already turned forty. 'Old Scot' of the convivial circles of Montgomerie and King James would be over sixty years of age.

This conjectural scheme makes sense at all points. Uncertainty still remains, however, as the sliding scale of marked years can nowhere be pinned to a particular phase in the life of the poet. But by great good fortune a quite new piece of evidence has been brought to light from family and Continental records and published by Mr John Durkan.[2] He reports 'Alexander Scott appears as student of the fife in Paris in 1540 besides being singer and organist with Canon's portion at the Priory of Inchmahome (Fraser Papers, 223. *Bibliothèque d'Humanisme et Renaissance*, XII, 113). He appears to be the poet of that name.'

The first reference is to an entry published from the notarial archives of Paris.[3]

---

[1] Professor John MacQueen favours an early birth date, claiming as Scott's, rather than Sir Thomas Wyatt's, the lyric 'Lo quhat it is to lufe' (B. CCCLXXV, 'quod Scott'). But the relevant Alexander Scott, eminent court official under King James V has the priestly title 'Schir': see, e.g. *Exchequer Rolls*, 1526, pp. 267, 280 (he may well be the poet's father). Such an early birth date does not accord at all with the life-span of the musician, or poet-musician, as recently revealed.

[2] 'Cultural Background in sixteenth-century Scotland.' *The Innes Review*, no. 2 (1959).

[3] '1540. 26 juin. Marché entre Jehan de Laulnay, joueur de tambourin de Suisse, rue Grenata, et Alexandre Scot, joueur de fifre, rue du Temple, d'une part et Claude Chorel, clerc du Palais, capitaine de la bande des Chevaliers

It is dated 26 June 1540 and refers to the Feast of Saint John the Baptist or some other aspect of midsummer festival celebration. 'Alexandre Scot' appears in the capacity of instrumentalist, 'joueur de fifre', along with a named player of the Swiss drum. (Fife and drum was a usual combination for music of ceremony to introduce a 'mumming' or 'play)'. An agreement is recorded between the two players and Claude Chorel, clerk of the Palace [Palais de Justice?], captain of the band of the Knights of the Table Round of the kings of the *Bazoche*. The *bazochiens* were the gild of law students of Paris, who were noted for the quality and splendour of their 'plays' and 'devices' as were their English contemporaries of the Inns of Court with their festival monarch, 'the King of Purpoole' or 'the Prince of Love'. The agreement concerns costume for some splendid appearance: a pair of hose of mouse-grey cloth doubled with green and trimmed with yellow taffeta, a 'cassock' or surcoat of yellow satin of Bruges and a grey bonnet with feathers. (It is to be remarked that the bonnet is not the red bonnet of livery of the 'official' musician.) A payment in cash is appended to the 'payment' in apparel. It would appear that the Alexander Scott of this entry was at one and the same time a skilled player of the fife and someone fitly included in the festival celebration of the *Bazoche*. An Alexander Scott, student of law in Paris, turns to good account his early musical skills learned about the court of Scotland? The year 1540 according to our suggested life-span would find Alexander Scott, poet, over fifteen years of age. This is just the age at which a youth in those days was sent 'abroad to the schools' or a musically gifted chorister was sent to France to further his study in music.

Some years later, in July 1548, an Alexander Scott 'musician and organist' was granted a Canon's portion in the Priory of Inchmahome, the monastery 'of St Culmoc' secure on its island in the Lake of Menteith. A word on its history.

The last of the strictly ecclesiastical priors, Andrew, died in 1528. During his tenure a lease was signed by him and by ten canons, probably the complete chapter. Thereafter the Priory, given *in commendam*, became practically the hereditary possession of the Erskines of Mar.[1]

The Priory of Inchmahome had been formerly united with the Provostry of Lincluden to the *mensa* of the Chapel Royal. King James V in a letter to Pope Clement VII in 1529 desires support in restoring this union. In 1537 a royal letter mentions the purity of life and devout zeal of the consistorial priory of Inchmahome. It is under the special care of the king.[2]

---

de la Table ronde du roi de la Bazoche, moyennant une paire de chausses de drap gris souris, doublées de vert bouffant de taffetas jaune, une casaque de satin de Bruges jaune, un bonnet gris à plumes et 21 s.t.' (XI, 2.) I take the last phrase to indicate a sum of money. Twenty-one 'sols tournois'.

[1] Margaret E. Root, *Inchmahome Priory* (leaflet H.M.S.O. 1947), 'History', p. 1.
[2] *Letters of James V, 1513–1542*, collected R. K. Hannay, ed. Denys Hay, pp. 161, 317, 338.

In 1537 also King James writes to Pope Paul III:

The monastery of St Culmoc or Inchmahome as it is commonly called suffered much damage to property while James V was a boy, partly by the negligence of the priors, partly by the action of the nobles. Robert Erskine, the present commendator, could not do anything in the way of restoration and at the same time support the convent because the rents are slender and in particular the Pope reserved a considerable pension to another for life. For this reason the commendator desires to resign to John Erskine, Chancellor of Moray, exchanging the priory for the Chancellorship. John can do much for the place owing to his friends and his resources. His ancestors were generous benefactors of the house; and he can recover alienated property, repair buildings almost in ruins and restore the old religious life.

Robert, commendator, was Master of Erskine. John his younger brother, succeeding in 1547 to the title 'Master of Erskine', held also the commendatory abbey of Cambuskenneth, site of the Chapel Royal in Stirling.

John the Commendator heads the signatories of a conventual chapter of nine persons in 1548 when granting the Canon's portion to Alexander Scott. From the wording of the grant Scott would appear to be already a figure well loved and highly esteemed in the community—or in the eyes of the Commendator. The chapter grants

to our lovit servitour Alexander Scot musitiane and organist for the decoir of our queir in musik and playing and for othir resonabill causes and consideratiouns moving us, ane channouns portioun of our said place with fyre, chalmer, candill, habit, siluer and uthir necessaris and casualities pertenyyng thairto aucht and wount in our said place of Inchmoquhomok for all the dais of his life, his entree in and thairto beginand at the day and dait heirof and thaireftir for all the dais of his life till enduire and sall cause him and his factour in his name to be thenkfullie ansuerit and obeyit alsweill in his absence as presens of the said portioun yeirlie...and mak na stop nor impedyment to him nor thaim thairin during his liftyme undir all hiest paine and charge that aftir may folow... providing all wayis the said Alexander be ane reddy gud seruand to us and our said place at all tyme quhen he may gudlie work therupoun.

The chapter bind their successors in strictest form to fulfil this grant in time to come, 'but frauds or gile na remeid of law nor exceptioun civile, cannon nor muncepall'. The document doubtless foresees the dispossession, dispersion or disestablishment that might ensue if the opposing forces should gain powers of government. (If their careful measures held good, a life tenure granted to the new Canon might well provide a sufficiency for the Alexander Scott, burgess of Edinburgh in the 1580s.)

'Our servitour' the musician and organist was appointed Canon in view of his outstanding musical skill and 'for othir resonabill causes and consideratiouns moving us'. What these were is not mentioned; nor is it clear whether service other than musical in the past is being rewarded or service other than musical in the future envisaged. Probably both are implied. Discretion prevails in the wording. Certainly the link with the community appears to be both strong and long-standing. The former Commendator, Robert, is said to have supported the education of George

Buchanan from grants on the Priory lands.[1] It may be that under the patronage of Commendator John who, it was hoped, would restore the substance and dignity of ecclesiastical life, another gifted young Scotsman had been helped to an education abroad in Paris, to further his musical training or to study law 'in the Schools'. The appointment as Canon of the musician and organist to enhance the service of God in the choir of the Priory by his skill is surely a gesture towards the restoration of the old religious order and may well have been at once the culmination and the harvest of earlier support and patronage.

The new Canon of Inchmahome was a musician of rank and dignity in the hierarchy of his profession, comparable in this for instance with Heywood, singer and keyboard player at the English court. On the contrary, the entry rewarding the fife-player in the revels of the law students of Paris eight years earlier refers to a musician of a very different rank and status. But this Alexander Scott's participation in the law students' mumming may have been entirely unofficial from the point of view of any Gild of Musicians. The playing of the 'quhissel' is not a skill exacting distinguished musicianship; it is possible, moreover, that some years earlier in the small court of Scotland a chorister of the Chapel Royal might have doubled on occasion as 'quhisselar' to the Household Music. 'Alexandre Scot, joueur de fifre' of Paris in 1540 (not 'student of the fife' as Mr Durkan would have it) may still be the prebend of the Chapel Royal of 1539 and also the Canon who rendered musical and other service at Inchmahome in 1548.

Alexander Scott, Canon of Inchmahome, entered into his musical 'life-fellowship' just one year after the Battle of Pinkie. The outcome of that conflict was so disastrous that the Castle of Stirling no longer offered sufficient security to the young child Queen Mary and her mother and they were consigned to the safekeeping of the Commendator of Inchmahome (the hereditary guardianship of the monarch lay with the Erskines). The royal mother and child resided for a time in the Priory on its island. Among the 'other good reasons' for the appointment of Alexander Scott as Canon may have been active services to the Commendator or the community, or loyalty in time of stress or field of battle to the Erskines and the Queen Mother. With such loyalty the poet Alexander Scott identifies himself in his 'Depairte'.

The poet Alexander Scott and the musician of the same name draw very close indeed to one another in this coincidence of time, of place and of loyalties. Is it not possible that the 'Depairte' was written by one who was himself involved in the leave-taking, before the battle, of the Master of Erskine?—that the piece was presented as a solace to the defeated and bereaved Queen Marie after the battle, embellished by music devised by the makar himself, performed by the musician and organist

[1] Root, *Inchmahome Priory*, p. 7.

in the island retreat in elegiac celebration of the Master's death? This matter we shall pursue further when considering the music of the songs.

In this amalgamation of the records of the poet and the musician one or two issues remain. First, neither as poet nor as musician is Alexander Scott ever styled Mr.; if the studies in Paris were in arts they did not culminate in a Master's degree. The 'Mr. Alexander Scott' of other entries in official documents refers to a different person.[1] Secondly, Alexander Scott the poet is credited at some point in his life with a wife— if we are to believe the note added by a later hand below his poem in the Bannatyne Manuscript 'To luve unluvit'—'Finis q Scott quhen his wyfe left him'. Scott of course could have married after Reformation, between 1560 and 1568: his wife may not have been the mother of the two boys legitimated in 1549, where no mother or marriage is mentioned. Marriage before Reformation for one in minor orders was not forbidden; the election of a former prebend to a Canonry of Inchmahome quickly followed by the legitimation of two sons is easily reconcilable with a wife who had run away.

Apart from these points, what we know of the poet confirms what has been gathered of the musician to a pronounced degree. Alexander Scott, I submit, whose poems were on occasion part-songs of a courtly nature, was not only brought up in the hearing of *musik fyne* sacred and secular; he was also—like his monarch—'ane gude musician himself' and more, a professional musician of the church trained in keyboard playing. An understanding, then, of the measure of pavan and galliard, of the underlaying of words to music was present in the mind of the makar himself. It is even possible that like Sir John Fethy, priest, poet and organist, Scott could write 'baith letter and note' of his songs. It was Sir John Fethy who first brought the new fingering of organs into Scotland. Scott may have studied law in Paris at a time when the future of a musician in the church no longer seemed an altogether assured career or he may have been both law student and musician, a combination not unknown.[2] His skill in organ-playing he may have acquired in Scotland. If, as seems very likely, these two trained organists in the pre-Reformation Church of Scotland who were both poets were acquainted with one another, then another link would be forged of transmission of style and skill in words and music through the medium of living personalities.

In the imagined life-story of Alexander Scott, poet and musician, such possible inking in the dimension of time and tradition is rivalled in interest by one possibility of coincidence in the dimension of space. Alexander Scott, if born in 1524, would be

---

[1] References to Mr Alexander Scott, *Register of the Great Seal 1546–80*, no. 686, 'M. Alex' and D. Alex Scot, testators (1551–2).

[2] Precedent exists for an 'advocate', presumably a graduate in law, who was also a musician: see Appendix II, Mr James Lawder.

exactly of an age with 'le divin Ronsard'. The boy Ronsard was a page in the train of Madeleine of France when she married King James V of Scotland in Paris on New Year's Day 1537. He came to Scotland with the royal couple on the 28 May in that year. The delicate and 'death-bound' Madeleine lived only forty days after her arrival in her northern kingdom. Ronsard, under the name of 'le Wandomoy' appears after her death in the accounts of the Lord Treasurer of King James (July 1537). He made the journey back to France but returned with Claude d'Humières, being in Scotland on 24 December. Some years later, in the April of 1540, Ronsard was in Paris; this was the year in which he first suffered loss of hearing.[1]

Did the boys meet? I find no evidence that choristers of the Chapel Royal of Scotland were in musical attendance on King James V when he set out on his wooing journey to France nor that they were numbered among the royal Household Music —'trumpetouris, tabernaris and quhislaris'—that went with the fleet early in May 1537 'to squyer the King of Scotland and his Queen through the sea'. We may not conjecture, then, a visit of Scott to France at this time, though 'whistler' is 'joueur de fifre'.[2] But during the long months the Queen's page spent in Scotland, through ceremonies of rejoicing and then of mourning, the French youth who was musical might well make friendly contact with an intelligent chorister of the Scots Chapel Royal. The company about the monarch was not after all enormous. Later, in Paris in 1540, the young Ronsard might not be liable to meet with a foreign student of law, but his path might well cross that of a young musician playing in the festival games of the *Bazoche*, who hailed from Scottish courtly circles with which the 'Vendomois' had earlier been acquainted.

The meeting of the boys who were to be poets famous in their nations must remain among the peripheral fancies of literary biography. But the figure of the Scottish poet we have modelled—chorister, organist and trained musician—not only picks up the tradition of Sir John Fethy in Scotland. It also looks across to a European line of poet-musician, Jean Régnier who missed his organ when he was in prison or Arnoul Gréban, organist of Notre Dame and Master of the Choristers, author of the 'Mystère de la Passion' whose poetry once had its music.

THE MUSIC OF THE SONGS

If poet and musician were indeed one and the same person then Alexander Scott was in himself an important vehicle of traditions of court-song, its creation, devising and transmission, and a vital factor in the interaction of skills of music with skills of

---

[1] I draw on the 'Chronologie' in *Œuvres complètes de Ronsard*, ed. Gustave Cohen, vol. I.
[2] *Accounts of the Lord High Treasurer*, vol. VI, pp. 399–400.

poetry in courtly Scotland. None so well as the singer understands the alliance of words and music in song. Let us look at his songs along with the music to which they were sung, bearing in mind the possibility that Scott as a trained musician could have been a maker of music as well as of words—and may have participated in courtly devising in the style of the *Bazoche* of Paris.

The music that is found associated with Scott's poems is *music fyne*, part-writing by a trained musician of the sixteenth century. Because of the lateness of record of the pieces *as song* we cannot be sure at what point Scott's words joined hands with the music, whether at the time of his poems' composition or at some later point in a long and lively currency. The poet or his poems could have met with such music at the court of King James and his French Queen Marie before 1542—provided he were old enough by then—or after the King's death at the reduced court of the widowed Queen Mother or in the circles of the Lord Governor, Lord Hamilton.[1] After 1562 in the gay but sporadic court-life of the daughter Mary, Queen of Scots, there were musicians Scots and continental in royal employment, Englishmen, Frenchmen and Italians. There was a stand of voices for part-singing. Taste at court was French, sophisticated, up to date. The Queen's 'Pompae', fragments of whose music may survive, were written in Latin by Buchanan.[2] Such information as we possess suggests that in the court circles of Queen Mary's reign the cultivation of Scots poetry in association with *music fyne* would have to make its way alongside poetry in other cultivated tongues and the skilled performance of contemporary music from Continental Europe.

From the records of these years, however, several figures emerge whose musical skill was to play a part in the *puy* of verse and song at the court of the next monarch, King James VI. The Hudson family 'Englishmen, violars' are first glimpsed when they are provided with royal liveries for Queen Mary's wedding to Lord Darnley. The musician James Lauder was in 1552 a young musician under the patronage of the Burgh Council of Edinburgh and in 1562 was rewarded 'by the Queen's Grace precept'. As musical *valet de chambre* he served Queen Mary in imprisonment and later was musical servitor to her son, King James VI.[3] A possible line of continuity

---

[1] Lord Hamilton, Earl of Arran, Due de Chastelherault. There was a play, by William Lauder, to celebrate the marriage of the Governor's daughter, Lady Barbara Hamilton in February 1549. There was festive celebration of the appointment of the Queen Mother as Queen Regent in 1554, and of the marriage (in France) of Queen Mary to the Dauphin in 1558: see *Works of William Lauder*, ed. Furnivall, introduction.

[2] Buchanan's 'Pompae': see *Opera Omnia* (1715), vol. II, p. 91; (ed. 1725), vol. II, pp. 399–405. His 'Pompae Deorum Rusticorum' marked the baptism of Prince James in 1566...'with musicians clothed lyk maidins playing upon all sortis of instruments and singing of musick'. There were Italian verses, and Latin verses from Buchanan in the *entremets* at the farewell banquet to Queen Mary's uncle in 1561. An account of French musicians at the Scots court of Queen Mary is in preparation. A 'stand' is a set of voices.

[3] The Hudsons and James Lauder are discussed in chapter 4, and Lauder in Appendix II.

in the cultivation of court-song can be traced in the musicians themselves under royal patronage. But with this court culture of music and poetry over the troubled years of the mid-century we cannot connect Alexander Scott more definitely than we have already done in noting his musical service under Commendator John of Inchmahome and Cambuskenneth (foundations that were linked with the Chapel Royal of Stirling) and his makar's bid for favour in 1562.

In what milieu, then, do we envisage Scott's poetry and song as written or as enjoyed during the years of unrest when the court-centred culture of court-song was largely in abeyance? A currency of part-song spreading outwards in the 1540s from the court of King James V, his Tudor mother and his two French consorts appears to have persisted despite troubled times: a repertory varying perhaps with political faction, changing as new items accrued yet showing itself singularly retentive of early favourites, survived until a court life grew up anew in 1579 around the young King James VI. In whose hands was it cherished over the intervening years?

The wider circles we can most plausibly suggest as having enjoyed this music are those of the lawyers and merchants of Edinburgh, groups within or about the colleges where private music-making is recorded, and here and there enthusiastic amateur music-makers in the great houses among members of the younger generation: it is from such that records later descend in manuscript collections of verse, song and music. But the manuscript tradition of the end of the century shows the important part that was played also by continuity of teaching and learning, practice and composition under the aegis of the religious institution. A body of skilled musicians educated in the extensive musical culture of the Catholic Church must have been disturbed and dispersed with the Reformation—however secure the provision made for their support. Some men like Andro Blackhall remained in the service of church music under the new dispensation retained as members of the Chapel Royal. Some like Wode and the writer of the contemporary 'Art of Music' sought to preserve the art of part-music, even to encourage new composition as the fabric of the old musical life gave way.[1] Some, no doubt, as in England, found service in great houses, making music for private devotions and for recreation and teaching the children. Some like Sir John Fethy passed on their skill of vocal and instrumental music as teacher in the song-schools. But the 'sang-schuils' of cathedral or burgh-kirk fell into decay with the troubled times. Fortunately however this desperate strait of music was rendered 'timeous remeid' by the royal edict of 1579 that ordered re-organisation. This came at the outset of the young monarch's personal effective reign. A resumption of teaching and practice of part-music with some composition in

---

[1] Wode commissioned part-settings of psalms. The 'Art of Music' gave 'examples' to be followed in composition. For music in the colleges see N. C. Carpenter, *Music in the Mediaeval and Renaissance Universities*.

Chapel Royal and burgh song-school alike is coeval with the fresh phase of 'Castalian' poetry and song in the court of the young King James VI.

The matching of Scott's verses with music could have happened, then, in courtly circles before the Reformation or in courtly company as it persisted despite warfare and disruption in a wider and dispersed cultivation of part-song during the troubled times or, in the case of some songs, over the years when the poet, as 'old Scot', was in contact with poet and musician at the court of King James VI. If we accept that Alexander Scott was both poet and musician he would provide in his own person both makar and musical milieu in whatever company he kept between 1550 and 1580. As Canon of Inchmahome he would have in his community his hours of recreation and would have singing voices to hand; he would be in touch with music of the Chapel Royal at Stirling. We know from the phrase in the legal document 'alsweill in his absence as presens' that the Canon-musician was not at all times resident in his island Priory.

4. DEPARTE, DEPARTE

SCOTT   ANON

De-parte, de-parte, Al - lace, I most de-parte From hir that hes my hart___ with hart full

soir, A-gains my will in-deid And can find no re-meid, I wat the pains of deid___ can do no moir.

Against this sketched background of part-music in Scotland, of court-song between 1548 and 1579, its currency and cultivation, let us consider the compact repertory of Alexander Scott's writing where one piece comments on another and each piece is stamped with his individual craftsmanship, whether it be love-song in stately style or its obverse, a 'remeid of love' in bitter or ribald vein. And let us look at the music for his verses that has survived from the sixteenth-century repertory of *musik fyne* in Scotland in order to determine in what ways the art of the poet and the art of the musician interacted and in order to discover if we can to what extent Scott was himself writing in a tradition of court-song, courtly verse linked with fine music.

First, to turn again to 'Depairte, depairte, depairte', one thing is certain. The music to which it was sung for well on a hundred years, a part-song to four voices in galliard rhythm, was matched with the words *after* the poem was written. Bannatyne's version, except for one puzzling line, is a clean text, obviously a complete poem, its first line 'Depairte, depairte, depairte'. But when the first stanza is found underlaid to the cantus part in the Quintus volume of Wode's part-books it runs thus: 'Depairte, departe, allace I most departe', as does the single stanza reported in the Taitt music-book.[1]

One iambic foot has been omitted from the text as it stands in the Bannatyne Manuscript. When I prepared the underlaid text for the version in *Music of Scotland* (no. 42) I had to subtract from the first line of the subsequent stanzas a phrase to correspond. (This a contemporary would have done without a qualm.) In some stanzas it could be managed only awkwardly. It may safely be concluded that embellishment with music was effected for Scott's piece after it had come into being, either close to the time of composition or at some later date. His poem could have been offered by him personally as *propyne* to his Erskine patron or commissioned from him for an occasion; and music could have been an embellishment of his poetic offering, or an embellishment of the performance on the occasion. Perhaps, as I suggested earlier, the poetic tribute was performed at a ceremony of departure and for this was matched with music to make a court-song. Or it may be that the poem was later acclaimed or valued for some special reason—the death of the Master created a profound impression—and music was *then* found for Scott's poem from among favourite tunes in the galliard style so that the piece could be sung. In either case the musical form prevailed over the verbal form and a corner was knocked off the stanza. If Scott himself found or composed music in dance-measure for his poem, he altered its first wording.

Perhaps a poem that had been a lovers' 'goodnight' was given ceremonial performance after the death of the Master in battle. Queen Marie bore his death 'many dayis in mynd'. This phrase in contemporary usage meant more than fond remembering: the day's mynd, the month's or year's mynd, was a ceremonial commemoration, which characteristically had its music, music linked in some way with the loved one mourned—as we shall see with 'The Mindes Melodie' for Montgomerie.[2] The fact that the music chosen for it is in the rhythm of a galliard, a spirited court-dance, does not preclude its being eloquent music for a lament if played or sung in solemn manner. The use of the dance-form for elegiac celebration is well attested. Indeed the composition of a pavan as deathpiece, with ceremonial playing among mourning friends, perhaps even solemn performance of the dance, has been suggested by Professor Dart.[3] The pavan was a slow and solemn dance, after all. But it is not beyond

---

[1] That stanza was kindly transcribed for me by Dr Rubsamen.   [2] Discussed in chapters 4 and 5.

[3] In a personal communication. For dancing as solemn ceremonial see James P. Cunningham, *Dancing in the Inns of Court*. ['The Queen's Goodnight' in Duncan Burnett's setting is in galliard rhythm: it is found elsewhere—in *The Dublin Virginal Manuscript*, ed. John Ward (Wellesley Edition no. 3, 1954)—'where the rhythm is that of the galliard' (K.E.).]

possibility that pieces in galliard rhythm were likewise composed or used in this way: 'The Queen's goodnight' certainly provides an instance of a piece in galliard rhythm whose title suggests composition and use on a similar occasion of farewell elegy or 'mynd'. In our Scottish example the double-play of galliard rhythm for a lovers' 'goodnight' as it had been, against the plangent farewell to the lover now dead would enhance the effect. The irony of 'My dayis ar most compleit Throw hir absence' in the new context would be poignant. The genre of a music or its provenance, the emotions or attitudes associated with a tune can be important factors in the whole meaning and effect of a song.

And we know something about the music from other sources. It is in Robert Edwards' Music Book among the early entries that are of music of the mid-sixteenth century. It appears there as a cantus part, entitled 'O ladie Venus heire complain' but this opening phrase is all the words we have. In Forbes' *Songs and Fancies*, however, we have the cantus part again and a full text of three stanzas

> 1   You Lovers all that love would prove
>   Come learn to know true love indeed
>   First, Love the Lord your God above
>   From whom all goodness doth proceed:
>   Pray to him faithfully
>   To grant his sp'rit to thee
>   Thy sins to mortifie
>   And that with speed.   (John Forbes *Songs & Fancies*, 1682, no. vi.)

This is a sacred song in dignified rebuke of earthly love and the 'cult of Venus'. It advises lovers not on how best to 'do love's observance' but on how to turn their thoughts to better things. This song, then, whose cantus part has elsewhere an amorous *incipit*, is very likely to be a spiritual version reflecting on the lost 'plaint to Venus'. The words of 'You Lovers all' exactly match the 'O Ladie Venus' / 'Depairte' music to which they are underlaid and they were patently written 'to the tune of it'.

Just such a plaint to Venus, a song to four voices, is called for in the great stage satire of 1540, David Lyndsay's 'Ane Satyre of the Thrie Estaitis'.[1] In the scene before Dame Sensualitie's bower, that great courtesan addresses her two companions— 'Now let us go sing a song to Dame Venus. We three shall sing and Fund Jonet [the porter] shall bear a bass'. If we translate the argument of 'You lovers all that love would prove Now learn to know true love indeed' back from spiritual into amorous terms, the result will fit remarkably well into this dramatic context.

The music to which Scott's 'Depairte' was so long enjoyed was clearly a very well-known tune current in Scotland already at the middle of the sixteenth century,

---

[1] See *Works of Sir David Lindsay*, ed. Hamer, vol. II, pp. 52–8. This matter was informally discussed in my 'What song did Dame Sensuality sing?', *The Scotsman*, 12 September 1959.

its character coloured by its use as a plaint to Venus—a favourite gesture of the courtly love-cult. It is significant that Scott's piece of about 1547 was afterwards matched with music in the rhythm and style of a galliard, a dance that with the pavan is believed to have come into Scotland 'brent new frae France' at the time of King James V's wooing journey to Paris and his wedding there to the King's daughter Madeleine on New Year's Day 1537.

The second song of Scott's that has its music is 'How suld my febill body fure' (B. CCCVI) The stanza in which it is written is not altogether new in Scots poetry; a near-variant was used by Dunbar. The stanza-form obtains with perfect regularity throughout the poem though the Bannatyne scribe is in two minds as to how to record the pattern on the page. The refrain element, a phrase repeated with variation, is a strongly marked feature of the poem, 'that suld be myne' or, at the close, 'As I did myne'. It throws back over the preceding stanza, now sadly now cynically now with rueful humour, the poet's sense of merit and service ill rewarded in love.

> For nobillis hes nocht ay renown
> Nor gentillis ay the gayest goun.
> Thay cary victuallis to the toun
>   That worst dois dyne.
> Sa bissely to busk I boun
> Ane uthir eitis the berry doun
>   That suld be myne.

The musical setting, which is made after the fashion of a French chanson, has a repetition of the last musical section. The musician has not felt bound to the poet's refrain but has included the preceding line of the stanza in his repeated element, 'Ane uthir eitis the berry doun that suld be myne' or 'To se ane uther haif in cure that suld be myne'. This bears witness to a sensitive reading of the poem, for the penultimate line gives in each stanza the varying circumstance that precipitates the poet's reiteration of his grievance. It argues, too, a cordial relationship between stanzaic and musical form at this time. (Did Scott make 'both letter and note'?)

In our findings on 'How suld my febill body fure' we leave it, then, as likely that in this case Scott's words were set to music. As to when this was done there is no evidence but there is a slight clue. The difficulty the Bannatyne scribe experienced in writing out the words of this song, unprecedented except for his slip in rendering 'O lusty May', suggests to me the likelihood that here too he was transcribing from a manuscript song-book where the words of the earlier verses were underlaid to musical parts. His first three stanzas are written down with the rhyming sections carefully marked off but the stanzaic form is rendered irregularly. By the time he comes to the later stanzas, which in the song-books were by custom written out as verse below the music or on the opposite page, the scribe renders them with gathering confidence as to the 'shape' of the stanza. It is very likely, then, that this piece was a part-song by the year 1568. This is in accordance with the chronology, based on musical style, suggested by Dr Elliott in *Music of Scotland*.

For 'Hence hairt with hir that most depairte' (B. ccxc) only the cantus part survives of what was possibly a four-part setting for voice or instrument. One source, Robert Edwards' Book, has the music alone with the *incipit* 'Hence Hairt', the other has one stanza underlaid. The triple time and the shape of the piece again suggest music for dancing though the rhythm is less spirited than other triple-time galliard-rhythm examples in Franco-Scottish song.

5. *HENCE HAIRT WITH HIR YOU MUST BE GONE*[1]

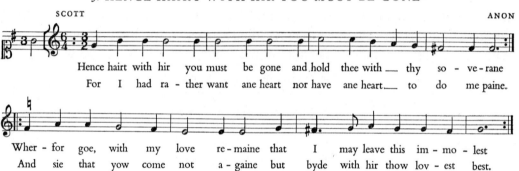

SCOTT   ANON

Hence hairt with hir   you must   be gone   and hold   thee with ___   thy   so - ve - rane
For   I   had ra - ther want   ane heart   nor have   ane heart. ___   to   do   me paine.

Wher - for   goe,   with   my   love   re - maine that   I   may leave this   im - mo - lest
And   sie   that   yow   come   not   a - gaine   but   byde   with hir thow lov - est   best.

Here one can picture Scott writing his words to match an existing dance-tune, or a dance-tune used for the poet's words or, equally likely, his words set after the galliard fashion. There is no deciding factor either way. The subject, the sending of the lover's heart, was a favourite theme in 'courtly love', present in ceremonial gesture and pastime.

The music for 'Hence hairt' will serve for another song of Scott's, an 'answer' to the first—'Returne the, hairt, hamewart agane' with the mocking refrain 'For feind a crum of the scho fawis' (B. cccxxvi). This makes a pair of heart-sending songs in a tradition long known and significantly used in medieval Europe. Its forebear was apparently a wooing game. The presence of a music matching both pieces, music in dance-rhythms, strongly suggests that these pieces were used in courtly pastime, a dance with significant costume and gesture, a 'play' for entertainment or the participation of a courtly company.[2]

---

[1] Music and text: a conflation of William Stirling's Cantus Part-Book (1639) fo. 22v and Robert Edwards' Commonplace-Book (*c.* 1650), fo. 4v. (K.E.); you, yow: thou.

[2] Other such groups of pieces, verbally interlinked or matching the same music or both, can be found in Scott's work. Discussion of these as possibly following a pattern of pastime, dance or 'play' will be included in a future publication.

These three examples have shown a variety of ways in which courtly verses by a known author could be associated with music to make a court-song. They reinforce examples we looked at earlier of ballats and their music. So far we have not seen a proved case where Alexander Scott's writing was done in terms of an existing court-song—where he can be shown to have made words to match the music. With the fourth example, however, we have more to go on. Scott's poem 'Only to yow in erd that I lufe best' (B. CCXCVI), which until recently stood alone, is now, thanks to the recovery of the music-books, companioned by two others related to it in subject and in opening phrase, 'Onlie to you my ladie bricht and schein' and 'Only to you in world that I loved best'. The three poems match one another exactly in stanza-pattern. 'Onlie to you my ladie' is found in the associated 'Alexander Forbes' and 'David Melvill' part-books of the early seventeenth century, three stanzas of words and the cantus and bass parts of a four-part music. The cantus part of the same music is recorded elsewhere, in William Stirling's Music-Book (1639) without verbal text but entitled 'Onlie to you my Ladie'. In Robert Edwards' Book the same cantus part appears again with the opening phrase only, 'Only to yow in world that I loved best' and Robert Taitt's Music-Book has four vocal parts and one stanza with the same first line. Two sets of words, then, were current to the same music, a polyphonic part-song, *music fyne*. The music, moreover, is French, that of a famous chanson, 'Maudite soit la mondaine richesse', the words by Clément Marot, the music by Claudin de Sermisy.[1] The Marot piece was known as a 'chanson' in 1525 and survives in print with its music from 1551.

There is no relationship that I can establish between the French words and the three poems in Scots. The Scots pieces, however, are close kin as will be seen by these stanzas. Here is the text of 'Only to you my Ladie bright and scheine' from Alexander Forbes' Cantus Part Book, 1611.

> 1   Only to yow, my Ladie bright and scheine
>   In quhome dois ly my comfort and my cair
>   Most plesand wight dother to Venus queine.

[1] The text of 'Only to yow my Ladie' was published and its kinship to Scott's poem discussed in H. M. Shire, 'Scottish Song-book, 1611'; also in K. J. Elliott, 'Robert Edwards' Commonplace-Book and Scots Musical History'. Here the music was identified as that of 'Maudite soit'. Printings of this song were noted in Lesure 'Autour de Clément Marot'; an important one is *Quart Livre de Recueil*: du Chemin, Paris, 1551: 'This volume was probably well-known in Scotland: it also has "Voyant souffrir," by Jacobin which is in Rowallan's song book and "Content desir" by Sermisy which is in Rowallan and Duncan Burnett' (K.E.). James Lauder was in France in 1552/3. '"Only to yow in world that I love best", 4 voices, 1 stanza and "Only to you my lady" 1 voice, no other text—the music of the second being exactly the same as that of the first, except for one note' in the Taitt MS.: W. H. Rubsamen, 'Scottish and English Music...in a newly discovered manuscript'. Dr Rubsamen kindly supplied me with the verbal text of the stanza. In Robert Edwards' Book the first line reads 'loved', which makes better sense.

O wight in quhome all bewtie hes repair.
Younge tender plant fairest of everie fair,
To yow the maker of my wo and end,
Unto your grace (unto your grace) my service I commende.

2 Of all my wo, yo ar the haill recuir
Off all my lampe, ye ar the haill light
Ane drope of grace schaw to your servitour
And loss me nocht your awin trew cairfull wight
Your servitour till all his strenthe and might
For pitie puir heartles I yow imploir
Or duilfull death, doubtles will me devoir.

3 Will ye me loss your avin trew innocent
Send that ye haiwe broght me in sik distres
And I to you ever obedient?
I yow exhort to haive pitie and grace
And banische now my wofull heavines.
Support my paine and my glaidnes restoir
Or duilfull deathe, doubtles will me devoir.

Of Scott's 'Only to yow' here is the first stanza and the last.

1 Only to yow in erd that I lufe best
I me commend ane hundreth thowsand syiss   [times]
Exorting yow with pensyfe hairt opprest
as ye ar scho whom in my confort lyiss
Gif I misuse my pen or done dispyss
Ocht at this tyme, will God I sall amend
protesting that this ballat ye attend...

6 Adew / rycht trew / adew my deirest hairt
fairest of hew / for this tyme haif gud nycht.
remord and rew / and pondir weill my pairte
Sen I persew / nathing of yow bot rycht   [perceive]
whilk gif ye knew / my mynd as it is plicht
ye wald subdew / your inwart thocht and mynd
and me reskew / whilk for your lufe is pynd.

'Onlie to you my ladie bricht and schein' by every token of substance, tone and manner belongs to the 'style King James V'. It is a sister-composition to such pieces as 'Lanterne of love' by Steill, or 'Support your servand peirles paramour' in its Scots dress.

Scott's piece is a making of a song on the same outset but in a new manner—'Scott's way'. His is a letter to the lady, cogently argued, appealing for a favourable response to devoted love. If one poem is an 'overgoing' of another there is no doubt in my mind but that Scott is the one who, with zest, élan and virtuosity in 'making', outplayed the earlier poet, whose rhythm is more staid, whose sentiments are limited to the gambit of appeal and celebration. Scott in his second stanza refers to ways in which other lovers strive to please their lady, some by diligence in service, some through 'fair facound speich blandit with eloquence'—which may glance at a comely poem of appeal already composed; some lovers lack a gracious response because they, through negligence, do not make their devotion known to her. As for himself (stanza 3), he is suffering great distress 'throw lack of speech' and his suffering devotion must find expression. Stanzas 4 to 6 are his appeal for an answer and his adieu. Scott's poem is of three-plus-three stanzas: in the second half there is an elaboration of artistry with multiplication of internal rhyming.

The third poem I take to be the answer made to Scott, opening with a greeting that repeats his first two lines and overgoes them—'world' is greater than 'erd'. It says that [his] message has put [her] heart to rest and rid [her] of sorrow; but the last line has an intimation of fresh distresses. (To me it is plain that the poem would continue beyond this single stanza.)

> Only to yow in world that I love best
> I me commend a hundred thousand sise.
> so far as yow have put my heart to rest
> and caused me from Languor to arise,
> I was alswell as any could devise
> Withoutin dolor dayly in yor sight,
> but now my noys augment both day and night.

Three poets pursue the same theme and the resulting verses constitute an 'argument of love'. All are found with the same music. If they were enjoyed aloud it seems highly likely that they were enjoyed to that music. If much of each poem's point lay in its being relished in terms of the others, then a presentation of all three together seems probable. There emerges a pattern of courtly entertainment that has in it something of bardic contest, something of a 'debating of love matters'. It is a 'play' of variations on a theme made piquant by poetic rivalry and, it may be, rivalry for favour in love, the whole embellished by presentation with fine music.

This then is my reconstruction: some courtly makar of the earlier sixteenth century wrote words of love-service in late medieval style in Scots to sing to the French music of the Sermisy–Marot song. Alexander Scott picked up the opening phrase of the makar's song and wrote to match it and its polyphonic music 'his' song 'Only to you'. Besides being a vigorous and lively argument in his own highly personal idiom, the whole piece will sing to the complex music of Sermisy, even Scott's flourish in the last stanza, a brilliant cadenza of redoubling rhythm and chiming rhymes. Other words were made, by Scott himself or by a separate hand, that certainly matched the part-music—'Only to yow in world'; these words betray their relationship to Scott's verses 'Only to yow in erd' in the reminiscent *incipit* of the first two lines. But which of these two poems came first or what is the precise nature of their relationship it is impossible to say for certain, for of the third poem we have only an initial stanza, a statement left incomplete.

With 'Depairte' we glimpsed the use of poetry for ceremonial performance in courtly love-service, in farewell, or 'mynd'. We know the piece had music and that that music was in dance rhythm. The possibility emerged that the song was 'danced' as a commemorative pavan death-piece may have been danced—that the totality of meaning was of words, music and movement, whether that music was shaped in ceremony or patterned in 'traces' of the figured dance or both together. With 'Hence hairt' we had a song and its answer in the same verse form and again the associated music was in dance rhythm. With 'Only to yow' we had a cluster of pieces, variations on a theme of love-service, not without an element of contest or rivalry. Such pieces found thus clustered—grouped to form a song with its answer, an amorous piece with satiric rejoinder or spiritual parody, or forming a series inter-linked by an echo in opening phrase or refrain, *where there is a shared rhythmic pattern and a music that matches it*—strongly suggest live performance to that music and a courtly company participating in ceremony, dance or pastime or assisting at a 'device' or 'play'. The motive of the devising in the first place may have been that of cele-bration, ceremonial tribute to a person of importance, for instance; but with years of currency and wider usage a piece might move from particular to general in its appli-cation, from occasional to recreative in its nature. Some pieces may have been re-creative from the beginning. Social pastime of the sixteenth century such as 'com-moning' or the Italianate *giuochi* featured the posing and debating of questions and matters of love in the medium of courtly speech. These may have had a counterpart in action-song, verses danced to song or danced in song, a song-dance game such as is delighted in to this day by those devoted retainers of old style, the children.

4

MUSICIANS AND POETS AT THE
COURT OF KING JAMES VI

THE REIGN of James VI, as King of Scotland only, falls into four phases. The first, of infancy and boyhood, begins in 1567 with his coronation at the age of a year and a half, and a sheltered life in Stirling Castle under the close guardianship of the Earl Marischal of the Realm, Erskine of Mar. His boyhood was spent in education by the great but ageing scholar George Buchanan and a gentler assistant, a severe and exacting schooling for a gifted and 'eident' pupil, a strenuous and Protestant upbringing for a lonely child bereft of parents.

The year 1579 brings a change, for the 'orphan' King was now thirteen years old, in Scots law no longer a child but enjoying the right to name his own 'tutor'. As King he could choose as companions and counsellors whom he wished. He emerged from the close protection of Stirling Castle and the authority of his childhood's mentors. The powers of Europe had their eyes on Scotland, expecting this moment. Scotland was 'the postern gate' by which England might be entered. Scotland was for the Catholic power-heads the realm of the imprisoned Queen Mary, its Catholic sovereign. The religion of the young King and his political affinities in his realm and abroad were of the tenderest concern in a Europe feeling the strong current of Counter-reform.

From France in that year there came to the young court of Scotland an informal embassy led by Esmé Stuart, Sire d'Aubigny, a kinsman of the King. Handsome, charming and ambitious, he brought with him other courtiers accomplished in horsemanship and arms and also in the airs, graces and dissipations of French princely style—a company well fitted to delight and divert a lonely youth. (The Kirk, alarmed, described them in very different terms.) Of Aubigny's company at the Scots court was Alexander Montgomerie, convert to and ardent partisan of the Catholic faith, royal favourite and leading poet and song-maker of Renaissance Scotland.[1]

---

[1] Alexander Montgomerie: *Poems*, ed. J. Cranstoun, S.T.S. 1887 and *Poems: Supplementary Volume*, ed. A. Stevenson, S.T.S. 1910. Life-records, etc., printed by Stevenson superseded much of Cranstoun's information; but only Cranstoun has edited, from the authoritative Ker (Drummond) MS., all lyrics, Miscellaneous Poems (1–49), Sonnets (I–LXX) and devotional poems. Montgomerie's life and activities at the Scots court were

From 1579 onwards the five years of the King's adolescence see a contest for ascendancy over his personality and character, his political beliefs and religious creed—indeed at times for the custody of his person. Aubigny triumphed for a time, gaining a dukedom and feigning a conversion to Protestantism on the way, but he was routed and driven out, to die abroad within the year. The victors were a band of elder Lords of Scotland, led by Lord Ruthven and backed by the power of the Kirk. The King was 'taken into cure' by force of arms and for a year royal policy was shaped by that party.

Then the young King escaped and in 1583 drew about him at court a company where different factions found a place. This, the third phase, lasts until 1590, and sees turn and turn again of faction in power. The tensions of the age of Counter-reform in Europe were strongly affecting a Scotland predominantly Protestant but with a King veering away from Presbyterianism as a state doctrine. The conversion of the King to Catholicism was still attempted by both open and devious means as was the rescue and return of his mother to participation with him in sovereign rule of the realm. The King meanwhile must at all costs keep on friendly terms with his 'cousin' and neighbour, Queen Elizabeth, whose throne he hoped to inherit. Crisis approached in 1587 with the execution of Mary, Queen of Scots, on the eve of the Spanish Armada, then the maturing of that great venture of militant Catholicism and its resounding failure.

A fourth phase is marked by the King's choice of a Protestant princess as consort and his marriage in 1590 to Anne of Denmark. The last thirteen years of his rule in Scotland saw a continuing of earlier pressures and counter-pressures but with a difference. That from France abated with the death of Queen Mary, scion of the Guises, and was affected by the change of monarchy in that country. The militant Catholicism of King Philip made other casts towards Scotland but with weakening power: the last was the project of 1596, the 'second Armada' when rebellion in Ireland was echoed by conspiracy in Scotland. In this last matter the poet Montgomerie was a moving spirit.

The King of Scotland's policy over these years was known only to himself: he 'practiced' with the powers temporal and spiritual of the Catholic faith and at the same time kept himself eligible as heir apparent to Queen Elizabeth's throne. This, in spite of other pretenders, he triumphantly inherited in 1603.

In this setting—a sequence of scenes alternating sometimes dramatically, in political and religious climate—song, poetry and dance had their being at King James'

discussed (Introduction and notes) by A. F. Westcott, *New Poems of James I of England*. Stevenson's discussion has to be reconciled at points with Westcott's. See Mark Dilworth, 'New Light on Alexander Montgomerie', and H. M. Shire, 'Alexander Montgomerie: The opposition of the court to conscience...'

northern court. Dance was anathema to the Kirk and unknown to the King's boy-hood education, but it came in with the visiting company from France. Poetry of the classics, of France and of Italy, the King knew well, for he had been superbly schooled in those tongues. *Scottis Poesie* he was to cherish himself as he came to see its com-position and publication as contributing to his country's presence in Europe. Cul-tured song was polyphonic song, drawing on the many-voiced music of the old religion. For sacred part-song patronage was now to seek elsewhere than in the Catholic Church, and the Kirk regarded it with disfavour. Secular part-song would flourish best if fostered in the King's presence. For musician and poet as individuals the politicial religious climate prevailing was a tender matter. Each had his creed, often persistently, sometimes covertly held. Each had his way to make, place or pen-sion to win or hold. How musician and poet fared while James was King of Scotland, how politics interwove with the maturing of music and poetry in this epoch of Counter-reform in Europe we shall see forthwith.

THE MUSICIANS

Andro Blakehall

Let us begin with the musicians and any music surviving from this time that can be certainly or plausibly attributed to them.[1]

The first to be considered is 'Andro Blakehall sum tyme ane chanon of the abbay of halyrudehouss; and eftir reformatioun wes minister of mussilburgh'. Andrew Blackhall, trained musician holding office under the 'old religion' must have been born in 1536 for he lived on to be 'minister of Gods word', dying in 1609 in his seventy-third year. Soon after the Reformation, in 1567, Blackhall was minister of Ormiston—a parish adjoining the abbey lands of Holyrood. He was in that year censured by the General Assembly of the Kirk—for what misdemeanour is not known, but quite possibly for aberration towards elaboration of church service.

He was certainly composing about this time sacred part-song in 'thir miserable pairts' so repugnant to the severer reforming powers. 'Giffin in propyne to the kyng' with the date 1569 is the inscription in the Wode Part Books for 'Of mercye and of judgement bothe', Blackhall's anthem for five voices, the words from Psalm 101.[2] The King was a little over three years old when, in August 1569, the government made preparations for his education. Two scholars were appointed for

---

[1] Earlier studies: H. G. Farmer, *A History of Music in Scotland*; J. McQuaid, 'Musicians of the Scottish Reforma-tion', *Music of Scotland*, ed. Kenneth Elliott and H. M. Shire, whose introduction and notes give detailed information not reproduced here.

[2] Unpublished. Edited by Hilda S. P. Hutchison in her Mus. Doc. thesis, 'The St Andrews Psalter; transcription and critical study of Thomas Wode's Psalter.'

his instruction in literature and religion, George Buchanan and Peter Young. Two Erskines of the family of the Earl Marischal were chosen to train him in horsemanship and the bearing of arms; they were lay abbots of Dryburgh and of Cambuskenneth, seat of the Chapel Royal near Stirling.[1] The musician's choice of this psalm for composition and dedication would bring him favourable notice at the time when the royal establishment was in formation around the child monarch. The words of the psalm could be read in the light of 'advice to the prince' but they also bear the sense of right-minded devotion to the virtues in the subject who devised the musical tribute. It is unknown whether this 'gift in propyne' was composed to mark any specific occasion.

Some years later the *propyne* of music is made to the young King himself, no longer an infant. A piece of *musik fyne* is commissioned as a gift for the boy King James made in an hour fraught with danger to the giver—the setting of a psalm that bears an urgent message. It can be found as no. 11 in *Music of Scotland*. In 1567 James Douglas, Earl of Morton, had championed the cause of the infant Prince and his murdered father Lord Darnley against his mother Mary, Queen of Scots. Under a banner bearing the words from the forty-third psalm 'Judge and revenge my cause O Lord' along with a portrayal of the babe and of his dead father, the forces had marched out from Edinburgh to confront Queen Mary at Carberry.[2] A bloodless but decisive encounter ensued and the words resounded thereafter in the Scottish mind. Douglas, Earl of Morton, was chosen Regent of Scotland in 1572. But six years later, hard-pressed by those who sought his downfall, he ordered the forty-third psalm to be set to five voices by 'Maister Andro Blakehall at the earnest sute of Lord Morton who presentit the samin to King Jamis'. It was an eloquent plea in words and music for grace in the present and for acknowledgment of devoted service in the past: 'Judge and revenge my cause'.

In *Music of Scotland* as no. 10 will be found his 'Psalme cxxviii set and send by blakhall to My Lord Mar at his first mariadge with my Lord of Angus sister' – 'Blessed art thou that fearis God', '1575'. Lord Mar and Lord Angus are two leading personalities in the moves for power during the childhood of King James VI; the *propyne* on the occasion of the marriage marks the Earl Marischal of Scotland as patron for a musician who had moved over to the new faith. In the years when direct royal patronage was in abeyance, then, the occasion of a noble wedding could elicit composition of sacred part-music from a trained musician, a setting of 'the wedding psalm'.

Andrew Blackhall also composed another anthem and a few psalm settings. He will come into the story again as having set to four parts 'the banks of Helicon', to

---

[1] Natural sons of the two Erskines who had been Commendators of the Priory of Inchmahome.

[2] See George Buchanan, *The Tyrannous Reign of Mary Stewart*, ed. W. A. Gatherer, p. 141 onwards. A drawing of the banner is shown in plate 1.

which was sung Montgomerie's 'The Cherrie and the Slae' of 1584. A musician trained in Catholic Scotland and now a minister of the Kirk, if uneasily so, thus employed his art, offering personal tribute to the infant King, celebrating a high religious and social occasion in the nobility, commissioned to express an urgent message in a crisis of rule, and drawn in to embellish a piece of courtly pastime—but one that had, as we shall see, an intention more profound and politically pertinent than recreation.

Other musicians there certainly were in Scotland over the difficult period of transition from the faith and musical culture of the old order to that of the new. For several pieces surviving complete from this time we know the composer. In sacred song there were, for example, John Angus and Andrew Kemp—and David Peebles, of whom we hear that he 'was not eident' when commissioned by Wode to set psalms plain; doubtless his musician's heart was not in composition in the 'contemporary' style.

In secular music we glimpse tantalisingly, as secret messenger to Queen Mary in prison, the figure of William Kinloch, composer of keyboard music, whose religious and political loyalties precluded the use of his skill in office either in the Kirk—where organs were here and there tolerated—or in the court of King James.[1] His existence must be borne in mind, however, as possible composer of some of the songs of the 1590s, an anonymous repertory that survives unfortunately in fragment only.

The Hudsons, Robert, Thomas, William and James: *'Sangistaris, Inglismen, violleris' and writers of verse*

When Prince James was crowned as an infant in 1567, his household at Stirling included with nurse, foster-mother and others a stand of musicians, 'Englishmen, violars', a family group of the name of Hudson, five in number.[2]

It is unknown from whence in England they hailed or where they were trained, but there were family connections with York. 'Thomas Hudson's father (that is) now with the King kent him weill' and 'Thomas Hutcheon...that is with the King knew him in Ingland' says Wode of Robert Johnson, priest and musician, who fled to England 'lang befoir Reformatioun'; this clue, however, has yielded no definite information.[3] The Hudsons had been first recorded in Scotland at the wedding of

---

[1] H. M. Shire, 'Musical Servitors to Queen Mary Stuart'.

[2] See Thomas Hudson, *The Historie of Judith*, 1584, ed. J. Craigie, for his translation from Du Bartas and other verses; Craigie's introduction gives life-records of the Hudsons, of whom he distinguished four. Only additional references are given now.

[3] These quotations from different part-books appear to mean that the father of Thomas Hudson (King's violer) had known Johnson when he was in England. Probably the phrase ''s father' has been concealed during binding in the volume cited second. McQuaid concludes that the father's name was Thomas also; this would explain the use of the distinguishing nickname for the son, Thomas, later Master of the Chapel Royal.

Mary, Queen of Scots to Lord Darnley and it is possible that they arrived in the north under the protection of the bridegroom's family. The Treasurer's Accounts of 1565 (fo. 87v) record this item after the wedding, 'the xxvj day of September be the king and quenis precept to Robert Hudson iii elnis of reid taffeteis to be v pair of gartanis' and 'v beltis to thame'. They also have their 'sarks' made. Livery for *five* persons is here indicated. The first payment to the Hudsons is £120 in part payment of their wages before February 1568, covering a period from late 1566 to early 1567. Here they are called 'sangistaris', singing-men or singing boys. (James Hudson must have been young as he lived on to request a pension in 1617.) Soon after Whitsunday 1566 the records show the 'five violers of Queen Mary' replaced by the 'five English violers.' A change of persons may be indicated but quite possibly both references are to the Hudson family, and only the designation has changed.

Thereafter we hear of four members only of the family group; 'Thomas Hudson's father' perhaps may have retired or died.[1] Thomas or 'Mickle' Hudson, Robert, William and James are thenceforward regularly recorded as violers, *familiarii* of the King until the 1590s. The fact that they were chosen to be placed about the infant prince under Lord Darnley's father as Regent and retained there under Lord Morton suggests that their affinities lay strongly with Protestantism, or with England rather than with Queen Mary and France, though Thomas Hudson we know was a good French scholar. Their loyalties are later seen as engaged to the young King James.

We do not know the exact composition of this family group but Robert Hudson was apparently a generation older than James.[2] Robert Hudson we shall find as a close personal friend of the poet Montgomerie, included in the writing game with the youthful King and himself able to pen out a couplet or two when he pleased—to use Montgomerie's phrase. He contributed one of the complimentary sonnets prefacing the King's volume of 1584 and he may be the 'Robin' and the 'auld crukit Robert' of the King's own youthful verses. He was made Treasurer of the Chapel Royal in 1587, served until about 1593 and retired to Dunfermline where he died in 1596.

Thomas Hudson called 'Mickle' (*big*) by reason of great height or girth received payment as one of the court violers until 1595. He played a prominent part in the royal *puy* of *Scottish Poesie*, the 'Castalian band', as we shall see. At the King's request he 'Englished' the *Judith* of du Bartas. This version was printed in 1584 in Edinburgh, and other verses have survived from his pen. In 1586 Thomas Hudson, musician, was appointed Master of the Chapel Royal and this appointment was ratified in 1587 by the Scottish Parliament and again in 1592 after the King's marriage.

---

[1] The 'fifth' and eldest Hudson (Thomas senior) apparently disappears from the records after 1572.

[2] In 1592 Robert and his wife were granted a pension for life to the survivor. His will: *Edinburgh Testaments*, 1597. (McQuaid.)

His was the task of building up again an institution fallen into decay and of directing emoluments, hitherto unworthily disposed, towards persons skilled in the art of music.

Of William little can be ascertained beyond the regular entries of payment to the violers, but in December 1579, he received a fee as his Majesty's 'balladine'.[1] Teaching the ungainly young Stewart to dance comes somewhat late in the education of this Renaissance prince, after his exacting training as scholar under Buchanan. We may read into this entry the influence of Esmé Stuart, come from France with his fine French manners, of whom we shall later speak at length. The entry is important for the study of court-song because it bears witness to a planned introduction into the King's presence of dance-music; court-dances like the pavan or galliard and dance-song tunes from Elizabethan England now sounded in Holyrood or Stirling, Linlithgow or Falkland Palace.

James Hudson served as violer with the others but from about 1583 he came to be relied on by the King as envoy, passing frequently between Scotland and London on the King's business 'on the English course' of policy. By 1596 Robert was dead and Thomas had passed from the records, William is lost sight of, but James's services as envoy continue into the new century and the new court.

There is no music directly attributed to any member of the Hudson family, but 'Hutchison's' pavan and galliard may well be the work of one of the group.[2] It is to be expected that trained singers and viol players, accustomed to purvey part-music vocal and instrumental for the young King's household devotions or entertainment, would be close to the practice of *musik fyne* in the court in his later years. The long residence of these musicians in the Scottish court may to some extent explain the retention there of old style in the repertory of song. It is possible, indeed, that one or other of them may have been concerned in the composition of new part-song or the devising of a fresh piece from known material. One sonnet by Thomas Hudson written to compliment the King on his *Essayes of a Prentise*, prefixed to the printed text with other admiring verses, was a song, a *propyne* not only of words but of music also, 'If martiall deeds and practice of the pen'. As a song to four voices it has survived albeit incompletely; a bass part bearing that *incipit* is in the Melvill Bassus Part-Book. It seems possible that a musician-poet would find or compose the music for his own offering to the King rather than request the other musician in the court, James Lauder, to do so for him.

Another part-song suggests by its content and its nature that it may have been used

---

[1] *L.H.T.A.*, vol. 1578–84.
[2] Unpublished. 'Hutchison's paven' (Taitt MS.) and 'Hutchison's galliard' (Taitt MS., Skene MS. and Rowallan cantus part-book). Spellings of the name Hudson include Hutcheonis, Hutchinson, Hutchison.

by the Hudsons on some occasion when the young prince was fêted, perhaps during festivities attendant on his coronation as an infant or on a birthday in his childhood. The most probable occasion, however, is in his thirteenth year when he entered in state into Edinburgh. We know that during the celebrations that day songs were sung and viols were played and among the shows was a figure of Bacchus with a fountain that ran wine, and while the King was accepting the keys of the city 'Dame Musick and hir schollers exercised hir airte with great melody'.[1]

This part-song for four voices was probably in the first place a festive drinking-song in praise of the art of part-music opening with a loyal greeting. In one version that has been noted, however, the words have been adapted to point a special salutation and wish for the sovereign. 'Nou let us sing to our yong King...That he may do some princely thing...'

6. NOU LET US SING

[HUDSON?]   [HUDSON?]

Nou   let us sing, Christ keip   our   King   Lord save our King, sing   al - to - gi-ther,

Christ keip his grace and   long   to   rigne That   we   may live   lyk faith - full bre - ther.

The second stanza addresses Dame Musick:

> Deame fill a drink and we sall sing
> Lyk merrie men of musick fyne.
> Tak Bacchus blessing it to bring
> So it be wight as any wine.

Then each of the four singing parts has a stanza in which he characterises his voice, Treble, Counter, Tenor or Bass, giving its particular reason for drinking deep. The song concludes

> Thes Art of Musick is richt dry
> Of all the seavene the merriest
> Deame ye ar sweir that lets us cry
> Once fill the stoup and let us rest.

The song is no. 48 in *Music of Scotland*.[2]

'Nou let us sing' in this metre and rhythm must have been a known song about 1578, for a spiritual version of it is found in the 'Gude and Godlie Ballatis' where it is a

---

[1] *The Historie and Life of King James the Sext*, pp. 277–9.
[2] Also reported in the Taitt MS., 3 voices, 11 stanzas.

Christmas song hailing the birth of Christ. The music may have originated in Scotland, composed by one of the Hudsons, or by James Lauder. But in idea the words may be connected with the French song of the parts and voices, 'Pour faire le bon contrepoint' otherwise 'Pour bien chanter le contrepoint' by Francoys Roussel, printed in Paris in 1577 by Adrien Roy and Robert Ballard: *Chansons Nouvvelles mises en Musique à iiii, v et vi Parties*. Several things, then, point to the song's use in Scotland in 1579.

The examples of court song we have discussed so far have all been *propyne* of words and music focused on the eminent patron or on the person of the monarch as he came of age and springing from political crisis or noble celebration, from royal or national occasion of ceremony.

James Lauder, musician: c. 1535– c. 1595[1]

James Lauder was musical servitor first to Mary, Queen of Scots and then to her son King James, but his loyalties personal, religious and political remained with the Queen as long as she lived. He came of a family where musical talent and trained musicianship can be traced from generation to generation. There may have been three men of the name, James Lawder, named early in the century as Chaplain of Abernethy 'well learned in music', a separate Mr James Lauder not specifically named musician but Dean of Restalrig near Edinburgh (a collegiate foundation where music flourished) and James Lauder, son of Gilbert Lauder burgess of Edinburgh, the musician with whom we are here concerned.

This was the James Lauder given permission in 1552/3 as prebender of the choir in Edinburgh to pass forth to England and France to further his study of music. As with Scott, the prebendency may have been granted to an older chorister, gifted musically, when his voice broke. In consequence of this reference a birth date of 1535 to 1537 seems likely. We do not know where he studied or when he came back to Scotland—but these were the troubled years of Reformation. In 1562, however, very soon after Queen Mary returned to Scotland, he received money 'on precept of the Queen's Grace and her special command', twenty pounds. This may have been for musical service or for music composed and presented 'in propyne'. In 1566, on the eleventh of August, a few months after Prince James was born, he was presented to a Chaplaincy in St Giles, the Burgh Kirk of Edinburgh—'the chaplainrie of St Nicholas alter foundit and situat for the tyme within the college kirk of sanct geill in Edinburgh'—with all the rents and duties pertaining to it when the present chaplain

---

[1] Lauder's life-records were first collected by McQuaid; Farmer distinguishes three men, separating 'Lauder' from 'Lawder'. Further references and discussion in Shire, *Music and Letters*. Life-records of the musician and his family in appendix II of this book.

Sir James Maxwell should resign or die. Here, shortly after Reformation while Queen Mary was still monarch in Scotland, we see a chaplaincy passing from a priest's tenure to that of a musician who was a layman.

The next news we have of Lauder is after the Queen's defeat. He is found in close attendance on her in custody in England, at Tutbury Castle, named *valet de chambre* in a document in a French hand, 'Jaques Loder'. He does not appear again in surviving documents as thus attendant on the Queen in prison, but his tenure of this office continued. In 1576 an entry in the Protocol Books of Scotland mentions 'James Lauder...vallet de chambre...200 livres according to the office where he is employed'. The musician's whereabouts, thus discreetly worded, are uncertain. By this time his bastard son, John Lauder, was personal attendant and musician to the imprisoned Queen, her 'panterer and player on the bass-viol'—and he was in trouble for bearing secret messages for her. Wherever James Lauder then was, there is certainly no record of his having at this time any connection with the household of the infant King.[1] To find an approach made by James Lauder to the court of Scotland we await the King's emergence from tutelage and the next move in international diplomacy.

Under the ascendancy of Esmé Stuart, Sire d'Aubigny, in the first year of King James' personal rule Lauder appears named in the accounts of the court of Scotland, not as retainer but as in receipt of reward or reimbursement. He has been on a mission for the King in London, commissioned as 'servitor' to purchase there on the King's behalf 'twa pair of virginells'. Lauder, like William Hudson, was obviously called into service in the education of the young King in the arts and graces of princely life. With this phase of music and poetry at King James' court, then, Lauder was closely connected. Indeed 'ane musiciane' listed in the royal household of 1580 may well be he.

Specific record is lacking but we can assume that the atmosphere of the court in Aubigny's time was propitious politically and artistically to this court musician as it had not been in the days when the schoolboy King was Buchanan's pupil. When Aubigny's bid for exclusive power was defeated and the King's person seized by the Ruthven party, dislocation of the royal household followed. The King in detention signed a draft scheme in 1582 for a new order of his household and Lauder is there named musician. He is, however, included not with the Hudsons at their table but at the end with the aviaryman and the washerwomen, among court servants who lived out and received their 'ordinary' in money.

He had by this time a wife and large family to support. A letter from Lauder has

---

[1] Lauder is not in the 'Scheme for the Royal Household' drawn up by the Regent in 1567/8. March, *MSS of the Earl of Mar and Kellie*, Hist. MSS. Commission (1904), pp. 18–19.

survived, dated 2 October 1582, soon after Aubigny's defeat and the capture of the King. It was written to his bastard son John, then with Queen Mary in captivity. Lauder there protests his faithful love to the Queen and prays for her health—'all the service he can do her at present'. At the same time he begs for her financial support 'whome of I hawe onlie help of her majestie and none others'. He asks for news of this year's pension and requests that it be sent him in the north, for his last journey to London 'made solely to fetch it' cost him more than the pension came to. We perceive Lauder's financial straits with both royal patrons in captivity but we perceive also a divided loyalty.

The arrangement by which James Lauder was servitor to the Queen in imprisonment was, as we saw, of some years' standing and it involved substantial sums. The 'service' he rendered may well have had a political aspect. In 1582/3 he declared himself to a sympathetic ear 'very affectionate to the Queen', a fact noted by de la Mothe Fénelon who had been sounding opinion for and against Queen Mary in the north. This being servitor to two opposed parties looks treacherous on first view, smacking of Catholic conspiracy in King James' court. But just over the years that followed the King himself was writing affectionate notes to his mother and there were those that hoped for a *rapprochement* between royal mother and son, rivals for a throne and strangers to one another since his infancy. Some indeed dreamed of their reigning together 'in association'. At one point King James indeed remarked that he had ever found most loyal to him those who had been devoted to his mother.

Where the policy of King James is so veering to outward appearance and his intention so baffling to read it is scarcely surprising that activities of his servitors are difficult to interpret, barely recorded as they are in report or account-book, covertly expressed in a letter or a poem. At one point Alexander Montgomerie made a sonnet for James Lauder bearing his name in anagram and also, I believe, including in its title the name of *Ma*[*ria*] *Re*[*gina*]. In this message concerning some great endeavour is expressed. It looks like a *propyne* in words and perhaps in music couched in terms of 'love service', concealing and revealing urgent information.

> James Lauder   *I wald se mare*
> I wald se mare nor ony thing I sie
> I sie not yit the thing that I desyre
> Desyre it is that does content the ee
> The ee it is whilk settis the hairt in fyre
> In fyre to fry tormentit thus I tyre
> I tyre far mair till tyme these flammis I feid;
> I feed affectione spurring to aspyre
> Aspyre I sall in esperance to speid
> To speed I hope thoght danger still I dreid

I dreid no thing bot ouer long delay
Delay in love is dangerous indeed
Indeid I shape the soner to assay
Assay I sall hap ill or weill I vou
I vou to ventur to triumph I trou.   (XLII).[1]

'I, James Lauder, would, more than anything I see, / like to see Ma Re, *Mariam Reginam*. To see her would feed the flames of my affection. Moved by my devotion I am making every effort to succeed yet I dread the danger that lies in overlong delay.'

Lauder's letter to his son John speaks of his longing to be with him 'and all the rest of his company' to remain and end his old days with them—'although I have a wife and seven children, God bless them, with sundry other servants' whom he is hard put to support in his difficulties. Money matters may be pressing, but the words of the sonnet reverberate with the anxieties of some greater endeavour.

It appears to me that in this sonnet the poet has clearly employed his art to serve the musician, his friend. (This is a reversal of the process that is frequently noted in these pages.) The reference to Marian policy is the more likely in that Montgomerie was involved up to his eyes in covert service to her cause.

One entry for 1586, 'James Lauder gone to France' is notable at that time and hour when conspiracy of European dimensions was gathering and threatened to make Queen Mary's workings an issue of her life or death with the Sovereign Elizabeth. Several noted Catholic agents had been dispatched abroad on business for the King, and Montgomerie too had leave to go and was entrusted with some mission from King James. Sympathy had waned by now between royal mother and son. Either the musician was too deeply involved in pro-Marian conspiracy and was got out of the way or permitted to leave as danger mounted or else King James, in full knowledge of his proclivities, employed him 'on the French course'. Quite possibly his departure signifies both things together and we have here, as with the missions of Montgomerie, Keir and other Catholic elements, James Stewart employing the double-handed implement in an ambiguous policy.

After the execution of Queen Mary and the crisis of the Armada Lauder was soon back in Scotland: a fee for his sustenance for 1588 is recorded and in 1590 his back-pay for three years. He is named musician in the new Order of the Royal Household of 1590 after the King's marriage, but his bid made at one point to win a place as *valet de chambre* to King James was unsuccessful. He lived on to examine in music in Edinburgh during the year 1593 and probably to see his son Robert placed in the service of the second Duke of Lennox in 1594.

Nothing further of him is known. But his early training in music sacred and secular,

---

[1] Here printed unpointed; mare (more) is normally spelt in Scots 'mair'.

his education in France and possibly also in England and later his comings and goings between both these countries and Scotland focus attention on his person as a live vehicle for the transmission to Scotland of fresh music from elsewhere.

Only one piece of music survives attributed to James Lauder, a court dance 'My Lord of Marche pauen set be Jamis Lawder, set 1584', no. 83 in *Music of Scotland*. The Earl of March was uncle to King James VI, being Robert Stewart, bastard son of King James V. He may have been musical like his royal father. On an earlier occasion he had been patron to a musician, for at his command David Peebles had composed his motet 'Quam multi, Domine' in 1576 when his patron is named according to his earlier style 'ane venerable Father in God, Robart Commendatour of Sanctandrous' ...(Peebles like his patron long retained affinities with the old religion and its music). Lauder's pavan, elsewhere called 'the gouden' (*golden*) pavan was a favourite piece, widely recorded.[1] As musician about the court or in court employment over the decade 1580 to 1590 and longer, Lauder rather than the violers was the likely person to be employed in devising pieces instrumental or vocal for occasions of court entertainment. His court dance was composed in the year that saw the publication of the first fruits of 'Castalian' poetry and poetic theory, as we shall see. It is very likely indeed that he was associated with the interests of 'the Castalian band', his zone of activity being music and the dance. He was certainly in close touch with Montgomerie, sharing his political leanings. The phases of his life at court keep time with those of the arch-poet. It is in the highest degree probable that where Montgomerie's poetry is found matched with music, his *propyne* in verse embellished by a 'gude musician', that musician was as often as not James Lauder. The burgeoning of court-song to *musik fyne* in Scotland under the young King James may be largely due to a happy conjunction there of the art of poetry and the art of music in two men who were friends.

POETS AT COURT

Early in the summer of 1579 the young King James, now in his thirteenth year, rode forth in state from Stirling Castle into the open countryside. The occasion was celebrated in a poem by Sir Patrick Hume of Polwarth, an official at court—*The Promine: on his majesties first going into the fields*.[2] Printed in Edinburgh, this weighty piece in substantial stanzas marked the beginning of the King's personal reign and the end of an epoch in *Scottis Poesie*.

In September of that year Esmé Stuart, Sire d'Aubigny, with his merry company

---

[1] In Wode, Melvill Bassus Part-Book, Robert Edwards' Music-Book and in Rowallan Cantus Part-Book, where it is called 'goldene'.

[2] Patrick Hume of Polwarth, *The Promine*, Edinburgh 1580; in Alexander Hume's *Poems*. His part of 'The Flyting' in *Montgomerie*, ed. Cranstoun, and *Montgomerie*, ed. Stevenson.

from France, arrived in the northern court. By the later autumn, if not before, Alexander Montgomerie had joined the royal circle.[1] Kinsman to King James through a Stewart ancestress, he was an acceptable courtier. Kin also to Aubigny he was, or became at this time, the French Stuart's servitor—for the poet was later to term Aubigny his 'umquhile master'.

Aubigny's success with the King was immediate, but Montgomerie quickly made his own bid for royal favour in his particular field, poetry. He challenged Hume of Polwarth, till then 'the' poet at court, to bardic contest in a 'flyting' or match of poetic invective, an ancient Scottish mode of courtly entertainment such as had delighted the King's great-grandfather when Dunbar 'flyted' with Kennedy.

It opens vividly:

> Polwart, yee peip like a mouse amongst thornes;
> Na cunning yee keipe: Polwart, yee peip.
> Ye look like a sheipe and yee had twa hornes
> Polwart, yee peipe like a mouse amongst thornes.

Three bouts of invective and counter-invective made the match. It was played in the King's presence with his Majesty as judge and Montgomerie was acclaimed the winner. He ousted Polwarth from the bardic 'chair' in the 'chimnaye nuike'. This ancient game, where outrageous and ribald personal abuse mingled with fantastic genealogy and accusations of vile versifying delighted the young King, for he happily quoted from it not long afterwards. By this stroke Montgomerie established himself in royal favour; henceforward he was 'belovit Sanders, maistre of our airte' and arbiter of *Scottis Poesie* and he came to be tutor to the scholar prince in the skills of poetic composition in Scots.

When he thus won place with the King, Montgomerie must have been in his late twenties, for pieces of his had been collected by Bannatyne ten years before. Of the same generation—and almost as good a poet as he—was John Stewart of Baldynneis;[2] he, too, could claim kinship with the King and distant 'cousinship' with his fellow-poet: witness his piece 'To his weilbelovit Cowsin and luifing Friend'

> Gif equall age, form, fortoune and degre
> Of yow and me Agment may our guidwill...

For a number of years cordial relations obtained between these two poets, though they parted company in time over politics and religion. Over the earlier 1580s Stewart was writing court pieces and interesting translations from French and Italian

---

[1] Montgomerie may have paid a visit to the Scots court the year before, presenting a book to the King on returning from military service abroad (Westcott, p. xxvi). An exploratory visit?

[2] *John Stewart of Baldynneis, Poems,* ed. T. Crockett, p. 169. Only vol. II (text) was published. Discussion: G. A. Dunlop 'John Stewart...the Scottish Desportes', *Scottish Historical Review,* XII (1915), 303–10; M. P. McDiarmid, 'John Stewart of Baldynneis', *Scottish Historical Review,* XXIX (1950), 52 and 'Notes on the Poems of John Stewart...', *Review of English Studies,* XXIV (1948), 12–18.

poetry. These he collected into a handsome manuscript volume and presented to the King in 1586—'Rapsodies of the Author's Youthfull Braine'. It closes with a farewell to the muses, and to 'brycht purpour Pean' ('the royal Appollo')—and marks the end of Stewart's bid for royal favour through poetry. Stewart's writing shows a distinguished mind and an accomplished technique in verse; but his poetry is no-where found in association with music and does not appear to have touched the development of court-song.

Somewhat younger than Montgomerie and Stewart and a cadet of the Humes of Polwarth was Alexander Hume, in 1579 a university graduate home from France and studying law in Edinburgh.[1] Though verse of high quality survives from his pen he failed to make his way at court, found the Aubigny régime uncongenial, sickened of suing for royal favour and is believed to have destroyed his early poems. He turned to the service of God in his Kirk and wrote thereafter only for the Christian muse as minister of Logie. The more is the pity for song at court in that we know he was musical. He played the lute and left a consort of instruments in his will.

A fifth poet, Master William Fowler, was nearer the King in age and enters the story somewhat later than the others. Of burgess background, he rose to favour by means of verse-writing and was for many years court official and a royal secretary. He had decided early on 'the English course' of political affinity as the most promising way up and he was over a long period in touch with Walsingham.[2] He it was who later ousted Montgomerie from place as Montgomerie had ousted Polwarth. Fowler as a poet was copious and determined, well-lettered and wide-ranging, his work bearing witness to the new interest in Italian poetry. Although for a time he was closely concerned with mounting ceremony and pastime in the court there is no link with music in his verse composition.

In the case of Montgomerie, both his poetry and his personal relationships show that he was at home with music and musicians. He was an intimate friend of Robert Hudson the violar, and in close association in art, politics and religion with James Lauder, as we saw. His major poem was set to music by Blackhall. He names 'old Scot' as his convivial companion about the court in the decade that was opening. He must himself have been musical, though probably not musically trained. His work in court-song, words matched with *musik fyne*, was so important that it will need a chapter to itself. James VI was not himself musical as his mother and grandfather had been.[3] In his court the impetus to the making of song must have come from the king's poetic tutor rather than from the monarch himself.

---

[1] Alexander Hume, *Poems*, ed. A. Lawson; biography in introduction.

[2] *William Fowler, Works*, vol. I, Poems, ed. H. W. Meikle, 1914; vol. II, Prose, ed. Meikle, 1933; vol. III (intro-duction, biography, notes etc.), ed. H. W. Meikle, J. Craigie and J. Purves, 1939.

[3] Fontenay, quoted D. H. Willson, *King James VI and I*, p. 53.

Montgomerie of all the poets who flourished at court was, moreover, nearest and dearest to the young King James, '*regi Jacobo carissimus*' if only for a time. Montgomerie's life-story, then, is worth retelling, for to do so will tell the story of court-poetry and song in Renaissance Scotland and illustrate vividly the intertwining of courtly making with issues of monarchy and state, politics and religion.

The Poet and the King

Alexander Montgomerie came of the Montgomeries of Hesilhead, a branch of the noble family of Eglintoun. There is no trace of his having been to college in Scotland. Indeed it is clear that he sought his fortune by his sword, like so many younger sons. Some early soldiering in the highlands is likely, for he earned the nickname of *eques montanus*, the highland trooper. He travelled as a soldier through many lands and commanded in war with distinction; he is frequently styled 'Captain'. Though brought up as a Calvinist he came to 'weary of passing all his days in darkness' and embraced the Apostolic faith under Spanish influence. 'Learned Spain taught him the laws of living with true piety': this may mean that he studied in Spain in a college such as that at Valladolid or, more likely, that he was converted by Jesuit teaching in Spain or elsewhere. 'He was noble in all his ways, in his birth, in his faculties of mind and in his endeavours.' 'He won favour in the circles of King Philip of Spain while at the same time being beloved and regarded by King James.' 'He assailed Protestantism with sword and song.'

That Montgomerie was a Catholic intelligencer and involved in the political activities of the age of Counter-reform had for some time been known to scholars and critics; but that he was ardent in the Apostolic faith with the zeal of a convert has but recently come to light.[1] This testimony, from which the above quotations are taken, comes in a series of Latin 'epitaphs' written in his honour by a monk of the Scots Benedictine brotherhood at Würzburg in Franconia.[2] Montgomerie was, then, a Catholic of the second generation after Reformation, a child of Counter-reformation Catholicism in its second phase—that of militancy and 'alarm spiritual'.[3]

He was converted apparently after years of wide-ranging military service. He may have entered Spanish circles in the first place as intelligencer on the Catholic side—as yet uncommitted in religious matters but coming to embrace the Apostolic faith thereafter. He may have been a Catholic already, if covertly so, when he arrived in

[1] Westcott, p. xxvi and Stevenson, introduction.
[2] Dilworth (1965) gives the five poems in Latin with commentary; Shire (1966) translates and discusses them.
[3] See John Bossy, 'The character of Elizabethan Catholicism'. The first phase, that of the first generation after the Reformation, was 'conservative, recuperative'; the third, 'meditative.'

the northern court; if not, he must have been converted very shortly afterwards.[1] (He was closely associated with Jesuit conspiracy in 1580 as we shall see.) At what point, however, the poet's ardent religious zeal was *avowed* or his paramount loyalty to militant Catholicism was discovered to or by the young King of Scotland, is a point at issue. (The dramatic effect of such an avowal and its far-reaching political repercussions may be seen in the life of the poet's friend, Henry Constable.)[2] Now that we know the strength of his creed and its driving-power, many aspects of his life in the Scots court must be reconsidered. The nature and motivation of his close relationship to the young King, his aims and intentions in many of the turns of fortune that that relationship involved and the meaning and tenor of many of his poems must be reassessed in the light of revelations in the Benedictine's verses of *éloge*.

The testimony to Montgomerie's presence in the court of Scotland by the autumn or early winter of 1579 lies in his own writing. Two poems of his, which may well be in sequence, 'The Navigatioun' (48) and 'A Cartell of the thre ventrous knichts' (49), are pieces for court entertainment apt for that year and for the thirteen-year-old monarch. Both speak of a company of several persons arrived by sea from afar to do honour to King James' northern court. The second, the 'thre ventrous knights', is the 'crying' of a tournament, a verse introduction announcing the three 'errant knights' come from foreign lands—as can be seen from their strange costumes—who offer contest that day in tourney or in jesting mimic-conflict. The first poem announces a company of four, the spokesman and three companions. It opens with a salutation to the young King:

> Haill bravest burgeon brekking to the rose,
> The deu of grace thy leivis mot unclose
> The stalk of treuth mot grant the nurishing   [thee
> The air of faith support thy florishing.
> Thy noble counsell, lyk trees about thy grace,
> Mot plantit be ilk ane into his place,
> Quhais ruiting sure and toppis reaching he   high]
> Mot brek the storme befor it come to the.
> They of they bluid mot grou about thy bordour
> To hold thy hedge into ane perfyt ordour
> As fragrant flouris of ane helthsome smell
> All venemous beistis from the to expell.
> Thy preachers treu mot ay thy gardners be
> To clense thy root from weeds of heresie.

---

[1] A Captain Montgomerie serving in the Netherlands was named as suspected 'of Don John's faction for the Scottish Queen's Sake' in 1578 (January 25). (Dr Wilson, agent for the Low Countries, to Davison.)

[2] *Poems of Henry Constable*, ed. Joan Grundy, introduction, p. 34. The news of his avowal and flight was said to have killed his father.

> Thy gardene wall mak the Neu Testament
> So sall thou grou without impediment;
> All lands about sall feir thy Excellence
> And come fra far to do thee reverence:
> As I myself and all the rest ye see
> From Turkie, Egypt and from Arabie...

The speaker goes on to declare himself 'ane German borne' and indicates his significant costume in that role. (Has 'german' a double sense, 'German' and 'german', Montgomerie 'sib to the King'?) These lines of salutation shadow forth a reality, showing the Stuart, Aubigny, already close to the King and ready to expel others from his side. But, diplomatically enough, the religious issue is veiled; extirpation of heresy may mean one thing or another, and here it is couched in terms of 'prechours' and the 'Neu Testament'. The watchful powers of the Kirk need not be outraged.

The piece is a monologue, its interest topographical and loyal. The spokesman tells how he fell into company with 'the Turk, and Moor and the Egyptian', who 'presently appear' 'in contrair clething', the various costume of their countries, to do honour to the King. (In accordance with the style of this devising, they probably brought gifts; are there overtones here of 'three wise men' of 'Tarsis, Arabie and Saba'?) In Constantinople news had reached them of the young King of Scotland just beginning his reign, and they voyaged to see him. The interest and perils of the voyage are described, from the Levant by way of Arragon [*nota bene*], Portugal and Ireland. On sighting the coasts of England he had exclaimed 'What if the Quene war deid? Quha suld be nixt, or to the croun succeid?'—a tell-tale phrase!

Once landed, they have come hotfoot to the King's gate:

> Quharas the court with torches all wes sett
> To shau the way unto your Graces hall
> That eftir supper we might sie the ball.
> My fellowis comes nou: I mon mak away.
> God blisse your Grace! I haif no more to say.

'The Navigatioun' obviously belongs to the celebrations of 1579, either to those attendant on the King's first entry into Holyrood in September or to a banquet and ball marking the official 'joyous entry' into Edinburgh in October, when civic homage was paid. Although the piece is patently a courtly devising, there may still be much of fact in the poet's narration of his coming.

By the time of these 'entries in state' Aubigny was already in high favour, riding by the King's side and loaded with honours—to be created Duke of Lennox in the following spring. The royal boy, parentless and affection-starved, gave his heart to the handsome cousin and accomplished courtier whose ambition was linked with the cause of Queen Mary and Catholic Europe, but whose private intent was personal domination.

These pieces for a court entertainment show Montgomerie as makar in a court in which his 'master' had gained ascendancy. In what must have been a carefully planned cultural and political operation to catch the fancy of the King, Montgomerie is soon seen fulfilling a specific role; it was one that he as a known poet was well able to perform—to provide the pleasures of poetry for the instruction and delight of a scholarly royal youth and by example and flattery to draw him into the pleasant discovery that he too was a poet. Certainly we can see with these Ronsardian *cartels* and other of his writings—the *Elégie* imitated from Marot and songs and sonnets drawing on the work of the *Pléiade*—that Montgomerie brought into Scotland afresh the famous and delightful poetry of France.[1] The King, an excellent French scholar thanks to Buchanan's teaching, was already acquainted with such poetry from his mother's library. Montgomerie brought, too, personal accomplishment in *Scottis Poesie* drawing on older traditions of the northern makar's art. Alliterative 'tumbling verses' and the 'Scottish Chaucerian' inheritance are now united in the same Scots poet, enlivened by fresh draughts from the new poetry of France. Above all he brought—as I hope to show—an interest in writing songs, words that were *amoene* to music, 'sonets' that could be sung. To have a known poet in residence in the northern court gave pleasure and prestige. That that poet was also a personable and distinguished young man, a witty and convivial companion who would rhyme you under the table in informal and ribald writing-game, was an added attraction for James Stewart, hitherto lettered in severity. That that poet was musical was of the first importance for the development of court-song in Scotland.

Montgomerie's residence in the Scots court as arch-poet was not uninterrupted. The winter of 1580 finds him on a mission in England involved in a transaction with one Henrie Gelis, merchant of Southampton, concerning the purchase by Montgomerie and two other persons of a vessel called the *James Bonaventor*.[2] This affair in all its sinister political implications and tangled finances was to pursue him years later and cause him trouble in the Scots courts of law. The legal records suggest that the acquiring of the vessel was connected with the Jesuit plan of that year for the overthrow of Protestantism both in Scotland and in England and the restoration to the throne of Mary, Queen of Scots. (To this it may now be added that a barque called the *Bonaventura* had in fact belonged earlier to Queen Mary herself, and this may be the same vessel now under an adapted title.)[3]

[1] L. Borland, 'Montgomerie and the French Poets of the early sixteenth century', pp. 127–34 and Stevenson, appendix C, 'New Sources of Montgomerie's Poetry'.

[2] Stevenson, appendix D. III and IV. See appendix III this volume.

[3] Mary to Elizabeth, recovery of the ship Bonaventure, October 1561 (*Cal. S.P.* vol. I, 1547–63).

Montgomerie in 1580 is not on court record as servitor to King James, but was presumably still owning Aubigny as 'master'. For whom then was he acting? As far as may be ascertained he was under the banner of Aubigny, for Queen Mary and in consonance with the Jesuits, having also won favour in the circles of King Philip of Spain. A key man? This visit to England may be the setting of the message poem 'James Lauder—I wald se MA RE'. Lauder, it will be recalled, was in London too this same year on somewhat double-handed business, for King James and touching his mother as well. This poem taken as written at this point would show Montgomerie apparently deep in 'double-play'—or should one say 'as yet unclear in politico-religious loyalties'? Firm conclusions here are dangerous, however, as the piece may date from a second visit some years later that marked another crisis in Marian conspiracy.

How long Montgomerie was absent from Scotland on this occasion of 1580 is unknown. There was indeed time for him to visit Spain or the Spanish Netherlands and to return. We must envisage him back in the north and resident in King James' court by 1581, for it was he who taught the King to 'mak' in Scots and by 1581, in his fifteenth year, the King had written his first poem—certainly his first verses publicly circulated. This is entitled 'Song' in the royal manuscript copy and it is neatly strophic, but no associated music is known. Here is the first of its three stanzas.[1]

> *Song. The first verses that ever the king made*
> Since thought is free, think what thou will
> O troubled hart to ease they paine
> Thought unrevealed can do no evill
> But wordes past out cummes not againe
> Be cairefull aye for to invent
> The waye to gett they owen intent...

The thought revealed here, consciously or unconsciously, is significant for King James' policy as we see it in these studies, the behaviour that was to earn him the angry phrase of Queen Elizabeth—'the false Scotch urchin'.

A relationship between poet and king is building up wherein poet can be 'double agent, Catholic intriguer, seducer of the King's youthful affections' or

convert to the Apostolic faith, burning with zeal to further the cause of Counter-reform but as yet not publicly avowed a Catholic, devoted to Queen Mary's cause and to the militant Catholicism practised by Spain as making for Catholic rule in Scotland, on terms of intimate affection with the young King and willing to use this influence to attempt the King's conversion to the Roman faith.

It depends on the point of view.

[1] Song. Westcott, no. LIII.

'Beloved Sanders' 1579–1582: the first phase of the 'writing game'

The instruction of the young King in the art of poesie and the pleasures of the 'writing game' as played by him with Montgomerie and others of the court are best seen in some of the King's own verses.

'An admonition to the Master poet to be war of great bragging hereafter, lest he not onlie slander him selfe but also the whole professours of the art' begins thus:

> Give patient eare to sumething I man saye
> Beloved Sanders maistre of our art...[1]

Montgomerie's state, the King writes, is poor and his royal pupil, a friend in need, must speak to help him as the mouse once did the lion in the fable. The literary play is here that of roles reversed, the schoolmaster admonished, the royal lion of Scotland playing mouse. The instance adduced by the King is in Henryson's fable, and that too, it will be recalled, was devised in royal style, perhaps for a prince of Scotland.

He continues:

> For all the poets leaves you standing baire
> Olde crucked Robert makes of you the haire
> And elfgett Polward helpes the smithie smuike
> He comptes you done and houpes but anie mair   15
> His tyme about to winne the chimnay nuike...

> For ye was cracking crouslie of your broune   25
> If Robert lie not, all the other night
> That there was anie like him in this toune
> Upon the grounde ye wold not lett it light
> He was so firie speedie yaulde and wight
> For to be short he was an A per se   30
> Bot yett, beleeve, ye saw an other sight
> Or all was done (or Robin's rithme does lie)...

Montgomerie had been boasting all one night of the speed and strength of his brown riding-horse, but when next day it was put to the test in the race it had run miserably, so far behind that the face of the poet was not even splashed by mud from the horses ahead.

> ...Ye bracke togither and ranne out the same
> As Robin sayes, it had bene fil'd your face
> It chanc'd ye were forerunne a prettie space
> A mile or more, that keiped it so cleene.
> When all was done ye hade so evill a grace   95
> Ye stoll awaye and durst no more be seene.
> [*alias* Ye stoll awaye and looked like Rob Steene]

Montgomerie's boasting of his mount seems to have been done in verse; it was certainly 'countered' by Robin in rhyme, from which a phrase is quoted in homely

---

[1] Westcott, no. LI.

Scots idiom. This sounds like verse used in ancient fashion for purposes of praise and denigration with a strong element of contest in it: other poets have turned on Montgomerie after his boasting of his horse has been shown to be vain, and are writing triumphant lampoons. Polwarth, ousted earlier from the bardic chair in the 'chimnaynuike', is now attacking strongly, hoping to prevail over him and win back the place of honour. The 'Flyting' is a recent memory, for 'elfgett' picks up a word from it.

Verse is used here in fun by a group of friends, King, poet and court servants. It is verse made after an ancient pattern but exercised in social undress. The tone recalls that of Marot's *Petite épitre au roy*. Yet this rhyming was enjoyed in a company where poetry was discussed seriously, witness the last phrase of the King's title 'the whole professours of the art' and the lines where he points out wherein lay the seriousness of Montgomerie's fault: he has given to Christian Lindsay, lady poetaster of the circle, excellent grounds for her accusation 'that poets lie'.

> Nor yett woulde ye not call to memorie
> What grounde ye gave to Christian Lindsay by it
> For now she sayes, which makes us all full sorie,
> Your craft to lie; with leave, now have I tried.

The last stanza of the admonition is signed by the royal versifier with his *nom de guerre* in the game

> I William Mow at after supper lawing
> With pen and drinke compil'd you this propine.
> I gat it ended long before the dawing
> Such pith hade Bacchus ou'r me, God of wine...

A William Mow really existed, known to the court some years earlier in Dalkeith; and Rab Stene was a pedantic schoolmaster of Edinburgh.[1] He is elsewhere called 'the King's fule'. But William Mow and Rob Steene are here, I suggest, the *personae* of the King and the 'schoolmaster' in the poetry-game. Further jokes about Rab Steen and his breeches and his style of versifying haunt the records and the verses of the company at court.

A play-world is built for a king around roles chosen from humble life; these verses are *lusus regius*, a proletarian pastoral.[2]

In similar vein of writing, of play between the King and his master-poet is the sonnet to Bacchus, 'O mightie sonne of Semele the faire'.[3] This begins in all solem-

---

[1] 'Letters served on William Mow in Dalkeith to compeir' before royal authority: *L.H.T.A.*, XI, 496. Rab Stene: *Scottish Historical Review*, II, 253–9, 480, VIII, 271; McDiarmid (1950) also believes Rab Stene 'was' Montgomerie, from premises possibly differing from mine. Montgomerie is called 'Rab Stewin' in 'The Flyting'; and 'Rob Stene's Dream' of 1591–2 though anonymous is obviously his. (ed. Maitland Club, Glasgow 1836).

[2] Compare the ludic *personae* of Robert Louis Stevenson and his friend in their 'Johnson–Tamson' correspondence.

[3] Westcott, no. XLV.

nity apostrophising Bacchus, as sister-pieces by the youthful royal poet had hailed Jove and Apollo. The octave celebrates the power of Bacchus over the five senses but the young poet is having trouble with poetic syntax.

> ...sume all five bereaved
> Are of thee, the greate Alexandre craved
> Thy mercie oft, our maistre poëte now
> Is warde by the...

Moving on in his sestet, on great men overpowered by Bacchus, he suddenly flits from earnest to jest. Like Alexander the Great, Alexander the master poet is 'warde' [overcome] by wine. Smaller poets then shall give up the struggle against the powerful god—and get drunk too. The king vows that the 'epitaph' for Montgomerie shall be

> Here lyis whome Bacchus by his wyne
> Hath trapped first and made him render syne

This has been taken in all seriousness to refer to the death of the poet. But surely it is done in game—an 'epitaph' for Montgomerie dead drunk, pronouncing his essential character. The writing of such 'epitaphs' in fun was a favourite vein in this epoch that produced in Latin or the vernacular many fine epitaphs written in all seriousness.

The obvious inexpertness of the verse and the outset as a 'sonnet to Bacchus' link this sonnet closely with the series of sonnets to the gods that the King was composing at this time and that he was to print in his *Essayes of a Prentise* of 1584. By all tokens a production of his apprenticeship in making under Montgomerie, it shows the convivial aspect of Renaissance writing, 'making' for fun, done here under the mantle of 'staitly style' and with classical apostrophe. Buchanan's teaching was laid under contribution now in a spirit distant from that of his stern schoolroom.

Like the 'Admonition' the sonnet was crossed out in the royal manuscript copy of the King's poems, considered indecorous or trivial by King Charles and Carey who oversaw the papers. But what was suppressed as undignified in a record of verses by the King of Britain lately dead was integral to the game of writing, the pleasures of poetry as enjoyed by James Stewart royal adolescent and his literary schoolmaster. The making of poetry was a serious art but could be indulged in for fun; Marot made a game of writing for his royal master. The composition of polyphonic music was a high and serious skill, yet it could be done as a game in puzzle-canon by an English king and his friends. And we have seen that the 'Art of Music' could be celebrated convivially with Bacchus' blessing in the song of the 'merrie men of *musick fyne*'.

What is the relevance to this social context of Montgomerie's writing? The 'Flyting' and the 'cartels', as we saw, were pieces of ceremony and entertainment made for the court. A deal of verse must surely have been written before he came back to Scotland in his late twenties, a known makar. Bannatyne ten years before had caught a merry lampoon against a highlander that looks forward to the 'writing game' in its jesting aspect (B. CCXXXI, Cranstoun 54).[1] Bannatyne had also collected the early love-lyric 'Irkit I am' (B. CCCXXIX) for which a score of companion pieces can be found among Montgomerie's poems close to it in manner and style (52). These would be available as sampler for the poetic schoolroom—poems 'treating of matters of love' in different aspects, celebration or 'regrate', 'remeid' of rueful humour or 'argument', 'I rather far be fast nor frie' and its answer (13, 14). Other examples of modes of rhetoric may have been expressly composed—a close rendering into Scots from sonnets of Ronsard or Constable or a translation with overgoing of Marot's 'Elégie'.

Was there in Montgomerie's making a closer pertinence to this phase of life at court? Some of the pieces treated of love as an ennobling force in man, an embellishing of social intercourse. These may reflect the education of the prince in the lighter arts and graces of life that was put in hand during the Aubigny ascendancy. Fontenoy thought such education was overdue: 'he [the King] dislikes dancing and music and the little affectations of courtly life such as amorous discourse or curiosities of dress'.[2]

> 3   Love maks men galyard in thair geir;
>   Love maks a man a martial mynd...
>   Love maks a couard kene,
>   Love maks the clubbit clene
>   Love maks the niggard bene...   (13)

There is, moreover, in Montgomerie's poetry an interesting consonance in metaphor which shows it keyed to the court of a young king. His poems are largely couched in terms of service to Cupid, Cupid's court and his laws, his bow, his darts, his well, his sacrifice. King Cupid, not 'Venus quene' is the image that integrates a run of lyrics. Poetry of the Renaissance court with its centripetal gaze coined significant metaphor for the monarch and in terms of that metaphor a coherent 'little world' was made. Raleigh was 'Wa'ter Raleigh', Shepherd of the Ocean to his Cynthia-Moon, the Mistress of tides and seafarers. Montgomerie's 'Cupid' poetry reveals a similar world of coherent conceit, though the metaphor for the monarch does not drive so deep into cosmic significance and the passions involved were somewhat different passions.

King James was not early debauched as his grandfather had been, plunged into the 'game of love' in his early teens, whether with 'leesome ladies' ambitious to bear a royal bastard or with wenches of the town or brewhouse. His adolescence was engaged elsewhere with his hero-friend, his French kinsman. Love billets, 'staitly' erotic or

---

[1] Printed and discussed in *The Cherrie and the Slae*, ed. H. H. Wood, pp. 86–9.
[2] The court under Aubigny: *Bowes Correspondence*, Surtees Soc. p. 136, discussed Westcott, p. xxv. Fontenoy, quoted in Willson, *King James*, p. 53.

bawdy erotic were not apparently a currency in his court life as they had been in the court of the 1530s, though critics asserted that the company around King James VI was lascivious and foul-mouthed enough. The 'prince without vice' was not the best patron for poetry voicing the service of Venus for its own sake. But the years of Aubigny's personal ascendancy over the young Prince, which were likewise years of close affection and apprenticeship of Prince with the handsome poet-friend, called from that makar a poesy whose world had its own geography, history and legend in which the poet's relationship with his monarch was expressed. Out from this world Montgomerie's major poem was to move, through an 'encounter with Cupid in the court', to a serious 'treating of matters of love' earthly and divine on a cosmic scale of universal and eternal values.[1]

In a maturer phase that was to follow, moreover, 'King Cupid' as an image of the King was to give place to 'the royal Apollo'—as we shall see.

'His maiestie in Fascherie': the Ruthven Raid, August 1582 – June 1583

By 1582 Esmé Stuart, Sire d'Aubigny, Duke of Lennox, had reached the zenith of his power in the Scottish court. In the eyes of the adolescent King he could do no wrong—even his conversion to the Protestant faith was believed possible. But certain Protestant Lords, Ruthven at their head, were outraged by the wide political dangers threatened by this ascendance. They took action in August of that year, seized the person of the King and, not long after, routed Lennox who retired in rage and despair to France, to die there in 1583.

King James was in the hands of the 'Ruthven raiders' for nearly a year and during that time he was segregated from his former companions. A few figures that had served at court before and were sympathetic to the 'Ruthven' point of view were now about the King, notably William Murray. The 'Montgomery' who was of his household during this period is certainly not Alexander the poet but in all likelihood a Captain Robert Montgomery formerly servant of Lord Morton, whose life-records have been confused with the poet's at several points.[2] Lennox's 'servitor' would be in the highest degree suspect to those now in power. Nor is there any sign of Montgomerie in the order of the household planned for 1582. Both the instruction in the art of poesy and the sessions of taking pleasure in it that the King had enjoyed with 'Sanders' were now in abeyance. Apparently the King was likewise without the musicians, the Hudsons, for their moneys failed in payment but were made up

---

[1] Discussed in chapter 5.
[2] Stevenson, Appendix D. XII, Westcott, p. xxviii; but this is not the poet.

later.[1] Lauder, certainly *persona non grata* with the Ruthven lords, was financially stranded for a time, as we saw. Of court-song, its making or its enjoyment there is not a trace. That the King took time over these months however to reflect on poetry and how it should best be written in Scotland, in this year and decade and at his court, is in the highest degree likely. It was most probably now and in his mind that the writing game of 'William Mow' and 'Rab Steen' advanced into the 'staitly style' of the game of the 'Castalian band', 'brethir to the sister nine' with himself the royal Apollo at its head.

There is nothing from the pen of the King or of Montgomerie coming certainly from this year. It is of interest, however, to note the approach made to the King over these troubled months by John Stewart of Baldynneis. The volume of his works he gave to his majesty in 1586 is carefully planned and in much of the verse a chronological arrangement can be discerned. An introductory sonnet to his majesty is followed by 'Ane prayer in adversetie' and 'Ane prayer and thankisgiving', 'To ane honorabill and distressit ladie' and 'To his rycht inteirlie belowit freind'; then comes a sequence of three pieces on a problem of matters of love—should, for example, a high-born lady love only one of a similar station or grant her love to one of inferior rank to whom nature and her emotions incline her? These poems for ladies are either frankly commissioned or they are nicely poised between 'making' on a stock theme and verse of social occasion. In all of them a known gambit seems to me to be used freshly to meet the real event.

After these follows a series directly pointing at life in the Scots court; first a piece 'To his familiar friend in cowrt'

> Heyis not ourhich in prosperus air
> Nor yit for stormie blast dispair...
>
> Lat Reson reull and do the best
> First serwing God and nixt our king
> With loyal hart abowe all thing.

Then comes 'To his maiestie in Fascherie' which surely refers to the king's detention by the Ruthven lords. We recall the young King's tears of anger at finding himself thus retained by *force majeure*, and the famous response of his captor 'Better bairns greet nor beardit men...'. The message in Stewart's poem is that this distress will surely pass

> Liwe still heirfoir in esperance alway;
> Maist plesour purchest is be pryce of paine.
> Thois that induirs the vinters scharp assay
> sall sie the seimlie symmer scheine againe.

With God's help his foes shall be beaten down.

---

[1] Hudson's moneys: Extraordinary Accounts, 1582–3 (XXI, 152, 1580): James Hudson paid £300 (fol. 128v), a retrospective payment to cover arrears during the King's absence. (McQuaid.)

The same message is contained in 'To his maiestie the first of Ianvar 1582,' that is the Yule of the year 1582/3.

> ...Ground the on God quho suir is thy defence,
> And he but dout your harts desyre sall send,
> My lyf in pledge, or this yeir cum till end.

For a New Year gift the poet has no jewel to send but only a faithful loving heart. The link between the occasion and the courtly making of Stewart is strong throughout. We should heedfully read a line from the earlier poem to his 'rycht inteirlie belowit freind' who is in all probability Montgomerie:

> The lyf is sad quhilk euir suffers paine,
> Strong linckit lyons quhyls begins to loup;
> Heirfoir with courage schaw yow blyth againe
> Schaik aff despair and confort yow in houp.

Lions even when strongly chained may sometimes begin to leap. God will by his providence

> conwoy
> Your noy and myn both schortlie till ane end.
> So ye and I sall giwe him thanks with Ioy.

The King's 'fascherie' in detention meant 'dolor' for both poet-friends, formerly his companions at court but now debarred his presence. But the young Stewart lion would not be always in chains.

The King's captivity stimulated the writing of consolatory verses, but it appears to have silenced the practice and devising of court-song for a while.

The Castalian Band 1583–1586

In June 1583 the King escaped and the power of the Ruthven lords was overthrown. The company about the King and the tenor of politics show a reversion to the state of affairs before the Ruthven raid. Bowes, the English Ambassador, noted that the King was now surrounded by nobles most of whom were Catholic, some partisans of Queen Mary and some in touch with Guise. The young King, however, had learned some lessons in detention and now declared his intention 'to draw his nobility to unity and concord and to be known as a universal king, impartial to them all'.[1] Beside the King, however, was the emptiness left by the death of Lennox. By December he had fetched to his court from France the young son, Ludovic, second Duke of Lennox, and he was celebrating in poetry the death of his beloved friend in 'Ane metaphoricall invention of a Tragedie called Phoenix', his best poem so far.

Shortly after the escape of the King the court servants were changed and in the

---

[1] Quoted Willson, *King James*, p. 47.

King's household freshly assembled Montgomerie had a place. In August 1583 the poet gained a royal pension. It derived from revenues of the See of Glasgow, some of which moneys had passed to Aubigny in 1580: Montgomerie would appear to have been rewarded from funds that had been in the hands of his 'umquhile master'.[1] These moneys proved difficult to uptake because of tangled politics, for the very identity of the rightful holder of the bishopric, whence they ultimately derived, was a hotly debated issue of politics and religion. That in the end the pension came to be a subject of grievance between poet and King was the result of forces to some extent out-with King James' control.

This getting of the pension, this becoming 'schervituour to his Majestie', was an all-important step and it was, I believe, celebrated by the poet in verse: Montgomerie expressed his thanks for a request granted in a *propyne* of poetry embellished with music, the song 'Before the Greeks durst enterpryse' (Cranstoun 38, *Music of Scotland* no. 50). The Greeks are remembered consulting the oracle of Apollo before their great endeavour and receiving a favourable answer to their request. Its last two stanzas run:

> 3   When they had endit thair requests
>   And solemnly thair service done
>   And drunk the wyne and kild the beists
>   Apollo made them ansueir soon
>   Hou Troy and Trojans haiv they suld
>   To use them hailly as they wold.

(In other words, the 'Ruthven' party were 'for it'?)

> 4   Whilk ansueir maid thame not so glad
>   That thus the victors they suld be
>   As ev'n the ansueir that I had
>   Did gritly joy and comfort me
>   When lo! thus spak Apollo myne
>   All that thou seeks, it sall be thyne.
>   (38)

King James cites a stanza from this poem as suitable for love matters in his treatise of 1584, but the piece is devoid of 'amorous' content. The idiom of the poem depends for its force on 'Apollo myne', and as clinching image for a love poem in the usual sense it is remarkably unapt, the lady figuring awkwardly as Apollo.[2] But this

---

[1] Stevenson, Appendix D. II. Aubigny soon after becoming Earl of Lennox acquired large revenues of the bishopric of Glasgow, to the rage of the Kirk; Montgomerie 'inherited' from his former patron, now dead, both funds from that source and the Kirk's opposition to the grant. Bishop Betoun, the pre-Reformation tenant of the see, had left for France and there acted as ambassador for the imprisoned Queen Mary. King James at one point contemplated the restitution of Betoun to the see of Glasgow (Register of the Privy Council 17 March 1586/7).

[2] (Du Bellay, however, uses the figure.) This concluding stanza is cited in the King's 'Tretis' as is the stanza (8) describing Cupido from 'The Cherrie and the Slae', both chosen, I suggest, because they directly figured the King himself—and the poets affection for him?

'Apollo' figure is the image of the King for the phase of courtly making that now ensudes, as King Cupid had been for the earlier years. Apollo was god of the sun, god of poetry and leader of the band of the Muses, poet himself and source of lifegiving force to other poets: du Bartas, presenting a poem of the King's in French translation, was to call him 'the Apollo of our time'!

With the approaching winter of 1583 the King's study and practice of poetry moved to public status and princely style. A programme must have been carefully thought out, for in the working library, selected to bring from Stirling to Holyrood in November for the winter's reading, poetry ranks with history and certain practical matters of jurisdiction as the monarch's serious concern. For poesy, besides volumes of the classics, he took Ronsard's *La Franciade* and his *Poèmes* containing 'L'Abrégé de l'Art Poétique françois', du Bellay's *Musagnœmachie* (the Muses' battle against Ignorance) and *L'Olive Augmentée*.[1] The poetic theory and practice of King James envisaging a new poetry for Scotland with Montgomerie at his elbow was based on reading of the best French models taken together with the native stock of earlier Scottish making. This latter may have had its own unwritten tradition of style and composition: the line can be traced back *in living contacts* from Montgomerie and Scott to the poetry of the court of King James V with Fethy, Lindsay and Inglis, and so to Dunbar and Kennedy and Henryson under King James IV.

Montgomerie was back at court and 'master of our art', the art now participated in by the King himself as a makar in his own right, witness his 'Phoenix'. To judge by the 'new' poetry, its theory and practice, as we see it coming from the pen of the King, the master poet and the other writers in the court, the young king now took the lead. The context for poetry as for politics recalled the days of Lennox's ascendancy, but in poetry as in politics the King would appear to be making a way of his own, one in which the importance of England does not go unacknowledged—a universal poetry, perhaps, like his policy, 'impartial to them all'.

The twelvemonth now beginning sees King James gathering round him in a literary project familiars of the 'writing game' of earlier years, Robert Hudson and his brother Thomas, probably with Christian Lindsay drawn in. James Lauder was in Edinburgh. 'Old Scot and Robert Sempill' are named by Montgomerie as sharing in convivialities of the circle but they were probably figures of Edinburgh or the Stirling region invited to court rather than servants or courtiers attendant there. Stewart of Baldynneis is of the company about the King at court and a new figure now enters the scene, William Fowler.

Nothing is more exacting to chronicle than a literary *puy:* the 'Areopagus' of the

---

[1] The King's library and reading-list, Westcott, pp. xxi–xxiv. In 'Musagnœmachie' there is a compliment to the young Dauphin, the first husband of Mary, Queen of Scots. This work probably helped to inspire King James to royal patronage of poetry.

Sidney–Spenser circle remains an elusive outline difficult to trace. In a literary coterie so much that is important may pass in conversation or be recorded only in the catch-phrase, pun or *nom de guerre*. It has been well suggested that King James' name for his poets at court, or their name for themselves, was 'the brethren of Castalian band'. King James was to use the phrase with affection years later in his epitaph on Montgomerie:

> What drousie sleep doth syle your eyes allace
> Ye sacred brethren of Castalian band...[1]

Of the Castalian band of muses' brothers, 'Apollo' was the leader. The creation of new poetry for Scotland was a project of the first importance yet it had a jesting aspect as the earlier project of poetry had had. Companionship and witty exchange of thoughts again make the name and nature of a play world. Now a mixed company of king, kinsmen and court-servants making poetry on the slopes of a Scottish mountain jestingly enjoy the parallel they present to the nine Muses on Mount Helicon, to the personified forces of creative composition in ancient times. They are 'brethir to the sister nyne', for Montgomerie; for Stewart they are the muses' scholars and his special devotion is to 'Paean', Apollo!

We know something of how the Castalian project was organised. Thomas Hudson tells us that the task of 'Englishing' the *Judith* of du Bartas was set him by the King following a table conversation about the problems of translation of French hexa-meter into native pentameter form.[2] William Fowler was inspired to translate the *Triumphs* of Petrarch.[3] In fact a certain zoning of interest can be discerned in the completed works of the group that have come down to us. It is just possible that—again half in earnest, half in jest—the activity of each of the nine sisters of the ancient world was followed predominantly by one of the northern brethren. Terpsichore: James Lauder is known to have composed a court dance and one of the Hudsons may have done so too. Montgomerie brought sonnets and songs of Ronsard, de Baïf and Marot into currency in the north and with them the suave grace of his own lyric pieces. Epic was served by Hudson's biblical epic from France and Stewart of Baldyn-neis contributed romance-epic, 'Roland Furious', rendered from Italian into Scots *via* Desportes' translation. For the comic muse there is the anonymous dramatic piece 'Philotus' printed only later but based as it is on a story printed in England in 1581, very probably belonging to this epoch and springing from this stimulus. As to authorship, the writer is '*aut Montgomerie aut diabolus*'.[4] Erato the muse of love-

---

[1] Westcott, no. XXXIV.

[2] Thomas Hudson's preface dedicatory to his *Historie of Judith*.

[3] *Fowler's Works*, I; dedicated 1587.

[4] Rudolf Brotanek listed parallel passages from this and Montgomerie's poetry: 'Philotus: ein Beitrag zur Geschichte des Dramas in Schottland'. Montgomerie's authorship is urged by M. P. McDiarmid in 'Philotus: A Play of the Scottish Renaissance'. He there agrees with my suggested dating.

poetry was certainly the mistress of Scott as well as being no stranger to Montgomerie. The King wrote a historical poem, 'Lepanto'. Polyhymnia, muse of sacred song, is well served in metrical versions of the psalms. Along with the muse Urania, once lady of astronomy but reinterpreted at the Renaissance, she was much favoured by the King's interest in poetry of the Christian muse. He translated the *Uranie* of du Bartas. For elegiac poetry in the sense of elegy there was the 'Phoenix'. The interests of all the muses was represented in their 'brothers'' work. The assignation of each brother to a particular muse cannot be worked out in detail, perhaps, but then we have no record of the work of Robert Hudson beyond a short poem or two of dedication, and according to Montgomerie he was in some sense the first of the brotherhood, the eldest or a founder-member

> Who first fand out of Pegase fut the flood
> And sacred hight of Parnase mytred hood. (xxix)

But whether he worked in song or psalm-setting, poetic composition, dance-composition or translation we do not know. He was a trained musician and he wrote jesting 'rithmes' and at least one sonnet of his has survived. He would 'pen out tua cuple' (turn a couplet) when he pleased, though his 'Homer's style' and 'Petrark's high invent' may well be the exaggerations of a friend's flattery.

The phrases 'Castalian', 'brother of the muses', 'Pegasus' recur in these verses as does the image of Apollo at the centre. Another glimpse of the language of the game can be caught in the metaphor of the smithy where poetry was forged, a variation of an accepted metaphor, used for instance by Wyatt. Montgomerie in exile 'upaland' longs to see the simple smithy smoke. He writes to Robert Hudson

> My best belouit brother of the band
> I grein to sie the sillie smiddy smeik. (xxv)

It comes again in Christian Lindsay's plea that Montgomerie's fellow poets at court are forgetting him:

> The smeikie smeithis cairs not his passit trauel
> Bot leivis him lingring, deing of the gravell.[1]

It may be that the pun of 'study' and 'stiddie', Scots for anvil, is an aspect of the same jest: the smiths, the poets, beat out their thoughts. Certainly the King uses the metaphor both of hammer and of poetry refined by fire to flowing smoothness,

> Such hamringe hard the metalls hard require
> Our songs are filed with smoothly flowing fire.[2]

The flowing smoothness was the quality he praised above all in the writing of his 'Castalians'.

---

[1] Cranstoun, xxx, 'Christen Lyndesay to Ro. Hudsone'; her identity traced in *Alexander Montgomerie: Selected Songs and Poems*, ed. H. M. Shire, p. 52.

[2] Westcott, no. XLVI.

The word 'band' is also significant. It may not have borne at that time the strong musical association that it now enjoys, but it had in Scots at this time a peculiar force, of a sworn brotherhood in league for violent action. The life of King James had since his babyhood been threatened by such 'bands' among his power-seeking nobles, and he was to be at the mercy again of the band of Earl Bothwell. Over against such leagues of destruction and death his Castalian band was a brotherhood of peaceful, constructive *making*. He tried on another occasion to effect reconcilation of fearful feuds by a gesture of peace, a social ritual: he ordered to take place a 'love-feast' in which certain deadly enemies among his barons were required to dine together and walk two by two, arch-enemies hand in hand, to church in symbolic procession of amity. 'There must have been some grim faces in Holyrood that night.'[1] Perhaps in this gathering round him of his Castalian band of poets we may read another such gesture made by James Stewart, King and peacemaker. It was for the twin qualities of King-peacemaker and King Phoebus, poet, patron of poets and source of their inspiration, that he was to be celebrated by Robert Ayton, the last Castalian. It may well be that the young King, just freed from 'fascherie' (distress) as captive of the Ruthven band, found solace, companionship and support and even a force for amity and concord in his Castalian band and their 'making'. Certainly their work in hand, the creation of a new poetry in Renaissance style for the Scottish tongue, was to serve the King's 'glore' and to add lustre to the nation. 'Lusus Regius', a courtly pastime, a royal recreation, is on the way to the printing house, and so on the way to attain European currency as literature.

The work of the Castalian band began to appear in print in 1584. Thomas Hudson had zealously completed his translation of *Judith*. Prefaced by a sonnet from the King and one from Fowler it was printed in Edinburgh by Thomas Vautroullier (or Vautrollier) who in the same year printed for King James his *Essayes of a Prentise in the Divine Arte of Poesy*. The royal volume had commendatory sonnets from Thomas Hudson, for one of which there was music,[2] from Robert Hudson and from 'M.W.' who may be William Murray, from Master William Fowler and from Alexander Montgomerie. The contents included the sonnets to the Gods—omitting that to Bacchus—with four on the seasons, du Bartas' *Uranie* translated, the 'Phoenix', where King James lamented his dead favourite, and 'Ane Schort Treatise, conteining some Reulis and Cautelis to be observit and eschewit in Scottis Poesie', with a sonnet on the perfect poet and a psalm version.

The King's 'Schort Treatise' was the manifesto of the new poetry of Renaissance Scotland. It was the work of a schoolboy, perhaps, and a prentice poet, but also of

---

[1] On the occasion of his twenty-first birthday. The comment is the late Agnes Mure Mackenzie's.
[2] 'Gif martiall deedis', discussed earlier.

Buchanan's gifted pupil and the King of Scotland. It is dogmatic in tone and concerned above all with techniques of verse composition but it bears already the imprint of his personality. The precept that matters of the commonweal are to be avoided by poets as 'to grave...for a Poet to mell in' has behind it the authority of a monarch; in writing of art *versus* nature and of invention he draws on Horace directly.

In the matter of his treatise and in the manner he was indebted to Gascoigne's *Notes of Instruction* (1575). He knew the work of the *Pléiade*, both their theory as expressed in Ronsard's *Abrégé* and their achievement in the poems of Ronsard and du Bellay. He knew, too, the other point of view in France that was displayed in the *Uranie* of du Bartas. He was much concerned that the new poetry of Scotland should be in touch with the new poetry in England and on the Continent, but national traits and traditions make themselves felt. Alliterative poetry in a medieval style was a live force in his court: he quotes from Montgomerie's 'Flyting' as an example of 'Rouncevalles or tumbling verse' by a master hand and it is possible that the term 'Rouncevalles' points to a solidarity still felt in this alliterative style with a remote epic-heroic past. For Gascoigne, on the other hand, alliteration is a rhetorical device divorced from any great tradition and the English critic warns the poet against 'hunting the letter to death'. Significant also is King James' praise of proverbs or moral aphorisms as making valuable contribution to a poetical composition. His care for quality in rhyme is seen in his strictures on 'rhyming in terms'; his own writing under Montgomerie observes this point with some care. In fact on these three counts as in the general tone of the treatise we feel Montgomerie at the young King's elbow, voicing a native way of *Scottis Poesie*. Furtherance of a national tradition is at least as important as the refreshing of that tradition from English and Continental sources. The examples the King cites are of course all in Scots, three unidentified, three from his own writing and seven from Montgomerie. Moreover in the section 'tuiching the kyndis of versis' the choice of stanzas he recommends for different kinds of writing is consonant with use in earlier Scottish poetry as we know it.

The national complexion that the treatise shows throughout is worthy of emphasis. It would go beyond the scope of these studies to discuss farther or to evaluate in detail the nature of the poetic lawgiving of the youthful royal rhetorician. To relate his volume to the matter of words and music, the King's sonnet on the perfect poet has no hint of any alliance of poetry with music nor has his own practice of verse-composition. Here Montgomerie's influence has not penetrated. But Montgomerie as master in matching words to music has made himself felt elsewhere. The King's treatise shows at several points an awareness of the discussions among the *Pléiade* of the kinship between poetry and music. To this we shall return in the later chapter, 'Montgomerie and Music'.

'Our daggs in horns of ink'

The gathering of the Castalian band and the manner of its play can be interestingly viewed in a verse-letter, fragmentary and unsigned but written to Robert Hudson, which announces the inauguration of the literary régime at court and expounds its economic aspect. The text was printed some time ago, along with the works of William Fowler,[1] but I have not seen its import commented on.

> *To Robart Hudsoun*
> Iff Ovid wer to lyfe restord
>   to see which I behould
> he might inlairge his plesant taels
>   of formis manifould
> be this which now into the court
>   most plesantlie appeirs
> to see in penners and in pens
>   transformed all our speirs
> and into paper al our jaks
>   our daggs in horns of ink
> for knapstafes, seals and signateurs
>   to change ilk man dois think;
> And every man that neideth leist
>   For more yet doth he crave
> some graips the things which ar not falley   [forfeit in law]
>   In that I think they reave.
> some meins there cace through mereits iust
>   some cravis without desert
> and both together cathces fame
>   off every thing a pairt...

The letter continues that reward comes not to him who will not ask or make an effort to obtain it, and that there is *one* way to get it...   [*the manuscript is here torn*]

The pictured metamorphosis of armed man into man of letters, armed band into Castalian band of poets, is most apt at the moment in 1583 after the rescue of the King. It would be far less credible placed at the beginning of the writing game in 1579 or 1580 or, I think, at any point in the intervening period. In 1583 the game of writing was being erected into something of serious public import. For the master poet it had been the way to success. In these verses it is seen as merged with the general game of court advancement. Poet now, not gamester as under the youthful King James V, is to 'play' with the King in order to win lands. It may surprise that these lines are written *to* Robert Hudson, by every token a sympathetic figure and 'in' the game from the beginning. But Fowler arrived back in Scotland only in

---

[1] *Fowler's Works*, III, appendix I, p. cli.

1583/4 and we do not know the exact whereabouts of the 'violars' during the Ruthven raid or when precisely they rejoined the court company. Fowler may be letting Hudson understand that he is 'in the know'.

By 1584 Fowler is in favour with the King, writing a complimentary sonnet for the first printed volume. In Fowler's eyes the metamorphosis of mailcoat to paper, dagger to inkhorn was indeed the way to power. But the sly rhyme that is probably his reflects, if obliquely, the young King's project of gathering a band of makars as a constructive gesture towards national prestige through poesy, towards peace rather than conflict of arms.

The Castalian band as glimpsed through the writing of Stewart of Baldynneis shows a pleasanter aspect. We take up his volume of poems where we left it in 1583, with the King looking to regain his freedom.[1] He records now a court ceremony devised during that first winter to honour the King as poet. The writing game is expressed in social ritual, a serious play of poetry and adulation. As *étrennes* for the New Year 1583/4, he not only sent the gift of a loyal heart in verse as before; he made a present to the King in person, a jewel and a *propyne* of poetry. 'To his majestie the first of Janvar with presentation of ane lawrell trie formit of gould, 1583'

> Lamp of all laud, resawe this laurell sing
> As mychtie Monarch and victorious king...

a costly present symbolising 'Apollo's' victory. There follows 'Sonnet, at command of his majestie in praise of the art of poesie' wherein peerless poesy is hymned in terms of Titan 'puissant and precellant', heavenly harmony from laureate poets and the verses of his majesty. This association of laureate poet and poet-King was not only a matter of verbal compliment or significant gift; it was a thing done, a ceremony performed, a reproduction in northern terms of Petrarch's coronation.[2] The very next poem is 'To his maiestie the day of his coronation vith laurell'—'O Laureat king be influence celest'—possessed of the crown imperial by thy birth, receive now this other crown as laureate poet, 'Deseruing now ane Doubill croune and moir'— the last line is interesting, as after rhyming with 'gloir' it glances towards another 'double crown' that one day, it was hoped, would grace King James' head.

The ceremony of the crowning with laurel may have been performed at the festival of Yule, New Year 1583/4, this season being always a propitious date for investiture. The King had just written his 'Phoenix'. Stewart's golden gift would then decorate the occasion, as his verses did. Or the ceremony may, as has been suggested elsewhere, have marked the publication of the King's poetical first-fruits

---

[1] *Stewart's Poems*, II, 128 onwards.
[2] In emulation of Petrarch's crowning, Conrad Celtis, arch-humanist Latin poet of the German lands, had been thus crowned by the Emperor in 1487. Scotland now enters the *Kulturkampf* of Renaissance Europe!

in *Essayes of a Prentise* during the year 1584. The two events may well have coincided.

Stewart by this time is clearly one of the close companions. His writing goes on to show knowledge of the 'Rab Steen' jest, so either the standing joke lasted on, as entries in the court records suggest or, possibly, Stewart may have been included in the writing game already in its earlier phase. In a laughable nonsense-rhyme to the King he burlesques the elaborate style of *rime coué*, showing his skill as a MacGonagall of the rhétoriqueurs.

> Ane new sort of rymand rym
> Rymand alyk in rym and rym
> Rymd efter sort of guid Rob steine
> Tein is to purchas Robs teine.

This may be playful reflection on the versifying of Rob Steen himself, the poetaster-schoolmaster. It is also a reminiscence of Marot's 'Petite Epitre au Roi.' But it is a wickedly clever take-off of a style favoured by Montgomerie and used in his message-poem and even of some sentiments therein expressed:

> Dalie to sie your grace is my disyre

The game is, I think, 'to purchas Robs teine', to 'get Montgomerie's goat'. Indeed, it is likely that the last two lines in all seriousness attack the masterpoet and the covert activities of the Lauder *Maria-Regina* sonnet as 'lourking', secret dealing. Stewart ends his poem

> Molestit be all quho luifs craftie lourking
> Lourking God disclois and gyd yow weill, our King.

The Protestant anti-Catholic vein of Stewart is seen in his writing, in small in a phrase against Rome or in large in the nature of his devotional poem 'Ane Schersing out of trew Felicity'.[1] Early friendship with Montgomerie, at one point his friend at court, may show still in his lines 'In praise of his friends vork'; the context is clearly the poetry of the Castalian band, the 'Muses' pupils'.

> Ye laureat scholers of the Sisters nyne,
> That on the hautie forkit pernass hill
> From sacred source soucks science maist deuyne,
> Giwe dew commend heir to the Authors skill,
> Quhois guid desert my sempill speitche may spill.
> Gif I the sam presum vold to recyt
> I langage laik, bot yit hes feruent vill
> Hiche till extoll his leirnit muse perfyt.
> Thocht ackuart yoile beir him at dispyt,
> Quhois coustum ay agains the best is bent,

---

[1] Indeed the poem may have been composed as a Protestant 'answer' to 'The Cherrie and the Slae'; it has a journey to the tree of salvation and figures the title to the sovereignty of Britain.

> Yit sall the sueitnes of his sound indyt,
> Imployed in vertew, prudent spreits content,
> Quhom from his youth I knaw vith bonteis blist.
> Lat vthers praise his volum as thay list.

Surely the same person is referred to here, a poet, and known from Stewart's youth. The friend whose volume of poetry is praised is in some serious trouble: 'yoile' is obscure; 'an awkward blow has him at a disadvantage' has been suggested, but more likely 'yoile' is *jowl* and 'ackuart yoile' is 'Malbec', 'Malbouche' the detractor, '*ungracious mouth speaks scornfully of him – always ready to turn against the best*'. A major Castalian work and an author in trouble point most plausibly to Montgomerie—as we shall see. By 1586, when Stewart's poems were engrossed, the arch-poet was in eclipse; the work may be 'The Cherrie and the Slae' quoted by the King in his 'Schort Treatise' of 1584 but not yet reached print. It sounds very much as if printing had been mooted—and the question of complimentary verses to accompany the volume had arisen. This sonnet may be Stewart's offering.

Stewart's own volume was most carefully groomed for his royal patron's hands; it had an allegorical 'aventure' with 'true felicity' as the King's lady, a 'Roland Furious' in decorous version and much timely and tasteful adulation. Though many courtly episodes and occasions are celebrated and court personalities are treated of, no names are named—save one court favourite (the Master of Gray) and his lady in compliment and Rab Steen in fun.[1] Alexander Montgomerie, I hold, is again and again the friend referred to, earlier in admiration and petition, later in counsel or criticism, but it is done tacitly. By 1586 devoted service to Mary, Queen of Scots, Catholicism avowed and militant, was no longer a passport to favour and trust with her son on the throne of Scotland. The winds of policy had veered from that quarter and Montgomerie is no longer '*regi Jacobo carissimus*'. Montgomerie was not yet 'out' but Fowler was 'in'.

The last poem in Stewart's volume of 1586 is 'His Fairweill to the musis'

> Fairweill my toynles trimbling strings
> fairweill, the Source quhair poems springs...

He bids farewell to his imperfect verses 'varpit vrang'. Some other will serve his patron, 'Pean'—the King, Apollo—better than he. Some suffer grief daily in the attempt to win the laurel tree, and if they succeed in part 'meschant mouth' will speak against them as the churl did against Venus when she danced. But he trusts his King who will purify his poetry and expel Thersites.

---

[1] *Stewart's Poems*, II, 144, ll. 55–6 of 'In commendation to tuo constant luifers'. There may be other references cryptically expressed, e.g. 'Ane Ansueir to the letter of ane honorabill Ladie' may be to Sybilla Stuart of Lennox, 'named' in stanza v.

For Stewart success at court came, in part at least, through his poetry and went through politics, for in the crisis that now ensued he appears to have been a supporter of the Master of Gray (whom alone he had named in his volume) and to have suffered with his fall. He passes from court life. Neither the schooling of 'rycht purpour Pean' nor the service of 'Apollo' had brought him lasting favour or high office or won him lands.

These sidelights have shown 'the Castalian band' as a game to win royal favour, and the entry into it of one player on his way to success. Another Castalian, John Stewart, has been seen in play. But devotion to the royal Paean, accomplished verses made for him and his court, loyalty to the Protestant cause and disquiet at Catholic activism detected in a fellow-poet and his writings—all these will not keep him in the King's grace when a twist of policy throws him out. We shall see how the master poet was to fare in the next turn of the game.

Montgomerie falls 'in Displeasur'

The years between 1583 and 1585, the years of the 'Castalian band' saw Montgomerie 'grit with his Grace'. He celebrated the verses of the royal Apollo in sonnets of adulation.

> As bright Apollo staineth eviry star
> With goldin rays when he begins to ryse...
> So, quintessenst of kings! when thou compyles
> Thou stains my versis with thy staitly styles. (xiii)

> Support me, sacred sisters for to sing
> His praise, whilk passis the antartik pole
> And fand the futsteppe of the fleing fole
> And from Parnassus spyd the Pegase spring...
> His brand all Brytan to obey sall bring... (viii)

With the new image of the monarch unfolds a fresh poetic landscape in a scheme of metaphor: Helicon, Pegasus and the Castalian sisters, 'the Weirds'—fates of the north, Echo's woods and Narcissus' well, Apollo's laurel tree—which, as we saw, had been planted anew in King James' court. Delphos, Troy and Thebes are visible in the distance and have their relevance. Well-trodden ground—or an evergreen region in which the way could easily be found and where points of reference to contemporary reality were discernible?

Figures in the landscape are recognisable, too: Good Hope and Melancholie and their fellows. Worn conventions—or a language still viable for expressing the pains and pleasures of love? In *Scottis Poesie* of 'staitly style' as practised by Montgomerie these figures in this landscape serve in poem after poem to convey and celebrate

1   A drawing of the banner carried at Carberry. Crown copyright

2 Sports and pastimes under King James VI; wood-carving for a press-bed, said to have come from Threave Castle

3 *a* A £20 piece of James VI (1578)

3 *b* Gold 'marriage medal' of James VI (1590)

THE III. SONG.

Nto a mirthfull May morning, As Phebus did upspring, I saw a May

both fair and gay, Most goodly for to see? I said to her be kind, To me that

was so pyn'd, For your love truly.

First there afore when I did you know,
You thirl'd my heart so low
Uncover your Grace: but now in cafe,
Banifht through falfe report:
But I hope, and I trow,
Once for to speak with you,
Which doth me comfort.

Wherefore, I pray, have mind on me,
True Love, where ever you be:
Where ever I go, both too and fro,
You have my heart alright.
O Lady! fair of hew,
I me commend to you,
Both the day and night.

Since Fortune falfe, unkind, untrue,
Hath exy'ld me from you;
By fudden chance I fhall advance
Your honor and your fame.
Above all earthly wight,
To you my truth I plight,
In earneft, or gain.

F I N I S.

4 'Into a mirthfull May morning' from John Forbes' *Songs and Fancies* (Aberdeen, 1662); a double-page opening
in the original, divided after the first stave

matters of state and matters of love. In plainer style differently figured he voices direct comment on public affairs or matters of personal concern. Here cogent argument, homely idiom or terse proverb drive his meaning home; or, his wrath aroused, his 'flyting' invective 'brings the flesh, lyk bryrie, fra the banes'.[1]

The master poet, we recall, was in 1583 rewarded with a pension as royal servitor —and was at the same time *persona grata* in the circles of King Philip. His was a rôle of great strategic potential but of no little danger. Not surprisingly there were rufflings of the waters in Scotland. In November 1584 he was in trouble in the law courts; the matter of the barque *James Bonaventor* and its purchase in 1580 was brought up. Had he, or had he not, satisfied the vendor by certain sums paid to meet his share of the purchase money? (The Admiralty of England were not uninterested.) The affair, perhaps until then a secret, now raises its public head and subsides in an unexplained manner. Influence from the powers at court may have been still favourable to him; but this was not the last he was to hear of the matter.[2]

Montgomerie's credit as 'regi Jacobo carissimus' saw some diminishing at about this time. There was a swing of power at court in 1585 towards the Protestant Lords again and this must have worked substantially to his disadvantage. The adumbrations in John Stewart's writing, of a friend's poem of high quality that had fierce detractors and of 'secret lourking' in 'Rab Steen', must now be laid beside the important assertion in the Benedictine's 'epitaphs', that Montgomerie assailed the Protestants or their doctrines with sword and song—'*Picarditas carmine Marte premens*'.[3] No surviving poem of his overtly matches that statement. Of course he could have written verses, of invective for example, that have not come down to us. But certain strange circumstances that attend his major composition *The Cherrie and the Slae*, a dream-vision whose meaning is couched in a 'dark conceit', strongly suggest that that was the *carmen* in question.

'The Cherrie and the Slae' though well begun by 1584 when the King quoted from it, exists in no complete text from that date; all the texts we have of it—in this, its early version—break off suddenly half through the sixty-seventh stanza and the matter is brought to no sort of conclusion. This piece was certainly a song, with Blakehall's music. And it assailed Protestant doctrines—if I read it aright. It presents to the dreamer, its narrator, a problem of choice in love, love earthly and divine, between the fruit of two trees, the bitter sloe of Calvinist doctrine on its bush (emblem of the Reformed Church of France) against the cherry of the eucharist on its

---

[1] Cranstoun (ed.), *The Poems of Alexander Montgomerie*, LXII.

[2] Documents in Stevenson, appendix B and appendix D. III, IV etc. and *Cal[endar of] S[tate] P[apers,] Foreign*, 1586, letter 437.

[3] Benedictine epitaph I, quoted at the head of chapter V; discussed Shire (1966).

Tree, the rood.[1] (This interpretation will be expounded in the chapter that follows.)

If a piece had music, above all court-style music for voices, or voice and instruments, devised especially for it, we must conclude that it was performed aloud or that such performance was planned. Publication of this piece in courtly circles or in the King's presence would amount to an avowal by its author of his creed—the Apostolic faith the only true goal for the seeker. In the year that the King quoted from it, 1584, the poem was at least passed about as work in progress and Stewart's lines appear to hint at projected publication in a volume. I suggest that enough of it was written and perhaps performed for its drift to be perceived and offence to be taken by the powers of the Kirk, its composition stayed or its completion forbidden; if a poem already finished was put on as courtly entertainment with its music, it was silenced at the moment when its inner meaning declared itself—and the conclusion quashed, even seized and destroyed. Such a conjecture meets the anxious lines of the fellow-poet and warrants the Benedictine's praise of a 'song against Calvinist doctrines'— and it would amply explain a falling-out between the poet and his monarch occurring only shortly after the piece had received royal praise.

James must have known for some time now that his poet friend was ardently Catholic. Indeed the poet may have tried directly to influence the King toward conversion as Henry Constable was later to try. The Ruthven lords during the King's first detention at their hands could hardly have left him unwarned of dangerous proclivities in Aubigny's servitor. As an ardent if covert Catholic, *persona grata* with King Philip, Montgomerie was an apt instrument for the King of Scotland to employ in subtle dealings. But a published avowal of enmity to the Kirk, however 'darkly conceited', put a different colour on the envoy's use and must entail a withdrawal of the King's close favour; the Kirk in 1585 was determined to remove 'undesirable company' from the King's presence.[2] Montgomerie certainly fell into the King's 'displeasur' about that year; he writes of his grief in a complaint of that title (46). He writes, too, the urgent plea five sonnets long to Robert Hudson to intercede for him, telling of his misery 'upaland', of his longing to be back at court with the convivial brotherhood making poetry and songs (XIV–XIX).

Nevertheless in 1586 Montgomerie left Scotland apparently with the King's good will and bearing his commission. The Privy Council document runs: '...oure soverane loird, for diveris gude causs and considerationis moving his hienes, and for the gude trew and thankfull service done and to be done to his maiestie be his gude

---

[1] G. D. Henderson, *The Burning Bush*, p. 4. The 'burning bush' was chosen as seal-emblem in 1583, to be used on all important letters. 'Seals' were talismans; the Scots court would notice.

[2] D. Calderwood, *History of the Kirk of Scotland* (ed. T. Thomson), IV, 401, etc.: Proclamation by the nobility of Scotland, 2 November 1585.

servitour Capitane Alexr. Montgomerie' having granted him a pension 'his hienes gave and grantit to [him] his maiesties licence to depairt and pass of this realme to the pairtis of france, flanderis and spane and utheris beyond sey for the space of fyve yeiris thaireftir' during which time the King guarantees to protect that pension.[1] This surely sounds as if Captain Alexander was commissioned for more than simple military service overseas. The year 1586 was a time when King James was sending forth or letting go other notable Catholic agents, Stewart of Houston and Barclay of Ladyland. We can add to that 'James Lauder, gone to France'. A crisis was approaching in the politics of Europe with the threatening power of Spain and the workings of Queen Mary in prison. The King could be ridding his court of dangerous elements, entrusting to ambiguous agents a subtly planned and double-handed policy or setting his envoys a task that of its very nature was impossible to fulfil. This last, it is now clear, was what he did with the embassy he sent to England in 1587: they were to plead for his mother's life at the hands of Queen Elizabeth, but not in such terms as would imperil his 'title' to the crown of England—an impossible task.[2] Any action of the King's, political or military on land or sea, that could be interpreted as taken against the English crown would debar James forever from the succession. An agent of his, courier or captain, was therefore at hazard.

In the May of 1586 a list was drawn up of captains and colonels 'that do offer to follow the Master of Gray into the Low Countries';[3] among the captains are named 'Montgomerie eldir; Montgomerie younger'. Without the Christian names it is impossible to be sure that Alexander was one; Ezechiel and Adam also soldiered abroad and there were other Montgomeries bearing arms. The document of 1589 cited above continues: in 1586 Captain Alexander accordingly 'depairtit of this realme' to the regions named, 'quheras he remanit continewalie sensyne deteynit and halden in prisoun and captivitie, to the greit hurt and vexation of his persoun attour the loss of his guidis'. This sounds as if he had been taken prisoner shortly after his departure.[4]

In June 1586, as Lord Cecil reports to Lord Burghley, an English vessel sailing between Gravesend and the Brill met with

a Scots bark...with six score Scottish soldiers within her and one Montgomery, one as he saith himself, near in credit and place to the King of Scotland: one that hath served in the Low Coun-

---

[1] Ratification of his pension by the Privy Council three years later, March 1588/9 Stevenson, appendix D. VI.
· In March 1586/7 James intended to restore Bishop Betoun to the see of Glasgow (Register of the Privy Council). So Montgomerie might well have carried papers, personal and otherwise, to Betoun, Queen Mary's ambassador in France.
[2] H. G. Stafford, *King James VI of Scotland and the Throne of England*, chapter I.
[3] *Cal. S. P. Scottish*, 1586, letter 437.
[4] 'Quheras' may mean 'in which', thus indicating imprisonment overseas; but it more probably means 'while on the contrary', which gives no indication of place.

tries and captain of that ship. There is great suspicion as the Scottish man saith that he was 'a taking man' notwithstanding his excuse, that being with out a pilot, he durst not put in neither to Flusing nor the Brill.

The Scots barque was boarded and contraband—seacoal and salt—discovered aboard.

We kept the Captain and master aboard of us and brought the ship into this haven [the Brill] where she is now. The captain is gone with letters of credit to his Excellency and I stay both men and ship until his return.[1]

This has every mark of being Captain Alexander, flourishing his credentials and protesting that he was lawfully in charge of a company of troops for the Netherlands —but discovered with his ship gainfully laden with contraband cargo. (Were these the 'guidis' whose loss he laments in verse?) 'A taking man', the phrase used apparently by a Scottish witness, may mean courier, runner of contraband or pirate. It is highly likely that from that interview with 'his Excellency' dated Montgomerie's imprisonment—whether he was confined in the Netherlands or brought back to England. (In November of 1588 one 'Montgomery' was being held in prison by the English authorities, apparently in England.)[2]

The poet in his verses 'No wonder thoght I waill and weip' (5) tells us of his sufferings in captivity, his ill-treatment at the hands of his fellow-prisoners. If his contraband running or his activities as secret agent had caused others of his company to be gaoled, the latter is understandable! A Scots pirate also would get rough treatment in an English prison. His reflections there may adumbrate the grounds of his imprisonment:

> 6 I sie and namely nou a dayis
>   All is not gold that gleitis
> Nor to be seald that ilkane sayis
>   Nor water all that weitis.
> Sen fristed goods are not forgiven
>   When cuppe is full then hold it evin
> For man may meit at unsetstevin
>   Thoght montanis nevir meitis.

[1] *Cal. S. P. Foreign*, January–July 1589, p. 189, letter undated (? late March). R. D. S. Jack ('Montgomerie and the Pirates'), thinks it likely that Montgomerie was 'one of the Scottish pirates encouraged by their King to give assistance to the Spaniards' and for that reason stood in credit both with King James and King Philip.

[2] 'Alexander was appointed Captain of a company of infantry on 24 July 1586 (*Algemeen Ryksarkiv Raad van State*, no. 1524)...', Boson Gabriel de Montgomery, *Origin and History of the Montgomerys*, pp. 208–16; but this genealogist is extremely unreliable, and ignorant of Westcott and Stevenson.

Westcott (p. xxxi) thought England, citing a letter of 25 November 1588 from T. Fowler to Archibald Douglas in London: 'Always if they [the English authorities] would deliver my house and stuff I shall be glad, and more of Montgomery's release which I beseech you to procure as much as you may, for he is honest and not acquainted with trouble and what they have to say to him God knows, I wot not, but I would gladly know whereupon they examined him and what he hath done with my books.' (Fowler was trustee for certain jewels of Queen Mary's and his house had been seized!) *Cal. Hatfield MSS.* pt. III, p. 374.

'Payment is exacted on goods got on credit'; 'one may meet, or be met with at no appointed hour', that is, by pure ill luck. Besides proved smuggling (of goods not yet paid for?) and suspected piracy, Montgomerie may have been discovered as bearer of secret papers or recognised as a dealer in the earlier affair of the debt on the barque *James Bonaventur*—a matter still unresolved. None of these counts would endear him to Cecil or Burghley. On any grounds he was safer in gaol.

It was some time after Queen Mary had been executed and the danger of the Armada had passed that Montgomerie was set free. In March 1588/9 he was still in prison—or so the Scottish Privy Council believed, to judge from their document. If so, he is in all probability not the 'Captain Montgomery' recorded in that month as bearing intelligence between Gitternebergen and St Omer.[1] (Captain Adam Montgomerie was, moreover, active in that area at the time.)

The poet returned to Scotland—probably in later 1589 or in 1590—seeking friends and trusting to have his pension again.[2] His verse-letter to the King four sonnets long puts his case and pleads the hardships he has unjustly been subjected to (XIV–XVII)

> 1 Help, Prince, to whom, on whom not, I complene
> But on, not to, fals Fortun ay my fo
> Quho but, not by, a resone reft me fro
> Quho did not does yet suld my self sustene.
> Of crymis, not cairs, since I haif kept me clene
> I thole, not thanks, thame, sir, who servd me so
> Quha heght, not held, to me and mony mo
> To help, not hurt, but hes not byding bene:
> Sen will, not wit, too lait—whilk I lament—
> Of sight, not service, shed me from your grace   [separated]
> With, not without, your warrand yit I went
> In wryt, not words: the papers are in place.
> Sen chance, not change, hes put me to this pane
> Let richt, not reif, my pensioun bring agane...

'Montgomerie had had the King's pass and letters of credit to be where he was (and to be doing what he was doing?); the documents exist to prove it'; or 'the documents were delivered according to orders, the mission was accomplished'. It was ill luck not bad faith that had brought him low.

But by 1589 the King was busy with the project of his marriage and was out of Scotland for nearly a year, from October 1589 till May 1590. The verse address comes more credibly after his return. In 1591 it was not the King who backed Montgomerie in his next step to recover his pension but the young Duke of Lennox,

---

[1] Argued by R. D. S. Jack, 'Montgomerie and the Pirates'.

[2] He honoured with an epitaph Robert, Lord Boyd, who died '3rd January 1589'; as the date is from a tombstone this is probably January 1589/90. This and other epitaphs dating from 1590–1 in Cranstoun, pp. 221–2.

who had been a royal deputy during the King's absence and was the son of the poet's earlier patron. This application won only temporary success. Lengthy and angry proceedings in the law courts, which are reflected vividly in the poet's sonnets, brought the enjoyment of the pension no nearer.[1]

The King would not or could not overrule the law-court findings. Perhaps he was tiring of the whole business. Queen Mary being dead and the political weather altered, a convinced partisan of the Catholic cause, especially one detected and imprisoned, had little to recommend him to the King as a familiar, however loudly he protested personal devotion or claimed ancient friendship—'for me, I love the king'. Since Montgomerie's first fall from grace new favourites had risen to power, companions in action like the Earl of Arran as well as associates in letters like William Fowler. The King had enjoyed a writing game in fresh circles where the influence of Italian poetry was felt. King James' love-verses were not a 'feygning of matteris of luve' in the style of *Scottis Poesie* transmitted by Montgomerie; his love poems for Princess Anne of Denmark as bride and Queen, however, still owe something to Montgomerie, once 'master poet' at court. His verses of poetic devotion to Lady Glamis in the early 1590s have left the 'maistre's' influence behind.[2]

The King was much taken up with his Scandinavian bride and the new double household was organised with enthusiasm. But Montgomerie is barred the court. The King's displeasure lay heavy on him and he writes of his grief. Muses may still sing some of his sonnets there, but the matching of his words to music, the live practice of court-song making, the fostering companionship of the Castalian days is lacking—as is the receptive audience, with its promise of live performance for verses sung as court entertainment. None of his plaints of 'displeasour' have music nor can be shown to have been presented as *propynes* embellished by a musician.[3] Indeed his appeals to the King are far otherwise expressed, in sonnets of close and cogent argument.

The years 1591 and 1592, moreover, show Montgomerie writing strongly worded sonnets in support of certain violent opponents of the King, Protestant preachers though they were (VI, VII). And 'Rob Stene's Dreme', anonymous but almost certainly the poet's, seems to side with Bothwell—whose own sympathies, religious and political, were widely veering, consistent only in serving his lust for power.

Montgomerie's exile 'upaland' was probably spent largely in the far southwest.

[1] Litigation: see Stevenson, appendix B and appendix D. VII–X.
[2] Westcott, nos. XVI–XVII; introduction, pp. vii–viii; nos. I–X, XIX, XX. Lady Glamis I take to be 'faire Anna Murraye mestres to the King'.
[3] It is possible to read 'Prepotent palme Imperiall' (Stevenson, p. 196) as an approach to Queen Anne, but for this strange poem to a royal personage I prefer an earlier date and occasion; the poet desires, but cannot hope for, presentation of his lines with a musical setting. (See chapter 6, p. 139.)

In 1591, and just before, his name is linked with Compston Castle in Kirkcudbright-shire.[1] A group of late sonnets suggest that the 1590s saw him often in the neighbourhood of Beath, where his convivial gifts drew around him a third 'band'—Lochwinnoch, Kilburnie and Semple, 'the bairns of Beath', 'the old master and the young disciple' (LXIX). There is a lively exchange of letter-sonnets among friends. Barclay of Ladyland 'in this winter win, with old bogogers, hotching on a sped, Draiglit in dirt whylis wat evin to the skin' greets sarcastically his friends 'birling at the wyne' on the far side of the moor—Ezechiel and Captain A. Montgomerie (LXVI–LXVIII). Their jokes, idiom and private language are caught: soldiers' jargon in Flemish, a new *nom de guerre* for the poet, 'Sir Icarus', and a farrier's phrase for a shot of satire that has gone home, which recalls the Castalian metaphor of 'the smiths'. The pattern of behaviour repeats itself. 'Sir Icarus', his wings melted by 'Apollo's' rays, has fallen and is in exile but takes pleasure in poetry with a band of friends. But it is a far cry from the court and the making of court-song. And among these friends was at least one of the leading Catholic activists of Scotland.

In 1592 the country was shaken by the conspiracy known as 'the Spanish blanks'.[2] The King was 'discovered' in touch with Spain. The extorted confessions of George Ker revealed a plot that caused the Kirk to cry for action against all Catholics. The King, however, had his own plans and sought to weave the action of the Catholic Earls into his over-all policy until early in the year 1595. Thereafter his policy veered and he was absorbed in the question of the English succession and his title to that throne.

We do not know whether Montgomerie was involved in the affair of 'the Spanish blanks'. Probably not. As long as any hope remained of salvaging his pension as royal servitor he may have held his hand. In 1593 the pension finally foundered in the law courts. Montgomerie's hopes of asserting his right to his moneys depended on the restitution of Bishop Betoun to the See of Glasgow and *that* depended, tenuously enough, on the Bishop's appearing in Scotland and attesting Protestant faith![3] Montgomerie's anger against the King was bitter indeed. Last sonnet of all in the sequence wherein the thoughts and feelings of his lifetime may be traced is that 'Against the God of Love'. This is not simply the 'flyting on Cupid' of poetic convention. As earlier in his poetry the convention of Cupid is pointed at the King. The lines are written with the rage and bitterness of affection once given and then betrayed. There is no mistaking the references, anger at the Muses betrayed, defacing of the winged figure and his 'staitly stylis'—so often a subject of adulation in Castalian days.

---

[1] See Cranstoun, introduction pp. xvi–xvii.
[2] See Willson, *King James*, chapters V–VIII and Stafford, chapter III.
[3] Stevenson, appendix D. X. By accidentally omitting a line of typed text, I misrepresented this document in 'Alexander Montgomerie', p. 149.

> Blind brutal Boy, that with thy bou abuses
> Leill leisome love by lechery and lust,
> Judge, jakanapis and jougler maist unjust
> If in thy rageing resone thou refuises;
> To be thy chiftanes changers ay thou chuisis
> To beir thy baner, so they be robust.
> Fals tratur, Turk, betrayer under trust
> Quhy maks thou makrels of the modest Muses?
> Art thou a god? No—bot a gok disguysit;
> A bluiter buskit lyk a belly-blind
> With wings and quaver waving with the wind;
> A plane playmear for vanitie devysit.
>   Thou art a stirk for all thy staitly stylis
>   And these good geese, whom sik a god begylis.[1]   (LXX)

'Against the Protestants with sword and song'

By 1595 reward or service with King James was impossible to seek or obtain. That way Montgomerie could further militant Catholicism not at all. True, King James continued to 'practice' with the Catholic power-heads, spiritual and temporal, and let it be known in these quarters that his ultimate conversion was 'not to be despaired of'. But neither as persuasive influence nor as confidential envoy was Montgomerie relevant. The year 1595 marks the founding at Würzburg of a community of Scottish Benedictines—a gesture in itself significant of this active phase of the Counter-reformation. Thither Montgomerie now bent his thoughts—and may have bent his footsteps also: 'St Benedict was calling him to Artaunum' says the Latin verse.

But the age of Catholic militancy in Europe was not quite gone by. King Philip made a late and desperate cast in the project of 1596 and 1597, the 'second Armada'. Armed rebellion in Ireland was planned under the Earl of Tyrone. Certain ardent Scottish Catholics with Hew Barclay of Ladyland as chief mover convened in Nantes with the Spanish ambassador in October and devised the taking of the 'Isle of Guyanna'—code name for the rocky Scottish islet of Ailsa Craig that lies out from the mouth of the river Clyde.[2] It was a useful stronghold, 'anes possessed nocht recoverable be no enemy out of the handis of men of warr' as they believed. It was victualled

---

[1] M. P. McDiarmid, '*Philotus*, etc.' showed the kinship of this sonnet to Watson's *Hekatompathia* (1582) sonnet XCVIII. 'The Author in his passion, telling what Love is, easeth his heart, as it were, by rayling outright, where he can worke no other manner of revenge'! Watson gives also a Latin version, which I find Montgomerie 'imitating' rather than the English text, adapting items from Watson's catalogue of metaphors against love and pointing them at *King* Cupid.

[2] *Cal. S.P. Scottish*, 1595–6, letter 454; J. Spottiswoode, *History of the Church of Scotland*, III, 61; Stevenson, appendix D. XI.

and manned to serve as a refuge to all distressed papists where mass could be celebrated. It would provide a place of relief and refreshment to the Spaniards, a port to
them in their arrival in Ireland, a base to supply the Earl of Tyrone. Support for the
venture was forthcoming from 'sundrie noblemen of France, England and Scotland'.
'Certain Montgomeries, Murrays and Stewarts, being papists' are named as concerned. They had an armed barque at their disposal, which was to report to Spain the
successful 'taking' of the island and to bring reinforcements.

By the early spring of 1596/7 Ladyland and others were in possession of Ailsa. But
the plot was discovered to King James by the Reverend Andro Knox, minister of
Paisley—the same who had exposed the earlier conspiracy 'the Spanish blanks' of
1592. James let this conspiracy ripen, the better to crop it. Early in March Hew
Barclay of Ladyland was alone on the island's foreshore, in the barque of the conspirators. The others of his company were away on a hunting expedition, perhaps on
the mainland, perhaps on the neighbouring isle of Arran. He spied a ship approaching,
but thought it friendly. On perceiving that those aboard were 'unfriends' he sought
his death in the sea rather than let himself be taken. (The confessions extorted from
Ker in the earlier conspiracy come vividly to mind.)

We do not know for certain whether Alexander Montgomerie was already of the
company on the island, escaping capture only because away with the hunters. He
may have been already ill and unable to join the conspirators: he suffered sorely
from 'the gravel' and a late sonnet speaks of him as 'a cripple'. He may have been
warned of the discovery and have avoided the rendezvous. But he was

arte, parte, at the leist upoun the counsale, divise and foirknawledge with the umquhile Hew
Barclay of Ladyland in the...treasonable interprise...; louked for and procurit be the said...
Hew...to have cum and arrivit in the saidis pairtis for subversioun of the trew religion, altera-
tioun of the estate and disturbing of the publict peace and quietnes of this haill Island [Britain].

He was accordingly summoned by the Privy Council in July to answer to these
charges and, failing to appear, was denounced as traitor and 'put to the horn'.
As outlaw every man's hand was against him and his life could be taken with
impunity.

The Privy Council's denunciation expected that he was still alive. Where and how
long he survived in hiding we do not know, nor whether in the end he succumbed
to illness, was killed or took his life to avoid capture as his fellow conspirator had
done. He did not reach Artaunum. The Latin epitaphs tell us: 'Montgomerie was
dying and the light of true religion was going out at the same time.' (Does this refer
to the death of King Philip early in 1598?) Montgomerie earnestly desired to join
the brotherhood at Artaunum; but 'inexorable death, meaning to render vain his
blessed intention cut off the devoted life in its prime'—that is, according to our

reckoning, about the forty-fifth year of his age, 1597, or at the very latest about the fiftieth, 1602.[1]

In the year 1597 his major poem *The Cherrie and the Slae* issued from the press in Edinburgh, the King's printers—incomplete and bearing his name but significantly bare of dedicatory or complimentary verses. One printing sold quickly and another appeared, with only minor differences of word or phrase, but 'Prented according to a Copie corrected be the Author himselfe'. The phrase suggests but does not prove that the poet was still alive at the time of the first printing. This dual publication—by undisclosed backers of an outlaw's poem, with text incomplete as it had been left many years ago—is a riddle I shall attempt to solve later.

Somewhere in hiding Montgomerie had been working on his poem. He still could assail the Protestants in song. 'The Cherrie and the Slae..., newly altered, perfyted and divided into 114 Quatorziems, not long before the Author's death'—*that* version was profoundly and significantly changed and was brought to its conclusion. What the poet now had to say about the rejection of the Calvinist sloe and the choice of the eucharistic cherry of salvation, his last word on his relationship with the King, the story of his long, intimate and painful involvement in the King's policies, will be expounded when the poem is studied in the chapter that follows.

We still do not know the exact year or the place of Montgomerie's death, but the Latin poems give us ample and sensational information as to the circumstances of his burial. (I summarise.)

When the poet Montgomerie was dying...dire rage seized the Calvinist dogs. The ministers would not let him be buried in consecrated ground and refused him burial rites. They shut the churches and would not let the bells be rung. The townspeople, moved to an unaccustomed pitch of riotousness, climbed the towers, man and boy—and the bells were rung. They carried their earnest entreaties to the palace. The Earls wished him to be fitly buried, friends and relatives brought funeral gifts, and it was the wish of the King himself. At last, with a royal escort [of soldiery standing guard?] he was interred and the funeral prayers were said to their end.[2]

'The King' is certainly King James and the scene Scotland—and somewhere near enough a 'palace' for an appeal to be carried thither and responded to. 'The Earls'— almost certainly 'the Catholic Earls' of current politics—and the common people or townsfolk in sympathy suggest the Westlands, but that region is remote. There were

---

[1] Dempster, *Historia Ecclesiastica Gentis Scotorum*, gives MDXCI, which is impossible; it is perhaps a misprint for MDXCIX—the manuscript original is lost.

[2] It is difficult to tell from the Latin poems whether the 'rage' was a state of unrest lasting over a considerable time during which the poet was dying or was occasioned by the crisis of the burial. 'Greeves' (grievances) were sent by the Kirk to the King in March 1598 protesting against burial inside churches. The King replied that every nobleman [possessing such rights of burial?] 'sould big a sepulture for himself and his owne familie', presumably outside the building (Calderwood, v, 685–6). The poet may have been excluded from burial in the family burying place.

scenes of general riot in Edinburgh in the summer of 1597, such that the King withdrew to Perth. These may be the scenes of riot referred to. The date of the funeral outrage is in all probability not long after the alarms of the 'second Armada' year. Such violence in the ministers is understandable in a time of indignation and fear, of Spanish attack and conspiracy in the realm. There was no reason why an outlaw, as outlaw, should be denied Christian burial. It was the papist, conspirator and traitor—perhaps suicide—whose body they thus harshly rejected.

The King, on hearing of the poet's death, grieved sorely. If the news came exacerbated with word of the outrage it must have struck deep into a King's conscience. He wrote an epitaph for the poet. He called on fellow-poets of Castalian band to honour in verse 'in any case' Montgomerie who had been 'Prince of poets in our land' and had gone 'thus' to grave unhonoured. It is the monarch of Scotland who is speaking —before the Union of the Crowns.

> What drousie sleepe doth syle your eyes allace
> Ye sacred brethren of Castalian band
> And shall the prince of Poets in our land
> Goe thus to grave unmurned in anie cace?
> No; whett your pens ye imps of heavenlie grace
> And toone me up your sweete resounding strings
> And mounte him so on your immortall wings
> That ever he may live in everie place.
> Remember on Montgomerie's flowand grace
> His suggred stile, his weightie words divine
> And how he made the sacred Sisters nine
> There montaine quitte to follow on his trace.
>   Though to his buriall was refused the bell
>   The bell of fame shall aye his praises knell.

Montgomerie's perfected poem was not printed for many years. It appeared in 1615 when the poet was long dead and the crises of Europe were other crises. It was this printing, the first issue of the *carmen* against the Protestants at full length and in all its strength, that inspired the young Scots Benedictine to write the funeral poems 'Of Montgomerie his death, his way of life and his devotion to religion'.

Meanwhile Montgomerie's death had been *kept in mind: The Mindes Melodie* was printed in 1605.[1] It consisted of versions of certain psalms 'applyed to a new pleasant tune' that we know was the tune for the poet's own court-song 'The Solsequium'. Two of these versions for certain, and probably all, had been made by the poet himself.[2] After the psalm-versions and in the same metre comes the *Nunc*

---

[1] Cranstoun, pp. 243–69.

[2] Montgomerie had at one point volunteered to translate psalms for the Kirk (Calderwood), and may have prepared more than these, from which his friends made apposite selection for his 'mynd' and so for this commemorative volume.

dimittis, there called 'The song of Simeon'; the volume ends with the *Gloria Patri*. This volume of words for music is 'the melody of the mynd', the pieces sung to commemorate the death of the poet in mourning ceremony—as the Master of Erskine, we remember, was commemorated. The psalms printed are a carefully selected and meaningful sequence, the voice of a man persecuted for truth, sorely distressed yet praising God, calling down His wrath on the godless nations, seeking deliverance from fierce and subtle enemies, in hiding in a cave like 'the chief musician', asking judgment and revenge on his cause, calling on all nations to praise God and lifting up his eyes to the hills. Last comes the 'wedding psalm', speaking eloquently of the poet who 'died untimely', a monk in intent.

Study of poets and musicians at King James' court has shown a close interweaving of poetry, music and politics, but seldom can poetry and politics have been more strongly interwoven, poet and monarch more intimately involved, than was the case with Montgomerie and King James. At the quick of their relationship lay the song *The Cherrie and the Slae*—to whose interpretation we now turn.

5

THE POET, THE CHERRIE
AND THE KING:
A READING OF 'THE CHERRIE
AND THE SLAE'[1]

Cheryse, of whiche many on fayn is.

The Romaunt of the Rose

Artibus ingenuis puer instituendus *amara*
    Calvinistarum mente venena bibi.
Ast ubi confirmata virum perfecerat aetas
    In tenebris totos taeduit esse dies.
Arma sequens, varias per martia praemia terras
    Vidi, Bellonae laude strategus eram.
Sed fidei ignarum me docta Hyspania leges
    Vivendi vera cum pietate docet.
Regis et exstabam pergratus in arce Philippi
    Semper honoratus Rex Jacobe tibi.
Hostis eram gravis haereseon semperque perodi
    Falsa, *Picarditas carmine Marte premens.*
Denique fatorum lege immaturus ad urnam
    Ossa dedi: mentem caelica regna tenent.

Benedictine Epitaph I on Montgomerie

But lo hou first my legacy I leiv:
    'To God I give my spirit in hevin so hie.
My poesie I leave my prince to preiv
    No richt can reiv him of my rhetorie
My bains to be bot bureit quhair I die...'

Montgomerie, 'Legacie'

---

[1] *The Cherrie and the Slaye*, Waldegrave (I), Edinburgh, 1597 (Aldis 300), and *The Cherrie and the Slae*, Wreit-toun, Edinburgh, 1636 (Aldis 871) were edited by Alexander Stevenson in *Poems of Alexander Montgomerie: Supplementary Volume*, S.T.S., Edinburgh 1906–7. A composite text, *The Cherrie and the Slae*, Waldegrave (II) Edinburgh, 1597 (Aldis 299), combined with Allan Ramsay's version from *The Evergreen*, Edinburgh, 1724 (believed to derive from the 'lost' Hart edition, Edinburgh, 1615) was edited by James Cranstoun, S.T.S. Edinburgh, 1887 .A composite text, Waldegrave (II) with Wreittoun, ed. H. H. Wood: *The Cherrie and the Slae* (London, 1937).

It falls now to justify my reading of Montgomerie's *The Cherrie and the Slae* as a poem of serious import, nearly concerned with 'mighty matters', religious and hence politic, in Scotland in the age of Counter-reform. The poem wears the dress of an 'allegory of love' and as such has long been belittled or dismissed as artificial, out-moded in manner and style and void of any important meaning.[1] The first editor of the poet's works, Cranstoun in the nineteenth century, regarded the makar as having failed. 'What the poet began as an amatory lay he ended as a moral poem; what he meant for a song turned out a sermon.'[2] An earlier critic, Pinkerton, had condemned it utterly: 'The allegory is thin and wire-drawn, the whole poem beneath contempt; let it then sleep.' Yet the piece in its final form was long a favourite in Scotland, reprinted throughout the seventeenth and eighteenth centuries, delighting the lawyers of Edinburgh by its deft and vigorous use of proverbs, its 'magazine of pithy wit'.

A writer of 1700 spoke of Montgomerie as one who masks 'his matter with such skill/As few perceave his drift'. He is conscious of not penetrating to the poet's whole meaning. By then the habit of reading allegory was receding, the powerful *genre* of the dream-poem was no longer in use and the tradition of posing a problem of con-duct—erotic, religious or moral—as a *questio amoris* was dimmed if not erased.

Voices nearer the time of the poem's composition, however, took it as a serious and important work. Dempster, discussing Montgomerie in a volume printed in 1627, spoke of his major work as *Cerasus et Vaccinium, Lib. I, poema divinum, quo amores suos descripserat; per cerasum amicæ sublimis dignitatem, per vaccinium contemnendos in-ferioris et fastiditae amasiae amplexus intelligens.* Dempster's information may have been at second hand and we do not know which version of the poem he had in mind—probably the 'early version'; but for him a piece treating of a 'question of love'—the choice of noble lady-love or lowly wench—was at the same time a divine poem.[3] A translation of the work into Latin verse, printed at Arctaunum (Würzburg) in 1631 and taken by some as originating in the Benedictine monastery there, was entitled *Cerasum et Sylvestre Prunum...De virtutum et vitiorum pugna. Sive electio status in adolescentia...* The translator, 'T.D.', who may well be Thomas Duff of the Latin epitaphs, indicates in a prologue that for him the poem concerns the choice of the religious life rather than the secular, heavenly against earthly love. The translator

---

[1] An honourable exception: Ian Ross, 'The Form and Matter of *The Cherrie and the Slae*': he discerns in the poem one level of meaning as being religious, but not as being specifically Catholic.

[2] Later editions and an account of critical opinion to 1887 in Cranstoun's introduction, supplemented in Stevenson introduction, appendices and notes.

[3] *Historia Ecclesiastica Gentis Scotorum* (Bannatyne Club ed.) II, 496. The date of Dempster's note on Montgomerie is uncertain; he claims to know little of the poet and his works, having lived long abroad (he may be being discreet). Himself a Catholic, he visited King James' court in England in 1615 or 1616, failed to obtain the position of Historiographer Royal and died abroad in 1623. His *Historia* was printed in Bologna in 1627.

knew the poem in its final version, but it is possible that his interpretation was coloured by partisan enthusiasm for Montgomerie, Catholic and Benedictine postulant.[1]

Near-contemporary opinion, then, was certainly conscious of a meaning in the poem beyond the foreground 'treating of matters of love' in the language of a courtly code. Montgomerie himself in the later 1580s protested that he was a love-poet pure and simple and did not meddle with 'mightie maters', 'copping courts or comonwelthis or kings'.[2] Such a protest, made in an anxious appeal for return to royal favour, would hardly have been voiced save to counter an accusation. Indeed his 'Legacie' bequeathed his poetry for 'his prince to preiv': James *shall not* escape its message! It is highly probable that the poem, dealing with religious matters, had a near-political pertinence.[3]

I hope now to expound the presence in the poem of such profounder meaning, religious and political. I speak first of the early incomplete version in the text of 1597 (second printing), that made 'according to a Copie corrected be *the Author himselfe*'. This I take to be as near as we can get to the poem as current in 1584 or 1585, when its composition was interrupted or its completion suppressed. Thereafter I review the late revised edition '114 quatorziems' long, 'newly altered, perfyted... not long before the Author's death'—rewritten and brought to its conclusion, that is, over the period 1593 to 1602, in all probability in 1597 or 1598. The text is that printed by Wreittoun in 1636, which is believed to reproduce Hart's printing of 1615 of which no copy survives.

In order to recapture the meaning the poem had for a sixteenth-century audience it is necessary to follow the professional poetic technique of 'the last of the makars' who was writing in a tradition of *Scottis Poesie* uninterrupted since the Middle Ages, and writing in confidence that his auditors at court were conversant with that way of poetry. We must learn to take the meaning that was then invested in image and motif, current in symbolism and figuration, discernible in a poet's use of this or that *genre* or in his tacit reference to this or that poetic forebear.

---

[1] 'Nunc rursus auctum et in Latinos versus translatum. Per T.D.S.P.M.B.P.P.' (? Professor at Salerno, Baron of Muiresk, Professor at Paris). 'T.D.' has long and credibly been claimed as Thomas Dempster, though no translation of Montgomerie's poem is listed in his *Autobiography* (see D.N.B. 'Dempster'). William Montgomerie in *The Montgomerie Manuscripts 1603–1706* states 'It was turned into Latin verses with the same number of foot and unisons as in the Original: a stupendious work indeed! fitt for the acute witts of that Scotish friary (beyond our seas) which undertook it.' If this refers (*a*) to this translation in hexameters and not to another (in stanza form) and (*b*) to the translation and not to the printing done at Arctaunum, 'T.D.' may be Thomas Duff, author of the funeral poems on Montgomerie, and the subsequent initials bear a different interpretation. Mark Dilworth concurs in 'The Latin Translator of *The Cherrie and his Slae*', and suggests T. Duff, Scotus Poeta, Monachus Benedictinus Professus, Presbyter.

[2] Sonnet XXVI, the second of five, 'To R. Hudsone'.

[3] Cranstoun, p. 27, 'Ressave this harte'.

The Scottish court of the early 1580s was retentive of old style in the patterns of poetry it enjoyed, witness the success of 'The Flyting' or the currency there as a favourite song of a *pastourelle*, a song of Maytime love-adventure, 'The gowans are gay'.[1] The pedigree of *Scottis Poesie* included 'The Romaunt of the Rose', Chaucer's dream-vision poems, 'The Kingis Quair,' Henryson's 'Testament of Cresseid', Dunbar's court allegories, Douglas' 'The Palice of Honour', Bellenden's 'Proheme to the Cosmographie of Scotland', David Lindsay's 'The Dreme' and his 'Satyre of the Thrie Estaitis'.[2] This tradition, moreover, was enjoying a new flowering. Discussion of the art of *Scottis Poesie* was lively in the court. New wine was being poured into old vessels. The author of a new piece could use nonchalantly a time-honoured poetic genre, confident of the expectations of narrative patterning it would arouse in his auditors. Or he could combine *genre* with *genre* in a new way, confident that the auditors would heedfully follow him in his new direction of their attention. A poesy could be sharply relevant to the present though devised as a complication of earlier patterns of imaginative composition, a variation on time-honoured themes.

What does the poem say? The matter may be expressed thus in bare outline:

On a bank in spring I lay alone and mused among the happy creatures of the season and the delights of sight and sound. I saw and heard a river run through a wild park-land by a high cliff, its waters plunging down from the rock. The sound of the rushing water was redoubled by the song of the larks, 'Nature's chapel-clerks'; both sounds rose to the heavens and wakened Cupido. He flew down to earth and came to rest beside me. I wondered at his appearance, naked, coy and smiling, and was much taken with his instruments for shooting and his wings for flying. Cupid noted my fascination and offered to lend me his implements. I donned wings and shooting gear and took to the air. I drew an arrow meaning to aim it at someone but wounded myself to the heart. Sorely injured I came down to earth where Cupid mocked me, despoiled me of the gear and flew up to heaven again with a noise of thunder.

I sighed, mused and raged and cursed Cupid, then I felt a sensation new to me, a surge of courage ['corage', élan vital] and desire within me, arising from the wound. I realised that my wilfulness, rashness and want of reason had brought me to this pass. Dazed, dizzy and half-dead, hoping to be cured of my stricken state yet despairing of it, I made my way [as in a trance] towards the river and the high rock. There there appeared to me [a vision of] hope and despair: it seemed to me that they grew there—a cherry tree flourishing high on the crag, its abundant and delicious fruit reflected in the waters, and below, close by me on the bank, a bush of bitter sloes.

I longed for the lovely cherries but saw no way of reaching them, inaccessible on their high tree, on a steep cliff beyond an impassable flood. Courage and Hope bade me attempt to reach them. Dread, Danger and Despair argued the vainness of such an attempt and the hazard to life and limb; they counselled me that I should pluck instead the simple sloe, that would serve to slake my thirst.

---

[1] *Music of Scotland*, no. 28 and note.
[2] I do not distinguish printed from manuscript currency.

These various powers, advocating the plucking of the cherry or the plucking of the sloe, advanced their 'contrarious' advice, urging opposed courses of action 'Risk all even lyfe and win a noble name' against 'Beware, take what you can safely have'. Between these courses I stood, 'swithering'.

> Quhillis minting, quhillis stinting
> my purpose changit oft.

Dread, Danger and Despair then took their leave, self-righteously disgruntled. Experience, Reason, Wit and Skill, Wisdom and Will came to join the debate. Will, who was blamed for the early rashness that brought about the fateful wounding, cried still for action.

As the dilemma was being argued out,[1] gradually some order was attained and indeed a measure of agreement. Reason judged that the cherries might after all be reached. Wit discovered how the cliff might be scaled. The tree was reached and then the fruit, still inaccessible on a high branch, suddenly for very ripeness fell. I, the dreamer, ate, my soul was refreshed, and 'I with you' and all nations give thanks to God for his love.

DREAM-POEM

Montgomerie in his new piece combines three *genres* or patterns of poesis, the dream-poem or love-vision, the love-adventure in spring and the *débat* or argument of contraries here rendering a 'contest of vices and virtues'. The narrator—the 'I' of the poem—'dreams', meets with a love-adventure and has his state of mind illuminated through an argument of contraries. The 'I' of the poem is-and-is-not the poet Alexander Montgomerie.

In this dream-poem there is no falling asleep elaborately described. There was none in 'The Romaunt of the Rose'. That a visionary state enters into the composition, however, is indicated clearly, and more than once. The sixth stanza has

> Bot as I mussit myn alone
> I saw a river rin...

In the same phrase David Lindsay had entered his 'Dreme', 'Than up/and doun I musit myne allone'.[2] At the moment where the river and the rock are first glimpsed there is thus an indication of transition to a dream-landscape which will be at once cosmic and 'inwart', significant of the innermost concern of the dreamer. The 'I' of the poem, wandering in the pleasant park (nature enclosed, the court) in spring (the season of love-adventure, the springtime of his days) entered a state of tranced meditation: he *saw* the river (of change) and the rock (of constancy, Petrus?) and *heard* the waterfall (the sound engendered by the opposition of rock to river?). This musical sound, 'corroborate' with the singing of the larks (nature's chapel clerks),

---

[1] At this point the 1584 version (printed 1597) breaks off: Waldegrave I and II, stanza 65. The rest is supplied from the version composed about 1597, printed (1615) 1636 by (Hart) Wreittoun.

[2] *Works of David Lindsay*, S.T.S. I, 7, l. 116.

rose to the Heavens and wakened the God of Love. Love, a cosmic force, 'leaving all the heavens above' in the form of Cupido, Desire, alighted on earth and confronted the dreamer. An encounter ensued, a love-adventure, with results disastrous to the dreamer-adventurer.

After this chastening, an experience of love's powers rashly misused, the dreamer was abandoned by Cupido. Almost out of his senses, in great disturbance of mind, he 'muissit' again (stanza 17). He cursed Cupido, a god of love. (Henryson's Cresseid had cursed Cupid and Venus, swooned and thus entered her dream, later to discover herself stricken with disease.) For Montgomerie's dreamer there ensued on the cursing an affliction of love-malady, severe and distressful. He was visited with dire thirst, an overpowering 'grening' (longing). Thus in a state of psychosomatic disturbance whence images arise from the subconscious mind he *saw* 'Betuix the river and the rok/Quhair Hope grew with Dispaire/A trie. . .' a cherry-tree on the cliff beyond the water and, at hand on the hither bank, a stunted bush of bitter sloes.

A contemporary audience would readily perceive Montgomerie's indications of penetration into a landscape of the mind whose features were spiritual landmarks, of an encounter there with a force at once cosmic and 'inwart' and its outcome in a further revelation—the emergence in visible terms of a dilemma that was the dreamer's own. The *genre* of dream-poem was well understood as a pattern of narrative *cum* meditation that showed a dreamer moving onwards through a landscape significant for his state of mind towards enlightenment and fuller self-knowledge. Through encounter, solution of a dilemma or overcoming of an obstacle, through choice made or course of action decided upon, he would 'come to know better' and might arrive eventually at a 'rationale of the universe': it had been so in 'The Kingis Quair' and in 'The Palice of Honour'.[1]

ENCOUNTER WITH LOVE

In the case of *The Cherrie and the Slae* a love-adventure is sited within a dream-poem. The encounter with *Cupido* is one of the stages on a dreamer's road to enlightenment.

Montgomerie himself must have known 'The Romaunt of the Rose', at any rate the early portion of it that Chaucer translated. There he found among the fruit-trees named in the orchard 'cheryse' and 'bullace' listed together though not in opposition —and cherries were 'the object of desire for many'.[2] There he found the dreamer meeting with Cupid, the god of love, but pursued and hunted by him, not confronted by him. There Love had a bow and a quiverful of arrows, some pointed with gold and some with lead. There Love's wound caused longing in the dreamer to

[1] See Andrew von Hendy, 'The Free Thrall: a Study of *The Kingis Quair*'.
[2] In Chaucer's translation, ll. 1376–7.

reach the Rose in its territory difficult of access, Montgomerie's dreamer, wounded by a deadly dart misused was afflicted with 'grening', thirst, to be quenched by attaining cherry or accepting sloe. Some of Montgomerie's auditors in the court of Scotland, the poetasters among them, might well have known, or known of, 'The Rose' and in that case would have noted the significant variations on theme, episode and motif that the late Scots makar was presenting in his new devising. And all would have been familiar, at least from the song of 'the gowans', with the general pattern of a love-adventure—encounter in a Maytime countryside with a figure significant of the season, a request of love and an outcome that was 'a coming to know better' and might be a chastening.

The *personae* encountered in a dream-poem appear in a form significant for the inward state of the dreamer. Montgomerie's *Cupido*, like Love in 'The Rose' vision, is not blind.[1] He is younger, however, a boy. He looks like a saint (stanza 8) while Love in de Lorris looked like an angel. He is winged, naked, coy and smiling. Seeing his 'shooting-gear' coveted he proffers his instruments 'somebody to beguile', at no cost but rendering them again. The overtones are erotic, that of a young man's first experience of sex. *Cupido*, then, is an aspect of Love—the cosmic force—conceived according to the capacity of the adventurer-dreamer at that time. We remark that he is not *Caritas* but *Cupido*, Desire, with something of egoism suggested. (We remark also that Venus is absent.)[2]

The meeting leads the dreamer on to a 'flight', aspiration for high endeavour, the wish to win a noble name. (So was many an earthly lover stimulated to noble endeavour.) 'Desyring impyring' he longs for power, imperial sway (stanza 12). The immediate outcome is disaster and mockery. Cupid spoils him of his gear and flies back to heaven. An encounter with love, however imperfectly conceived the love, however disastrous the adventure, may yet lead on to a profounder understanding of love, a fuller realisation of the nature of the high endeavour. (In 'The Kingis Quair' —to cite a northern example of a great mediaeval theme—an experience of earthly love by a prisoner had led on to an understanding of heavenly love and of true freedom, and thence towards a rationale of the universe.)

To Montgomerie's audience, moreover, the figure of Cupid was already established as King Cupid in his court. There is no doubt at all that this episode in *The Cherrie and the Slae* as read or performed in the Scots court of 1584 would bring vividly to mind the crowned head in their midst—and his dealings with his *carissimus*.

The poesis is thereafter concerned to show how out of such disaster came

---

[1] 'Cupid not blind' could see and enjoy the result of wounding by his weapons (see C. S. Lewis, *Studies in Medieval and Renaissance Literature*, chapter 12).

[2] Venus (heterosexual love?) is named only fleetingly as 'Cupid's mother' at some time wounded by his 'deadly dart'. Note the revision of this reference, Wreittoun, stanza 12, discussed p. 133.

bewilderment, agony of mind, a new consciousness of a powerful longing and a further vision: his own dilemma, of choice between two possible objects of his 'grening' and determination of course of action to obtain one or the other. This vision 'where Hope grew with Despair' is of the cherry and the slae.

THE VISION OF THE TWO TREES AND THEIR FRUITS

Against what background of themes and conventions would the vision of cherry tree and sloe-bush be understood by Montgomerie's readers or listeners? First, they knew the pairing or opposition of plant to plant—thistle and rose, holly and ivy. Then widely current in the Middle Ages was the theme of the inner battle, the contest of the virtues and the vices; associated with it on occasion was found Desire, Cupid throwing his darts.[1] From early times this contest had been expressed in the figure of two trees in opposition, the tree of old Adam and the Tree of Christ, the trees of the Old and of the New Testament. As branches from the first grew the vices and their fruits, for example Fear and Despair; as branches from the second sprang, for example, Hope. It was for man to choose between them. (A poem written for a French king had shown Desire, that is egoism, as the root of the first tree and Love, that is charity, as the root of the second.) Such ideas lived long and were widely expressed both in the written word and in plastic art. It is beyond question that Montgomerie could count on his auditors' familiarity with the theme of the two trees. They appear, for example, in a woodcut illustrating *The Kalendar of Shyppars* (shepherds) translated into Scots about 1503 from a popular French work printed and reprinted in the late fifteenth and the sixteenth centuries.[2]

Montgomerie's two trees are fruit trees bearing the Cherrie and the Slae. Both these fruits had medicinal properties: the sloe served to slake thirst for a time while 'a medecine of cherries' was the phrase for a dose that was at the same time effective and delicious. The cherry in 'The Romaunt of the Rose' was *the* delectable fruit 'of whiche many on fayn is'. In the Scots makar's poem the fruits are presented from the moment they appear as in opposition. Their contrasted nature, sweet or sour, is reinforced by a contrast between the parent plants, tree and bush, and between the places on which these grow: each berry is the natural fruit of the parent plant in its significant habitat in the dream landscape. What is more, the Tree bore throughout the Middle Ages the full significance of the Rood. Here the fruit of the Tree grew on

[1] See Emile Mâle, *L'art réligieux du troisième siècle en France*, trans. Dora Nussey as *The Gothic Image* (London, 1961): Book III, 'The Mirror of Morals'.

[2] *The Kalendar of Shyppars*, trans, and pr. Antoine Vérard (Paris, 1503); English tr., R. Pynson (London, 1506) (from *Le Compost et Kalendrier des bons Bergiers*, Guy Marchand, Paris 1493). Modern version ed. G. C. Heseltine (London, 1930): woodcuts, pp. 96–7.

the Rock (Petrus) beyond the water of change in the territory difficult of access. The fruit of the Slae-bush grew on the near side of the water-barrier. (In 'The Palice of Honour' immersion in such a water-barrier signified baptism.)

The cherry as a single image was frequently the love-cherry; as such it survives today in American slang as 'the maidenhead'. Erotic connotation was there for the makar to use if he wished. But the cherry was heavenly fruit.[1] It was the object of craving in the Mother of God before Christ was born—in the well-known 'Cherry-tree Carol' that is a variation on the early legend of Mary and the date-palm on the flight to Egypt.[2] A 'bob of cherries' was one of the meaningful gifts for the infant Christ in the Wakefield shepherds' play: offered along with bird and ball, these gifts pointed at the Son, the Holy Ghost and the Father, Ruler of All—the Trinity.[3] Else-where in a mystery cycle, that of Coventry, a cherry tree bears fruit just before the birth of Christ.[4] There was that in the nature of the cherry, the white and red of its flesh and juice, that could eloquently figure the body and blood of Christ, of the sacrament. It is so used in plastic art to indicate the eucharist.[5]

Thus from the Middle Ages onwards a wealth of cherry symbolism was there for the makar to draw on in order to render his meaning profoundly and precisely. Edmund Spenser writing the 'Mutability Cantos' of *The Faerie Queene* drew on it for the meaningful love-gifts of 'Queene-apples and red cherries from the tree' offered in his fable by Faunus to Molanna. They figure the sovereignty and the Catholic eucharist, the 'small boone' offered to the people of Ireland by the Earl of Tyrone if by its help Cynthia could be seen naked—Elizabeth be stripped of her Irish provinces. The 'reinette' apples and cherries were recognised symbolic gifts of earthly love; but now defined as 'Queene-apples and cherries of the Tree' and signi-ficantly paired their reverberations of meaning were profound—and politically pertinent.[6]

By a similar stroke of artistry Montgomerie—and he preceded Spenser here—drew on the symbolism of the cherry and of the two trees to show the two fruits in contest: the cherry/delicious/lovely and refreshing/delectable/high and inaccessible/fruit of heaven/Christ-eucharist symbol on its Tree—against the Slae/bitter/black and

---

[1] Herbert Friedmann, *The Symbolical Goldfinch*, Bollingen Series, VII (Washington, D.C.), p. 95, 120 and plate 125.

[2] F. J. Child, *The English and Scottish Popular Ballads*, no. 54.

[3] 'Secunda Pastorum', stanza 80: *The Wakefield Pageants in the Towneley Cycle*, ed. A. C. Cawley, p. 62 and note, where the explanation is incomplete.

[4] *Ludus Coventriae*, 'The Birth of Christ' (E.E.T.S. ES. 120; 31–42).

[5] E.g. the tapestry (fifteenth-century Spanish) in York Minster, where the table of the Last Supper is strewn with cherries and roses.

[6] 'The VII Booke of the Faerye Queene', composed 1596–9. Spenser presenting the Tyrone rebellion, is likely to have known of the Ailsa conspiracy and may well have read Montgomerie's poem, printed 1597. The Molanna fable is interpreted in J. L. Stampfer, 'The Cantos of Mutability'.

uninviting/harsh and unpleasing/thirst-quenching only for a time/low and accessible on its Bush. And in the year 1583, we remember, the bush, the 'burning bush', was chosen as heraldic badge on the seal of the Reformed Church of France. Montgomerie's Cherrie and Slae, motifs from which the poem took its name, thus sited within the pattern of a dream-poem and significantly paired in opposition had reverberations at once profound and politically pertinent.

THE CONTENTION OF THE VOICES

The narrative-meditative pattern of the dreamer on his way to enlightenment progresses; beyond the vision of cherry tree and slae-bush rises the argument of the voices that emerge at the same moment of perception. (A revelation can come through ear as well as eye, witness the voice heard in the Maytime garden in 'The Palice of Honour'.) 'There Hope grew with Despair.' Hope and Despair already belonged to the theme of the two trees and their contest. As used in Montgomerie's poem they speak; their voices rise from within the dreamer, externalising his inner conflict. Other voices soon join them, Corage and Will on the side of Hope, and Dreid and Danger reinforcing the arguments of Despair.[1] At a later point the debate is joined by Experience, Reason, Wit and Skill. All these voiced *personae* argue among themselves and with the dreamer in a varied and progressive pattern of contention, devised on the lines of the poetic *genre* of *débat*. They are 'contrarious' aspects of human character and behaviour, as such they are used in a contemporary sonnet of King James.[2] They can be understood as forces for good and forces for ill. They urge on the dreamer different courses of action, to risk all in order to reach the delectable cherry which alone offers ultimate satisfaction of soul or to play safe and pluck the available but bitter sloe that will serve but to slake his thirst for a time.[3]

The argument explores all aspects of the situation in the dreamer's mind. The 'I' of the poem listens and learns, as the protagonist of other dream-poems listens and learns from persons—or emanations—whom he meets on his way. A certain progress is discernible in the pattern of the argument, towards a mean; extremes are discarded.[4] And there are castings back and recriminations in this life-like rendering of a human argument. At the moment when the poem breaks off our dreamer is moving towards a point where conviction will have an outcome in choice and in decisive action. No

---

[1] Cf. *amara venena Calvinistarum* of the Benedictine epitaph 1. Despair's bitter berry touches on the doctrine of predestination?

[2] 'A sonnet when the King was surprised by the Earle Bothwell' (Westcott, no. XXXVII).

[3] Dreid, Danger and Despair are glimpsed as three long-winded 'preachours' (stanza 44), which reinforces earlier pointers to the slae as Calvinist fruit.

[4] Will runs mad and Despair hangs himself (stanza 57).

'psychopomp' advises the 'I' of *The Cherrie and the Slae* in his dilemma or helps him find a way into the terrain difficult of access. That rôle, characteristic of the dream-poem *genre*, is here fragmented into the voices of the inner debate. (In the revised and completed version the dreamer will accept Skill's prescription of the cherry as sole remedy for his thirst and will be guided over the water and up the rock by a band from among his voices. Reason at their head—ordered and consonant at last.)

It is difficult to pronounce on the meaning of an unfinished poem or a truncated text. Nevertheless we have gone some way towards recapturing contemporary understanding of the piece and some observations may be made as to the impact Montgomerie's verses may have made on his courtly audience of 1584 or 1585.

First, the arch-poet who was also *carissimus* and also confidential envoy had something profound and pertinent to say. He 'mask'd his matter' with some skill. It was couched deliberately and discreetly in 'dark conceit' that challenged penetration. Multiple meanings would be expected. Within the form of a dream-poem a *questio amoris* was presented that was designed to stimulate discussion. In the foreground of meaning the piece 'treated of matters of love' and marked a progress in understanding the nature of love. Perhaps the early version intended to trace progress through an immature experience of love/*cupiditas*, homosexual love 'for the noble friend', towards an apprehension of heterosexual love and a right choice therein, noble spouse to be won through high endeavour against the embraces of a vile and available mistress—as Dempster's Latin title suggested. As such it would be apt indeed in that year and in that court, understood as a piece in the eminent kind of 'admonition to the prince'.[1] Just such an admonition on choice in love had been offered to King James' grandfather, King James V, as a preface to Bellenden's 'Cosmographie of the Realm of Scotland'. There in a Maytime scene the young red-bearded Stewart and a group of friends espied the approach of two ladies, Virtue well dowered with lands (the noble spouse) and Delight, the 'fairy mistress' offering 'warldis blisse' and goods that would vanish at a touch. Choice had to be made between them. This piece was prologue to the cosmic description of the realm the prince was to rule. Montgomerie and his Scotland were, moreover, no strangers to traditions of Celtic culture; there the King's love/desire of attaining true sovereignty had long been figured as 'the King's wooing of the fair'.[2] The 'grening' of King James for the sovereignty of all Britain, his 'wooing of the realm' was at the quick of his policy. In both these directions Montgomerie's auditors could take bearings on their monarch when considering the central conceit of the poem.

[1] Various consorts had been suggested for King James; by 1585 the choice had narrowed to a princess of Denmark or Catherine de Bourbon.

[2] This theme was closely associated with the Stewart dynasty. See Daniel Corkery, *The Hidden Ireland*. For 'literature of the sovereignty' in the Scots court, see Willson, *King James*, chapter IX.

And Montgomerie's piece treating of love was also a divine poem. The makar had made clear from the first moment of his vision that he was 'treating of Love' in its full range of significance—earthly and heavenly together as understood by the allegorical temper of the Middle Ages. The choice of cherry or slae when it came could not be of erotic love-cherry alone, for the cherry was heavenly fruit. The whole issue of a right choice in love as it faced the young Prince of Scotland was of 'true spouse' embraced in the double sense of the Apostolic faith in religion and the Catholic princess as consort. This Montgomerie's 'rhetorie' showed. In this complex issue was involved the 'true sovereignty' of the realm, and perhaps not of Scotland only, but of Britain also; and that aspect of the matter too was rendered in the poem's complexity.

To test this opinion let us look at the central passage of the poem, the *descriptio* of the cherries, high on their tree on the cliff, dangling temptingly over the river, gleaming in the light of the sun, its rays reflected upwards on them from the waters of change. This passage thus devised is strategic—not decorative or fortuitous. Again, the dreamer perceives the cherries to hang 'half-way to Heaven'. To obtain them is a task like Apollo's to obtain his laurel—which was a striving for noble name as much as for the lady. Moreover, they hang above his head like a round of rubies—suggesting the ruby crown of the realm; the phrase was used by Montgomerie elsewhere in his poetry with this meaning.[1]

22

> With sober pace I did approche
> Hard to the river and the roche
>   Quhairof I spak befoir;
> Quhais running sic a murmure maid
> That to the sey it softlie slaid:
>   The craig was high and schoir:
> Than pleasur did me so provok
>   Perforce thair to repaire
> Betuix the river and the rok
>   Quhair Hope grew with Dispaire:
>   A trie than, I sie than
>   Of CHERRIES in the braes
>   Belaw, to, I saw, to,
>   Ane buss of bitter SLAES.

23

> The CHERRIES hang abune my heid
> Like twinkland rubies round and reid
>   So hich up in the hewch
> Quhais schaddowis in the river schew

[1] Sonnet XXXI, 'To M. J. Murray', discussed further in chapter VII.

Als graithlie glansing, as they grewe
  On trimbling twistis tewch,
Quhilk bowed throw burding of thair birth
  Inclining downe thair toppis:
Reflex of Phoebus off the firth[1]   ['of' WII corrects 'in' WI]
  Newe colourit all thair knoppis;
    With dansing and glansing
      In tirles dornik champ
    Ay streimand and gleimand
      Throw brichtnes of that lamp.[2]

24

With earnest eye quhil I espye
The fruit betwixt me and the skye
  Halfe gaite almaist to hevin;
The craig sa cumbersome to clim,
The trie sa hich of growth and trim
  As ony arrowe evin;
I cald to minde how Daphne did
  Within the laurell schrink
Quhen from Apollo scho hir hid:
  A thousand times I think:
    That trie then to me then
      As he his laurell thocht: [corrected from 'as hich as
    Aspyring, but tyring,   laurell' 1597, I.]
      To get that fruit I socht.

25

To clime the craige it was na buit
Lat be to presse to pull the fruit
  In top of all the trie:
I saw na way quhairby to cum
Be ony craft, to get it clum
  Appeirandly to me:
The craige was ugly, stay and dreich,
  The trie heich, lang and smal;
I was affrayd to mount sa hich
  For feir to get ane fall:
    Affrayit to say it
      I luikit up on loft:
    Quhiles minting, quhiles stinting
      My purpose changit oft...

---

[1] Stevenson, *Montgomerie*, prints Wreittoun and Waldegrave I, on which he notes variants from the latter found in Waldegrave II; some of these are important corrections.

[2] Compare the use of sunlight or its absence in book I, *The Faerie Queene*. 'Light reflected up on them from the waters of change lent them a new colour, their radiant and changeful motion suggesting the lively patterns of Dornik weave (and lively and complex activities in Flanders field?).'

In the early 'unfinished' version of *The Cherrie and the Slae* this vision of a right choice in love was presented in terms of a narrative progress of a dreamer who was, and was not, the makar. And in that makar a flight of high endeavour undertaken from imperfect experience of love for his Prince had brought disaster; from suffering had issued a vision of high endeavour more perfectly understood—the delectable cherry of love and of the eucharist to be won through dangerous and courageous venture. The revelation of the choice of the cherry was for him, for his King, for all. Makar and prince had been intimately involved one with another in issues of diplomacy with Spain, wherein the King's conversion, his choice of consort and the 'true' sovereignty of the realm and of the future realm of Britain were all implicated. 'Mightie maters' indeed...'copping courts and commonwelthis and kings'. It is as a mimesis of such matter, both mighty and complex, that I read *The Cherrie and the Slae*.

The composition of such a piece would have been watched with keen interest in the newly assembled court of 1583 and 1584, and approved by many. Its drift detected by a fellow poet might well cause him unease. With the turn affairs took in 1585—towards Protestant dominance at court—it comes as no surprise that the poem was severed or the makar silenced.

THE POEM PERFYTED

The Cherrie and the Slae
Composed into Scottis Meeter be Alexander Montgomerie.
Newly altered, perfyted, and divided into 114 Quatorziems
not long before the Author's death.   Title-page (Wreittoun, 1638)

The 'perfyted' piece, '114 Quatorziems' long, was the poet's last word on the matter of the cherry and the slae. Strangely little interest has been shown in how his last word differed from his making in the earlier form; indeed the printing by Cranstoun and by H. H. Wood of an amalgamated version, early with part late, has served to obscure the issue. But the poet's revision comments sharply on the earlier version as well as supplying a conclusion. Indeed the nature of his alterations will be seen to confirm again and again the interpretation that has here been offered of his poem in its early, incomplete version.

The poem revised gives the first twenty-six stanzas to prelude, encounter and vision—one important stanza has here been added. Eighty-two stanzas develop and extend the 'mental fight' in its progressive stages until with the last six a way is found, the Tree reached, the cherry falls and is tasted, and the poem ends with thanksgiving of 'dreamer' and all nations for health restored. Differences between the revised poem and the earlier version as far as it goes, vary from addition of a stanza, alteration of stanza-order and interpolation of a passage to significant recasting of the opening, rewording of several stanzas and alterations here and there to word or phrase. These had been enumerated, but no serious attempt has been made to catch the poet's intention in thus altering the presentation of his vision—no critical comment save a word of regret that he had spoiled the freshness of his first making.[1]

But a change of tone is strongly evident at the outset, and with it a change of intention. What he wished most urgently to say must now be said differently. In the early prelude the 'I' had been in tune with nature's happy springtime mood; only the turtle sang sadly and Echo replied, bewailing Narcissus' love-death.[2] An adventure of love was expected. (This opening stanza is quoted on p. 165.) The late version begins also with spring and the birds, in two stanzas that now stand together. But they are different birds.

I

About a Bank with balmie bewes
Where nightingals their nots renews
   With gallant Goldspinks gay
The Mavise, Mirle and Progne proud
The Lintwhite, Lark and Laverock loud
   Saluted mirthful May.
When Philomel had sweetly sung
   To Progne she deplored
How Tereus cut out her tongue
   And falsely her deflorde:
     Which storie so sorie
      To shew asham'd she seemde.
    To hear her so near her
     I doubted if I *dream'd*

Thus early the 'dream' prevails. And first among the birds to be heard are now the nightingale and goldfinch, paired. They are both birds that had strong associations with the Crucifixion and Passion, in legend, poetry and iconography; the linnet, also a 'Passion' bird, is now linked to lark and laverock.[3] The Maytime happiness of other birds is saddened when Philomel sings of her suffering *and the fact that her tongue was cut out;* this, and not the harmony of the birds' joy with nature, is what now impinges on the listening figure and precipitates the dream.

The second stanza is sinister throughout. Cushat sings but the lone crow cries. Magpies mock the cuckoo. Other birds are hostile or of ill omen; they 'deave' the

---

[1] Differences between early and revised texts listed: Stevenson, introduction § 10.

[2] These examples—'true wedded love bereaved' and 'self-love punished'—do not argue against true love.

[3] F. J. E. Raby, 'Philomena praevia temporis amoeni' in *Mélanges Joseph de Ghellinck*, pp. 435–49, and Friedmann, *The Symbolical Goldfinch, passim;* linnet p. 7.

dreamer with harsh cries. The peacock has Argus eyes to spy and the turtle wails on withered trees.

The stanza of beasts has altered in tone too. 'The Hurcheon and the Hare, Quha fed amangis the flowris fair' in the early version, now limp furtively in hiding-places here and there. 'The Con, the Conny and the Cat' have 'stiffe mustaches'. The fox is now 'false'. The Buck is bearded, the 'Baires and Brock' are bristly; 'bair' (boar) is an addition. The snares are not now 'sudden'; they are 'Hunters' subtile snares'. (Why the characterisation by facial hair? The creatures were 'downy' before, and happy among the flowers. Are wild beasts, 'the passions', now 'horridae'? Is a system of animal figuration at work to which we lack the key? Did a courtly 'you know who' attach to the creatures 'of the park' perhaps, as animal nicknames obtained among Queen Elizabeth's courtiers?)[1]

The weather has changed also, to '*sober*, soft and sweet'. Where Nature had nourished the flowers before, now they are sprinkled with many a tear, shed by 'Apollo's paramours'! Stanza 7, of the music of Echo answering the sound of the running water, ends not with Helicon and Amphion (whose song helped to build Thebes), but with 'the Musis that usis, To pin Apollo's harpe'. Does 'pin' mean *support* and point at the important activities of 'the Castalians', the state-function of poetry?

A stanza has been added to the description of Cupido—and here also the tone has altered.

10

His youth and stature made me stout;
Of doublenesse I had no doubt,
　　But bourded with my Boy.
Quoth I 'how call they thee, my child?'
'Cupido, sir' quoth he and smilde:
　　'Please you mee to imploy?
For I can serve you in your sute
　　If you please to *impire*
With wings to flee and shafts to shute
　　Or flames to set on fire.
　　　　Make choice, then of those then
　　　　Or of a thousand things:
But crave them and have them'.
　　　　With that I woo'd his wings.[2]

The next stanza begins '"What would thou give, my *heart*," quoth he'. The earlier version had 'friend'. The new emphasis is on Cupido's 'doublenesse' from

[1] In his animal catalogue in both versions Montgomerie may be alluding overtly to Henryson's fable 'The Parliament of Foure-futtit Beists' under the Scots king. Allusion to members of the court in a beast fable is made in *Rob Stene's Dream* (1591), which is probably by Montgomerie.

[2] Cupido offers choice of mode of endeavour—wings of an envoy, shafts of a soldier or flames of propagandist?

the beginning and his mockery after the wounding is strongly in character. Does this change of aspect to the dreamer signify a change of feeling in the poet—Montgomerie burning now to show the doubleness of Cupido, desire, *on earth?* Is Montgomerie, longing in his heart to become a monk of St Benedict, now dispraising earthly love in itself, although experience of it may still lead on through distress, vision and inner conflict, to knowledge of heavenly love? Moreover, does the form of the dispraise glance back at the 'temporal happenings' of his own passages of love and trust to Cupido/James Stewart, since 1584 so bitterly betrayed?

Again, as in the earlier version, the dreamer mounts like Icarus and now we recall how in the late exchange of sonnets Montgomerie was called 'Sir Icarus' after his fall from royal favour. We recall, too, the poet's last sonnet, his furious and heart-broken invective on Cupid/King James for 'betrayal under trust'. The 'doubleness' comes in again—

> First forth I drew the *double* dart
>   Which sometimes shot *his mother*...[sometime(s), at a point in past time]

As far as I know, Cupid in legend or picture had not a dart that was 'double'.[1] (The outstanding example of King James' doubleness in diplomacy was, we recall, in the matter of his mother's life, in 1587.) The stanza of Phaeton (77) has now 'his fathers chaire', not 'cart' as earlier—perhaps a step nearer 'throne'.

In the encounter with Cupido/Desire/Love appearing on earth, the experience that engendered the thirst for high endeavour 'to win a noble name', the image of Cupido has been defaced. Earthly love experienced in the court is marred by false-ness. Cross-reference to the poet's writing elsewhere has suggested that in the Cupido encounter there was a sharp glance at the King. Now the cumulative effect of numerous and extensive alterations impresses on the reader that changes in the poet's circumstances have led him to change correspondingly the presentation of his matter. He is no longer 'carissimus', no longer servitor and envoy, no longer acting in any sense *with* the King; he depicts his 'endeavour' as encouraged by the King himself, as used by political doubleness. That doubleness shall be exposed in 'rhetorie'.

Prelude and encounter have been significantly transformed, but the sequences that follow stand virtually unchanged—the 'disease' and thirst from the wounding, the vision, and the emergence of the inner forces to contend as voices. Then in the course of the debate (58) there is an insertion nine stanzas long. It is the moment when

---

[1] A 'deadly' dart before, it is now 'double', perhaps drawing on Cupid's two arrows, *Metamorphoses*, I, 462 ff. Cupid's two darts, lead-tipped and gold-tipped, inflicting disdain and love are used by Montgomerie else-where (Cranstoun, p. 153. Apollo and Daphne are wounded). Compare Love's arrows of two types in 'The Romaunt of the Rose'. Watson, *Hekatompathia*, LXIII, quotes Conrad Celtis, *Odarum*, lib. I, 'spicula Quae bina fert saevus Cupido', which Montgomerie knew and may have interpreted wrongly.

Experience and Reason are urging the dreamer to banish Will and Despair, the two extremes of the contending parties. Will now retorts that the dreamer should have plucked the cherries when aloft on Cupid's wings, but Reason counters that *he had not yet seen them and did not know that he needed them*. This stroke serves to integrate an earlier and a later sequence of the poem. The passage is a contest between Reason, master of men, and Will, creature of the senses and master of the 'bruital beasts'. In terms of the 'foreground' of courtly love, the lover should have striven to attain the beloved by high endeavour in the first flush of amorous feeling, but had he not yet discerned the object of his desire? Can we read this insertion as making clear what was only hinted in the early version, that during Montgomerie's first phase as *carissimus*, his first essay for high endeavour flying on the wings of an envoy in 1580, he was not yet a Catholic and did not yet perceive the true nature of the goal to be reached—the eucharistic cherry, noble spouse and true religion to be embraced, with its aspect of royal reference, Catholic sovereignty?

Small changes all tend one way; for example, in the stanza where the dreamer's drouth and disease are described in terms of love-distress (60, 70), 'The persing passion of thy spreit' thus carefully corrected in Waldegrave II, has now become 'The peircing passions of the spirit'.

In the portion of the poem that is new (77–114) the argument of the voices proceeds according to a pattern that was already discernable in its earlier phases, confrontation of one force or group of forces with a 'contrarious' opposite in a progressing series, with a working from extremes to the mean. It is a vigorous mimesis of a human argument, and a psychiatrist has commented on its interest as a figurative rendering of disharmonious 'voices' in the mind working towards composure. The opposition of 'courage/action towards the desirable but dangerous of access', to 'caution/making do with the available', persists but with diminishing force. The stages by which Experience and Reason gain sway in the dreamer's mind mark his progress in ordering the contrarious forces in himself—not without further castings-back and recrimination. Only when leadership of 'the famous four' is established can he receive Skill's prescription for his disease. Only when that has been allowed and all voices, albeit with mutinous murmurings from some, have accepted guidance can Wit devise the plan of action. The voices now in consonance speak as psychopomp.

During the argument-sequence of the dreamer's progression the landscape of the vision, whose features defined the issue—fruit tree, water and rock—is kept in mind by light references. 'Who wats, sir, if that, sir, Is sowre which seemeth sweet' (79). Hope is an anchor that grips fast only if the ground be good (85), which anticipates the 'sound bottom' necessary for the eventual wading of the water. Hope and Courage reiterate 'Our counsel is, he clim' (87) and cherry and slae are insisted on as incompatible in their view (88). Skill prescribes the Cherry as sole remedy (99); it is unique and heavenly fruit: 'No Nectar directar/Could all the gods him give'. Since the stanza of the break there has been no affirmation of matters of earthly love: the direction of attention towards heavenly love is plain.

When the dreamer's mind is ready the geography of the dream-landscape asserts itself strongly (110). The final action is shortly described but carefully delineated. The issue has become clear. The way to cross the river, whose waters grow always deeper and more dangerous the farther they flow from the linn where water of change interacts with rock of constancy—*is to go to the source*. There above the linn is firm bottom and the dreamer, all his voices orderly, can cross the water. The cliff is steep but is surmounted. The Tree is reached but remains unscalable. The cherry, for ripeness, falls: grace cannot be taken; it comes down. The dreamer tastes the delicious fruit and his health is restored. His rejoicing involves the thanksgiving *of all nations*.

Since the 'broken' stanza there has been no glancing at temporal happenings that I can discern, no relation to contemporary issues other than the main issue of conversion to the Apostolic faith, for poet, for King, for all, with which was bound up the true sovereignty of the realm. (In 1596 and later, the Papacy was directly involved in political manœuvring by King James in his efforts to secure his 'title' to the succession, and his conversion was there still hinted at as not inconceivable.) As the revised poem reaches its end there is no re-entry of the theme of 'winning a noble name', as there is none of the earthly aspect of love. None the less, when the revised poem is read as a whole, the effect of the lovely *descriptio* of the cherries lingers throughout the later sequences, cherries as tempting fruit of desire, earthly or heavenly, cherries as 'round of rubies' dangling overhead, lit by the sun's rays reflected from the water. And the thanksgiving of all nations for the health-giving fruit at last attained is not meaningful unless the dreamer's attaining the fruit of grace is felt to have universal and international significance.[1]

To me it seems that in composing the completing portion of the poem the author has drawn the issue clear of running reference to 'temporal happenings'. In the end the winning of the cherry is felt as an individual attainment of grace; achieved by the dreamer and the poet, urged on the King and on all. Others could reach it, that had shared the vision and followed the argument.

113

As Reason ordeinde all obeyde;
None was ov'r rash nor none affraide,
Our counsel was so wise:

---

[1] The last stanza renders verses from Psalm 117, which is present in *The Mindes Melodie*.

As of our journey Wit did note
We found it true in every jote:
   God bles'd our interprise.
For even as wee came to the tree,
   Which, as yee heard mee tell,
Could not be clum, there suddenly
   The fruit for ripnes fell.
     Which hasting and tasting
      I found myselfe relievde
     Of cares all and sares all
      Which minde and body grievde.

114

Praise be to God, my Lord, therefore,
Who did mine health to mee restore,
   Being so long time pinde;
Yea, blessed be his holy Name,
Who did from death to life recleame
   Mee, who was so unkinde.
All nations also magnifie
   This everliving Lord;
Let me with you, and you with mee,
   To laude him ay accord;
     Whose love ay wee prove ay
      To us above all things;
     And kisse him and blesse him
      Whose Glore eternall rings.

The Cherrie and the Slae, then, is a narrative meditation, conveying, in a 'dark conceit' that could nevertheless be penetrated by sharp eyes, the innermost concern of the poet Montgomerie—Catholic convert and, confidential envoy, intimate as few others were with the workings of his monarch's mind in his complex and devious policy. Montgomerie is seen to be a Catholic poet of the Renaissance, the only one in Scotland. He is a counterpart to Southwell, who was an isolated figure in Elizabethan poetry. Southwell voiced the spirit of Elizabethan Catholicism in the third phase of Counter-Reform—the meditative, and his work anticipates the spiritual poetry of the age to follow. Montgomerie writes from the second generation, that of 'alarm spiritual', of Catholic militancy, conversion and monastic orders refounded. 'He assailed the Protestants with sword and song.' In this, I think, he stands unique. His friend Henry Constable was diplomat then convert, poet and prose propagandist, and for years he attempted the conversion of King James.[1] Like Montgomerie 'he did not at first sho himselfe al together a papist'.[2] Like Montgomerie he had to face a crisis

[1] See chapter 4, p. 83, n. 2.
[2] King James on Constable, who was in 1589 writing his *Examen Pacifique*. P.R.O., S.P. 52, LXIV. fol. 37.

of conscience, loyalty to religious creed against loyalty to his monarch. As with Montgomerie, his avowal of Catholicism meant 'displeasur', exile and the end of a career. But his poetry does not match the whole endeavour of the man. Montgomerie's does, though the old-style manner of his poetic expression has meant that for long his drift lay unperceived.[1]

THE POEM REACHES PRINT

That this poem in its early version was silenced in 1585 is not surprising. But that this same version patently lacking its conclusion should in 1597 issue from the press of Waldegrave, the King's printer, is more difficult to understand. Montgomerie was sensationally in the news in that year, involved in conspiracy in its opening month of March and outlawed in July. That sympathy for the poet was felt in some quarters is clear from the crisis of his funeral. Obviously to print his work at that moment would be a paying proposition; the first edition must have sold out rapidly for it to be followed by a second in the same twelvemonth. But the printing of this, Montgomerie's major poem, in that year by the King's printers is comprehensible to me only if the poet were by then near death or dead—and King James, pricked by conscience or moved to deep grief at the news of his death and dishonoured funeral, wished to make amends. 'On hearing of the poet's death he was stricken with grief' and called on fellow Castalians to honour in verse the prince of poets in Scotland; by the same token he may also have ordered or permitted the printing of Montgomerie's major poem as tribute to the admirable makar who had once been his dearest friend. The verse published, after all, did not proceed to its conclusion and was veiled in 'dark conceit'. The poem was not new. Any historical pertinence detected could be referred to a situation now more than ten years old; if the King was shadowed forth it was in pleasant guise. The Kirk could withold its censoring pen. Watching powers of Europe need not take alarm.

A further puzzle lies in the relation between these printings in 1597 of the early incomplete version and the poet's composition 'not long before his death' of a text strenuously altered, that commented vigorously on that early version and drove the poem's meaning through to a conclusion. The difficulty is that we still do not know for certain the year and month of Montgomerie's death; late 1597 or early 1598 is most likely. His decision to revise his poem, expose the King's doubleness and make the work's conclusion known could have been taken at any point after his break with the King in 1595. The writing of the revised version may have preceded

[1] Summary comments only are possible here on style and matter in these three Catholic poets; a fuller comparative study is in preparation.

the printings and may have been unrelated to their appearance. If, however, Montgomerie, believed alive in the denunciation of July 1597, lived on in hiding for a time, then the decision to 'alter and perfyt' his major work may have been touched off by the poem's appearance in print in a form that did not give the whole meaning and presented earthly love and the King in a pleasant guise. That missing ending should be supplied, that image defaced. Montgomerie may have retained somewhere in secret a copy or outline of the poem's conclusion. To 'alter and perfyt' it could be the work of one furious week.

At all events the late version is the work of a poet who rejected slae for cherry, who fought with song against Protestantism as he was ready to fight with sword in the Ailsa conspiracy. It is, too, the work of a poet now on his way to Arctaunum. It is self-vindicatory in accusing the King of past doubleness and perhaps of present doubleness also.[1] The main interest is confessional and hortatory and the matter is still sharply relevant to the monarch: as late as 1599 James was negotiating for Catholic support in his succession claim, allowing it to be believed that his ultimate conversion was not to be despaired of. Montgomerie was now writing far from the court but

> My poesie I leave my prince to preiv
> No richt can reiv him of my rhetorie...

'I leave my poetry for my Prince to sample' *and* 'to try my prince'—to put him to the test. He shall be forced to face the truth of the issue of conversion and Catholic sovereignty.

The poem and its revision sprang from tensions between poet and King wherein, in terms of an intensely personal conflict, was fought out an issue of the Counter-Reformation. But the poem had universal significance on another plane. The dreamer has reached the cherry—and the reader, having shared the dilemma, the decision and the perilous journey, is with him:

> Let me with you and you with me
> To laude him ay accord
> Whose Love ay we prove ay
> To us above all things.

[1] It is possible that the King's duplicity over the Ailsa conspiracy involved the poet.

6

MONTGOMERIE AND MUSIC

THE STUDY of song-writing at the court of Renaissance Scotland centres on the work of Alexander Montgomerie. Music survives for more than thirty poems known to be his or attributable to him and there is reason to take the matching of his words with that music as contemporary, as effected during his lifetime, in many cases during his presence as 'master poet' in King James' court—to be a circumstance, in fact, of the social enjoyment of his poetry there. When we enquire how the court-songs came to be made we find that the question of how the words and music came together is apt to embrace the question of social occasion. Consideration of the Montgomerie songs raises issues familiar from earlier chapters but there are new topics also: when is a sonnet a song, when is a dance-song a danced song, what was the influence from France and what from England in this new phase of song-making at the Scottish court?

More than once Montgomerie refers to the singing or setting of his songs and on each occasion the context is courtly. Recalling, in Sonnet XXVI, happy days at court before he lost the King's favour, he says

> I wantonly wryt under Venus wings.
> In Cupid's court ye knau I haif bene kend
> Quhair Muses yit some of my sonets sings
> And shall do aluayis to the world's end.

And Cupid's court, as we saw, was the court of the young King James as well as 'the god of love his conclave'.

In a panegyric in high style and 'Scottis meeter', 'Prepotent palme Imperiall', a poet, by every token of internal evidence Montgomerie, vows love-service apparently to his lady's 'pulchritude preclair'. There is, however, no indication of female sex in the poem. He uses terms of royal greeting, 'your Grace', and wishes his contrition and constant devotion to be made known through the arts of rhetoric and of music. (The piece could mark an approach to Queen Mary or King James from the poet who is in prison literally, not only 'love's prisoner'. He is in misery because by his 'grosness' he has given offence.)[1]

> Quhairfore I humele pray your grace
> Latt my complaint cum peirss your eareis...
>
> O happie war the Rethoriciane
> That with sueit wourdis wald lament it
> Alss happie war the gude musiciane
> Wald sett and caus it to be prentit
> And in your grace's hand present it
> Sua that ye wald reid and perus it
> To knaw so soir I am tormentit
> So that my grosnes war excusit.

Presentation with music furthered the message in words, made more telling the lover's or the courtier's plea.

Were songs of Montgomerie's ever 'prentit'? His renown at the time of his death, as poet as well as partisan, suggests that poems of his, love-songs no doubt among them, were widely known beyond the royal circles of their origin. A book of love-songs, 'Cantiones amatoriae lib. I' is listed among Montgomerie's works by Dempster.[2] No such volume is known to have reached print and certainly during his lifetime printing of such songs with their part-music was highly improbable in Scotland. The Mindes Melodie of 1605, however, made known to a wide public his psalm-versions for singing and indicated the music for them. Manuscript song-books of the time bear ample witness to the singing of his 'sonets' not only in courtly circles but also in castle, in college and song-school, not only during his lifetime but for generations to follow. When court-song of sixteenth-century Scotland did eventually reach print in Forbes' Songs and Fancies of 1662 to 1682, four of Montgomerie's songs were included, although without his name. Music of Scotland 1500–1700 gives 8 musics that match 27 sets of verses, sacred or secular, from his pen.

Some of his songs survive in such imperfect musical text—one part extant of a four-part composition—that reassembly for Musica Britannica, volume XV was not possible. Yet those items extend the repertory of his extant song-making and increase

---

[1] Stevenson, pp. 196–8, anonymous; attributed by him to Montgomerie. The sense runs thus: 'I don't know how to tell you how grieved I am, how constant my devotion. I would rather die in storm at sea or in battle than have to explain matters and confess my painful plight. I pray you pity my misfortune. Why should an armed knight vent his rage by killing one who has yielded to him and is in his power? Forgive and help "your bundman now and evir moir".' The first verse praises 'your perfyt pulchritude preclair', which declaration of 'perfytnes' he hopes will be rightly understood (taken 'in gude pairt')! The message is couched—perhaps for safety and secrecy?—as a lover's plaint. Signature would be superfluous: the lines shout 'Montgomerie'.

[2] See Appendix III. A volume entitled 'Amoretti or sonnets' printed in Edinburgh in 1595 (Aldis 261) of which no copy survives, may or may not be Spenser's Amoretti; it might be Montgomerie's 'Cantiones Amatoriae'.

our knowledge of his varying practice in the art of wedding words and music. One such song, its music incompletely recorded in surviving Scottish music-books, is 'A bony *No*'. A treble part is thus entitled among the 'delectable French songs' in the carefully planned anthology of part-song made for the family of Mure of Rowallan, great-nephew of the poet Montgomerie. The music is the treble (*superius*) of 'Ung doux nenny', Clément Marot's epigram set as a four-part *chanson* by Orlando de Lassus. It was included in two French song-books that were favourites, widely reprinted between 1565 and 1587.[1] Montgomerie skilfully translated Marot's words to match the four-part music and also wittily 'continued' the poem's sense for another couple of eight-line stanzas; this lyric of his is in the Ker manuscript.[2] Montgomerie's making afresh in Scots of this French *chanson* is done in the tradition of 'Support your servand' which was discussed in chapter II.

For a second instance we have manuscript record of music for four voices and we have two sets of words by Montgomerie, one a courtly love-song 'In throu the windoes of myn ees', the other 'The seconde Psalme. To the Tone of—In throu the etc.'—'Quhy doth the Heathin rage and rampe'. Clearly for the inscriber in the Ker manuscript 'In throu the' was a known music and the writing of the psalm-version was secondary.[3] We know that 'the tone of In throu the' was part-song because it was widely recorded as such in manuscript music-books and described as 'to four voices' in one source. The music has not been found associated with other words or inscribed without title or verbal text.

There is a good case, then, for claiming the song as Scots in provenance—as Montgomerie's writing of a stanzaic lyric and its subsequent setting to four-part music. The verbal-metrical form is basically nine lines of tetrameters, five rhyming *abbab* then, with a pause in sense, four rhyming *cdcd*, of which the *c* lines rhyme on *c* also at mid-line.

1 In throu the windoes of myn ees
   A perrillous and open pairt
   Hes Cupid hurt my hevy hairt
   Quhilk daylie duyns bot nevir dees
   Throu poyson of his deidly dairt.

---

[1] *Mellange/D'Orlando de Lassus/contenant/plusieurs chansons/tant en vers Latins qu'en ryme francoyse//A quatre, cinq, six, huit, dix parties//A Paris//par Adrian le Roy et Robert Ballard/Imprimeurs du Roy/1570;* (reprinted La Rochelle 1575, Paris 1576 and 1586; reprinted in London in 1570 by Vautrollier, who later moved to Edinburgh); from the same French printers *Quinsième Livre/de Chansons/à quatre, cinq et six parties/de plusieurs autheurs./Imprimé en quatre volumes/à Paris 1565; 1569, 1571, 1575, 1578, 1587.* See F. W. Sternfeld, 'Vautrollier's Printing of Lasso's *Recueil du Mellange, London 1570*'.

[2] Cranstoun, p. 195; manuscript record provides no authority for underlaying stanzas 2 and 3 to this music. '"Un doux nenny" had been set earlier by Créquillon' (Lesure). The matter is still under discussion. Verbal texts French and English also in H. M. Shire *The Thrissil, the Rois and the Flour-de-lys*.

[3] Cranstoun, p. 161 and p. 226; *Music of Scotland*, no. 53. This need not have been the order of writing; but one or the other of the sets of verses was written to match words-and-music of a part-song.

I bad him bot
To sey ane shot } I smyld to se that suckling shute:

Boy, with thy bou
Do vhat thou dou } Quod I, I cair the not a cute.

Thus written on the page of the Ker manuscript it shows up as one of the 'much cuttit and broken' stanzas 'devised daily' in the court. The music takes up the cue of the verse-form, rendering the rhyming half-lines in lively musical points of imitation. Concert performance has shown that the setting conveys marvellously well the vigour and humour of the love-adventure—and also that it serves excellently to render the strife and wrath of the second psalm.

A third example of Montgomerie's song-making proves to be a complication of the first two analysed. 'Lyk as the dum solsequium' is a love-song and there are psalm versions in the same measure, while for the music there is a link with printed song from France.[1] 'The Solsequium' is found underlaid to charming music for four voices—a homophonic part-song, a busking air with subtly varying rhythms. Three strains of music make up the song; matching this, the long stanza is of three self-repeating sections—a three-trace pattern characteristic of the dance-song. The words on the page show the stanza to be again one 'much cuttit and broken' in outline, but when sung the words move nimbly in the intricate pattern. Shadings of mood succeed one another as meaning and music unfold, trace by trace of the measure, section by section of the music.

Lyk as the dum
Solsequium   trace A
With cair ouercum
And sorou, vhen the sun goes out of sight,/
Hings doun his head
And droups as dead   A'
And will not spread
But louks his leavis throu langour of the nicht,/
Till folish Phaeton ryse   B
   With vhip in hand/
To cleir the cristall skyis   B'
   And light the land:/
Birds in thair bour
Luiks for that hour   C
And to thair prince ane glaid good morou givis;/
Fra thyn, that flour
List not to lour,   C'
Bot laughis on Phoebus lousing out his leivis:

Sometimes there is a strong contrast between one strain and the next, as at the sudden sunrise above (line 9). The second hearing of a strain of music can continue or

[1] Cranstoun, p. 148; *Music of Scotland*, no. 54.

intensify the first, as in the opening lines of the song. Again, the second hearing of a strain may mark, by alteration in tone and tempo of the singing, a vivid contrast—as in these lines of stanza 2:

> I die—I duyn
> Play does me pyn—
> I loth on euiry thing I look—alace!
> Till Titan myne
> Upon me shyne
> That I revive throu favour of hir face.

'Though the four voices "keep together" one beneath the other, the varying pace and rhythm offer great scope for subtleties in the poet's meaning to be conveyed in the music.'[1]

The vocal parts of the part-song in manuscript and printed record are found with the secular words of 'The Solsequium'; but psalm versions in the same highly idiosyncratic stanza are associated with the sunflower lyric in more than one fashion. As late additions to the Bannatyne manuscript these pieces are grouped together: 'The first pshalme—Montgumry', 'The XXIII sphalme translait be him', 'Lyk as the dum solsequium—finis q. montgomery' and his 'Peccavi pater miserere mei'.[2] These two psalm versions appear, somewhat anglicised for printing, in *The Mindes Melodie* of 1605 along with thirteen other pieces in the same metre—a choice of psalms with the 'Song of Simeon' and the Gloria Patri. This volume, as we saw, gave the words of the 'mynd' for Montgomerie and the music of the 'mynd' was indicated: *The Mindes Melodie./Contayning certayne/Psalmes of the Kingly Prophete/David, applyed to a new pleasant/tune, verie comfortable to/everie one that is rightlie acquainted therewith.*[3] That the 'Solsequium' music was 'the tune' prescribed was never in doubt, but a recent discovery of the music written into a copy of the volume clinches the matter.[4]

The phrasing of the title-page is important, and may be cryptic. 'Certayne' points to significant selection; 'applyed' implies that the metrical form has been matched to an existing measure; 'verie comfortable...' appears to mean that the versions fit the tune featly if you know the 'right way' of the tune, but at the same time 'verie comfortable'—which had the force of the modern 'comforting'—may refer obliquely to the whole solace offered by the sequence of chosen psalms.

'New' in any such song-book prescription need not mean recently composed. The 'Solsequium' music was 'new' in the sense of freshly devised for, as Kenneth Elliott has shown, it is a decorated version of the 'tune' of a French *chanson*, a setting by de la Grotte of words by de Baïf, 'Or voy-je bien qu'il faut vivre en servage'. This was

---

[1] The critical opinions quoted on the music of these songs are from Kenneth Elliott's Doctoral Dissertation (1959), 'Music of Scotland 1500–1700', I.
[2] Bannatyne Manuscript, ed. S.T.S. I, 85 ff.   [3] Aldis 389; Cranstoun, pp. 243–69.
[4] Dr Elliott found the tune thus inscribed in a copy in Glasgow University Library.

first printed in Paris in 1569 in a famous song-book reissued five times by 1580.[1] Here is the first of its ten stanzas:

> Or voy-je bien qu'il faut vivre en servage
> Adieu ma liberté.
> Dans les liens de l'amoureux cordage
> Je demeure arresté.
> Iay cognoissance
> de la puissance
> D'une maitresse
> Qu'amour adresse.
> O bien fut nommée une beauté.

The song was also in Chardavoine's *Voix de villes*, six stanzas long.[2] The words of the French *chanson* are not rendered in Montgomerie's sunflower lyric nor will his words sing to the music in the French song-books. The music itself has been altered. We cannot tell by exactly what process in the hands of poet and musician there came about the perfect matching of words and music we enjoy in the 'Solsequium' song. Montgomerie may have met the music already altered from the printed French song-book into a decorated version—now in a three-strain pattern like a dance-song, perhaps indeed for use as such—and he may then have devised words that matched the 'new pleasant tune' at all points. Conversely, Montgomerie may have devised his 'Solsequium' in a 'much cuttit and broken' stanza made in three traces like a dance-song from England and the musician of the court, casting about for music with which to embellish the sun-flower poem, may have adapted with discrimination the music of de la Grotte's well-known song.

These three instances show under Montgomerie at the court of King James a reassumption of a Franco-Scottish tradition in court-song making that had flourished earlier in the century. Precedent in contemporary printed song-books from France is clear at times, but as clear to see is a live collaboration between the Scots poet and a 'gude musiciane'. We can observe, too, among the ways of court-song devising in this northern court a convergence of the French *chanson* style with the pattern of the three-trace dance-song prominent in England.

There are some seven or eight poems, sacred or secular, by Montgomerie that are strophic songs whose music is recorded nowhere furth of Scotland and which may in consequence be taken to be Castalian song, in all probability of Castalian musical composition. 'Before the Greeks durst enterpryse' existed by 1584, as we saw, and I

---

[1] *Chansons//de P. de Ronsard,//Ph. Desportes, et autres//mises en Musique par N. de la Grotte//vallet de chambre et organiste de Monsieur//frère du Roy*, printed by Roy et Ballard; the collection was reissued with modifications in 1570, 1572, 1575 and 1580.

[2] Chardavoine, *Le Recueil des Plus Belles et Excellentes Chansons en forme de voix de villes...Paris 1576* (Bibliothèque Nationale, Paris).

144

suggested the occasion in 1583 for which it may well have been written, the moment of the King's escape and reunion with former friends that was marked by the granting to the poet of a royal pension. The tune to which the words were sung was widely known: it was recorded in Straloch's 'Playing book for the lute', though it does not survive today; as a four-part arrangement for instrumental playing without title it is in Rowallan's lute-book, which was largely of dance-tunes; it is in Robert Edwards' Music-Book as part-song and in *Songs and Fancies*.[1] It is reported also in the late Robert Taitt manuscript, words and music. Thurston Dart remarked on a kinship of rhythm between this piece and 'O lustie May'. It would be reasonable and agreeable to claim the music for Montgomerie's poem as originating in the Scottish court.

I have, however, a residual doubt in this case. The title or *incipit* of the song as music appears not as 'Before the Greeks durst' but as 'Whenas the Greeks did...'. This may be chance or mistake; or it may mark the passing of the piece from particular occasion to general currency. ('The Greeks'—the King's party?—did proceed to 'take Troy town' later in 1583.) Variation in wording of an *incipit* is on occasion due to blending with the name of the tune. The poem is in 'common metre', as King James called it, like very many broadsides; it may have been written to match a broadside tune, or such a tune may have been found for the words so that they could be sung. Now one very famous broadside tune 'When that Apelles dwelt in Greece', prescribed for scores of ballads in England at the time, is not now to be found in English sources.[2] The titles are near enough for confusion or blending to have taken place, and the piece was present *without title* in one Scottish source. It is possible, then, that in this case an English broadside dance-tune happens to survive in the north only, associated there with a famous set of words from the chief makar of the Scottish court.

Of songs that are love-songs pure and simple there are several, most of them surviving complete in musical text. One, however, is musically incomplete and corrupt. 'Remember rightly, when ye reid' was recorded in 1612 by David Melvill in his manuscript 'Ane buik of Roundells', among Scottish part-songs at the end. Alas that this song is difficult to salvage as it looks to have been a fine one.[3]

'Evin dead behold I breathe' is no. 55 in *Music of Scotland*, where the musical text was assembled from scattered parts.[4] It is reported with four vocal parts in the Taitt manuscript of 1676, still enjoyed nearly a century after its probable date of composition; this late text is unfortunately not yet available for study alongside the vocal parts recorded much nearer the poet's own time. A three-trace stanza appears again

---

[1] Straloch's copy of this song was not copied by Graham and is therefore not extant: see Source List.
[2] John Ward, 'Music for *A Handefull of Pleasant Delites*'. The Ker MS. had 'Before the greeks durst...' (Cranstoun, p. 188).
[3] Cranstoun, p. 197.   [4] Cranstoun, p. 158.

in this song; 'this stanza is sympathetically set in three sections of music of different rhythmic patterns though the poem's metre is constant throughout—iambic tri-meters'. Dr Elliott found in this song's music certain antique features that brought to mind an earlier tradition of part-writing, possibly English. The setting, he suggested, might be the work of one of the Hudsons.

'What mightie motion' won enthusiastic praise when it was first heard in modern concert and broadcast programmes.[1]

It is another part-song that achieves variety by being set in three sections of different rhythmic structure within a duple-time context. But how much more sensitively are the words set from both melodic and harmonic standpoints! The opening pair of balancing phrases both begin with the same melody notes in the soprano but each receives different harmonic treatment. They recall some of the French and French-inspired psalm-tunes, but the harmonizations are on a far more intimate level. In the second section (bars 7–14) sensitive declamation of the text is a primary consideration...The last section (bars 15 onwards) is a refrain of great beauty and subtle structure with a falling fifth in the soprano and contrary motion in a sequence of soprano and bass. This almost perfect little song owes much of its success to a fine lyric by Montgomerie.

> 1   Quhat mightie motione so my mynd mischeivis?
> Quhat vncouth cairs throu all my corps do creep?
> Quhat restles rage my resone so bereivis?
> Quhat maks me loth of meit, of drink, of sleep?
> I knou not nou vhat countenance to keep   [continence]
> For to expell a poysone that I prove.
> *Alace! alace! that evir I leirnd to love.*

Near neighbour to this song both in words and music, but anonymous in both, is 'No wonder is suppose my weeping eye'.[2] 'Again there are three sections: the style, too, is similar and both compositions may be the work of the same composer. Moreover, the musical language, if not the structure itself, is the natural development of "Richt soir opprest".' The same affinities and pedigree could be claimed for the poetic language. This rueful love-lament or 'regrait' has a skilled playing on words and ideas that suggests Montgomerie's authorship—as well as using certain of his favourite turns of phrase. To my mind the words are as fine as the music.

> 2   As with the wind oppressèd is the corn
> The stone thirlèd with rainy droppis great
> And with the worm the scarlet rent and shorn
> So is my heart o'erthralled and overset.
> My salt tears mingled are with bloody sweat.
> Pale is my face and faded is my hue.
> Of Lovis lair alace that ev'r I knew!   [lore]

[1] Cranstoun, p. 135, *Music of Scotland*, no. 56.
[2] *Music of Scotland*, no. 52 and note.

3 I seek remead unto my deadly wound
  As fire in ice and heat in marble stone.
  I find a quadrant in a figure round
  A deaf sophist a problem to expone.
  I seek the truth in heart where there is none
  As who would fish upon the mountain hie
  Or go and gather berries in the sea.

Of the Castalian part-songs published in *Music of Scotland* one remains to discuss and a very fine one both in music and words. Musically it belongs to this epoch and perhaps to the same musician as the two just reviewed; but no claim can be made for Montgomerie as author of the words, which are late medieval in manner, 'style King James V'. In 'My bailful briest' the musician apparently chose to set words written some time before.[1]

Several songs of Montgomerie are devotional pieces.[2] His penitential lyric, 'Peccavi Pater, miserere mei' already mentioned, is in all likelihood the text for the part-song with that *incipit* which was recorded by Melvill in his part-books—as far, that is, as can be judged by the sole surviving part, the bassus. Another sacred lyric of his is a teasing example from the point of view of content, meaning and possible social intention. 'Come, my Childrene dere, drau neir me', a poem of five stanzas as it appears in the Ker manuscript, is the only text there for which music is included with the words; the 'tune' for it has been written into the manuscript apparently by the same hand that copied the poems, a hand unskilled in musical transcription.[3] In *Music of Scotland* Kenneth Elliott has provided an instrumental accompaniment (no. 57). The same tune apparently was recorded in the late Taitt manuscript as a song to three voices, the lyric now having a sixth stanza.

In content it is a love-song of the soul to Christ, an ancient mode indeed, current elsewhere in Renaissance poetry.

1 Come, my Childrene dere, drau neir me
  To my Love vhen that I sing;
  Mak your ears and hairts to heir me
  For it is no eirthly thing

---

[1] *Music of Scotland*, no. 51 and note.

[2] To be discounted in our review of Montgomerie's practice in court-song making are two devotional pieces whose words have recently been taken as his by Dr Rubsamen ('Scottish and English Music...') although earlier scholarship had carefully refrained from doing so. 'Away vain world bewitcher of my heart – to the tune of *Sal I let her go*' certainly appears in the Ker MS., but so do other pieces demonstrably not by Montgomerie. The tune was a famous one from England and the words rightly belong to Elizabeth Melville, printed in her *Ane Godlie Dreame* (Edinburgh, 1603). 'O Lord my God to thee I cry' was printed by Stevenson from Laing MS. 477, where it is anonymous; he does not attribute it to Montgomerie but to Hume (pp. 229–31 and introduction, §21). Dr Elliott draws attention to it in the Douglas–Fischear part-books of the mid century, words and stave but no musical notes; the inscription of this item, however, may be late. ('Church Music at Dunkell', *Music and Letters*, July 1964).   [3] Cranstoun, p. 238.

> Bot a love
> Far above
> Other loves all, I say,
> Vhich is sure
> To indure
> Vhen as all things sall decay...

In the fourth stanza of the five-stanza text the 'I' of the song is wed to Christ with a ring. The ceremony this brings to mind is the espousal to Christ of one taking religious vows. The piece may reflect Montgomerie's own desire in the last years of his life to enter the religious life and the song may date from his years of exile and hiding—'my Childrene dere' being his companions 'the Bairns of Beath'. On the other hand the verses might have been written for presentation to a religious or for devotional use by a religious community. One need not look far among the poet's acquaintance for a possible recipient. A daughter of his dead patron, Gabrielle d'Aubigny, was for a time betrothed to a Montgomerie kinsman but did not marry, becoming instead a nun at a convent in Berry.[1] ('My Childrene dere' may be members of the community and the imagined singer mistress of the novices.)

The accruing of the sixth stanza turns the poem into a penitential lyric, urging a change of heart from earthly to heavenly love. This stanza may have been the original close of the lyric; but it may on the other hand mark its redirection from a particular to a general use—perhaps from use in private Catholic devotions to currency in the Protestant milieu of Robert Taitt's Sang Schuil at Lauder.

> O my soul therfor repent the
> Of the love thou hadst befor.
> Let his countenance content the
> Since he is the king of glore.
> So shall he/be to the/
> all the being that thou wouldst have.
> In his Love/shall thou prove
> quhat thy heart can voise or crave.[2]

Love-song and song of good life declare their own social context; but we have seen two pieces of Montgomerie's where song may have been instigated in an individual hour of ceremony and of personal concern—to pass later, with a slight modification of wording, into general currency. With the last strophic song of Montgomerie's to be considered, however, the social context is clear. This is a court piece to mark the dawning of a day of tournament, a song of 'joyous entry' to a running at the ring. There is sound precedent in early Tudor music and poetry for

---

[1] Balfour Paul, *The Scots Peerage*, v, 356. Montgomerie's sonnet XXXII is to Gabrielle's sister-in-law, the Duchess of Lennox.
[2] This, the sixth stanza, was kindly transcribed for me by Dr Rubsamen.

the use of song as an aspect of celebration of such contest of arms. John Stevens has shown that the carol 'My soverayne lorde for my poure sake' needs such a setting and he cites another example, which is patently a 'summoning' to the play of arms.[1]

Montgomerie's piece is such a summoning, a kind of martial *aubade*. It gives the rousing joy of a summer morning felt in sound and colour through all nature. 'Corage' is surging up in bird and flower, in human lovers and in contending knights. The climax is the clang, the stamp and the jostling of horses and armed men. Critics of the poem have found it inconclusive, but the piece is by its very nature an 'introit' and the rest is action.

Probably 'the tune' was a popular tune with this opening line known as far back as 'The Gude and Godlie Ballatis.[2] Music for 'The day dawes' was recorded in Straloch's lute-book and appears to match Montgomerie's words. It survives now only as sketchily transcribed in the nineteenth century, however, and reconstruction is unfortunately not feasible.

1 Hay! nou the day dauis
    The jolie Cok crauis
    Nou shroudis the shauis
      Throu Natur anone.
    The thissell-cok cryis
    On louers wha lyis.
    Nou skaillis the skyis:
    The nicht is neir gone.

2 The feildis ouerflouis
    With gouans that grouis
    Quhair lilies lyk lou is   [flame]
      Als rid as the rone.   [rowan]
    The turtill that treu is
    With nots that reneuis
    Hir pairtie perseuis:
      The nicht is neir gone...

5 All curageous knichtis
    Aganis the day dichtis
    The breist plate that bright is
      To feght with thair fone.
    The stoned steed stampis
    Throu curage and crampis
    Syn on the land lampis: [gallops]
      The nicht is neir gone...

[1] *Music and Poetry in the Early Tudor Court*, pp. 241, 392, 405.

[2] 'Hey now the day dawis' was discussed in chapter I as spiritual 'parodie' of a known song; Cranstoun, p. 193.

Sonnets as Song

The Franco-Scottish tradition of court-song making extended from strophic song to include the sonnet in the strict sense of fourteen-line piece. Renaissance poetry in England displays on the whole a distinction of sonnet from song, a separateness of one from the other or a conscious interspersion. The sonnet proper was of course written very frequently as a single-standing piece; but the sonnet sequence, sometimes with songs intermingled, presenting an extended concatenation of poems under some aegis—directed to the same patron or loved person or concerned with the same theme or congenial themes—is rightly regarded as characteristic of Elizabethan England. In Scotland the case is different. Later Castalian writing was to naturalise the sonnet sequence there by translation and imitation from Italian; but Montgomerie introduced the sonnet to *Scottis Poesie* by 1582 at the latest, for a piece for a wedding belongs to that year (L).[1] His sonnet writing looks significantly to Ronsard and, while Ronsard's sonnets were widely known as a sequence in print from 1552 onwards, that first edition included musical settings: *Les Amours de P. de Ronsard, Vandomoys. Ensemble le cinquiesme de ses Odes...le dict livre avec sa musique mise en fin d'iceluy.*[2] It was not as a sequence but as a book of sonnet part-songs that *Les Amours* made its impact on Montgomerie, master maker of the new poetry in Scotland.

Montgomerie wrote seventy sonnets, but they are in no sense a 'sonnet sequence'. They are very varied in matter and style, in tone and in social intention, many of them being occasional pieces. His life-story can indeed be read in them but they were not composed in grand series to present a case or to embody an aspect of his inner concern. Within this variety there are several interesting sonnet-groups or short runs, indicated as such in the Ker manuscript by careful numbering. The longest is of six sonnets, entitled 'A Ladyis Lamentatione' (XXXIII–XXXVIII). There is the verse-letter of five sonnets to Robert Hudson and another to the King, each presenting a closely argued case. In these and in other groups of four the sonnet is virtually a long stanza, and not the longest by any means in Montgomerie's repertory.

We noted that for another Castalian, the musician Thomas Hudson, a complimentary sonnet was a part-song, its music and *incipit* recorded in Melvill's surviving part-book. Such explicit documentary proof, of words underlaid to music or heading a musical part, is not found for any sonnet of Montgomerie's. For several of them, however, there is interesting indication of musical association; all of these are trans-

---

[1] There is one sonnet, an English one, in the Bannatyne MS. Fowler's 'Tarantula of Love' for example, derived from Petrarch, was made presumably after he joined the court circle.

[2] See *Œuvres Complètes*, ed. Paul Laumonier, IV; the music, pp. 190–247; lists of 'sonnetz qui se chantent sur la musique de...', pp. 248–50.

lated, imitated or adapted from sonnets by Ronsard where the French original was in some sense a song.

From their first being made known to the public Ronsard's *Amours* had been seized on by French musicians as apt for setting.[1] In the first edition it was explained that the poet envisaged the pieces as sung and that, accordingly, fine music matching them was made available at the end of the volume, music to four voices by Certon, Le Jeune, Jannequin, Muret and Goudimel. There could be enjoyed to its music the opening sonnet of *Les Amours de Cassandre*—'Qui vouldra voir comme un dieu me surmonte'. Composed by Jannequin, this was a master-setting prescribed also as music to which many other sonnets could be sung: '"Pardonne moy Platon" se chante sur la musique de "Qui vouldra voir".' Later there is a similar directive for 'Heureuse fut l'estoile fortunée'. All three sonnets were translated by Montgomerie (LVII, LVI, L).

For the last we know the social occasion that the Scots poet had in mind, and there is reason to believe that live performance with music graced that day's celebrations. In 1582 'the Lady Margaret Montgomerie' was married to Lord Seton. She was the poet's young kinswoman and Alexander Montgomerie wrote a wedding piece of praise and felicitation, 'Luiffaris, leif of to loif so hie/Your ladyes...' Sir Richard Maitland has this recorded in his manuscript collection, entitling it 'Sang on the Lady Margaret Montgomerie' while its companion piece there is entitled 'A Poeme on the same lady', 'Ye hevinis abone, with heavinlie ornamentis.'[2] Evidently he knew of music to the first, had heard that the epithalamium had been sung. Of such music, however, no trace survives. Now the fiftieth sonnet in the Ker manuscript is entitled 'Of my Lady Seton/M.M.', opening 'O Happy star at evening and at morne' and it is a deft translation of Ronsard's 'Heureuse fut l'estoile fortunée' in the text of 1552.

> Heureuse fut l'estoille fortunée
>   Qui d'un bon œil ma maistresse apperceut:
>   Heureux le bers, et la main qui la sceut
>   Emmailloter alors qu'elle fut née.
>
> Heureuse fut la mammelle emmannée
>   De qui le laict premier elle receut
>   Et bienheureux le ventre, qui conceut
>   Si grand beaulté de si grandz dons ornée.
>
> Heureux les champs qui eurent cest honneur
>   De la voir naistre, et de qui le bon heur
>   L'Inde et l'Egypte heureusement excelle.

---

[1] *Les Amours* in the *chansonniers*: see F. Lesure and G. Thibault, *Bibliographie des Editions d'Adrian le Roy et Robert Ballard*, (*1551–1595*), (C.N.R.S., Paris, 1955).
[2] Cranstoun, pp. 214 and 216. The Maitland MSS. are edited for the Scottish Text Society.

Heureux le filz dont grosse elle sera
  Mais plus heureux celuy qui la fera
  Et femme et mère, en lieu d'une pucelle.

OF MY LADY SEYTON
M.M.

O happy star at evning and at morne
  Vhais bright aspect my maistres first out fand
  O happy credle and O happy hand
  Vhich rockit hir the hour that sho wes borne.

O happy pape, ye rather, nectar horne
  First gaiv hir suck in siluer suedling band.
  O happy wombe consavit had beforne
  So brave a beutie honour of our land.

O happy bounds vher dayly yit she duells
  Vhich Inde and Egypts happynes excells
  O happy bed vharin sho sall be laid

O happy babe in belly sho sall breid
  Bot happyer he that hes that hap indeid
  To mak both wyfe and mother of that maid.

Montgomerie's version renders skilfully the substance of Ronsard's poem but turns the thought differently in one detail and extends two ideas, perhaps for the rhymes' sake, perhaps to meet the particular circumstance of the occasion celebrated. 'Silver suedling band' and 'O happy bed...' are added and 'Si grand beaulté de si grandz dons ornée' becomes 'So brave a beutie honour of our land'.

Does Montgomerie's version sing to the music prescribed for that sonnet in the volume of 1552, the setting for four voices by Jannequin of 'Qui vouldra voir'? A practical test of performing the Scots words to that music shows at once that it does, very comfortably.

The musician has set the two quatrains as stanzas, to the same music. In the French music of the sestet, almost every line of the text has a phrase that is prolonged or repeated in one or other of the voices. The corresponding phrases of Montgomerie's version that fall to be repeated are these: 'yit sho duells', 'O happy bed', 'sho sall breid', 'Bot happyer he', 'To mak both wyfe'. The joyous iteration of these phrases is central to the celebratory nature of the wedding piece. In musical illustration (7) the phrases repeated within square brackets are in a different category. These are editorial, introduced to accommodate the extra syllable of the feminine rhymes, where the mute 'e' is sung as a separate syllable.

Musicians other than Jannequin set 'Heureuse fut', notably Anthoine de Bertrand. The text he uses is that of 1552 except that it reads 'fruit' for 'filz' in the twelfth line.

7. O HAPPY STAR[1]
(Heureuse fut)

MONTGOMERIE (RONSARD)　　　　　　　　　　　　　　　　　　　　　　　JANNEQUIN

[1] Music: *Les Amours de P. de Ronsard* (1552), facsimile in *Pierre de Ronsard: Œuvres Complètes*, ed. Laumonier, IV 230–5. Bar 5, alto, note 3: F. (K.E.)

His setting was current in a French song-book that was in high favour at the time of the wedding, printed in 1576 and 1578 and again in 1587.[1] When we submit Montgomerie's version to the test of being sung to Bertrand's music, however, we quickly find difficulty in underlaying the words. Again the musician has set the quatrains as strophes but there are repeated phrases, the first two iambs in the second and third, sixth and seventh lines. Montgomerie's version does not match this rhythmic structure: 'Vhais bright aspect', 'First gaiv her suck' would sing to the music of the repeated phrases; 'O happy wombe' would pass but 'O happy credle' necessitates a split at the stressed syllable 'cred' which makes nonsense to the listening ear. There is a similar difficulty at the tenth line where 'Egypts' must be split. Montgomerie's sonnet is not 'amoene' to Bertrand's music.

The famous first sonnet to Cassandre 'Qui vouldra voir comme un dieu me surmonte', whose music by Jannequin is a 'master-setting' prescribed for many others in the *Amours* of 1552, is rendered by Montgomerie as 'Vha wald behald him vhom a god so grievis' (LVII). The Scots poet's version is close in matter; he has, however, chosen a different rhyme scheme in the sestet, *cc, dd, ee* against Ronsard's *ccd, ccd*. The rhythmic structure has been reproduced and the Scottish version is

---

[1] *Les Amours de Ronsard Mises en Musique à quatre parties par Anthoine de Bertrand*, printed in Paris. Modern edition: H. Expert, *Monuments de la Musique Française au temps de la Renaissance*, v, no. XXVI.

amoene to the four-part setting of the French sonnet, as a comparison of the verbal phrases repeated in the music will show. Montgomerie has also sought to reproduce that alternation of masculine and feminine rhymes advocated by Ronsard.

This sonnet was one much revised by Ronsard. When set by Bertrand the piece closes with the figure not now of 'the poisoned dart' but of 'the dying swan'. The last revision, as printed in 1584, gave as the concluding lines

> Et cognoistra que l'homme se deçoit
> Quand plein d'erreur un aveugle il reçoit
> Pour sa conduite, un enfant pour son maistre.[1]

This version was certainly known to the poets of King James' court for it lies behind the ending of the famous sonnet by Mark Alexander Boyd

> But twice unhappier is he, I lairn...
> Led by a blind and teachit by a bairn.

Again we note that it was not the up-to-date musical setting or the recently printed volume that Montgomerie knew, but the words with their music from the 'song-book' *Amours* of the mid century.

Montgomerie translated another sonnet for which the music of 'Qui vouldra voir' was prescribed, 'Pardonne moy, Platon'. These two sonnets are far apart in Ronsard's sequence, but with Montgomerie they come side by side, third and fourth in a numbered group of five; the other three are apparently original pieces and the whole presents an argument of love. 'Excuse me Platon if I suld suppone' (LVI) has Ronsard's substance in the octave while the French sestet has been adapted to new argument in Montgomerie's little sequence. This shows at least that a link existed in Montgomerie's mind between 'Qui vouldra voir' and 'Pardonne moy Platon'—and such a link must surely have lain in the music the two French sonnets shared. The existence of French part-music for two of the five sonnets may well have enhanced this little 'handful' if it was designed for presentation to a lady.

Other sonnets of Ronsard rendered into Scots by Montgomerie had musical associations in France. 'So suete a kis yestrene fra the I reft' (XLI) is from 'Harsoir Marie', a piece in extended sonnet form—seven quatrains and a sestet—entitled by Ronsard 'Chanson'.[2] A *chanson* music matching this longer form (the quatrain's music being repeated) would be viable for Montgomerie's piece, but such a setting is yet to be traced. 'Suete nichtingale in holene greene that hants' (LI) entitled 'To the for me' is linked with Ronsard's 'Rossignol mon mignon qui part cette saulaye'.

---

[1] *Les Œuvres de Pierre de Ronsard*, Laumonier, I. I owe the recognition of Boyd's line in Ronsard to Mr Robin Lorimer.

[2] 'Harsoir Marie' is one of several *chansons* and other pieces interspersed with the sonnets in 'Amours de Marie': 'Le Second Livre des Amours' in *Œuvres Complètes de Ronsard*, ed. Gustave Cohen, I, 162.

This had been printed in the *Continuation des Amours* of 1555 and was a favourite song of the time, set by three musicians.[1]

Critical discussion of Montgomerie as a translator initiated by earlier scholars went seriously astray when the Scots versions were laid beside the Ronsard sonnets as they appeared revised in later printings, say that of 1584.[2] (That edition was of course too late to be relevant to the nuptial song of 1582.) Montgomerie was accused of extensive 'stealing' from the French poet. He can now be shown as a gifted and accurate translator 'par lettre' who may yet groom his new Scots version for an occasion in mind or divert the argument of a French sonnet to suit the whole sense of a new poetic unit. His departure at times from the rhyme scheme of his original may be caused by exigencies of language—but it may be the result of adaptation of the sense. He shows himself aware of many of Ronsard's recommendations for fine sonneteering.

A new claim may now be made, that on occasion he certainly reproduced in his Scots poem the rhythmic structure of the French, traceable as it is in the placing of the caesura in the line; this made his version usable for singing to the part-setting devised for Ronsard's piece by the musicians of the 1552 volume. Such reproduction of rhythmic structure may have been regarded as an aspect of the makar's skill in translation/imitation or it may have been undertaken expressly so that the resultant text should be a song to the French music. In either case a consideration of Montgomerie's work has brought to notice a consciousness of rhythmic structure in the sonnet among French and Scottish poets of this time. The topic will be enlarged on in later pages. (By the way, this question of rhythmic structure is one worth raising for Italian–English sonneteering earlier in the century.)

I am not one to deny, withal, that Montgomerie was on other occasions in makar's debt to Ronsard for theme, idea or turn of phrase. Thus at the Renaissance was admiration expressed. Thus did a nation's 'new poetry' grow in substance and skill.

'THE TUICHESTANE IS MUSIQUE': PRACTICE AND THEORY

Montgomerie, master poet in the Scots court, learned his art not only from earlier traditions of *Scottis Poesie* but also directly from the poetry of France, above all from the work of Marot and Ronsard. In the court of Scotland before the Reformation it had been a skill of court-song devising to render into Scots strophic song from Marot's French in a form that matched the music of existing part-song or was

---

[1] The music by Boni was six times printed between 1576 and 1594, that by le Jeune in 1572 and twice later, that by Maletty in 1578. Montgomerie's introduction of the sonnet form as song in Scotland comes at the peak of this printed song's currency.

[2] E.g. Stevenson, *Montgomerie*, appendix C, 'New Sources of Montgomerie's poetry'.

amoene to setting in a *chanson* style. A generation later Montgomerie exercises this skill in strophic song sometimes from Marot, as has been abundantly shown. I have suggested that this skill is exercised also in his sonnet-writing where he is naturalising in Scots sonnets of Ronsard that were famous part-songs.

This skill amounts to the reproduction of the rhythmic structure of an original along with the reproduction or variation of the metrical form and the re-creation of the meaning. This skill we have glimpsed, already, in translation or in *parodie*, in 'answer' or in *imitatio* and likewise in the matching of words to music. It may be lightly dismissed as a technique easily picked up or as a knack coming naturally to a poet with a fine sense of rhythm and, in all likelihood, an excellent ear for music. I believe there was more to it than acquired knack or happy talent, that certainly by the mid century this skill was regarded as a professional one consciously exercised, developing at the point where the art of poetry touched the art of music. As such it was patently considered in the edition of Ronsard's *Amours* of 1552.

The nature of this link as it was regarded in France at that time was made clear in the introductory matter of that volume, the 'Avertissement au Lecteur' signed by Ambroise de la Porte, son of the editress.

Ayant recouvré le livre des Amours du Seigneur P. de Ronsard et le cinquiesme de ces Odes avec aultres siens opuscules: Et puis après entendu que pour ton plaisir et entier contentement il a daigné prendre la peine de les mésurer sur la lyre (ce que nous n'avions encores apperceu avoir este faict de tous ceux qui se sont exercites en tel genre d'escrire), suyvant son entreprise avec le vouloir que j'ai de lui satisfaire et pour l'amour de toy, Lecteur: J'ai faict imprimer et mettre à la fin de ce présent livre la Musique sus laquelle tu pourras chanter une bonne partie du contenu en iceluy.

As 'sonetz qui se chantent sur la musique de *Qui vouldra voir* (Jannequin) he names ninety-six of the pieces, sixty for *Nature ornant* (Jannequin) and four for *Quand j'aperçoy* (Goudimel).

Reviewing these, the modern editor of the critical edition adds several more to these groups as 'singable' to their master-setting and withdraws one or two others as having been listed in error; these last, however, he notes as singable to *J'espère et crains* by Certon, which is also printed in the 1552 volume. The modern editor's criterion is clearly stated: he includes or reassigns items 'leur structure rythmique étant identique à celle des autres sonnets de cette liste'.[1] No doubt he has also submitted the words to the practical test of singing to the part-music. This one can do for oneself with any of Montgomerie's versions which have been suggested as singable to such or such an air.

The 1552 *Amours* contains also 'Le Cinquiesme Livre des Odes' and the writer of

---

[1] *Œuvres Complètes*, ed. Laumonier, IV, 189.

the 'Avertissement' goes on to say 'Au reste saches, Lecteur, que tous les Strophes et Antistrophes de l'Ode a Monsieur de l'Hospital se chantent sur la Musique du premier Strophe *Errant par les champs*. Et les Epodes de l'Ode mesmes sus la Musique du premier Epode *En qui respandit le Ciel*.' Both these musics, to four voices by Goudimel, are printed in the volume.

The avowed association of ode and sonnet with music, the writing of these novel forms as 'lyric', 'vers mésurés sur la lyre' was regarded as one aspect of Ronsard's genius as innovator. As a young poet he invited the collaboration of musicians and their art with his. It was natural to suppose that Montgomerie, who knew *Les Amours,* was conscious of the extensive link with music presented in the 1552 volume and of the significance of the listing there of Ronsard's sonnets and odes for singing with this or that part-music; it was natural to suppose also that he should perceive the several patterns of rhythmic structure according to which the sonnets grouped themselves for musical association and that he should seek to reproduce such pattern in his Scottish versions.

It is highly likely that this topic of words and music, the relation of poetic to musical form and of the musician's art to the poet's was among those discussed in King James' circle of poets and musicians. The Castalians had to hand 'brethren' professionally trained in music sacred and secular in Blackhall, Lauder and the Hudsons. Preserved in the memory of 'old Scot', poet and musician, or in their memory of his pieces, they had the tradition of court-song making from an earlier Scotland. They had also to hand the custom, current in contemporary Scotland, of making parodies of courtly part-songs, the 'changeit' songs of 'the Gude and Godlie Ballatis' reprinted in 1578, 1600 and 1621. Now it would appear that through Montgomerie, Lauder and Thomas Hudson with their French background, as through the perfect French scholarship of the King, the Castalians had access and indeed recourse to the influential precedent of a volume of sonnets (and odes) of the new poetry of France whose pieces grouped themselves according to their rhythmic structure under one or other of several master-settings of part-song to four voices. This would mean that they were cognisant through de la Porte's words of this skill—of making 'vers mésurés sur la lyre'—as an avowed practice in words for music by the renowned poet of the Pléiade which he was to proceed to apply to new forms of poetry.

A consciousness of this topic and of ample and distinguished examples illustrating it may explain one of the young King's findings on poetic practice expressed in his 'Reulis and Cautelis...for Scottis Poesie' of 1584. King James treats of the importance in making poesie of 'flowing', by which he appears to mean the management of the rhythm. He says that the poet, having observed certain regularities of stress, must in this matter go on to trust his own ear, but that 'the tuichestane [thairof] is

Musique'. His treatise devotes a substantial paragraph to 'sectioun', which may be equated with *caesura*. He indicates the place at which the 'sectioun' should fall in shorter or in longer lines and recommends that it come always on a long syllable, a long monsyllable or the long [and presumably final] syllable of a polysyllable.

The reason why it must be the one or the other is for the sake of the Music, because when your line is either of fourteen or twelve feet it will be so long drawn out in the singing that you must rest in the midst of it, which is the sectioun. If the sectioun fall, say, at the first syllable of a poly-syllable the music shall make you rest in the midst of the word in such a way as to cut the one half of the word from the other.

This was above all to be avoided. 'For shorter lines the Music makes no rest in the midst of them. Only take heed that the sectioun in them show somewhat longer than any other foot in the line—except the second and the last as I have said before.' He appreciates, then, the importance of the caesura in shaping the rhythmic structure of the line. From this would follow that the placing of the caesura plays a part also in the rhythmic structure of the whole poem.

King James did not himself write words to match part-music, nor was he musical. He may mean by 'Musique' the quasi-musical sound-pattern of verses intoned aloud. (He was accused of chanting the numbers when he read verses aloud, in accordance with his early teaching under Buchanan.) I think it is very likely, however, that by 'Musique' he means music and that he is envisaging the verses sung. If this is so he may have in mind a correspondence of words with music in any of several styles of song known at his court, words made to a tune, the single vocal line with instru-mental accompaniment or the single vocal line in a homophonic part-song apt for voice and instruments. In any of these cases the musical phrasing following the rhythm of the words would make a breathing-space at the 'sectioun' of the longer line. His argument that sound and sense must be consonant at the pause or breaking-point, that the splitting of a word fatally interrupts the sense, holds good even more strongly if he had in mind the four-part settings characteristic of Castalian song-making in the Franco-Scottish tradition. Such consonance is crucial where phrasal units of words and music may be repeated by one voice-part or another with points of musical imitation. That such phrases should be verbal/musical units momentarily isolable without destruction of the sense is indeed 'the touchstone' of successful song-making. It is by recourse to this touchstone that the majority of the sonnets of *Les Amours* may be separated out and grouped into one or the other list with its master-music. By it may be tested whether such and such a translation, parodie or 'answer' was written with the part-music of the original in mind. By it may be tested whether a poet writing a strophic song had a particular part-music in mind to which all his stanzas should be singable or, another possibility, whether a poet made subsequent stanzas of a piece each to match his first stanza and so be *amoene* to part-music that might be devised for it.

The examination of the different structural patterns of Ronsard's sonnets in *Les Amours* of 1552 revealed that the differences lie in the placing of the caesura within the lines of the octave and the sestet. The variation of pattern made by these 'isolable' phrases, often repeated in the music, sometimes showing points of musical imitation, operates within part-song that is over-all of the *chanson* form. Indeed, such variation of musical patterning within the form has been described as characteristic of the *chanson* style. I hazard the suggestion that in the developing *chanson* style of the mid century there was, running alongside the skill of the musician, a related interest and skill in poetry, both French and Scots. This is seen demonstrably in Ronsard's sonnets as printed in 1552 where it has arrived at conscious expression in the grouping of the sonnets. It is perceptible at roughly the same time in *Scottis Poesie* where a northern poet is translating a *chanson* or where Alexander Scott is matching words to *chanson* music. Alexander Scott, we recall with added interest, was in Paris in 1540, conceivably in touch with musical circles there.

The craftsmanship of Scott, this makar who we believe was a trained musician, served as a bridge from the earlier to the later phase of Franco-Scottish style in the making of court-song. It is possible that, in addition, Scott's work provided during the intervening years of troubled history and disrupted court culture a sensitive line of contact between skills in *Scottis Poesie* and developing styles in French court-song. In this matter of court-song devising, Alexander Montgomerie's friendship with 'old Scot' (possibly as early as 1567 or 1568) may have been as fortunate and as fruitful as was his association with James Lauder or other musicians of the court.

For the Castalians music was 'music practical' not 'music speculative'. This was natural among court musicians practically trained with a King widely learned but not himself musical and a poet who was surely profoundly musical but was as surely not instructed in music at an academic level. Only in Blackhall, educated in the music of the Catholic Church, might an awareness of 'music speculative', be presumed: it is possible that his setting of the Helicon tune to four voices 'for' 'The Cherrie and the Slae' was meant in part to advance the tune—and its words—to participation in 'four-part perfection' and thus in universal harmony. The nearest approach to 'speculative music' is probably the young King's phrase 'the tuichestane...of all is Musique': it may have looked beyond Ronsard's theory to the reference in Plato. But of overt consideration of music in its philosophical aspect there is none on record. The 'Art of Music' surviving incomplete from this epoch is eminently practical.

A Franco-Scottish tradition in court-song devising has been displayed in terms of skilled musicianship and of printed part-song, of *chansonniers* from the French printers of royal privilege that disseminated to a wide European public the courtly part-song of France. Such song was composed predominantly in the *chanson* style, a style, be it said, that was based ultimately on the court-dance. We have seen three 'lyric' forms, strophic song, sonnet and ode, touched by this way of song-making in France and therefore apt to be conditioned by it as Franco-Scottish style developed in Scotland. We turn now to another quarter whence influence was felt in the devising of Scottish court-song.

LOOKING TO ENGLAND: THE DANCE-SONG TRADITION

While much of Montgomerie's court-song making was done in traditions present in an earlier Scotland with bearings taken on France, two extended and accomplished stanzas he used have no overt affinities with the *chanson* of French printed song-books. For them parallel or forebear must be sought elsewhere. One is the fourteen-line stave in which Montgomerie couched his major poem, the meditative-narrative *The Cherrie and the Slae*. The other, that of 'Melancholie', is the longest and most intricate of his verse forms and has a certain affinity with the ode. To both a pattern of three traces is fundamental, a pattern of dance and dance-song prominent at the time. The first, being made as was Maitland's ballat 'to the tune of the Banks of Helicon', has links with the dance-song tradition of broadside currency in England. For the second the music *as song* has not been found outside Scotland but appears in English instrumental sources, where it has strong associations with the dance. To study Montgomerie's devising of poems in these stanzas, then, we must look to England and to the dance-song tradition there.

Castalians concerned with the devising of court-song were well aware of the poetry, music and dance of Tudor England and not only from the printed page. Montgomerie and Lauder both spent time in England in the early 1580s, the years that saw the dance and its music introduced to the ruder habits of the northern court. The court violars were 'Inglismen', though one of them was a good scholar of French.

The currency of dance-song widespread in England in the sixties, seventies and eighties of the sixteenth century was not a currency of printed music. No extensive printing of part-books recorded it like the *chansonniers* proceeding in their hundreds from the King's printer in France. Indeed, as music of the dance it was of a different ambience; it was only informally committed to paper at all, and then the 'tune only' —other parts being improvised. If the tune reached print it was only rarely—and then roughly at the foot of a broadside sheet, appended as the tune to which the ballad was to be sung. The words—thanks to broadside circulation—were kept before a wide public. The tunes were used as a basis for instrumental compositions and these were committed to paper—but that takes us from our theme.

The words of such tunes enjoyed a printed currency beyond the broadside sheet. Over the years that saw the flourishing of this way of song-making there was printed and reprinted more than once a miscellany of verses matching such tunes. This was *A Handefull of Pleasant Delites* compiled by Clement Robinson and others, the first poetical miscellany to appear since Tottel's of 1557. Where the verses in Tottel were courtly in provenance, those in the *Handefull* were, many of them, more popular in origin and appeal.

Robinson's volume gives us valuable insight into the nature of the dance-song tradition as a way of song-making. Its title runs:

> A Handefull of pleasant delites
> Containing sundrie new Sonets and delectable Histories
> in divers kindes of Meeter
>
> Newly devised to the newest tunes that are now in use, to be sung;
> everie Sonet orderly pointed to his Proper Tune.
> With new additions of certain songs to verie late devised
> Notes not commonly known, nor used heretofore.

(1584; earlier issues 1566? 1568?)

A number of the tunes named for the verses in this important popular collection were dance-music, as we can tell by the titles given: the Quarter Braules, the Cicilia Pavin, the Blacke Almaine, the New Almaine. The remaining tunes are almost all of them 'derived from dance-tunes frequently of foreign origin and often in a musical style first cultivated by continental instrumentalists'. This John Ward has shown in his study 'Music for *A Handefull of Pleasant Delites.*'[1]

As far as we can discern, the practice of song-making worked in this way: for a known tune, that was characteristically a dance-tune, words would be written; in some cases several sets of words for a tune were circulating at the same period, on occasion reaching print as broadsides. Such a set of words thereafter could be set to a new tune—the measure of the dance, its essential sequence of rhythms, significantly persisting. In such a chain of music-and-words, words-and-music, it is the instigation of a form that we are interested to discover; thereafter, the impact of that form on poetic composition. Such of instigation form not infrequently arose with the introduction or devising of a novel pattern of the dance, and its use spread as the dance became the fashion. A well-attested instance of composition in this mode by a court poet is Ben Jonson's poem 'Hear me, O God' which was written to Alfonso Ferrabosco the younger's 'Four-note paven'.[2]

[1] *Journal of American Musicological Society*, x (1957), where the dates of Robinson's volume are discussed.
[2] *Musica Britannica*, IX, no. 63.

The Helicon/Cherrie stanza

About ane bank, whair birdis on bewis	A
Ten thusand tymis thair notis renewis	
Ilke houre into the day,/	
The Merle, and Maveis micht be sene,	A'
The Progne, and the Phelomene,	
Whilk caussit me to stay:/	
I lay and leynit me to ane bus	B
To heir the birdis beir,/	
Thair mirth was sa melodius,	B'
Throw nature of the yeir:/	
Sum singing, sum springing,	C
With wingis into the Sky:/	
So trimlie, and nimlie	C'
Thir birdis they flew me by.	

The famous Helicon/Cherrie stanza has been much discussed.[1] In 1898 T. F. Henderson gave an account that long proved influential: 'Montgomerie's metrical invention consisted in adding to a ten-line stave, very common in England from the beginning of the fourteenth century, a peculiar wheel borrowed from a stave of the old Latin hymns. It may be that the song was written to fit some old sacred tune or the tune may have been written by some court musician.'[2]

Recent discussion of the stanza by Ian Ross is couched in terms essentially literary although he suggests that it is related to music and the dance.[3] Analysing the stanza on the page as of three sections, he brings forward interesting forerunners for each metrical section. Indeed the three traces of the measure, separately or combined with others, are easy to find in poetry Scots or English of the period (1566–1600); but it is the concatenation of precisely these three paired rhythmic units that makes the particular character of this measure in whatever medium it be found. It may survive in words without music or musical association, in words underlaid to music or designated 'to be sung to' a named tune. It may be found recorded in musical notation as a 'tune' or as a cantus or other part of a composition designed for voices and instruments or for instrumental playing only. Expressed in any of these ways the measure will be recognisable and will declare or maintain its rhythmic identity. Our study, then, must be of the currency in Britain at this time of this rhythm-sequence in words and in music and of the part Montgomerie's pieces play in that currency. We can observe the impingement of this measure on poet or musician as a stimulus or a shaping spirit in creative composition.

[1] By Sibbald, Stenhouse and Laing.
[2] *Scottish Vernacular Literature: A History*, pp. 256–7. 'The dumb wyff' is not in this stanza.
[3] 'The Form and Matter of *The Cherrie and the Slae*'.

Currency in England. The earliest text from England in the pattern we have called the Helicon/Cherrie stanza is the broadside ballad *Of the horrible and wofull destruction of Sodom and Gomorra. To the tune of the Nine Muses:* 'The Scripture playne doth show and tell', printed about 1568 in London.[1] The matter—scriptural, moral and admonitory—does not consort well with the name of the tune which, to be thus quoted, must have existed before and must have been at the moment at least moderately well known. In fact this ballad has the air of morally upbraiding certain ladies of Parnassus Hill, who may well have figured in an earlier courtly-amorous set of words to the designated music. The moral ballad was printed more than once about this time.

The next example comes in Robinson's *Handefull* of 1584 and it may have been included also in the earlier issues of the volume those presumed as of 1566 and 1568: 'A proper sonet/of an unkinde damsel to her faithful lover/To the—Nine Muses.' A popularity of some twenty years is established in England for this measure, for its named tune (which in these entries may well be a dance-tune) and for its stanza.

'The Nine Muses' was the title of a dance also. Choreography for performing it is included side by side with pavans and galliards, in the 'way of making basse-dances' described in the first part of the manuscript Rawl. Poet. 108 in the Bodleian Library.[2] This choreography has been linked with the 'proper sonet...to the Nine muses' by John Ward in his article mentioned earlier, though he does not try out the one against the other. He suggests as a possible occasion of the devising of the dance 'A maske of huntars and divers devisses and a Rocke, or hill for the ix musses to Singe uppone with a vayle of Sarsnett Dravven upp and downe before them' given before Queen Elizabeth, 18 February 1565.[3] John Ward, however, working perhaps from the Rollins index and not from the ballad texts, has missed the clue that leads to other words for the 'Nine Muses' dance-song, and thence to matching music. He reports with disappointment that music matching 'The Nine Muses' has not been found.

The stanza is found with an interesting extension of its pattern in a printed volume of verses of 1581 that was near-courtly in style: *Devises: Delightful Discourses* of Thomas Howell, a poet on the fringe of the Sidney circle. An old-fashioned makar, this his third volume of poems differs little in manner or content from his first book of 1568.[4] Although untouched by the new poetry of England that had declared itself in print in Spenser's *Shepheardes Calender*, Howell's *Devises* was widely popular and

---

[1] *Stationers' Register*, ed. Arber, I, 439; reprinted in Lilly, *Ancient Ballads and Broadsides* (2nd impression 1870), pp. 125–9.

[2] See Appendix IV for choreography and interpretation.

[3] See A. G. Feuillerat, *Documents Relating to the Office of the Revels in the time of Queen Elizabeth*, p. 117.

[4] *The Arbor of Amity*, 1568; *New Sonnets and Pretty Pamphlets*, 1581; *Devises*, 1581 (reprinted 1906, ed. Walter Raleigh, with a biography in the Introduction); 'A Dreame', p. 80.

had its importance. His poem in the 'Nine Muses' stanza, 'A Dreame', is a miniature love-vision in late medieval style. The poet sleeps and sees in a pavilion a goddess decked in green and white (the Queen's colours). She is Venus in her court and to her come lovers male and female to make their pleas. He himself presses forward to plead his case, but there is a thundering and he awakes, wondering what is the meaning and what the validity of vision or of goddess in her court. He concludes that 'fansie' is persuading him to be ever faithful to his love.

This poet was at one point in the service of 'Bess of Hardwick' who was for years 'gaolar' to Mary, Queen of Scots. The year of the volume's publication saw Montgomerie in England, in all probability on business touching Queen Mary. The poets may have met. At all events it is clear that Montgomerie knew Howell's book. Not only does 'A Dreame' have the stave and the love-vision genre in common with the poem maturing in the Scots poet's mind, but on another page of *Devises* he would find a poem of two trees that were converted from bearing hard or sour fruits to bear 'fruites of more delight'.

Metrically 'A Dreame' is in eight stanzas of two patterns alternating: stanzas 1, 3, 5 and 7 exactly match that of the 'Nine Muses' ballads—that of 'The Cherrie and the Slae'. The others are in a different measure, of two traces—the first self-repeating, the second single. No tune is named for 'A Dreame' but elsewhere in his volume Howell writes 'to a' named tune that is characteristically a dance-tune.

Two stanzas will take us once through the metrical pattern:

1 To clime the high and hauty hyll
  Where Poets preace for praise by skyll
    I list no labour waste:
  The water Nimphes I never vewde
  Nor Ladies of the Lake persewde
    That poore Acteon chaste:
  King Arthurs knights long since are fled
    In force that did excell
  And all those Ladies nowe lye dead
    Whose lyves olde Poets tell;
      Revealing their dealing
        I purpose not to wryte
      But dreaming a straunge thing
        Loe heire I doe recyte.

2 A fayre Pavillion finely pight
  In sleepe appeared in my sight
  Amidst whereof in greene and white
    The goddesse sate of all delight
  Beset about with Ladies true
  Which did to her suche service due

167

As few I deeme the like hath seene
Idone to any earthly Queene.
Her Nimphes all they were
Of such comely cheere
Helen's face may give place
Where they appeare.

In choosing for his 'Dreame' this twofold strophic verse-pattern Howell, drawing on the dance-song tradition for a first stave, may have invented the second as a kind of metrical companion or variation of the first. It is also credible that he invented the very idea of a twofold stave, which appears for the first time in this decade. (It had appeared earlier in the music for Ronsard's odes in the 1552 *Amours*.) But to me it seems overwhelmingly more likely that it was from one and the same line of tradition—that of dance-song—that he drew all three, the idea of a twofold stave, the 'Nine Muses' dance-song measure and the pattern of the second stave, conceived as counter-measure.

The dance-pair—the *double-danse* of France—was a mode long established in England; the pavan-and-its-galliard had come in during the 1540s. There the pavan, a stately dance in duple time, was followed by its galliard, a lively dance in triple time usually to a related music. By 1580 the strict dance form of pavan-and-galliard, characteristically a measure of eight bars each, is found alongside the dance-pair in other forms of which the *passemesure-saltarello* is one.

No music has come to light that matches precisely Howell's second stanza. But it remains possible that he knew the double pattern as the tune, or the music, for a dance-pair based on 'the Nine Muses', the tune in duple time followed by a related music with change of tempo. Such tune or music may already have had a set of matching words—may already have been in currency as a dance-song.

This extended twofold stanza of Howell's has been curiously misjudged by a distinguished critic who missed entirely the poet's metrical intention. Sir Walter Raleigh in his edition of the *Devises* believes the poem to be composed in the same stanza throughout. He describes it as

written in a Quartorzain stanza the invention of which has commonly been attributed to Alexander Montgomerie who used it in his poem of *The Cherrie and the Slae*. The *Devises* were published some sixteen years earlier than Montgomerie's poem but the clumsiness and imperfection of Howell's handling of the metre show that he was not the inventor of the stanza. Perhaps it came to him from Scotland in the retinue of Queen Mary; perhaps both Montgomerie and Howell are copying with very different degrees of metrical skill from some unknown original.

As Raleigh believes the poem to be written in the same stanza throughout he naturally finds clumsiness and imperfection in the metrical execution! Certainly Howell is not the delicate metrist that Montgomerie is. Certainly there is slight variation, say in presence or absence of internal rhyme, between one matching stanza and another; but this is to be found elsewhere in words written to a tune. Howell's metrical patterning is over-all regular, though his stressing is pleasantly informal rather than severely Tudor-iambic. The nature of the 'unknown original' I have tried to indicate as without doubt entailing music. Hence Raleigh's 'copying' is better described in the phrase 'writing to a tune'.

The extension of the 'Nine Muses' stanza by Howell may well testify to a development about this time of the 'Nine Muses' dance measure into the longer pattern of a dance-pair.

The measure of a dance-song might be abbreviated as well as extended, witness the rubric for the broadside ballad 'Philosophers Learnings', 'A proper newe Ballad... songe to the tune of Lorde Marquis Galyarde or the first traces of Qui Passa'.[1] An abbreviation of the Nine Muses/Cherrie measure, its trace one and trace three along with their matching sections of music, make up the music of 'Now God be with Old Simeon', which is printed as a catch in Ravenscroft's *Pammelia* of 1609; this was known also as 'Hey Jolly Jenkin' and as such is referred to in 1592 and is current in 1604.[2]

This break-up and reassembly of the tune and its stanza form may mark a decline in England of the 'Nine Muses' measure following on a falling from favour of its dance. In 1592 also William Warner used for his 'My Mistresse' the Nine Muses/ Cherrie stanza, but adapted: line 2 and line 5 are now omitted which means that the words are no longer 'orderly pointed' to match the music; indeed the words may have been written at several removes from the tune.[3]   There is no suggestion in Warner's volume of musical association. By this time the whole tradition testified to by the reprintings of Robinson's volume would be overcast by the vogue of more recent dance forms. In some circles, moreover, the musical ear was already taken by the rush into favour of the printed madrigal.

Currency in Scotland: measure and words. It was in 1568 that Bannatyne recorded Maitland's ballat made to the tune of the 'banks of Helicon'. Not long afterwards in the north the same stave was used for a rough soldierly satire on the side of Queen Mary and against the Congregation, 'Ane Ballat of ye Captane of the Castell' concerning the determined defence of Edinburgh Castle in February 1571.[4] The measure is precisely that of the contemporary English broadsides 'to the tune of—the Nine Muses'. Therefore from 1568 onwards there were either two separate tunes matching

---

[1] By W. Elderton in *A Collection of 79 black-letter ballads and broadsides*, ed. Lilly, p. 138; i.e. alternative musics for the 'new ballad' were the whole measure of the named galliard or the dance-tune 'Qui Passa', the opening sections only.

[2] Chappell, II, 484, 784.   [3] Warner, *Albion's England*, book VII; in Ault, *Elizabethan Lyrics*, p. 164.

[4] *Satirical Poems of the Time of the Reformation*, ed. J. Cranstoun, I, 174–9, III, 117–22; also in *The Green Garden*, ed. J. Fergusson, p. 102.

this dance-measure, each widely known, one in the south and one in the north; or there was one such tune that was current under different names in England and in Scotland. Both titles are such as might accrue to the tune after its performance on a notable occasion with pageantry illustrating Mount Helicon and involving dancing. The case for the origin of dance-measure and tune in the 'devisse' with 'a rock or hill and nine muses' made for Queen Elizabeth in 1565 is strengthened rather than weakened by the currency of the northern ballat to the second-named tune. Both names point to the existence of a verbal text treating of such matters, as did the moralising ballad against the ladies of Parnassus Hill.

This very text may be the poem preserved in the anthology of Mary Maitland, Sir Richard's daughter, compiled about 1584.[1]

1   Declair ye banks of Helicon
Parnassus hills and daills ilkon
And fontaine Caballein
Gif ony of your Muses all
Or Nymphis may be peregall
Unto my Lady schein
Or if the ladyis that did lave
Thair bodyis by your brim
So seimlie war or (yit) so suave
So bewtiful or trim
Contempill exempill
Tak be hir proper port
Gif onye sa bonye
Amang you did resort.   (11 stanzas)

'Declair ye banks of Helicon' has the measure, the matter of the muses, and Helicon, 'a rocke, or hill' and its text celebrates some great lady. Of Montgomerie's pieces in this measure one is his delightful love-farewell 'Adeu o desie of delyt' which will be found under-laid to the 'Helicon' music as 49 of *Music of Scotland*.[2] There is no way in which the date of this lyric's writing can be established. But the poet's decision to use the measure for 'The Cherrie and the Slae' can now be attributed to the year 1583 or 1584. It was used on another occasion for a long poem, by Burel, Master of the Scots Mint, his *Ane Passage of ane Pilger*.[3] This poem was printed, but in what year is unknown; it is more likely that a minor poet used the stave after, rather than before, Montgomerie's 'Cherrie' made its way to fame in the court.

Scotland shows, then, a currency of the measure—its tune referred to as 'the banks of Helicon'—in a variety of verses, moral-scriptural ballat, popular satirical broadside

---

[1] *The Maitland Quarto Manuscript*, ed. W. A. Craigie.

[2] See musical example no. 3.

[3] Burel's 'Ane Passage of ane Pilger' or 'The Passage of a Pilgremer' dates from about 1590. The unique copy, B.M. c.21.b.39 has lost its title page.

and extended narrative piece, over the years 1568 to 1584, the years that marked Montgomerie's progress from early verses to poetic 'mastery' in the circles of King James.

Currency in Scotland: music. No music, as we saw, has so far been found either entitled 'the Nine Muses' or associated with any of the texts in the English currency.[1] Such music, however, may well lie unrecognised as yet in English manuscript record —a quite separate tune, distinct in melodic outline from the music known in Scotland yet also answering exactly the sequent rhythms of the measure under discussion. The tunes may have been different though the dance-measure to which they corresponded were the same. The identity of the two tunes is equally possible, as was mooted earlier—a tune that was well known in England wherever it originated happening to survive only in musical compositions of Scottish provenance.

An early record in Scotland of the tune in musical notation is its occurrence as a tenor *cantus firmus* in a manuscript of about 1570, an 'Art of Music' associated with song-school teaching.[2] Here the 'tune' is preserved; coming in long notes in the new composition it does not there reproduce, though it does represent, the rhythm-sequence of the measure. Then it was current as the tenor part in an instrumental setting believed to be of the same decade, where it bore the title 'the bankis of Helicon'.[3] As the tenor voice in a four-part setting it was inscribed by Thomas Wode in one set of his part-books between 1575 and 1584, as 'About the bankis of helicon, blakehall'; in a later hand in the sister set of Part Books it appears as 'About a bank where birds on bews'; Wode's Quintus Part Book has the tenor part where the text is, explicitly and by directive, 'The Cherrie and the Slae'. The tenor tune in a separate source of 1630–40 is there entitled 'About the banks of Helecone'. The late MS of Robert Taitt has a version of the song to four voices with the first stanza of 'The Cherrie'.

The 'Helicon' tune had already stimulated fresh musical composition, then, on more than one occasion when it was set afresh to four voices by Blackhall of the Scots Chapel Royal in, or shortly before, the year in which we first hear of 'The Cherrie and the Slae'. Both the tune and words to match it were in high favour in Scotland when Montgomerie chose its stave for his major poem and precedent for that stave's use for a love-vision piece was to hand in a recent book of poems from England. Most probably Blackhall's fresh setting was made especially for Montgomerie's new piece, perhaps against its presentation to the King.

Perhaps Blackhall's four-part setting for voices was prepared explicitly for a performance of the piece at court. An instrumental setting already existed well suited to such a project: the music was for the stave, i.e. strophic, and enabled any stanza or any group of stanzas to be sung by a single voice with viols. Blackhall's 'new'

---

[1] Ward, 'Music for *A Handefull*'.   [2] AM in Source List.   [3] See notes to no. 49, *Music of Scotland*.

setting was specifically for four voices. Passages from the poem could be sung in either manner or the instrumental music be played on four viols to introduce and vary the presentation of this dream-encounter and *certamen*, the main body of the work being recited by a narrator and the lively argument of the *débat* 'acted' in character parts. The 'abstractions', Hope and Despair, Danger, Experience and their fellows, may have worn significant costume or head-dress. Passages that suggest themselves for singing are the spring prelude with its 'dream' and the vision of the river and the two trees. (In staged drama music was used to mark the visionary moment.) In the complete version the hymn of thanksgiving at the end would be most impressive if rendered by four voices in part-song—the 'four of perfection' whose concord signified universal harmony.

The question of the poem's performance apart, there was distinguished precedent of music 'for' a long poem, music matching its stave. Such music existed for the romance-epic *Orlando Furioso* itself. Montaigne heard peasants 'throughout Italy... with lute in hand and even the pastoral poems of Ariosto on their lips'. Probably the music he heard used was the 'Italian dittie' matching the stave of Ariosto's poem, 'Rugier qual sempre fui'. This 'dittie' was one of the most important ballad and dance tunes of the sixteenth and early seventeenth centuries, as John Ward has shown.[1] The tune was popular in England as 'the new Rogero' and verses to it appeared on broadsides and in the *Handefull*. Such a precedent may indeed have influenced Montgomerie's choice of a stave for his long poem from among those current with their music in the tradition of dance-song and broadside ballad.

The Helicon/Cherrie music continued a favourite in Scotland until well on in the seventeenth century. Robert Taitt's manuscript, in which it makes its latest appearance, is dated 1676. Over the years that saw *The Cherrie and the Slae* printed four times and once in Latin translation also, the music survived recorded in the part-books of Scottish gentleman or musician, both the Blackhall part-song and the earlier setting for voice and instruments. In England, however, the second decade of the seventeenth century was to see a change in musical thought marked by the coming of the declamatory style in song-writing. With this the long-standing marriage of the Nine Muses/Helicon/Cherrie measure with its stanza form was broken. Patrick Hannay, Scots poet and would be courtier, wrote his long poem, an Italianate-Ovidian romance called 'Philomela', in the *Cherrie* stanza which in the world of *Scottis Poesie* was still an accepted medium for extended narrative. When, however, he had his poem printed in London in 1622 the music he included for it was a fresh composition in the new style.[2] Here the Helicon measure of sequent rhythms, the

---

[1] 'Music for *A Handefull*.'

[2] *The Nightingale...Songs and Sonnets* (London, 1622): copies in B.M. and National Library of Scotland. The title-page is reproduced as plate 1 of this volume.

living shape of the stanza, was no longer operative in the music: you could not dance to it now. This new setting is decorated, Italianate and declamatory. The music for the stanza—it is still only one stanza long—is through-composed, ignoring or overriding the earlier traces and their repetitions. Even the rhymes in their fall are now played down instead of being dwelt on as before. Music and words for Hannay's 'Philomela' are in *Music of Scotland* as no. 65, 'Walking I chanc'd into a shade'; but with this piece the 'Helicon stanza' is no longer the living shape of the poetical/musical form.

This gesture of Patrick Hannay's in presenting with a long narrative poem music to which its stanza could be sung has been misunderstood and made fun of. Agnes Mure Mackenzie quizzed 'a fine pair of Galloway lungs' in Hannay if he could sing one hundred and twenty-four stanzas.[1] But music for the long poem matching its stave, such as was reported in Italy in the sixteenth century, is found in Scotland well into the seventeenth—witness the recording in manuscript music-books of items that, to judge by their entitling, must be music for the old-type romances such as 'Graysteil' or 'Sir Lemuel' or for some rehandling of these knightly adventures going under their names. Music for 'Graysteil' was in Gordon of Straloch's 'Playing book for the lute' of 1627. Music for 'Sir Lemuel' is in Robert Edwards' Music-Book of the 1630s.[2]

We noticed earlier that in England the measure, the significant rhythm-pattern, that was the soul of the Helicon stanza form, was falling from use by 1600. Northern taste was more retentive of old style. In Scotland the cultivation of courtly music after the court itself had departed continued but ceased to renew itself in new writing or composition and gradually declined. A conservative taste retained the Helicon music, but this music, though still current as part-song in 1676, never reached print. It was probably at this point that the tune passed from a context of part-song taught in school into oral tradition in Scotland, meeting there that other live tradition of dance-song, the 'Scots native air'. And in this milieu of native air the tune would appear to have persisted while over the same period its matching stanza form was printed again and again as the popularity held of *The Cherrie and the Slae*. Certainly the tune lived on, as did its stanza, into the eighteenth century and so into a new chapter in the tradition of song-writing in Scotland.

'MELANCHOLIE, GRYT DEPUT OF DESPAIR'

The long stanza in which this poem is written is the most complex 'devised' in King James' court. The piece is the epitome of the makar's craftsmanship of which the monarch was so proud; but such complexity of patterning was not always

[1] *In Scottish Poetry*, ed. Kinsley, p. 62.　　　　[2] Printed and discussed in Elliott and Shire, *Scottish Studies*.

173

invented by his makars—was not always devised in terms of words and metre alone, as the full story of the Nine Muses/Helicon/Cherrie stanza has shown.

'Melancholie' is written out in the Ker manuscript as four staves, the first exactly matching the third, the second the fourth. In other words it consists of two identical double-stanzas, the first part of each stanza contrasting in metrical pattern with its second part. These two contrasted patterns are of much the same duration in time; the second part has something of rest or finality in its close, both in metre and in sense. In form over-all the piece shows a kind of movement and counter-movement, strophe and antistrophe, twice performed. The poem as a shape on the page immediately suggests to the eye an ode.

Kinship with dance form is again fundamental: both stanza patterns used are of three traces or self-repeating sections and the movement and contrasted movement encompassed by the long double-stanza strongly suggests the dance-pair of the epoch that we have already seen embodied in words in Howell's 'A Dreame'. It calls to mind also that movement and counter-movement present on a larger scale in masque and anti-masque.

From this double-stanza used by Montgomerie we can take bearings on the 'new' and 'learned' verse form, the ode, and at the same time on a pattern prominent in contemporary courtly dance. Ronsard's *Amours* presented the ode (his fifth) as part-song along with the double 'aire' to which it should be sung. In England a convergence can be seen of the idea of the ode with the rhythmic patterning of a dance in performance—and that in the work of a learned court poet whose practice has already proved relevant to our enquiries. Ben Jonson's piece 'To the immortall memorie and friendship of that noble paire, Sir Lucius Cary and Sir H. Morison' is in form a sequence several times repeated of three staves entitled 'The Turne', 'The Counter-turne' and 'The Stand'. These are the strophe, the antistrophe and the epode of the regular Pindaric ode, but the terms Jonson uses are, significantly, English terms of the dance.[1]

While no music survives underlaid to the text of 'Melancholie' or bearing its name, verses in precisely the same stanza form are found as part-song in Robert Edwards' Music-Book. The song is there incomplete in musical transcription, words, underlaid to a cantus part: the text is 'The flaming fyre that in the furnace fries' one double-stanza. The matching bassus part survives in the Melvill Bassus Part-Book, marked 'four voices'. The song, its two inner parts reconstructed, is no. 47 in *Music of Scotland*; the words, two double-stanzas, are from a manuscript collection of

---

[1] Jonson's is a 'death piece' for Morison and therein may lie the kinship with dance, which featured in such ceremonial commemoration. It is at the same time 'the most truly Pindaric' of Jonson's odes (R. Shafer, *The English Ode to 1660*).

Castalian poems, where the piece is entitled 'Songe'.[1] Mure of Rowallan had 'The flaming fire' in his family part-book, grouped with songs to four voices among the Scottish items. To its music he wrote a spiritual song, 'Help, help O Lord, sueit saviour aryse'.[2] I have not the slightest hesitation in taking Montgomerie's 'Melancholie' as words matching this music also.

The music was well known in England of the times, but as instrumental music only. It appears in the Fitzwilliam Virginal Book as Edward Johnson's 'Old Medley' set for keyboard by William Byrd.[3] An arrangement for lute entitled 'Johnson's Medley' can be studied in *An Anthology of English Lute Music* (1953) edited by David Lumsden, who gives details of other settings and sources. Well-known music, then, existed in the very pattern of the Scots poet's metrically intricate piece and that music had, in its nature as in its title, a strong affinity with dance.[4]

The interesting form of the music is remarked on by David Lumsden in his commentary. He describes it thus:

$$\text{MINOR } \tfrac{4}{4} \text{ AA' BB' CC'} \qquad \tfrac{3}{4}\text{ DD' } \tfrac{6}{8}\text{ EE' FF' MAJOR GG'}$$
$$\text{eight bars each} \qquad\qquad \text{four bars each}$$

The double-dance or dance-pair is clearly present in this form, which declares itself as a movement in duple time then a counter-movement in triple time, the last section, Major G G' (four bars each), being somewhat in the nature of a coda or 'stand'.

The part-song version current in the north has a slightly simpler structure:

$$\text{MINOR } \tfrac{4}{4} \text{ AA' BB' CC'} \qquad \tfrac{6}{4}\!:\!\tfrac{3}{2}\text{ DD' EE' FF' GG'}$$
$$\text{8 bars each} \qquad\qquad \begin{array}{cccc} 2 & 4 & 4 & 4 \end{array}$$
$$\text{bars each}$$

G G' is still in the nature of a coda or 'stand', but not major. The change of time is here not quite so complex, for there is in the song no change of time-signature within the triple-time section such as apparently occurs in the lute music.

The term 'medley' was known to the Renaissance epoch as a way of presenting or grouping forms of the dance, a type of dance-arrangement—witness Francis Bacon's simile 'as when galliard-time and measure-time are in the Medley of one Dance'.[5]

---

[1] National Library of Scotland: MSS. Hawthornden, XIII, fols. 16a–35. This manuscript is discussed in detail in chapter VII.

[2] *Works* of Mure: S.T.S. ed. Tough; see chapter 8.

[3] *The Fitzwilliam Virginal Book*, ed. J. A. Fuller Maitland and W. Barclay Squire, no. CCXLIII. See also *Tisdale's Virginal Book*, ed. Alan Brown, p. 188; he notes a setting by Byrd in 'Forster's Virginal Book'.

[4] E. W. Naylor, *An Elizabethan Virginal Book*, p. 206, described the piece as there recorded as a pavan and galliard; but Professor Dart points out that the 'pavan' betrays its incompleteness by not consisting of eight bars.

[5] Bacon, *Sylva* (1626), §113. The musical form called 'the medley' has not yet been completely studied, but see the notes to Lumsden's edition. It is a kind of instrumental piece based on dance-pairs, consisting characteristically of five sections: dance-pair, dance-pair repeated or second dance-pair, and coda. (A resemblance to the pattern of the ode is apparent.) Scottish examples extend the medley to dance-song and suggest a kinship with the '*fricassée*' of France. See *Music of Scotland*, nos. 30 and 36 and notes.

Measure means in this context a grave or stately dance if not the pavan itself. 'Medley' as a musical form analysed by David Lumsden reflects exactly the sequence of sections in Montgomerie's poem and in the other sets of Scottish verses mentioned. The music matches the words rhythm for rhythm, note for syllable, long note for heavy stress. In 'Melancholie', moreover, such musical matching is not the end of the artistry: the sense of the words corresponds with the spirit of the music, for the course of the poem as its meaning unfolds changes emotional temper in sympathy with change in musical time. Even the feeling of repose, finality, in the musical coda or 'stand' is present in the content and tone of the corresponding lines of verse.

Here is the text of the poem marked in self-repeating sections, the 'traces' of the dance:

1 Melancholie, gryt deput of Dispair   A
  With painfull Pansing comis apace
    Acompanyde with Cair,/
  Quhais artalyie is Anguish shooting sair   A′
  Of purpose to perseu the place
    Vhair Plesur maid repair./
  Presuming to prevaill
    A muster grit they mak.   B
  Amids thair battell bitter Bail
    Displayis his baner blak,/
  Quhais colours do declair
    To signifie bot smart   B′
  Quharin is painted cold Dispair
    Quha wrings a hoples harte;/
  Quhilk armes on far so uglie ar   C
  And ay convoyd with Dolour and with Duil/
  That Hope micht skar if they com nar   C′
  And fray ane hart perhaps out of his huill/

At D D′, the change to triple or 'galliard' time, Montgomerie's words quicken pace; battle is joined with shooting by Sighs and Sobs that burst the bulwark of the lover's breast. At E the triple time gives the attack and stout defence by Courage and Constancy.

2 For Sighis and Sobbis of shooting hes not ceist/   D
  Quhill they haif brasht the bulwark of my breist/   D′
    And cryis, 'Go to, the hous is win   E
    Melancholie, cum in!'/
    Thoght Rigour then he rekles rash   E′
    Yit Curage bydis the brash;/
  And then the hairt whilk never yeild   F
  Of Constancie hes maid his sheild,/
  Quharon thair shaftis and sharpest shottis   F′
  Lyk hailstanes aff ane studie stottis./

Yit pairties proudlie baith pretend   G
The victorie in end:/
And so the tyme but treuis they spend   G'
To assaill and to defend./

The counter-movement in galliard time ends with F'. In GG' the conflict is commented on; this pair of traces is the 'stand'. The piece continues:

3   The rendring reid whilk bouis with everie blast
In stormis bot stoupis, when strongest treis
   Ar to the ground down-cast;
Bot yit the rok whilk firmer is and fast
Amidst the rage of roring seas
   He nevir grouis agast:
   The busteous blast he byds
     With watring wavis and huge
   Whilk ramping ouer his rigging ryds
     Bot can not caus him budge.
   What reks then of the reid
     Or of the trees what reks?
   The rok remanes a rok indeid
     Whilk nather bouis nor breks;
So sall my harte with patient parte
Remane a rok all rigour to resist
And sall not start to suffer smart
For ane quhom to obey I count me blist.

4   Yea tho' I had a hundreth thousand hairts
And eviry hairt peirc't with als mony dairts
   And evirie dairt thairof also
   Als mony shafts and mo,
   And eviry shaft thairof must needs
   To haif als mony heeds.
And evirie head als mony huikis
And evirie huik als mony fluiks
And evirie fluik in me war fast
So long as breath of lyf micht last
   I suld not seme for shame to shrink
   For hir, of death to drink
   Whais angels ees micht ay, I think,
   Revive me with a wink!

The second half of the poem takes us through the music again. In stately 'measure' time the rock remains unyielding, the heart firm, and strong single syllables matching the long notes mark the patient resistance. Again at DD' comes a change of rhythm and the 'galliard time' is a spirited protestation of love. The conclusion, the 'stand', is grandiloquent—but not solemn. The medley dance-song ends with a compliment and 'reverence', looking to the lady, catching her eye in whose honour the piece was devised.

Montgomerie's poem is words-for-music and the music is music-for-movement, an arrangement of dance measures. So too is 'The flaming fire'. It is overwhelmingly likely that Montgomerie's sensitive ear and the ear of the less gifted anonymous poet met the music of the 'medley' and each devised a dance-song to match it, words to be sung for a company dancing or to be sung by the dancers themselves. The relationship of the danced movements to the words may have been formal association —the dancing being of figured dances of the time, combined, perhaps of a pavan-galliard. But in the case of Montgomerie's medley 'Melancholie' the meaning of the words is so intimate to the movement implicit in the music that I strongly suspect we have in his lyric the residue of a particular 'devisse', a pastime or danced mime. In 'Melancholie' a conflict of matters of love has been embodied in words that match the dance-and-counterdance pattern. 'Abstractions'—Melancholie, Despair, Hope, Heart; even the rock, the winds and the waves—advance or retire, endure or prevail as do figures in a masque. Montgomerie's piece may have been not only words sympathetically framed to sing to the dancing of figured dances but an action-song, the movements performed to the music enacting the sense of the song. The dancing performers may have worn significant costume or head-dress.[1]

'The Flaming Fyre' is a dance-song with words that address a lady. But in 'Melancholie' we have, I suggest, the device of a conflict of love enacted in her honour, an action/song/dance. With it we may step across a threshold from 'medley' dance-song into the world of *ballet de cour* and masque.

Montgomerie's courtly making was the chief source of words for court-song of the Castalian epoch but it was not the only source. Poems in an earlier style, by another member of the company at court or by an unknown hand also found their music at this time. Of the songs whose words are by Montgomerie fresh composition in the court can be claimed in some cases for music as well as for words; in others, derivation from earlier song can be established for words, for music or for both.

Final judgment on the quality of the songs as songs had better wait the day when access to the music in the Taitt manuscript can be granted and the nature and merits of the settings found there, inscribed late in the seventeenth century, can be studied together with the records made much nearer to the time of the songs' first devising. But it has proved possible to outline and characterise a repertory of northern court-

[1] Precedent for my conjecture of a device with participation of costumed figures moving significantly to music is to be found in the 'magnificences' in the Scottish court celebrating the baptism of Prince Henry. Fowler's description of these in his *Works*, II, 169–95.

song enjoyed under the young King James and to link it at points with song-writing in contemporary England and in earlier and contemporary France. Transmission of influence has been traced operating in various modes, through the journeying poet who was musical or the musician foreign-trained and travelling abroad, through the far-disseminating broadside, the wandering tune and the fashionable dance with its intricate matching stanza, through verse in printed collection or miscellany from England and the *chansonniers* from France, especially the influential *Amours de Ronsard* of 1552 with its music.

Several topics have emerged: that the intricacy of the stanzas devised by the Castalians and praised by the King had, at times, sources other than the metrical ingenuity of the makars; that the *Amours* of 1552 made known in Scottish courtly circles the sonnet as part-song, drawing attention to rhythmic structure as a feature to be embraced in translation or imitation; that the planning of 'vers mésurés sur la lyre' apparent in Ronsard's volume and its preface, though phrased in the classical vein of the Pléiade and its new poetry, yet corresponded to a practice long established in France and in Scotland in the devising of courtly part-song and its spiritual 'parodie'; that a poem cast in a dance-song stave was thereby apt for live performance in divers ways, from strophic song or dance-song for figured dances to modes of greater complexity involving words and music, movement and 'acting', modes which may have provided entertainment in a northern court of small resources such as was provided in the circles of wealthier monarchs by the developing *ballet-de-cour* and court-masque. With several of these topics discussed, gates have been opened rather than avenues explored—the medley form, musical affinities of the ode, and the live presentation with music and action of pieces by Montgomerie in the Scots court.

For some of Montgomerie's songs the nature of the social occasion they voiced has proved discernible. Sometimes a particular piece has seemed most fully explicable in terms of words and music devised against some special day, such pieces passing later into general currency with minor but significant changes in the words. As the songs were reviewed the notion built up of an audience both in the court of the time and beyond it that took pleasure in part-song, 'love-song or song of good life' enjoyed for its own sake.

The happy conjunction of poet and musician at court together and in the King's grace seems to have been the factor that contributed above all else to the flowering of court-song in Scotland—Montgomerie in touch with Lauder, with the Hudsons or with Blackhall. The possible presence about the court of 'old Scot', poet and in all probability trained musician, with his experience in France and his memories of court-song in the earlier years of the century, is also significant. The time of flourishing was short. The years after the King's marriage in 1590 to a Queen who loved diversion and had attendant ladies from Denmark and from France would seem to offer warm encouragement to musician and poet and frequent demands for dance or fresh devising. But in the later 1580s and 1590s Montgomerie was in displeasure or absent in prison abroad and Lauder much abroad. 'Old Scot' if he lived so long, would by this time be old indeed. The poet in royal favour was Fowler, whose verses give no sign of being *amoene* to music. He it was who then planned the court 'Maskardes' and all record of his work has perished save for fragments of the descriptions of the celebrations at the Queen's coronation or the Prince's birth. Perhaps there was indeed a fine repertory of songs in this later decade also and they were thrown aside in 1603 when the courtiers took horse for England. Perhaps here a repertory was thus lost before it passed into wider currency as the songs of Montgomerie had done. Such ill-luck in timing may explain the fewness of the extant *airs-de-cour* as well as the failure to survive intact of the madrigals of the northern court—for which we have bass-parts and titles only.[1]

Certainly we are remarkably ill-informed about court-song and its making between the time of Montgomerie's falling into royal displeasure and the year when the King and his court left Scotland. An attempt to throw light on court-song making after Montgomerie, however, will be made in the next chapter, which treats of two younger Castalian poets, hitherto little known, of whom one certainly was praised for his songs.

[1] In the Melvill bassus part-book.

7

YOUNGER CASTALIANS: A COURT-TRADITION OF POETRY AND SONG-MAKING CONTINUES

THE ROLE played by Alexander Montgomerie in the making of court-song has been traced to its last expression in his lifetime—his song-allegory that assailed the Protestants and was revised to impugn the King. To that King Montgomerie had been 'maistre of our airte' of poesie and leading makar of the Castalian band. Who else learned the art from him? Can we see his skills in sonnet- and song-making transmitted to any younger poet with whom he was in personal touch? If so, the court tradition of *Scottis Poesie* and song can be shown descending to a second generation.

Twice in Montgomerie's poetry there is mention of a young disciple. In 'Displeasur', a lament written while he was in disfavour and 'barred the court', he calls on a younger poet to help him bring his verses to a telling close. (Such an invitation was a recognized form of compliment between one makar and another.)

> Nou, Sone, since I must smart
> Thou of my age that art
> The staffe—
> Evin MURRAY myne
> Len me a lyne
> To end my epitaph.
>
> Cranstoun, pp. 200–2

Again, among the sonnets of the last group evidently composed when Montgomerie was in exile in the westlands there is one prefaced by the couplet

> To my old Master and his yong disciple
> Tua bairnis of Beath, by Natur taught to tipple

A disciple is to seek, a poet who was a generation younger and closely associated with him both in life and in art. In the affair of the taking of Ailsa Craig those named as confederates were 'certain Montgomeries, Murrays and Stewarts, being papists'.[1] The young disciple of the late sonnet could credibly bear the name of Murray and be one and the same with 'Murray myne', poetic 'sone'of the lament.

For Montgomerie's 'Murray myne' we lack a Christian name. Can he be convincingly identified with the M[aster] J. Murray to whom an earlier sonnet had been addressed—the sonnet 'Flie louer, Phoenix', that warns a courtier-poet against flying too high in pursuit of the King's favour—of being 'burned out' in his service? This was written evidently after Montgomerie had himself had a taste of such destruction, say after 1585.

> Flie louer, Phoenix. Feirs thou not to fyre
> Invironing the aluayis-upuard ayr?
> Which thou must pas before that thou come thair
> Wharas thy spirit so spurris thee to aspyre
> To wit, above the planetis to impyre
> Behind the compas of Apollo's chayr
> And twinkling round of burning rubies rare
> Quhair all the gods thy duelling do desyre...
>
> Cranstoun, XXXI.

The terms are discreetly figured but intelligible if we note Montgomerie's recurrent idiom: Apollo's chair, as we saw earlier, is not only the sun-chariot and seat of poetry but also the throne of King James of Scotland and the 'twinkling round' the ruby crown of the realm.

To establish the identity of this Master J. Murray from references in court records proves difficult because of a ubiquity of Murrays in royal service. He must be distinguished from John Murray of Cockpool, who rose quickly to favour from about 1580 onwards, gained a place in the Bedchamber of the Scots court and won lands, later to enjoy great influence in the English court of King James as Viscount Annan: *that* John Murray nowhere is styled Mr (Master of Arts), nor is it clear that he was a poet.[2]

References to a Mr John Murray, however, appear in state papers of the year 1592.[3] He is in disrepute, named as a follower of Lord Francis Bothwell, that flamboyant and ambitious adventurer, cousin to the King, who after bouts of high favour at court was finally outlawed for conspiracy.[4] Bothwell fled abroad in 1595; several of his associates were taken and imprisoned. It is not impossible in that age and day that the Mr John Murray found as Bothwell's companion in desperate exploits should appear also as companion of Montgomerie's years of exile—even as confederate in the affair of Ailsa.

So far the matter of identifying Montgomerie's poetic disciple, Murray, has proceeded by conjecture. Fortunately precise news of a Master John Murray, Scots

---

[1] *Cal S. P. Scotland*, XII, no. 454.

[2] Balfour Paul, *Scots Peerage*, I, 227.

[3] *Cal. S. P. Scotland*, X, no. 769; XI, no. 257.

[4] Bothwell, see Willson, *King James* p. 100.

poet at one time in royal favour, is easy to find at the other end of a life-span which was, apparently, shortened by disease and misfortune. In 1615 there died in London in miserable circumstances a M. John Murray not in good odour with the King but beloved and admired by literary Scots both at court in England and at home in the north—'John Murray, Albiones sweetest swaine' 'He died the 11 of Aprile, 1615'. This note in the hand of the poet Drummond of Hawthornden is written below a sonnet on John Murray's poetic worth composed by Sir William Alexander of Menstrie and sent in a letter to Drummond:

> Mourne Muses, mourne, your greatest gallant dyes
> Who still in state did court your sacred traine
> Your Minion Murray, Albiones sweetest swaine
> Who soor'd so high, now low neglected lies.   [(low) or 'sore']
> If of true worth the world had right esteemd
> His loftie thoughts what boundes could have confind?
> But fortune feard to match with such a mind
> Where all his due and not her gift had seemd.
>   Faire nymphes, whose brood doth stand with Tyme at strif
>   Dare death presume heavens darelings thus to daunt?
>   To flattering fancies then in vaine you vaunt
>   That you for ever will prolong a lyf.
>   He gracd your band and not your bayes his brow
>   You happier were in him, he not by you![1]

Sir Robert Ayton, too, wrote moving lines on Murray, the poet and his ill fortune:

> *Epitaphum Joannis Moravi*
>
> Huc quicunque venis, disce hoc ex marmore quam sit
>   Invida virtuti sors et iniqua bonis.
> Moravius nulli Musis aut Marte secundus
>   Post varios casus hâc requiescit humo.
> Primum aulae malefida fides, mox carceris horror
>   Tandem hydrops misero fata suprema tulit.
> Hydrops crudelis, carcer crudelior, aula
>   Saeva hydrope magis, carcere saeva magis;
> Unica mors clemens, quae hydropis carceris aulae
>   Tot simul et tantas finiit una cruces.
>
>   (*Deliciae Poetarum Scotorum*, 1635)

And J. Dunbar in his *Epigrammaton*, printed in London in 1616, paid tribute to the poet recently dead.

[1] Hawthornden Papers, vol. XIII: printed in *Works* of Drummond (1711), p. 151. See *Poetical Works of Sir William Alexander* ed. Kastner and Charlton (1921), reissued by S.T.S. 1929, II, 540.

Centur. III. LXXV.   Io. Moravij Epitaph.

Mortuus haud ille est magnus Morravius: ille
Mortuus est quem mors imperiosa rapit:
At morti in Musas, aeternaque munera Phoebi
Imperium non est; ille Poeta fuit.[1]

A poet, a Master of Arts and a soldier, his life at court bringing favour then disgrace followed by imprisonment and disease: this is surely the same we glimpsed earlier soaring rapidly and dangerously into royal favour in Montgomerie's cautionary sonnet, surely the same that was poetic disciple to the older poet. The motivation behind his conduct remains unclear—how he rose and why he fell. But exploits shared with Bothwell or confederacy with Montgomerie—either could have earned him a harsh prison sentence and the King's lasting disfavour; the King in 1615 thought that Alexander praised his verses too highly.

Something of a life-story has emerged of a younger Castalian who learned his art from the 'maistre' and shared a similar course of fortune. What of his poetry has survived?

Certain sonnets signed 'I.M.' or 'John Murray' did reach print, all of them congratulatory pieces prefacing the work of fellow poets who were fellow Scotsmen. One greets the publication in Edinburgh in 1603 of Sir William Alexander's *Tragedie of Darius* and includes the lines

Yet none of all hath so divinely done
As matchlesse Menstrie in [his] native tongue.

Murray praises Menstrie as a Castalian writing neo-classic poetic drama in Scots. We do not now value very highly as poetry the *Monarchick Tragedies* of Alexander of Menstrie and we may doubt whether such mutual admiration of the Scots at court implied either acumen in the critic or excellence in the poet. A sonnet by John Murray 'To my louinge Cousin Da. Murray' prefaces '*The Tragicall Death of Sophonisba*' printed in London in 1611 by Sir David Murray, Scoto-Brittaine.[2] (It was dedicated to Prince Henry in whose household he served.)

Faire Sophonisba on her tragike stage,
(To death, or bondage worse than death design'd)
Doth shew the greatnesse of a proud grieu'd minde,
Th'ambitious thoughts of *Scipio* to asswage:
With courage farre aboue her sex and age,
She quafs the cup her loue-sick Lord propin'd.
By which although her liues-thred was untwyn'd

---

[1] Dunbar has also (*Cent.* III: LXXI) '*Epigrammaton*: Ad Ioannem Morravium, Jacobo regi à cubiculis int. etc.', but this may well be Murray of Cockpool and its phrase 'o Musae spes' signify patron, not poet.
[2] Sir David Murray of Gorthy, *Scots Peerage*, I, 465. His *Poetical Works*, ed. T. Kinnear (Bannatyne Club, 1823).

Yet she triumphs aboue the Roman rage:
Thrice happy Queene, and more than happy thrice,
Who finds a rare Physition with such skil,
To rob the Fates of thee there lawfull prize,
By vertue of his euer-liuing quil,
  And makes that poyson which bereft thy breath,
  By power of his pen, to poyson death.
        Your louing Cousin
        John Murray

Below it stands a sonnet 'To my kinde friend Da. Murray by M. Drayton'.

When Sir David prints his CAELIA, *Containing certaine Sonets*, probably in the year 1611, he includes two 'to the right worthy Gentleman and his louing cousin M. Iohn Murray'.

While Eagle-like upon the lofty wings
Of thy aspiring Muse thou flies on hie
Making the'immortall Sprites in loue with thee,
And of those Ditties thou so sweetly sings,
Where quaffing boules of their Ambrosian springs
And sweetest Nectar, thou divinely stayes:
Low by the earth (poore I) sings homely layes,
Till like desire of fame me upward brings,
Then borrowing, from thy rich Muse, some plumes
Icarian-like beyond my skill I soare,
While coming where thy songs are heard before,
My lines are mockt, that thine to match presumes:
  And thus I perish in my high desire,
  While thou'rt more prais'd, the more thou dost aspire.

                    Idem

Inrichèd sprite by great *Apollo* crown'd
With cirkling wreaths of stately laurell Bayes.
Scorning as't seemes that thy inchanting layes
Should haue their praise but of immortall sound:
For heau'ns seeing earth so be thy songs renown'd,
Draw up thy sweetest Ditties to the skies,
Whose well tun'd notes *Phoebus* t'his harpe applies:
While as his chariot wheels about the Round.
And thus thy divine-sprite-inspirèd Muse
Hath made thee here admir'd, belou'd aboue,
She sings so sweetly that she doth infuse
Wonder in mortals, in the godhead loue:
  No maruell if thy songs b'admired then,
  That yeeld both musicke unto gods and men.

The examples we have of John Murray's sonnets come from print in England after the Union of the Crowns: all three factors may have affected the form and style of the poet's writing. The patterns of the sonnet he uses are not the Castalian—*alias* Spenserian—but two varied schemes of his own. These variations are reproduced in the pieces of compliment by his 'cousin' Sir David Murray, no doubt as a gesture of admiration. Both Murrays show the current fashion for the compound word, 'lives-thread', 'divine-sprite-inspirèd'; in both writers the language is English though traces of Scots grammar remain. The important point is the emphasis on Murray as a writer of 'songs', 'that are sung', 'that yeeld music'; 'ditties' meant specifically 'words for music'.

Even allowing for rhetoric, pity and sentiment, blood-relationship and the clan-nishness of the 'poets of Scoto-Britaine', we may conclude that Master John Murray was a goodish poet and a respected sonneteer rightly celebrated among them for his songs. Some body of songs and sonnets must have been known beyond the few pieces surviving with his name. Indeed, a volume of his work in manuscript was owned by Drummond of Hawthornden and presented by him to the library of the University of Edinburgh. It appears in the catalogue of books made in 1626 as 'John Murray. Certaine Sonnets' but unfortunately there is no volume now traceable to correspond to that entry.[1] Verses of his, however, may have survived elsewhere.

Of a Castalian poet, Master John Murray, we know the reputation and the life-span, say before 1570 to 1615. The poet's 'cousinship' to Sir David Murray of Gorthy implies at least a kinship with Sir David's forebears, who were the Murrays of Abercairney on one side and on the other the powerful Murrays of Tullibardine.[2] The poet's parentage, however, remains in doubt; he may have been illegitimate. If he is the Master John Murray of Montgomerie's 'Phoenix' sonnet he was rising in favour after 1585 and the same man was very probably in disgrace by 1592.[3] On both counts he is very likely to have been the poetic 'sone' of the older poet named in 'Displeasur' and possibly the 'young disciple', a 'bairn of Beath'. Is there anywhere a corpus of poetry of this era lying anonymous containing pieces that might on these findings be claimed as his lost work?

[1] No. 26 in the catalogue. Mr Finlayson, Keeper of Manuscripts, most kindly made a fresh search, but in vain.
[2] G. H. Johnston, *The Heraldry of the Murrays*, reveals no full cousin that can be he; nor does *The Scots Peerage*.
[3] Stevenson, *Montgomerie*, introduction, §22, identifies Master J. Murray of the 'Phoenix' sonnet with the 'Maister Johnne Murray' who 'partyed' with Bothwell and with the sonneteer of the lost Drummond MS. Westcott, *New Poems*, introduction, pp. ix, lxxxvi, lxxxvii, identifies John Murray, sonneteer and cousin of Sir David, with 'John Murray, a gentleman of the King's privy chamber (no authority cited) and with the poet who died in 1615. The bedchamber reference may derive from Dunbar's epigram *Cent.* III, LXXI and be inapposite. See chapter 7, p. 184, n. 1; 'John Murray, groom of the bedchamber', *Register of the Privy Seal*, VIII, 594 (anno 1609) is Cockpool.

AN UNCLAIMED REPERTORY OF CASTALIAN SONGS AND SONNETS

The most extensive collection of Castalian poetry whose authorship remains unknown is a book of some thirty poems, originally a separate manuscript, now bound with miscellaneous papers of Secretary William Fowler.[1] It is gathering of verses carefully compiled in a clear hand of the seventeenth century—the same throughout but for a possible change at the last few items. There is no formal title, but an inscription 'Sindrie verses and some of his ain (own)' appears to belong to this collection. Its contents were printed along with the *Works of William Fowler* as 'poems of doubtful authenticity'. The editor judged them 'too good to be his'.[2]

On the last page of the manuscript is a monograph, hitherto unnoticed: M, with W or, possibly, I. W.M. is probably William Murray of Dysart, courtier to King James in England and to King Charles, known as a writer of verses and Sir Robert Ayton's friend. The manuscript appears to be a collection of verses by more than one Castalian poet, verses valued by W.M. to which pieces of his own have been appended at the close. It contains sonnets and lyrics some of which can be shown to have musical associations. This repertory, manifestly Castalian in language, style and content, has until now stood apart; none of the poems was known elsewhere in manuscript or print save one of the closing pieces—a fine song found in another context set as a declamatory air. The language of the verses is literary Scots, here and there 'Englished' as if in expectation of publication in print. The entitling is probably contemporary with the compilation.

The book opens with an 'Ode' on May.

> 1 As Maye most worthy we doe call
> Of all the moneths in the year
> As Maye doth comforte creatures all
> And make them looke with lyvelye cheare
> As Maye so brave the soyle adornes
> With bewtye that the heaven it scornes
>
> 2 Right so my love most worthye is
> Of everye lyffe that I have seene...

In matter and in stanza-form this recalls the famous piece, favourite part-song of the Scottish courtly repertory, 'O lustie May'. It has no overt refrain; nevertheless the words could sing to the part-music. There is, moreover, in its second line a complimentary echo of the earlier song, the quotation of a complete line.

---

[1] National Library of Scotland: Hawthornden Papers, XIII, fols. 16–32, 35. This volume also contains the sonnet on Murray's death. The papers are bound in some disorder and the letter with the sonnet may have been closely associated with the collection of poems.

[2] *Fowler's Works*, I, 337–90; the poems are numbered I–XXXIV. Commentary in vol. III.

The literary style is that of the last quarter of the century in Scotland. The earlier 'Hail May' poem had kept an aureate glitter from the end of the Middle Ages, the years of 'The Thrissil and the Rois'. Instead of the visual glistering of 'Phoebus schene' this poet uses abstract qualities and argues with them well, stanza by stanza: May is worthy of praise, right so my love is worthy, the pleasures of May, the virtues of my love, May is 'maie'. Proceeding by parallels in a sound tradition of rhetorical verse that recalls Tottelian making, the poet knows how to sum his thought in a conceit, where the growing tips of qualities flowering forth become the manifold tongues of praise for his lady, Maye.

The last stanza is an interweaving of May the month, 'maie' the May-lady of festival, May the girl beloved, 'may' the verb of hope or expectation and 'maying' the flower-festival and joyous entry. This knot is made with poetic artistry, for in the verb 'unfold' is summed the effect on the winter cold, on the lover, in the fresh shoots of living things and in the feeling of celebration with which the whole poem moves.

> 5 And as she is the maie that maye
> Transform to Maye my winter colde
> So nowe in Maye some mayenge daye
> I hope she maye my cares unfould
> That I in prayse of hir maye saye
> 'Loe, all my ioyes began in Maye'.

This is a Scots Castalian song—there are Scots rhymes—possibly written with 'fine music' in mind, deriving consciously and gracefully from a tradition of Scots song-writing that had been established by the midcentury and recalling Scott's skill in the virtuoso cadenza. With this tradition is now combined the rhetorical patterning familiar in Tudor poetry. Where Scott flourished rhyme and alliteration in his climax, this poet shows concentring power. The outcome is a fresh style of Scots making, based on a Renaissance pun.

Number xx of the poems 'The flaminge fyre' is entitled 'songe'. Indeed it is a courtly part-song and one in the forefront of Castalian song-making, as we saw. With these words to the four-part music it continued a favourite into the seventeenth century. As words written to match music this is a prentice piece beside Montgomerie's, as we suggested earlier. If the words are read aloud apart from the music, rhythms and metrical patterns declare themselves as component parts; heavily iambic hexameter or fourteener, even 'Poulters' measure remodelled as to rhyme, are felt in which the words had first arranged themselves, the lines first taken form. The poem bears one or two characteristic turns we shall come on again—the interposed 'madame', the unhackneyed rhyme, the telling close.

Court-song, Scots or English, is seldom far from this poet's mind. He is fond of quoting a famous line or phrase in a new context, with the conscious gesture he made in 'Maye'. This seems to be done not so much from a wish to 'crib' or to sport peacock feathers as in a spirit of artistic solidarity. Number x, for example, is in theme and content related to the Tudor song 'If cair doe caus men cry'. This piece, recorded in England as early as 1558 for lute and included in Forbes's *Song and Fancies* in the later seventeenth century, was long-lived and in widespread currency in Scotland as well as in England, perhaps disseminated as a broadside.[1] The Castalian poet echoes the well-known title-phrase in his last stanza but he develops the theme in a new way, referring it to the power of time and making it personal.

He pursues the theme in a fresh verse form; the earlier poem was in 'Poulters' measure'.[2]

> 4 If solace make me singe
> Or cares doe cause me crye
> Or if dispayre me stinge
> Or hope me hoyse on hye,
> If hote desyre me frye
> Or coold releive my smarte,
> With bothe content am I,
> And pleased in eche part.
> No tyme shall change my harte;
> My will is in your powers;
> What euer me astarte,
> My harte is onely yours.

The stanza he chooses looks uncommon, a twelve-line stave of iambic trimeters rhyming alternately in quatrains, the rhymes interlinked. To an ear attuned to Scots Renaissance song, however, it has a familiar ring, recalling strongly Montgomerie's well-known 'Evin dead behold I breathe'. Indeed both this piece and no. III in the collection, 'Epigrame', would sing to that music (*Music of Scotland*, no. 55).

His no. VII, 'My dolefull harte the tombe of deadly care', picks up at one point a phrase of the famous Tudor song 'O death rock me asleep'.[3] It is in rhyme royal, the last line repeated as a refrain. Two musics were current for this pattern in the repertory of Scots court-song, that of Montgomerie's 'What mightie motion' and the fine anonymous 'No wonder is suppose my weeping eyes' (*Music of Scotland*, no. 52). Of this second piece there are verbal echoes in the Castalian's song—the 'duilful hairt', the 'sword of sorrow' and the 'storm of woe', but such phrases may of course be poetic clichés common to a group of poets at court.

---

[1] B.M. Stowe MS. 389, for lute, dated 1558 and in B.M. MS. Roy. App. 58 (early half of sixteenth century). See also David Lumsden, *An Anthology of English Lute Music*. The song is in Wode and Melvill's *Roundels* and is reported in the Taitt MS. Words by Surrey.

[2] x. 'If tyme might cause me tyre'; it has no title.

[3] 'O death rock me asleep', words attributed to Anne Boleyn. Stevens (1961): index, no. 231.

This no. VII has further links with court-song of Scotland. Its first stanza opens thus

> My dolefull harte, the tombe of deadly care,
> My wearye ghost, that flickereth to and fro,
> My bailfull breste, the den of darke dispaire
> May witnes well my deip ingraved woe...

The third line appears as the title or *incipit* of a song in Thomas Wode's Quintus Part-Book, entered in the list of additional songs.[1] Unfortunately the section of the manuscript to which this entry refers is now missing and Wode's song remains a 'ghost'. We cannot determine finally what is the relationship of Wode's recorded song to the Castalian's piece. It is just possible that the song in Wode's volume had as its text this very Castalian poem and that one transcriber or the other transposed the two rhyming lines: such slips do occur. If this is not the case then one song echoes a whole line of the other. Altogether no. VII looks like a learner's piece with admired phrases woven in; it bears testimony to the world of poetry and music in which a young Castalian was learning to write songs.

On the strength of this, moreover, other verses in W.M.'s collection can be claimed as sister pieces showing a familiarity with the songs we have discussed, though there is nothing to show that they themselves were associated with music. In these the presence of Montgomerie's influence is tangible, his phrases or his stanzas, often his brand of rueful humour in treating of matters of love. In III, 'Epigrame', the corpse of the lover murdered by disdain declares the approach of the cruel beloved by fresh-bleeding wounds; a new turn of thought is given here to the frequently murdered lover and the 'green wounds' of Montgomerie's verses. IV, IX, XII, and XXIII strongly recall the master poet as do XV, XXIV and XXV, and these last three conclude with an 'advice' or an 'epitaph'. XXIII, 'Enigme', on receiving the gift of a jewel, the lady's picture, has many stock phrases in common with 'The Flaming Fyre' but the thought is more firmly shaped. Why it is called 'Enigme' is not clear to us, but probably we are to understand the golden archer, the bow and the blossom of crystal in which the poet figures the lady's beauties as embodied in the form of the 'jewel' given to her and the lines as presented with the gift. Again the poet gives a new turn to the thought, though we can see clearly the tradition on which he is drawing, that of gifted allegorical gem and matching lines of poetry.

This review is displaying a poet imbrued in court-song with a good feeling for its technique; but I hope a rehearsal of echoed phrases and shared song-patterns will not give the impression of a makar writing altogether at second hand. The feeling that grows firm as one reads on through the collection is of a poet of individuality,

---

[1] Wode Quintus Part-Book: index, 'My baillful breast the den of dark despair'. Straloch's 'My beelful breest' (title-list only) could refer either to this or to a completely different song, 'My bailful briest in blood all bruist' (*Music of Scotland*, no. 51).

emerging from a formative background of late medieval and Tudor poetry joined with the example of Montgomerie. The habit of strophic song we saw in the May ode is marked in poems rhetorically patterned, with the meaning concentrated at one point in verbal conceit and drawing to a close on a pronouncement—an 'epitaph' or 'epigrame', an avowal of constancy or a shaft of ironic humour. It vividly suggests Montgomerie's phrase 'len me a lyne To end my epitaph'. This style is close also to that of the song surviving with its music 'Since that my siches' printed as no. 58 in *Music of Scotland*, whose words are anonymous. And the kinship noted with 'No wonder is' may be interpreted the other way round: what we called 'echoed phrases' may in fact be anticipations, and our unknown Castalian, rather than his master Montgomerie, may be author also of that fine anonymous song.

A song-writer has come to light, then, who was demonstrably a disciple of Montgomerie's and in touch with the styles of part-song that we know were current in the court of King James in the later 1580s and the 1590s. This was before the *air de cour* came in from France, before the madrigal made its belated impact there some time towards the close of the century. 'Thy songs renound' and 'thy sweetest ditties', the praise given to John Murray by his kinsman, could very credibly have been earned by pieces such as these devised in the Scottish court or in the styles of its song-making during the last decade or so of the sixteenth century.

In conclusion no. XXXI, which comes near the end of the collection along with three short pieces manifestly later, could be claimed as a mature production of the 'John Murray' poet, a piece in the 'staitly' style. It celebrates the union of a noble or a royal pair. The occasion described might well be the wedding of Princess Elizabeth and Frederick, Elector of the Palatinate, in 1613, celebrated with great pomp despite Prince Henry's recent death—discharge of ordnance, bonfires, music and dance, the playing of fountains and the pealing of bells. The poet has embodied each festive phenomenon in his verse, the 'brazen bodies' of cannon, the 'symbols of ambiguous voice' and joyous creatures of fire, air, earth and water. He ends with an 'epitaph'— the voice of the bells inviting all to sing with them the words of rejoicing.

The planning of the poem recalls earlier style in its unfolding of the meaning in terms of the four elements—thus implying universality and cosmic concord, but the couplets have a concentration and balance in meaning and rhythm that are an advance on 'Maye'. Here again is the accomplished verbal conceit—'enlightening fame' for the beacons, and for the dance 'joy doth beat the measure of our love'. The organisation of the poem towards a pronouncement at the end is marked. It was clearly a great Castalian interest. (From their work in sixteenth-century rhetoric Sir Robert Ayton learned what he was to do later in the deft concluding paradox of his graceful Cavalier style.)

Whilst brazen bodies breathing flames of fire
So fierclie charge than euen themselves retire,
The noice seemd that which doth so fearfull proue
When lightning guides the thunderbolt of Ioue;
But thowtes more lowde then it did soundes conuoy,
Which shew loue lightned, and the clapp was joy,
    A joy by rauish'd myndes so reall proud   [prov'd]
As proues some mightie influence it mou'd.
This uniuersall sympathie of mynds
10 A great conjunctioune most stronglie bindes;
The lights most glorious of our undersphœres
Are joyn'd in one yet no eclipse appeares:
For both propitious as to cleare our dayes
Doe shyne while thus combyn'd with doubled rayes.
    No wonder then though all thinges act a part
Where joy so naturall is and needes no art:
The fire, the aire, the earth, the water, each
Showes that it feeles the same though wanting speach.
The fire (so scorning a confined flame)
20 Doth blaze in publict as enlightning fame;
The aire, glade messenger of joyfull soundes,
Proude to be beaten entertaines their woundes;
The earth (else dull) is nowe constrain'd to moue,
Whilst joy doth beate the measure of our loue;
The water too, as to confyne them all,
Is link'd to heauen by liquid chaines that fall;
Yea, euen those symboles of ambiguous voice
(For some bells sing, some howl with equal noice)
Now as inspir'd with joy speak clearelie thus:
30 'Joy rings our rowling rounds then sing with vs:
    "Day neuer shin'd so cleare as doth this night,
    Whilst hearts all fir'd with zeale as sunnes give light."'[1]

There are seven sonnets in W.M.'s collection, two of them notably good poetry (XIX, XXI). Another two are set-pieces on the 'heart' theme—one as 'full of hearts' and of alliteration as the poem sent by the lady to Alexander Scott. No. XVI is an anagram sonnet written with deference as to a patroness, one 'Ieane Stuart' of high rank.

Lyke as the heavens with dowries hathe you dect
Aboue the common course of humaine race, . . .
So wish I you (A TRUSTIE ANE) to chuse:
And, mistris myne, if ye my truthe will trye,
Ye shall not fynde a trustier then I.

[1] Corrections on the text read: l. 10, powerfullie bindes; l. 19, whilst scorning.

The lady addressed is very probably the wife of Ludovick Stuart d'Aubigny, second Duke of Lennox, whom she wed in 1598: she had previously been married to Robert Montgomerie, a kinsman of the poet.[1]

Further hints of affinities at court are forthcoming. Two sonnets, XIII and XIV, make a pair, being an exchange of sentiments, the first written covertly as if from a man's hand but embodying acrostic-wise a name in anagram:

A M. A G E M U R N S A Y. A M

This I interpret as Agnes Muray, 'faire Mistris Ann Murrey the Kinges Mistres', to whom the young King James paid service in poetry.[2] (She is named variously as Ann, Agnes or Annas Murray of Tullibardine when her marriage in 1595 to Lord Glamis is discussed in despatches to England.)

The first of the pair is a sad sonnet of a lover forlorn:

> My hart not myne, my harte is from me gone
> Unto that hart first set my harte on fyre
> Regardlesse nowe of all my plaintes and more
> None now companions me but cares alone...

That the writer was actually a woman becomes clear from the poet's reply, which is in affectionate jesting tones as if to a close friend or kinswoman. It begs that the writer will cast off mourning and appear again brightly in company where her beauty gave such pleasure.

> Let us not mourne to lack thy lonesome sight
> Uppon whose lookes so many lookes do reste;
> Hoyse upp our hartes, and cast from the thy geere;
> Tis AGE MURNES AYE and not younge ladyes fayre.

The easy and charming sonnet XXI celebrates a lady in the court whose name is Anna—not the Queen herself, for the terms of praise fall short of royal though the 'peirles pearle' is styled as pre-eminent among a 'troupe of Ladyes' at court. Here again I think it is certainly fair Anna Murray, at one point reigning beauty in the court of Scotland.

> And as she walkt with grave and comly pace
> I askt her name of one came last of all.
> 'Hir name' quod he 'a nimphe of heavenly race'
> 'Thatis trew' quod I 'but what shall I hir call?'
> Quod he, 'if thou so curious be to knawe,
> hir name beginis and endeth with an A.'

---

[1] Or IEAN STEUART: see Scots Peerage, V, 356. An appeal for patronage after the disastrous conspiracy of 1597?
[2] Anna Murray, Scots Peerage, I, 470. See chapter IV.

The inset comment at the end is here not an 'epitaph' or 'epigram' but a naturally worded query and its answer. A Castalian poet of the later 1580s is moving towards simplicity and social 'adresse', along the path to be taken later by Robert Ayton.

One sonnet remains, XIX, which is entitled '4 Sonet. Haruest'. It is the fifth sonnet in the collection, the fourth if we except the acrostic piece that was by a woman: the figure 4 may indicate this as the fourth sonnet from one man's pen. Its delicacy and smoothness enhance our conception of Castalian style.

> Then, Madam, if this longe desyred springe
> may once haue holde within your tender hart,
> What Ioy shall suche automney to vs bringe,
> when bothe shall reape the frute of loues desert?
> howe soone than shall these stubborne stormes depart
> That misted hath the mourninge of myne eyes?
> howe soone may ye, sweit sommer, slake the smart
> That cold dispaire lyke winter made to freise?
> Allas, howe longe with tyme our tyme we leise!
> The springe dothe passe, the sommer dothe expyre,
> Autumnye reapes, with winter all thinge dyese:
> yet for my part no guerdon I requyre,
> Saue with your will I wist to reape the rose,
> For which I haue sustaind so manye woes.

All seven sonnets in the collection are in the Castalian (*alias* Spenserian) form of Scots court-writing of the time. John Murray's printed sonnets, coming from a different epoch and milieu, are not in form Castalian, show a current fashion in language and are no longer in Scots: but this does not preclude his possible author-ship earlier and in Scotland of these pieces. Their prominence in this collection made, as I have suggested, by a kinsman, their intermingling there with lyrics that have musical association—'ditties'—the identity of the court ladies there addressed and the apparent date of composition of some of his poems—all these persuade me to conjecture that here may be a record of 'certaine sonnets—John Murray', who was about the court in the late 1580s, that same that was famed for his songs.

A SECOND 'YOUNGER CASTALIAN'

In the pages of W.M.'s collection, intermingled with pieces in the style we have linked with the name of John Murray maker of songs and sonnets, is a second strain of writing. Again a group of poems declare themselves as one man's work. They are four in number: XVIII, 'Eligye', II, 'Pastorell', XXX, 'Letter of Creseyde to Troyalus' and XXVI, 'His Ladies Dreame'. All four are in the same metre, 'fourteeners', but fresh and freely running like a ballad stanza and once (II) rhymed like a ballad stanza also. Beyond this metrical unanimity there is a lively poetic idiom, an idio-syncratic turn of phrase that marks them off from the pieces that companion them in the volume.

They are neither sonnets nor songs. Their author is not palpably a disciple of Montgomerie's. His work bears no resemblance to the rhetorically patterned Scots–Tottelian style. Yet here, too, is a Castalian writing in literary Scots that has been, in the record we have of it, somewhat 'Englished'. He, too, is composing in the court of Scot-land because one of the poems says so. As was the case with 'Murray', however, this poet's work shows kinship at points with verses the young King James was writing.

With the poetry of this second strain inspiration is seen to come from a different quarter, from medieval poetry—for example Chaucer with Henryson—as relished at first hand, not as passed down through Montgomerie. The choice of words is more catholic than in 'Murray' and suggests that the poet had learned to gather vocabulary more widely and with a freer hand: this he may have learned from the practice of the *Pléiade* or from the new language of Spenser's *Calender* of 1579. He has felt the touch of the sugared fashion, the golden poetry of Elizabethan England, and one or two southern word-forms have been brought into use. (This is integral to the poetry and distinct from the 'Englishing' traceable in the manuscript collection as a whole.) He has drawn, then, from different founts, some earlier and some later than those that served John Murray; we shall see that other influences also were at work.

Of the four pieces of this second strand 'Eligye' (xviii) is a happy child of Scots cultural belatedness. The medieval lyric pattern of a love-adventure on a May morning is enriched by Renaissance mythological interest: Venus 'clarks' are joined by 'Pandion's daughter', the nightingale

> Scarce PHOEBE of the flowers had drawne
>   The mantle blacke of night,
> Scarce had the morninge opened yett
>   hir husbandes windows bright,
> Nor PANDIONS daughters plaintes lent place
>   For VENUS clarkes to singe;
> On buddes and flowers AURORAES teares
>   As yet lyke perles did hinge;
> And still the sillver streames did slyde
>   On christall gravell sweit,
> The topps of tremblinge trees and herbs
>   In balmye dews did fleit,
> The warblinge tunes of birdes about
>   In broken ayre reboundes,
> And echo throughe the woodes and rockes
>   Ther latter notes resoundes;

The soyle was sweit, and pleasant was
    The sweit and pleasant ayre,
The season pleasant, and the daye
    moste pleasant cleare and fayre,
When I to doe myne observance
    To maye, as is my guyse,
was ranged forth with hauke on hande
    To see APOLLO ryse.
And even as EOUS in the east
    kept vp his crimson crowne,
And PHEBUS on the ocean old
    Spred out his golden gowne,
Another sonne I sawe whose beams
    So peirst me in eche part,
That with the sight I thoght my self
    depryved of a hart.
For pluckinge vp the blossoms of
    The beames of hir regardes,
I felt that loue al soddaine tooke
    Me captyve in his wardes.
That she some goddesse was I demed,
    Or nimph of heavenly race,
With VENUS bewtyes, IUNOES welth,
    And with dame PALLAS grace.
Devynlye was inspyred me thought—
    AURORA pale and colde
Did blushinge hyde hir head so rare
    A bewtye to beholde.

Several traditions have met here. The ground-plan of the poem is still the medieval *pastourelle*, and it is the truer to the old mode in being couched in terms of spring rite and celebration: we expect that the poet ranging forth will meet a lady or a country lass and will celebrate her beauty, make a love-request or otherwise undergo the love adventure. This poet-lover goes out very early on May morning, hawk on hand pursuing the sport of the month, to do his observance to May. According to ancient rite, social, magical and 'folkloric', he is to view the sun rise on May morning. What he sees is 'another sun arise' that outshines the real one, in his lady's regard: here seasonal rite meets literary conceit of the beloved's eyes. Then, with recourse to Renaissance mythological colouring he makes a good end to his poem by involving the break of day, the reddening Aurora, in the tribute to his lady.

In the same measure, but rhymed and lined into a ballad stanza, is his piece for St Valentine's Day, a festival still celebrated in courtly circles and famous since Chaucer as the setting of a poem. The plan of the poem is that of the *reverdi*, as old as

196

the *pastourelle*. In a spring scene marked by joy of beast, bird, fish and insect the 'I' of the poem feels the first rising of 'corage', and initiation into Venus' service is looked forward to as young men hail St Valentine and maidens gather the first flowers and dance their ring-dances of the season.

Medieval themes and motifs long familiar here spring to life in newly minted phrase or fresh alignment, 'motlaye grounde' or 'galliard king'. He has robin and wren and goldfinch as well as nightingale; he has northern spring felt in the snowcap melting on the hills and running water and he has the leap of the salmon, 'the silver harvest people dive'. The rhythm of creature answers the rhythm of Creator in the spiders' webs against the weft of new spring leaves. The poet finds he is ready to leap into the spring dance of love.

1   Why should not pleasures plant in me
      And hoyse aloft my harte
   Since that eche liuinge thinge I see
      dothe playe the semblie parte?

2   The vglye darke and werye night
      Is fettered fast in chaine;
   Nowe brings the blisfull EOUS bright
      The dawninge sweit againe.

3   The winter with his stormes is past;
      The somer dothe repaire;
   From mountes the snow distills as fast,
      And lyvelye lookes the ayer.

4   The skyes with PHEBUS beames are clad
      In clokes of golden hew;
   The siluer fountains dull and sadd
      Ther course againe renewe.

5   The trees with natures tapistryes
      Are hunge in budes and leavs;
   The spyder for to catche the flyes
      hir webb and nettes now weaves...

9   Nowe flockes they breake, and couplinge springe
      Eche little one by his make:
   With sugred throates they sonnettes singe,
      Eche for his swetings sake—

10   The Robin, Wraine, and whutinge quaill,
      The lennett and the Larke,
   The goldfinch and the nightingall
      That sighs in shaddowes darke.

11 The siluer haruest people dive
    In christall channells cleare,
    And euerye wight ther sprittes revyue
    As newe revyves the yeare.

12 Nowe ZEPHIR sweit dispercheth from
    The topps of buddinge trees,
    And honye from eche pleasant blome
    Nowe suckes the bussinge bees.

13 'Saint Vallentyne! all haile to the!'
    These louers loud they shout;
    Nowe bagpypes blawes to warme on he   [?warne]
    These younkers rownde about.

14 The wenches spoyle the motlaye grounde,
    And primrose garlandes plett,
    And hand in hand in ringes full rownde
    About the grene they jett

15 And nowe I thincke I feile in me
    A newe desyre to move,
    And eche one saithe, for ought they see,
    The cause thereof is loue.

16 Then if that love so shott his darte
    That none his bowe maye flee,
    I would to god I knewe that arte,
    Or might the manner see.

17 Nowe that my love woulde me resaue,
    That would I first assaye,
    What other sportes these louers haue
    Then woulde I learne the waye.

18 For loue, they saye, is Lord of Ioye,
    Whence lyvelye bloode dothe springe;
    He liues beneath a lawlesse boye,
    Alofte a galliard kinge.

19 My weides of woe, my mornfull mynde,
    And cares I caste asyde;
    To loue a seruant I me bynde;
    So VENUS be my guyde.

So personal is the note, so distinct the impression the poem makes that it is a shock of surprise for the modern reader to discover that the piece is 'not original'. Besides the voices of medieval poetry and of contemporary making, the young Castalian has heeded the 'other voice' with which Renaissance poetry spoke in

Scotland—Latin. The Castalian's poem is an 'overgoing' of George Buchanan's 'Valentiniana', at points a close translation but different in mood and in intention.

> Festa valentino rediit lux: frigora languent
> Et liquat horrentes mitior aura nives...[1]

Buchanan's pieces for St Valentine's Day may have been linked to pastime at court as closely as was the Castalian's. It is printed with verses of compliment after his 'Pompae' for various state occasions. But his is the comment of the old man, the onlooker at the game of love, the young revels and chaste joys of the spring festival (Buchanan died in 1582).

> Quaeque suis vicibus nascentia sufficit annus
> Munera, temporibus non aliena suis.
> Nos quibus et iam flos melioris decidit aevi
> Nec niteant horti, nec renovetur ager...

The Castalian's introduction and conclusion are new and the description of the season is extended; phrases and couplets grow out of suggestions in the Latin or motifs are significantly changed. Violets and roses become primroses. In fact, the Castalian poet's is a young man's 'answer' to the old poet's 'elegie'. This is not derivative writing but a joyous response and lively negative delivered in a fresh tongue.

This Castalian's longest poem is the 'Letter of Creseyde to Troyalus', a 'heroic epistle' of over three hundred lines. It is in fourteeners, a measure liked by King James for a narrative. Here a young poet celebrates the heroine he has met in Chaucer's and in Henryson's poetry. He takes up the motif of the letter and the ring from Henryson:

> This royall ring set with this rubie reid
> Quhilk Troylus in drowrie to me send
> To him agane I leif it quhan I am deid.

The ring and the letter are now sent to her lover by the dying Cressida. She rehearses her story, pleading her cause piteously enough, crying not against the planetary powers or the gods, but against the Fates, that through Paris and Helen and the Trojan War brought it all to be.

> O! rather wish I that the sorge[2]
> Of sousinge seas had drencht
> The leiches twayne, and all the fyre
> Of loue by water quencht...

55

---

[1] George Buchanan, *Opera Omnia*, II, 99; *Georgii Buchanani Scoti Poemata*, fol. G10.
[2] No. xxx, l. 53: I read 'sorge'; S.T.S. editor prints 'songe'.

She lays some blame on Troilus,

115
> Why slewest thou not thy mortall foe,
>   And fled with me awaye?
> No, thou extemed myne honour soe
>   Myne honestye to blott;
> Thou was affrayde, or ells thou shouldst
>   Haue done it well, I wote.
> For thou no sooner tooke thy loue
>   Of me, nor from me went,
> When DIOMEDE with his sleated lipps
>   Hathe faste my bridle hent.

She pleads her terrible dilemma,

215
> My father olde, Sir TROYALUS loste,
>   Then must I bear eche wronge.
> Nowe this, nowe that, I ryfle vpp
>   Within my buissy brayne;
> Whyles will I with my father staye,
>   Whyles steale to TROYE againe.
> A sevenight thus I liued—huge fight
>   was dayly still without,
> Stronge garde within—eche thinge presentes
>   Vnto my harte a doubte...
> But loue in mowld of memory
>   Imprintes in perfitt harte
> The loued, so that deathe it self
>   Can noght the same devert...

Here the Castalian cannot devise an 'epitaph' to finish (who could?) after Henryson
had inscribed
> ...Crisseid of Troyis toun
> Sumtyme countit the flour of Womanheid
> Under this stane, lait lipper, lyis deid.

In the epistle we find proofs of a young makar's response to the two earlier poets
rather than any new vision of Cressida. He has, however, essayed a *combination* of
Chaucer's telling and Henryson's with a comment on both and has presented the matter
in a fresh guise. The letter form has something of *epitre galante*, something of 'testament' and something of Ovidian heroic epistle.[1]

There is no 'ancientry' about Chaucer or Henryson for this northern poet though
the date of his writing was very possibly later than the appearance of the *Shepheardes
Calender*. His work shows no conscious assertion of literary lineage but rather an
effortless '*innutrition*', evidence of uninterrupted poetic inheritance.

[1] Imitating 'Briseis to Achilles'?

So far the characterisation of the poet in this second repertory has been stylistic and the world revealed has been that of his reading and his imagination. But in one poem we glimpse also the actual world of the Scottish court and its courtiers. In XXVI, 'His Ladies Dreame', the poem, the dream and the lady are located exactly:

25

> Farr in that ysle which the ocyan old
>   Imbracethe lyke a wall,
> Which thanciantes names thother worlde,
>   Nowe BRITTAINE we it call—
> Of which the middowes partes bespreides
>   The hardye Inglish knight,
> The Northern boundes is bordred by
>   The warlyke Scottish wight—
> Wher rears the dreadfull mownt so styled
>   Of olde, who on his breast
> The broughe of Sterlinge beares, and high
>   The Castell on his creaste,
> When IANUS tooke his Inn at signe
>   Of CAPRICORNUS colde,
> In hope that thou, O PHEBUS great,
>   Thy Ryottes ther should holde,
> Lo! in this ysle, this tyme and place,
>   As ther my Ladye slept...

Great Phebus who should hold riots there at New Year refers to the feast of the winter solstice but at least a glance is cast at the King, 'King Phoebus' with his Yuletide revels held at Stirling Castle.

The dream is interpreted by the poet lover as masterly to his own advantage as Chanteclere's was. It is of a perilous journey, and one of the fearsome beasts that beset the lady's way brings to mind the resident lion of Stirling Castle (left out of the revels once lest he 'fricht the ladies') though here he is a dream-fear and a beast subject to allegorical interpetation.

> As hapened hir who thought hir selfe
>   drawn from all danger deipe,
> And tickling Ioye began about
>   hir quakinge harte to creipe.
> Behoulde a dreadfull beast she thought
>   She sawe of portlye state,
> Who capteu of his owne accorde,
>   stood penned in a grave;

He moves to attack, but is abashed by her 'high regarde' and gives way

> Lyke one who at a soddaine meittes
>   his better in the streit...

Interpreted, after the serpents of slander, the 'gaillard beist in wilful warde' turns out to be the poet-lover fettered by lawlesse love, who

> Beleyved at first she linckt her mynde
>   Vnto his lassyve lace;
> But pondringe well hir stately race,
>   Hir witt, and manners grave,
> he sees that loue and bewtye made
>   Throughe luste his hart to rave;
> So nowe with tyme he hopes to win
>   Which haste drewe in extremes.
> Iudge thou the rest: so fare the wele!
>   Thou vexest me with dreames.

In subject and treatment a late variant of the medieval 'dream poem' fashion, in form and metre using the 'fourteener', this poem finds a counterpart in King James' 'A Dreame on his Mistris my Ladie Glammis'—'Whill as the silent shaddie night Did with her courtens blacke' but the Castalians is on all counts the livelier poem.[1]

None of these four poems is linked to a court personality of discoverable identity, but the courtly setting emphasised in the 'Dreame' is implicit in the style and tone of the other poems. The literary background is constant throughout. A marked characteristic of this second 'unknown Castalian' is the presence in his writing of the dimension of time and season. His poetry grows out of the festive cycle of New Year's Day, St Valentine's Day and May Day; the observance of the day contributes to the action of the poem. This happens naturally and unselfconsciously, treating of such 'secular' festivals apparently needing no defence against the puritan aggression. So marked is this that one might be tempted to assign the poems to the earlier half of the sixteenth century—and the 'Troyalus' piece in consequence nearer to the 'Troilus' vogue of the late 1530s; but against such back-dating is the reference to the 'ryottes' of King Phoebus in Stirling Castle and there is the glint of new Elizabethan gold in the poetry. This poet, it would seem, was writing out of reach of reforming zeal that cried against idolatry and pastime.

The songs of 'John Murray' showed close links with known personalities at court and they declared their own context of Castalian song, but they are not rooted in courtly ceremony or celebration. He wrote a song on 'Maye' with only the lightest mention of 'may lady' or 'some mayenge daye'. William Fowler composed a poem 'For his Valentyne' and it was based on the customs of that day, the giving of a ring or a pair of laces ('poynts') woven from silken strands of different colours that signified good or ill fortune in love. But he made a tremendous fuss before he would

---

[1] Westcott, *New Poems by James I*, no. XVII and note p. 78. In addition, both poets have a piece entitled 'Enigme'.

let himself write a piece for the day of a saint, even one of such frivolous and amorous disposition.

> Prepair and prease as papists dois
> o poetts your ingyne
> And celebratt the memorye
> off blist saint valentyne.
>
> Sound furth your voce, and sing his praise
> with learned verses fyne
> Ane with my dames resound the glore
> off blist saint valentyne...[1]

It sounds to me as if a celebration of St Valentine's Day was proposed in the court and more than one poet composed a piece. One may read between the lines of Fowler's verses that there was a lady of that name in courtly circles whom it pleased the company to honour in this way: his poem is 'for his Valentyne', his chosen lady of the day whatever her Christian name was, whereas the unknown Castalian's 'Pastourell' is a celebration of the day by one who is ready to 'enter Venus service' in time-honoured style.

Who was this second 'younger Castalian'? We can only surmise. One good poet was about the court in the 1580s who is believed to have written verses then that are not now to be found: fruits of his youthful 'fantasie' did not survive his later recantation of amorous verse and his withdrawal from attendance at court. These pieces might be early work of Alexander Hume, cadet of Polwarth.[2] Returned from studies in France, heir to the poetry of earlier Scotland and aware of the new style of Renaissance Europe, is he found here offering service to Cupid in verse and compliment to the King in court? Later his style was chastened with his decision to serve God and the Christian Muse only; but he made—and allowed to survive—the beautiful piece celebrating Midsummer Day, 'Of the day Estivall' with the invocation 'O lovely Light'.

> ...The gloming comes, the day is spent,
> The Sun goes out of sight,
> And painted is the occident
> With pourpour sanguine bright.
>
> The skarlet nor the golden threid
> Who would their bewtie trie
> Are nathing like the colour reid
> And bewtie of the sky...

The poet who wrote in his prentice verses of 'the silver harvest people' and of Phoebus laying his golden cloak on the ocean could strike out the descriptive felicities of 'Estivall'. In both poems the aptness of every detail to cosmic order is outstanding.

---

[1] *Works, Fowler*, I, 312–15. The celebration of St Valentine's Day was apparently not then tied to a particular day.

[2] *Poems of Alexander Hume*, ed. A. Lawson, pp. 25–33; 'Recantation', pp. 11–16; biography in introduction. The same criterion is used to attribute a poem to Hume by Stevenson, *Montgomerie*, p. xl.

Alexander Hume, minister of Logie, who dedicated to God the celebration of the summer solstice, might in his years of youthfull 'fantasie' have composed a Maytime *pastourelle* for his love.

If we have not come upon four lost poems of Alexander Hume's courtly making, then the second 'younger Castalian' must remain unknown! Nowhere else have I found his fresh running rhythms, his particular touch. Meanwhile this handful of distinctive and vivid verse enhances our idea of *Scottis Poesie* at the Renaissance Court of King James.

CASTALIAN CONTINUITY: W.M. 'AND SOME OF HIS AIN'

The repertory of poems valued by W.M. and engrossed with some of his own appended is important evidence of continuity of poetic tradition in *Scottis Poesie*. One poetic personality has been isolated and limned in outline who was early in his life a maker of court-song. Another is glimpsed as an idiosyncratic and gifted young poet in the court deriving in his own way from poetry of an earlier Scotland. The linking of these verses with named poets must meanwhile remain conjectural but with the estimation of the corpus of poetry as 'younger Castalian' we are on sure ground. Now the substantial indebtedness to poets of the Castalian band in song or sonnet now the parallels with poems written by Buchanan or by King James himself at this time, place the work as *Scottis Poesie* of the Renaissance. Influences from England have been discerned, Tottelian Tudor in the dance-song style and 'golden' Elizabethan poetry and also—and importantly—fruitful contact of *Scottis Poesie* with Renaissance verse in Latin in a piece fit to companion the work in two tongues of Mark Alexander Boyd. But the lines of lyric style are seen to be evolving in ways distinct from those observable in the southern kingdom though at points in touch with them—and finally to merge with them in the great and varied lyric of King James' southern court.

In the music with which the poems are associated W.M.'s collection spans a considerable space of time. It embraces verses written in Scots to match music that was current in England in the earlier years of Queen Elizabeth's reign; it has songs in the Castalian repertory and it ends with three fine lyrics framed for music in the style of madrigal, Jacobean lute-song or declamatory air. Dearth of material for the last ten years of the century prevents a complete history of court-song in Scotland being written here and now. Nevertheless, W.M.'s collection serves to illustrate from one man's taste one line of descent in northern song-writing—from the 'younger Castalian' compositions of the 1580s and 1590s cherished by W.M. to 'some of his ain', which may well be work of William Murray, perhaps kinsman of 'John Murray', certainly friend of Sir Robert Ayton, Scots cavalier and wit and author of the impressive song that ends his verse collection.

8. IF WHEN I DYE[1]

[WILLIAM MURRAY?]

[FERRABOSCO?]

1 If when I dye to Hels e - ter - nal shade as an I -
2 And for thy great - er plague two hells shall prove The one the

-do - la - ter con - demn'd I bee be - cause a mor - tal beau — ty that doth
trew, where - in thy self shalt be My hat - ed lookes the o — ther, pale with

fade, I have to long a - dor'd in cru - - el thee, thinke not to
love Shall seeme each day and houre new hell _____ to thee But I be -

[1] Words and music: Bodleian Library MS. Mus. Sch. F. 575, fo. 7 r, stanza 1 underlaid; accompaniment in lute tablature. Bar 16, notes 5–6: octave higher in original. Also in Christ Church MS. 87, fo. 2 r, a highly decorated version of the tune with stanza 1 underlaid and a different bass. (K.E.) Also in Gamble MS. and B. M. Egerton 2013.

scape, for,   for thy ty - ran - ny,   thou there shalt bee con - demn'd _____
- hold - ing   thy bright shyn - ing eyes   Shall heav'n en - joy a - midst _____

_____ as _____ well as I.
_____ hells _____ mi - se - ries.

8

FROM COURT TO CASTLE

SIR WILLIAM MURE OF ROWALLAN 1594–1657

This Sir William was pious and learned and had ane excellent vaine in poyesie; he delighted much in building and planting, he builded the new wark in the north syde of the close and the battlement of the back wall and reformed the whole house exceidingly.

The Historie and of the House of Rowallan.[1]

A GENERATION was born in the castles of the north that grew up into a Scotland without a court: Drummond of Hawthornden, laird, poet, historian and lute-player; a Sempill of Beltrees whose family had the habit of verse-making; Duncane Burnett son of a modest branch of Leys, a trained musician; Robert Gordon of Straloch, cartographer and lute-player; William Stirling of Ardoe, owner of the fine music-book; Alexander Forbes of Tolquhon, heir to a great castle and musical amateur; and William Mure of Rowallan, heir likewise, musical amateur and poet.[2] As they came to manhood they inherited an age of courtly poetry and music and a memory of court and kingship that had been their fathers'. Father or uncle or head of the family had been about the court or had known King James, for they were of the King's own generation. But of the contemporaries of his son Prince Henry few seem to have gone south to court favour as did the poetasters who were intermediate in age, men like William Alexander or Robert Ayton.

The family of Mure of Rowallan had been long lodged on the banks of the Carmel Water south of Kilmarnock in Ayrshire. The Queen of King Robert II had been of their blood and they had played a powerful part in political history. The castle, built large in 1562 after the French fashion of Falkland Palace, was extended by this Sir William. His planting and building speak of a life rooted in the north. His 'vaine of poyesie' was rooted, too, in northern tradition: his great-uncle was Alexander Montgomerie, master of *Scottis Poesie*, and in the art of 'making' Mure was his devoted disciple. Like him, too, he wrote songs.

Of William Mure's early years and education little is known beyond what we

---

[1] In *Works of Mure of Rowallan*, ed. W. Tough, II, 256.

[2] Their music-books in Source-List. Duncane Burnett (of Craigour), who was master of the song-school in Glasgow c. 1630, made a music-book largely of keyboard music. See Thurston Dart, 'New Sources of Virginal Music'.

gather from his own writing. He may have been at college in Glasgow as his younger brother was or, as heir, he may have been sent 'abroad to the schools'. He was certainly well educated, witness his 'Dido and Aeneas', a version from Vergil in dignified stanzas; witness too his verses in Latin, in a modified Scots and in English, and his knowledge and practice of music that is seen in manuscript music-books of his and of his family that have survived. His poetry was published long since for the Scottish Text Society (1898) but the editor, Tough, knew of only one of the music-books. It falls to us now to lay his verses together with the evidence of the music cherished in his family, a lute-book and a set of part-books of which only the Cantus is extant. We may then see whether there is in his writing any link between music and poetry, any continuation of Montgomerie's tradition of song-making in his young kinsman's practice.

I suggest the study of Mure's early poetry alongside the music because his writing falls into two distinct parts, poems written before the King's visit to Scotland in 1617 —when the poet was twenty-three years of age—and other poetry very different in tone and style written for the most part much later, after his recantation of his youthful vein of courtly and amorous making. This is serious and protestant, religious or political in matter, sometimes metaphysical in temper and often dark and satiric in mood. But for his good and interesting metrical versions of the psalms, this later writing has little to do with music, and is out of our story.[1]

At the time of his change of heart he took formal farewell of fancy, of 'Love's false delight and beautees blasing beame'—renouncing Cupid:

> Blinde Dwarfling I disdaine thy deitie
> My pen thy Trophees neuer more shall write
> Nor after shall thine arts enveigle mee.
> With sacred straines reaching a higher key
> My thoughts above thy fictions farre aspire...[2]

His early poems are not here advanced as important intrinsically but as vital to the tracing of ways of song-making in Scots from the practice in King James' court down into a Scotland that lacked that meeting-place for poet and musician, that possibility of patronage and performance that a court and its company could so well provide.

The original manuscripts from which the Scottish Text Society edition of Mure's poems was made are not now to be found, but that edition is carefully arranged, apparently following the original in grouping of unprinted pieces, and presenting

---

[1] The spiritual history of William Mure and its impact on his poetry has yet to be written. See R. S. Jack, 'Scottish Sonneteer and Welsh Metaphysical', *Studies in Scottish Literature*, III, no. 4, p. 240 and discussion in subsequent numbers.

[2] Fancies Farewell. Sonnet 1. *Mure*, I, 195.

printed works in chronological order. Of the pieces all apparently written before 1617, some are precisely dated and they are assembled in chronological sequence. I give the numbers there allotted them. 'Dido and Aeneas' and his dozen sonnets we set on one side, noting only that they bear witness to the extent to which the nephew leant on his uncle's precedent, whether in turn of courtly phrasing or in shaping of a sonnet for praise or vituperation. Like Montgomerie he 'flytes' pungently in sonnet form.

Of the twenty-one numbered poems ten are epitaphs or royal addresses, none of them in any sense songs. Poetry on the death of the Archbishop of St Andrews or the fall of Somerset (cautiously worded, this one) are found side by side with pieces for Scottish neighbouring gentry. Poem xx is for the eyes or ears of 'the most hopeful and high-born Prince Charles, Prince of Wales'. Here he declares his pride in his great-uncle, court poet to King James, and offers his modest service in poetry to the new heir to the throne. (Nothing, however, came of the offer.)

> Machles Montgomery in his native tounge
> In former tymes to thy Great Syre hath sung
> And often ravischt his harmonious ear
> With straynes fitt only for a prince to heir.
> My muse quich noght doth challenge worthy fame
> Save from Montgomery sche hir birth doth clayme...
> Pretending tytyls to supply his place
> By ryt hereditar to serve thy grace...
>   Quhen thy auntcestors' passiouns I have schowne
>   Iff, (but offence) Great Charles Ile sing thyne owne.

This sounds as if Mure were contemplating something ambitious in the epic or historical strain on the house of Stewart, but nothing of that nature has survived.

Like other poets in Scotland he bursts forth into verse of welcome to celebrate the visit of King James to his native land in 1617. In 'Burst forth, my Muse' he uses, it is interesting to note, the Apollo image

> 2   Since our much lov'd Apollo doth appeare
>   In pompe and pow'r, busked with golden rayes
>   More brigt heir shyning on our hemispheare
>   Nor that great planet, father of the dayes;
>   With boldness offer at his sacred shryne
>   These firstlings of thy weake and poore ingyne.   (xxi)

In 'Ane Conflict tuix Love and Ressoun' (i) three voices play a part in a debate that could be a courtly devising. The matter is close to that of *The Cherrie and the Slae* but the significant and picturesque 'cadre' of spring is absent. The vision of Cupid comes with approaching sleep but this is no 'dream poem'. The stanza form is not taken from Montgomerie but is much in accordance with his style. No music is known to match this pattern; it is not in dance-song style nor does the poet observe the exact matching of stanza and stanza that would make it amenable to setting as part-song.

Mure's second poem, dated 1615, has a French title, 'Mes Amours et mes douleurs sont sans comparisoune'. This title is not explained nor is it fully substantiated in the verses that follow, and it may well be the title of a French song or poem that was in some way a forerunner of the text or of the stanza. Again the poem is in part in quasi-dramatic speech, [B] eutie, [A] uctor and [C] upeid and the manner suggests a courtly devising. Mure has varied the iambic pentameter six-line stanza by a reminiscence of Horatian metre. Indeed he may be experimenting in *vers mésurés*. Here is one stanza; its pattern, the interesting rhythm and the clue of the French title may yet lead to the discovery of a forebear among French *chansons* or *airs de cour*.[1]

> 2 Quhill Beutie by a pleasant spring reposes
> With fairest schads of trees o'reschadoued, under;
> Ye cooling air, with calmest blasts rejoyses
> To sport hir with hir locks o'rcume with wonder;
>   So then admiring hir most heavinly featour
>   I mervel'd much if scho was form'd by natour.

'Chansoune' is the title of the fifth poem. Again this may be a Scots version for singing of a French song, or it could be an original composition in French *chanson* style.

> 5 Calling to mynd the heauinly featour
>   The baschfull blinks, and comely grace
>   The forme of hir angellick face
> Deckt with ye quintascence of natour
>   To none inferiour in place
>   Oft am I forc'd
>   Altho divors'd
> From presence of my deirests eyes
>   The too slou day
>   To steil away
> Admiring hir, my smairt quho sies...

In VIII and its variant IX as in X, XI and XII Mure makes known that he is writing to match music already in existence. No. XII is his 'Hymne', 'Help, help, O Lord', that has the stanza of 'The Flaming Fyre'/'Melancholie'. It is a sacred song to match part-music in the dance-song style, as we have seen, the music being recorded in Mure's part-book. XI is entitled 'Ane letter to ane musicall tune' and is written to match the music of a song that was a favourite in the repertory of early seventeenth-century

---

[1] The association of *vers mésurés* with stanzas under a French title may prove important, especially in a context that suggests associated music.

Scotland, recorded in several of the manuscript collections and in Forbes, 'Joy to the persoune of my love' (*Music of Scotland*, no. 59). That Mure's is a secondary and not a primary text for this part-song is suggested by his echoing of phrases from the well-known piece—'Hands forbeare to tuich/Oght your tuiching can bewitch', for instance, after 'Shall I strive to touch/...the beauty that did me bewitch'. Where one or two details of rhythm in Mure's poem do not precisely match the music surviving for one version of this song their exact counterpart can be found in a variant from another music-book. 'Joy to the persoune' with its lovely freely ranging tune has melodic leaps that bring to mind the 'native air' of Scotland. We find Mure carrying forward his uncle's practice of writing new words for courtly part-song into a later style where courtly song is touching hands with 'native air' in a regional and indigenous style.

With VIII, X and III we come to an important departure. Again these are pieces written to a tune but the music is no longer courtly song in known European style but a 'native air' of Scotland, dance-song still, but music of the Scottish regional dance of which Mure recorded several in his playing-book for the lute. In VIII, 'To the tune of Pert Jean' the name is certainly 'Port Jean' or 'Puirt Jean', 'puirt' being a Celtic word for a rhythm of music or a kind of musical piece that could be vocal or instrumental; it was of a march-like nature and was much used in pipe-music. It may well be that the music for this piece is the 'Port Jean Linsay' of the 'playing-book for lute' of Gordon of Straloch, whose musical text is no longer extant.

Though the type of music mentioned in the entitling has now changed to the 'native air' there is no corresponding change in the matter or style of the poetry.

'*To the tune of Pert Jean*'

Fair goddes, Loadstar of delight
Natour's triumph and beuties lyfe
Earth's ornament, my hopes full hight
My only peace and pleasing stryfe
Let mercie mollifie thy mynd
If Saturnes hert sould Venus have?...

The matter of Montgomerie at his most formal with a touch of Tudor and an echo of Henryson comes from Mure's pen with very little mark of individuality. Only towards the end of his long stanza is his work enlivened by a rhythmic echo from 'The Cherrie and the Slae':

Natour's due so sall we pay
Bathing in boundless pleassour
Inioying
That toying
Quhose sueits exceid all meassour

x is 'to the tune of and new lilt' and 'lilt' is again a name for a type of native air. Beauty and Cupid of courtly tradition are used for love's vows, and rather dully, but the rhythm of Mure's lines written to the lilt goes lightly, in trochee rather than iamb, sped by the fall of the feminine rhymes. It is likely that the enlivening of rhythm came from a spirited 'Scotch' air.

> Beutie hath myne eyes assailed
> And subdued my saulis affectioune
> Cupid's dairt hath so prevail'd
> That I must live in his subjectioune
> > Tyed till one
> > Quho's machles aloue
> > And second to none
> > In all perfectioune
> Since my fortune such must be
> No change sall pairt my love and me.

This enlivening power of the native dance-song rhythms is seen most clearly in III, 'Ane reply to *I caire not quither I get hir or no*'. Here we have as forebear of Mure's song not the indication of a tune only; we have evidence of the words, for a version has luckily survived.[1]

> '*I cair not quhither I get hir or no*'
> I hate the esteat of that Lover's conditione
> > Who pynes for hir, regards not his [pain].
> I hate the esteat of that foolish ambitione
> > Who fondly requyts true love with disdaine;
> I love them that love me my houmer is such
> And those that doe hate I'll hate them as much
> And thus I resolved [how] e're it doe goe
> *I cair not whither I get hir or no.*   (3 stanzas)

Mure replies to the words and responds to the rhythm:

> To pleid but quher mutuel kyndnes is gain'd
> And fancie alone quhair favour hath place
> Such frozen affectioune I ewer disdain'd
> Can oght be impair'd by distance or space?
> My love salbe endles quhair once I affect
> Ewin thoght it sould please hir my service reject
> > Still sall I determine till breath and lyfe go
> > *To love hir quither scho love me or no.*   (3 stanzas)

[1] Printed in the *Paisley Magazine*, xx, 104, from a MS. of 1673: in *Works of Mure*, II.

THE ROWALLAN MUSIC-BOOKS

Let us place beside the early verses made by Mure for singing the record surviving of the music and song he knew. Two music-books have come down to us that belonged to the family of William Mure of Rowallan, both in manuscript of the earlier part of the seventeenth century. The first is his own playing-book for the lute made over the same years when as a young man he was writing his songs, that is before the year 1617. It is dated 1615 and bears the name 'William Mure'. It is now in the library of the University of Edinburgh, MS. Laing III, 487.

It is an album of some fifty items, dances, tunes and songs. There are no words. The contents range from 'Wolt' and 'Spynelet' through music in dance rhythms for the words of his great-uncle's 'Whenas the Greeks', to tunes for the Scots native air, some of them names and airs in use to this very day for Scottish dances, 'Corne yairds' or 'Katherine Bairdie', the 'Battel of Harlaw' that is both ballad and dance-tune, 'O'er the dyke, Davie' and 'In an inch I warrand you' that come in other seventeenth-century collections and 'Gypsyes Lilt'. 'For Kissing for clepping for loving for proving' occurs twice, once with the note 'set to ye lute be Mr Mure'. The tunes that he played on the lute, then, span the same range as the music to which he wrote words, from courtly dance-song to regional, indigenous airs and rhythms. The *air de cour* type and the *chanson* straight from France are not, as far as we know, represented here but the nature of the collection, an album of dance-tunes, makes their presence unlikely.

The second music book was, as we saw, the 'Cantus' volume of a set of part-books, sole survivor of four, five or six volumes. This book bears the name 'Sir William Mure of Rowallan' and the inscription 'Robert Muire with my hand'. The first would refer to the poet's father until the year of his death, 1639, and after that to the poet. Robert Mure is the poet's younger brother.

The contents are almost entirely part-song; only in one case are any words included, but many entries bear title or *incipit*. The arrangement is careful: first come songs for four, then for five, then for six voices: then for two, for three and for four voices. English, Scots and Continental pieces are included, those of Scots provenance being grouped together. In this part of the repertory are to be found 'The bankis of Helicon' and 'The flamming fyre', associated with Montgomerie's song-making. There are pieces substantially earlier than the Castalian song-making under King James and pieces belonging to it in its latest phases.

Within the arrangement of the book can be traced groups of pieces taken from printed song-books: Morley 1595, then Jones 1608 and Wilbye 1598; then Hilton 1627, followed by Weelkes 1598 and Jones 1609. Psalms in the volume have been identified by Kenneth Elliott as drawn from the *Psalter* of 1615 and some from the later psalter of 1635. 'Delectabill Frensh songes', which are widely represented, range from a song-book as early as 1558 (Attaignant) through many pieces by distinguished composers. Among these is found 'A bonie no' translated by Montgomerie. The recording of the repertory of part-writing enjoyed by the family of Mure of Rowallan, then, with arrangement as to number of parts and chronology, bears witness to a systematic engrossing at some time after 1627. It is suggested that these fine part-books may have been made from music in the family's possession for the musical education of the poet's children.

The song-making and lute-playing of young William Mure of Rowallan early in the seventeenth century is an important aspect of the last stage of a court culture of music and poetry: the music and song is cultivated and created at one remove from the court. The impetus was royal precedent and family pride, the great forebear Montgomerie and his poetry and song made for King James. The scene has passed from court to castle, where there were music-books in print and in manuscript to hand and where there must have been skilled music teaching. Words are written to match monophonic song and in one or two cases song that was for several voices, to match native air or regional dance-tune, broadside or dance-song originally from England. The natural verbal medium is courtly Scots, somewhat modified towards current English, and the style looks back to masters of *Scottis Poesie*.

William Mure remains in the north to plant his policies. The King's visit to Scotland and the poetry he devised for it did not sweep him into royal attendance. He wrote verses offering poetic service to Prince Charles and the line of Stewart, but without success. It was William Murray of Dysart, brought up as Prince Charles' companion, who became Cavalier wit and song-writer to the southern court. Mure's progression was from Castalian-by- family-tradition to sombre puritan. As had been the case earlier with Alexander Hume, William Mure forswore the amorous making of his younger days; he turned to poetry of meditation not uncoloured by devotions of the Counter-reformation—and hence to anti-Catholic propaganda and partisan defence of the Covenant. Some hand—in all probability the poet's—blotted blackly from sight the titles of the delectable French songs in the family music-book. The fierce current of history here drove through the castle-culture of courtly song and broke the hereditary continuity of *Scottis Poesie*.

9

THE LAST CASTALIAN:
SIR ROBERT AYTON

Brave Murray ah is dead, Aiton supplies his place   Lithgow

SIR ROBERT AYTON, Scotsman and writer of courtly words for music, was the last
Castalian. Secretary to two queens, Anne and Henrietta Maria, he was friend of Ben
Jonson and for many years a well-loved figure of the Jacobean and Caroline court. A
gracious personality and an elegant poet of compliment in Latin and the vernacular,
he has been called 'the father of the Cavalier lyric'. His witty verses were favourite
entries in the commonplace-books of the time and appeared in the printed miscel-
lanies of the mid century and the Restoration. Lovely songs of his were set by musicians of the age, Lawes, Playford and others.[1]

His poems in the vernacular were collected after his death by his nephew, Sir John
Ayton.[2] They were conscientiously recorded in manuscript probably with publication in view, but these were troubled times and they did not reach print. Latin verses
of his, however, were brought together in the *Delitiae* published in the seventeenth
century, but not since reprinted;[3] others lay among unpublished papers or as dedica-
tions inside rare printed books of the time. The poems in Greek or in French that
Ayton was said to have composed have not been found.[4]

The poet himself had taken no thought to preserve his writings: 'Vita verecunda
est; musa jocosa mihi' appears motto-wise on Sir John's collection. Ayton's best
verses in the vernacular paid the price of their popularity. They were handed about,
copied, misread and copied again, learnt by heart and repeated wrong, or appropriated to deck some new occasion of compliment and altered accordingly. To his

---

[1] See *Musa jocosa mihi*, Twelve songs for voice and keyboard by Lawes, Wilson, Blagrave, Playford and anon.
to poems by Sir Robert Ayton, ed. by Kenneth Elliott; cited as Ayton/Elliott.

[2] B.M. MS. Add. 10308 with a preface by Sir John Ayton worded as if to prepare the book for print, but later
revised; B.M. MS. Add. 28622, also a collection of Ayton's poems, is written by a 'young' hand probably
about 1700. Cited as 'the Ayton MSS'.

[3] *Delitiae Poetarum Scotorum* (Amsterdam, 1637).

[4] Dempster: *Historia Ecclesiastica...*, article 112; Bannatyne Club Edition I, 62. 'Ejus sunt stylo omnia tersissimo
raraque inventionis felicitati. Poemata Graeca lib 1...Latina lib 1...Scotica lib 1...Gallica lib 1.'

more provocative lines 'rejoinders' were devised whose words became in time entangled with those of the original. It is no surprise that verses of his appeared in print 'in other men's names'.

All this speaks of lively enjoyment of his verse but it militates against the survival of the poet's work. There was no printing of his collected poems until the nineteenth century, when two editions appeared, marred by unworthy scholarship and gratuitous 'improvements'. Within the last few years, however, poems and songs of Ayton have been printed in valid texts and have appeared in anthologies of verse and of song. A choice of his vernacular verse, *Poems and Songs of Sir Robert Ayton*, was prepared by the present writer as volume III of the series 'The Ninth of May', Cambridge 1961. Now there is a new volume from the Scottish Text Society called *The English and Latin Poems of Sir Robert Ayton*. Edited by Dr Charles B. Gullans it includes 'the Life 1569–1638', compiled largely from the life-records of Ayton the court servitor and from letters by him, or alluding to him, in his official capacity. Here Sir Robert the man can be glimpsed through Sir Robert the official, as he can be heard or overheard in the poems of compliment or the lines of love-song. To have the Latin poems side by side with the vernacular enables certain qualities in both to be felt, charm and integrity even in panegyric, a clear argument and a light touch in both verse media and the presence of that charity of heart which inspired affection. But there are questions to raise.[1]

The vernacular poems in this volume for the Scottish Text Society are presented as 'The English Poems'. This titling, unqualified, is surprising. Dempster described Ayton as author of poems in Latin and Greek, French and Scots. Sir John Ayton in his preface to the poems in manuscript was careful to say that some were 'old Scots pieces done in his younger days'. Recent scholarship has pointed out verses by Ayton recorded in their original language of literary Scots as well as songs of his continuing Scots in a northern currency.[2] Ayton regarded himself as a 'Scoto-Briton'; the legal step of 'denization' which he took in 1614/15 would safeguard his property in England but would not undo his northern poetic youth.[3]

Furthermore, in presenting the vernacular poems Dr Gullans is concerned first and foremost with textual mutation. He has taken up the challenge to establish 'the text' for the favourite poems from informal currency. He has not, however, seen that certain other issues are important in themselves and most pertinent to his purpose— in the matter of verbal mutation, the inter-influence of words and music, in the matter of anglicisation, the possible presence in variant readings of Ayton's own

[1] For these editions by Charles Rogers see Ayton/Shire and Ayton/Gullans.
[2] M. P. McDiarmid, 'Some Versions of Poems by Sir Robert Aytoun and Sir William Alexander'; *Music of Scotland* no. 68 and notes; Ayton/Shire (1961) texts, notes and commentary.
[3] See Ayton/Gullans p. 37, note 5.

revising hand. The original version is not of necessity 'the' version of a lyric that was a song. The revised version is not of necessity 'the' version in the work of a poet who refashioned in current English verses conceived in literary Scots. The editor of Ayton's poems and songs needs to consider his policy deeply.

These two issues—the interest of Ayton as exponent of Scottish courtly poetry in its latest phase and the significance for his verses of association with music—are aspects of the poet's work that make him the fitting subject of our final chapter here. I attempt now to display Robert Ayton as grounded in a tradition of *Scottis Poesie* and as being, like Scott and Montgomerie before him, like Hudson, Mure of Rowallan and John Murray, a maker of verses *amoene* to music, apt for devising as courtly song.

ROBERT AYTON AND THE LATE CASTALIANS

Robert Ayton, born in Fife about 1570, student at St Andrews, then scholar and poet publishing work in Paris, seeker then holder of great place in the royal household in England under King James VI and I and his son Charles, became himself in his turn a patron of poets and scholars. His life-story spans changes in time and in place that are significant for the argument of this book, from the Scottish kingdom of his youth to the realm of 'Britaine' in whose court he later flourished. What can his vernacular poetry tell us about the writing of *Scottis Poesie* during the last decades of the sixteenth century? What can his verses written in the new court show us of change or continuity in such poetic tradition? What can his songs tell us about ways old and new of relating words and music?

First, who was he? His paternal grandmother was a Stewart of royal if illegitimate line. This same grandmother took as a second husband John Winram, the famous sub-prior of St Andrews who was bastard half-brother to Mary Queen of Scots, and by the same token half-uncle to the King of Scotland. For Robert Ayton, therefore, from his birth the door of entry as servitor to a Stewart monarch was at least ajar. A second son, by no means poorly endowed with worldly goods and well primed in faculties of nature, Robert Ayton chose a way to achievement through learning and letters. His education at St Andrews completed by 1589, he inherited substantially from his father in 1590. Thereafter the story breaks off until the year 1603 when he was in Paris, writing and publishing poetry of state compliment and request aimed at the new monarch and court of England.

Search has been made in Paris and in the records of the French universities in vain. But the only testimony to his having spent some or all of the 'lost' years in Paris is Dempster's phrase, that in France he 'for long cultivated the arts and left there a name for virtue and distinguished proof of his achievement'.[1] This is sufficiently indefinite and may do no more than refer to the Latin verses that were printed there in 1603, the panegyric on King James. Search should obviously be made elsewhere also for traces of Ayton as a young man. A clue to his comings and goings would exist among the documents of 'passport' if he travelled furth of Scotland alone, but evidently no such reference has been found. In 1591, however, an interesting possibility arises. In that year the poet Spenser in Ireland dedicated his 'Colin Clout's come home again' to Sir Walter Raleigh. In his poem he gave an impression of the literary-courtly England he had recently visited through a catalogue of named poets and patrons he had encountered there. Some items are actual surnames, like Alabaster; some are *noms de plume* or nicknames and some are couched in 'dark' or riddling terms. Towards the end of the list after a tribute to 'Amyntas' comes one to 'Aetion'.

> And there though last not least is Aetion
> A gentler shepherd may no where be found
> Whose Muse full of high thoughts invention
> Doth like himself Heroically sound.

(ll. 444–7)

The first couplet might let us dally with the thought of a young Scots pastoral poet spending a year in a nobleman's service in Queen Elizabeth's realm. But the second couplet sounds too grand, does it not, for anything Robert Ayton is likely to have achieved by the age of twenty—certainly if the reference is to 'Heroick' verses already composed and known? But 'Aetion' has been construed as a Greek pun on α-ἥττων *less, inferior to none* and pastoral verses from a gentle poet whose name had a heroic sound just brings it within the realms of possibility.[2] Early pastoral verses of his certainly exist—'Amyntas on a summer's day'.

Robert Ayton could well have been in England about 1589 or 1590, having crossed the border in the train of some eminent person, his passage thus going unrecorded in official document. Of course it must be admitted that Spenser's poem could enter into the matter in another way once it was printed in 1595—as an influence. A poetical-pastoral pseudonym so luckily conceiting Ayton's surname—he himself always spelt it 'Aiton'—may have been seized on and appropriated by the young Scots poet or his friends; along with the neighbouring 'Amyntas' it may have contributed to the building up of the poetic personality of the young poet of Kinaldie. He was much given to the practice of surname-conceit, as we shall see.

Robert Ayton was three or four years younger than King James. He was a student

---

[1] 'Nobili loco natus, summa eloquentia incomparabili morum suavitate ac modestia, diu in Gallis bonas artes excoluit et praeclarum suae virtutis specimen nomenque reliquit.'
[2] 'Aetion', see *Works of Edmund Spenser*, I, 472–3.

in Scotland when Mary Queen of Scots was executed.[1] No trace has been found of a Mr Robert Ayton as servitor or suitor for service at the court of Scotland either with the bachelor monarch before 1590 or in the double household newly organised when King James brought his royal bride Anna back from Scandinavia. Ayton's presence as a young man at the court of Scotland or at the court of England is unproven. His access to courtly making, however, English and Scots, in manuscript and in print, is manifest.

What was the literary climate in Scotland when Ayton was a student? In courtly circles Montgomerie was still 'arch-poet' in 1584 but soon bound for 'France, Flanders and Spain' and subsequent personal disaster. By 1589 or 1590 Montgomerie was back in Scotland but not restored to royal favour. It is not surprising that the influence of Montgomerie's poetry is found in Ayton's early writing. Over these years, however, one literary event is likely to have outrun all others in interest: the very year Ayton went to college saw the printing and publication of King James' *The Essayes of a Prentise, in the divine art of Poesie* with 'Ane schort treatise, conteining some reulis and cautelis to be obseruit and eschewit in Scottis Poesie'. A lead had now been given from the throne to any young Scot whose mind turned to writing poetry. And there were young poets about. Along with Ayton at St Andrews was, apparently, Alexander Craig of Rosecraig. Some years later William Alexander of Menstrie was at college, in all likelihood at Glasgow, which was probably the university of William Mure also; Drummond of Hawthornden studied at Edinburgh.[2] All of these wrote verses. All at some point in their lives made a bid for the King's favour, but only some attained it. In patterns of acquaintance Mure stands alone, linked only with his great-uncle, Montgomerie; William Alexander was close friend of the older poet Alexander Hume, and preserved links of cordial acquaintance with Drummond for many years.

Poems of Ayton and Craig show mutual admiration and encouragement and a shared interest in genre and style of poetry. In a way characteristic of the age, the development of a poetic personality is marked by the conceit on the surname. Ayton's early 'dier' (lament), 'My temperate style at first' figures 'hills and Craigs' as 'his wonted Secretaryes' in whom he confides; later his fellow poet is to be 'the Craige whence flows that sacred well, Where Phoebus reigns, where all the Muses dwell'. Later still, Craig is to bid *Aethon* sing again as his voice has not been heard for long; *Aethon* is chief of the steeds of Phoebus' chariot—a leading poet under King James.[3]

[1] As of kin he might have been among the numerous 'Aytons', some not particularised, recorded in State Papers as present at her funeral.

[2] Dr Gullans (p. 266), following Rogers, mistakenly states that William Alexander of Menstrie was at St Andrews along with Ayton. Alexander's date of birth is now 'not later than 1577', see T. H. McGrail, *The Life and Works of Sir William Alexander, first Earl of Stirling*, chapter 1.

[3] Ayton/Gullans no. 10, no. 27 (1604) and no. 34 (1609).

Others probably joined forces with them in the enthusiasms of their college days and participated in exchange and dedication of pieces. Two manuscript collections of poetry made in the last years of the old century or in the early years of the new show us this generation of young poets at work, late 'Castalians' in style and a 'band' but not, as far as we know, in direct touch with the court. One such source-book is an extensive manuscript volume where after several substantial entries—Poems of Alexander Hume of Logie, Burel's 'Pilgrimer' and a pamphlet of 1601—comes a group of seven poems.[1] Some of these seven are subscribed 'Semple' but in such a way as to suggest that he was compiler or owner of the manuscript rather than author of the poems; the phrase of direct attribution, 'quod so-and-so' is absent but there are some signs of authorship all the same and these link the pieces closely with young Ayton and his 'band'.

These seven poems composed in literary Scots have been printed as the opening items in the Scottish Text Society edition of Ayton, but only two of them are with any certainty Ayton's work, no. 2 and no. 6, 'Quhen Diaphantus knew' and 'Will thow, remorsles fair', which are in the Ayton manuscripts. 'Diaphantus' was acclaimed as his on more than one occasion. 'Let not the world beleeve' (no. 4) is by William Alexander of Menstrie while 'Evin as the dying swayne' (no. 5) is likely to be his also.[2] The title of no. 3, 'Craiges passionado' is surely a clear enough indication of authorship though this long lament, 'Quhy did the gods ordaine', is not to be found in the printed volumes of Craig's poems. 'Let him whois hapeles state' (no. 7) is very much a sister piece to those of Ayton, Craig and Alexander; unknown elsewhere, it is 'signed' within the poem by that favourite device of the pun on the surname:

Rest thee in thy wnrest and murray be thow still
The maike where meneles miseries directes there endles ill.   (ll. 43–4)

(This may well be the John Murray we know.) The first poem of the collection, a sonnet, gives no such clue to its author.

Two poems by Ayton written in literary Scots are found, then, in a collection made at the turn of the century; they are Scots in accidence, in vocabulary, in forms and spellings of words. They are indigenous 'making' and companioned by kindred pieces by other poets writing in Scotland. We have in this handful of young men's poems a late gathering of *Scottis Poesie*. Ayton's 'Scots pieces done in his younger days' were done in a live tradition and not in isolation.

All seven poems are laments of love—for absence of the loved one, for her lack of love or her inconstancy. The poet is writing in the first person—of actuality or of amorous 'feygning'—in all but the verses of 'Diaphantus and Charidora'. The

---

[1] National Library of Scotland: MS. 19.3.6.   [2] McDiarmid, 'Some Versions'.

opening sonnet makes the lover's plaint for absence with some skill, using phrases and cadences that rouse in us echoes of earlier Scottish courtly songs—

> Oche loyell saull, is this ye fates decreete?
> May I nocht have your presens as befoir?
> Adew contentment till thow me intreit!
> So sall be sene ay till thow me restoir.

The summing couplet, however, turns from fates and thousand hearts to something nearer the voice of affection

> No worldlie pleasure can expell my paine
> But presence of my deerest deere againe.

This may well be Robert Ayton, Cavalier song-writer of the future, first finding his own voice—using phrases he was to use again.

This sonnet apart, all these 'Semple' poems couch their love-lamentation in the genre of the 'dier'. The meaning of this word has never been fully explained and investigation is called for. Used as a title for two of the pieces it is rendered 'Ane Dyor' and 'passionado' appears to be a synonym.[1] The verse form is 'poulters' measure' and the style highly rhetorical. Neither the metre nor the genre under one name or the other is characteristic of *Scottis Poesie* of the earlier sixteenth century. They are not found in Montgomerie's writing nor are they represented in the King's printed volume of 1584, either in his own verses or in those examples chosen to illustrate his 'Schort Treatise'. Nor would their metre, 'poulters' measure', qualify as one of the 'sindrie kyndes of haill verse, with all thair lynis alyke lang, quhilk I haue heir omittit' of his conclusion. The King's second printed volume, *His Maiesties Poeticall Exercises at Vacant Houres* of 1591, has little variety in verse form—two long poems in fourteeners rhyming in couplets and several sonnets. But some time after his marriage the King wrote just such a love-lament in 'poulters' measure' and it was entitled 'A Dier on her Majestie', Altered to 'A Dier at her majesties desyer'.[2] (The entitling was done, we should allow, many years later yet it may still have been supplied by the King.) Queen Anne's request for a 'dier' to be written, met by the King's love-lament in 'poulters' measure', marks this as a kind of poem enjoying high prestige in the years following 1590. The King's poem begins

> If mourning micht amende my harde unhappie cace
> or if complaining coude appaise dame fortonis frouning face
> then shoulde I neuer cease by songs and sonnets still
> uith my too iust conceaved regraitts the earth and aire to fill

---

[1] 'Passionado' is used for the same kind of poem by William Lithgow in his *The Pilgrimes Farewell* (Edinburgh, 1618).

[2] Westcott, no. XIV and note pp. 76–7, where 'dier' is discussed.

and it continues in like vein for some fifty lines. A sonnet is appended, however, explaining that the grief is feigned passion, done to please his lady by one who is in reality happy in love; how much more piercing are the cries of those that love unloved, the royal poet observes.

The fashion in love-complaint that took the fancy of Queen Anne had been prominent in England for at least ten years. Howell's *Devises* of 1581, for instance, had an excellent example called 'Sorrowe disclosed, somewhat eased':

> Sithe kindled coales close kept continue longest quick
> And secret smarte with greater power the pensive mind doth prick
> Why should I cloke the griefe from whence such passions grow
> Unlesse my braine by pen I purge, my brest they overflow[1]

The measure had been in high favour in England long before this. Verses in this mode were found congenial for setting by the early master of English song, William Byrd.

The best explanation that could be found by earlier critics for the title of the King's poem was 'a careless spelling or contraction of "*dirige*" the first word of a penitential psalm becoming "dirgy" or "dirge"' (Westcott). Dunbar's mock-penitential had been entitled 'Dregy' in the Bannatyne Manuscript. But there is more to it than that. 'Dier' though unknown as anything like 'complaint' in the *Oxford English Dictionary*, bears there the meaning of 'one who dies, is ready to die' and 'one who dyes'. This ambiguity had already been exploited in print in the 1580s in the name-conceit of a poet. In Geoffrey Whitney's *A Choice of Emblemes* the emblem of a dyer is entitled 'In colores' and the verses describe the work of the dyer, playing on his colours and the colours of rhetoric. The climax is a tribute to Edward Dyer

> Yet Englande hath her store of orient dies
> And else therein a DYER most of fame
> Who alwaies hathe so fine and freshe a hew
> That in their landes the like is not to vewe.

The name-conceit is taken one step further in a manuscript version of one of Byrd's *Psalmes, Sonets and Songs*, 1588, no. xxxv, 'O that rare breast', a funeral song for Sir Philip Sidney. The last two lines run

> O heavi tyme! that my daies drawe behind thee:
> Thou dead dost liue, they dier living dieth.

The printed version is anonymous, reading 'they friend here' for 'thy dier'; in the manuscript the name-conceit gives the author, Dyer, who lives but dies of sorrow at Sidney's death—and the death-poem, the 'dier' whose verses will live.[2]

[1] Howell's *Devises*, ed. Raleigh, p. 40.
[2] Whitney, *A Choice of Emblemes*, p. 134: see Philip Brett, 'The English Consort Song, 1570–1625', *Proceedings of the Royal Musical Association*, LXXXVIII (1961–2), 82. Manuscript version (Christ Church, Oxford, MS. 984) see *The Collected Works of William Byrd*, ed. E. H. Fellowes, XII, revised Philip Brett (1964), p. xxxviii.

Sir Edward Dyer was known for his love-complaints of which only two are now to be found and these are not certainly assigned. Francis Meres names him as among those who 'are the most passionate among us to bewaile and bemoane the perplexities of Love'.[1] I submit that the kind of lament whether funereal or amorous, that was associated with Dyer at just this time may have come to be known as a 'Dyer' or 'dier'—to yield, in Scotland at least, a name for the genre of lament where the poet declares he is near death for love. Certain it is that a kind and measure long known in England and used as late as 1581 in the *Devises* (a volume that Montgomerie knew) was in fashion in royal circles in Scotland in the early 1590s. Passing outwards it obviously influenced the young poets of Ayton's generation whom we have called 'the late Castalians'. Two more examples in the same measure and genre are found in another manuscript from Scottish aristocratic circles of the 1590s belonging to one of the Murray family.[2] They are significantly entitled, the one 'English Dyare' and the other 'Murray's Dyare'. The use of the titles marks a moment of conscious adoption of the southern mode by a young practiser of *Scottis Poesie*.

For the young 'late Castalians' the 'dier' was a favourite genre with royal cachet. Among these young poets Ayton was a leading figure. Of the 'dier' he was an enthusiastic exponent.

FROM CASTALIAN TO CAVALIER

Robert Ayton commenced poet, then, in the courtly tradition of his own country, witness 'Diaphantus' and 'Will thow, remorsles fair' in the 'Semple' versions. How Ayton revised his 'Diaphantus' for presentation to an English public can be clearly seen by setting the Semple version beside that in the Ayton manuscripts.[3] In brief, Scots accidence and spelling have been modified and northern words uncouth in the south have been dropped. Some northern vigour has been lost, alas, in the polishing process.

> Yet peradventure to
> For Diaphantus saike
> Sum rectles bodie cumming by
> will homage to the make

is the early version; the Englishing has changed the nonchalant passer-by, the 'rectles bodie', significantly, to a 'civil person'. Again, several lines have disappeared that look forward to the Ayton of the Cavalier lyric.

[1] *Palladis Tamia or Wits Treasury* (1598); see *Francis Mere's Treatise on 'Poetrie': A Critical Edition* by Don Cameron Allen, XIX, p. 79 and note on p. 136.
[2] A manuscript copy of Lydgate's 'Troybook', part of it in the hand of [Sir] James Murray of Tibbermuir (1612); it contains additional pieces from the sixteenth and early seventeenth century (Cambridge University Library MS. Kk.v.30). Murray may be John Murray of chapter VII. Another 'A. Dyer', thus entitled, is no. LVII in MS. Laing III, 436, 'the Scots cavalier's anthology', Edinburgh University Library.
[3] They are juxtaposed in Ayton/Gullans. The comparison is made by McDiarmid.

That day sall nevir daw
  nor sunne sall never schyne
Sall quarrell me for appostate
  for naucht remayneing thyne.

It would seem that 'Diaphantus' or 'Diophantus' (thus spelled in the Ayton version) reached print, for Drummond of Hawthornden possessed a copy that cost sixpence.[1] But a 'dier' in early Tudor style that pleased Queen Anne in Scotland in the early 1590s was quite out of step with taste in a London that had known the blossoming of Elizabethan lyric poetry. The Castalian poet of the north was betrayed by the 'Scottish time-lag'; language could be modified to please but the onward movement of taste in poetry could not be made to turn back upon itself.

Other 'old Scotts peeces' done in his younger days we may recognise partly by their closeness to pieces in the Semple collection, partly by traces they bear of having been composed in the first place in literary Scots.[2] Two other 'diers' must surely date from the Scots Castalian period of 1584 onwards to the close of the century, 'My temperate style at first' and 'My heart exhale thy greife'. The first has a punning reference to Craig. Both retain many Scottish characteristics in vocabulary or accidence, 'greete' for weep, and the northern plural verb form in 'Now tragick trumpetts blowes'. Here and there, however, a Scots word that would be incomprehensible or a spelling that might be misunderstood has been corrected in his manuscript by the hand of Sir John, 'hinmost' to 'latest', 'waine' to 'vayne'. Whether Sir John was correcting on his own initiative or from another copy of the poet's writings it is impossible to tell. Probably both processes are at work in all the poems we shall consider. Sometimes a Scots word survives in one 'Ayton' manuscript and has been changed in another, 'bairnlyness' to 'modesty'. Sometimes the Englishing of a rhyme-word has involved further modifications and in such cases it is probable that the amending hand was the poet's own. Sir John may have been faced by no neat final draft but by a poet's working papers.

'Will thou remorsles fair' is in the style and metre of the 'dier' but shorter and better organised in argument. The poet is concerned less to pour out his woe than to communicate a train of thought to the beloved. The poem is clinched in a paradox, if somewhat clumsily:

Then to prevent thy schame and to abraige my woe
Because thou wil noucht love thy freinde I'le cease to lufe my foe.

Another piece of the same rhetorical texture 'If high excess of irrelenting smart'—in pentameters this time, organised into substantial stanzas—emerges at the end into

---

[1] For this Gullans has another explanation: Ayton/Gullans, p. 264.

[2] A chronology of Ayton's vernacular poems is suggested in Ayton/Shire and in Ayton/Gullans; these agree substantially but differ at points.

wording that is simple and direct, if naïve. These poems stand half-way between the 'outpouring' of the late Castalian 'dier' and the succinct *adresse* of the Cavalier lyric.

In the sonnet, too, we can see development and advance from the work of the student poet influenced by Montgomerie and enamoured of obscurer classical references—'Cephisus' son', 'Thurinus' smoke'—to the mastery of two royal pieces written, one perhaps for King James as King of Scotland, the other certainly for James VI and I of Britain.[1] To both the 'Phoebus' figure is central. 'Where Thebes' staitly towres did threate the skye' has the poet likened to the statue of the sun-god at Thebes that can give forth a 'vitall-vocall' sound when struck by the beams of Apollo. 'The old records of analyzed fame' celebrates the coming to rest of the floating isle of Delos when Apollo graced it with 'the bliss of his birthday': King James the peacemaker brings stability to 'that Ile' 'our Albion' formerly racked by strife. The image of the king long favoured in northern circles is now used with distinction *in aula britannica*. Ayton has arrived in London.

In the year that marked for *Scottis Poesie* the end of court-patronage centred in Scotland Ayton was an accomplished exponent of lyric and of sonnet conceived in a milieu of royal ceremony and touched by national concern—witness two pieces reflecting the departure of the King and his company from Scotland. The sonnet on the River Tweed marks the crossing of the border by the King and his company at the Union of the Crowns. The occasion was momentous and marked by ceremonial farewell—by writing of verses that were cast into the waters. (William Fowler had a record of some of them among his papers.) The Tweed—'Faire famous flood, which sometime did devyde And now conjoynes two Diadems in one'—is in Ayton's lines invoked to bear on its waters news of 'our Captiver's last farewell'—downstream to the ocean and thence to the whole world and also upstream to Melrose Abbey where lay the heart of Robert the Bruce, long ago champion of Scotland's independence. ('Captiver' in Scots is 'one who leads a band into captivity'. The poet's awareness of the moment is sensitive.)

Similar scenes of ceremony fraught with emotion marked the King's entry into the border town of Berwick—in a thunderstorm that cleared to sunshine later, which the King interpreted as a happy omen.[2] It is very likely that this moment's emotion informs the lyric of personal leave-taking which Ayton wrote: 'Thou wilt not goe and leave me heir' has the lines

> The sun's depairting clouds the sky
> Bot thy depairting makes me die.

(This 'depairt' will come into our story again later, as a song.)

---

[1] Readings and gloss to this effect in Ayton/Shire.

[2] See Wilson, *King James VI and I*, p. 162: 'The sun before the rain represented his happy departure, the rain the grief of Scotland, the succeeding fair weather the joy of England at his approach.'

The tenor of Ayton's life once he was established in the English court as documented from letters and entries in official papers is interestingly at one with the concern of his poetry. Indeed in one letter to the Duke of Buckingham he moves from verse to prose and back again with nonchalance:

> Arch-miracle of men, in whome wee see
> Things joyned, which never could, but now, agree
> Both great and good, both fortunate and wise
> The Darling both of Prince and People's eyes
> My noble Lord...

Suffer these lines to do that which my self, partly for feare of importunitie dare not and partly for want of opportunitie can not do, that is, to put your Lordship in mind of him who, without your faithful and speedie remembrance is in danger to sink and perish...[He appeals in prose for help to secure from the King the 'seacoles patent' ending the letter in couplets of compliment.]

Were 'these lines' simply the verse in the letter? Or were there lines enclosed, the sonnet 'Loe how the sailer in a stormy night'? There is between letter and sonnet a remarkable concordance, in the mood of despair—the loss of the star 'whose situation and assured light' should guide him, and in the matter of shipwreck. Queen Anne had died in 1619 and her Secretary had now to look elsewhere for revenues and patronage. Buckingham, Master of the Horse, was created Master of the Fleet in 1620. Both the Queen's death and Buckingham's double command were honoured by Ayton in Latin verses.[1]

The art of *quémander avec grace* Ayton understands to perfection, whether in prose or verse, whether in Latin or the vernacular. He writes with loyal love to Queen Anne on New Year's Day 1603 or 1604 playing on the theme of the 'gift of a heart' and the renewal of pledge at Yule. He writes to King James on the Fifth of November. Other accomplished pieces are penned to patrons (Sir James Hay) or to fellow-poets (Alexander Craig or Sir William Alexander), or they concern friends like Thomas Murray. Those in the vernacular parallel poems in Latin, to Ralph Thorius or Sir John Murray. Scottish names predominate. The letter appealing for material help merges into the poetry of *propyne*. Latin is a sister medium of the vernacular. Such poetry is the voice of court ceremony, of the conduct of affairs, the muse of a court poet in the service of *vita verecunda*—despite the chosen motto!

Many other verses, however, belong to *Musa jocosa*, being teasing pieces of court-frippery, 'Lov's like a game at Tables', 'Upone a Gentle-woman that painted' or 'Upon Platonick Love: to Mistress Cicely Crofts, Maide of Honor'.[2] This last reflects the fashionable pose of the 'Platonicks' in King Charles' court and must have

[1] Ayton/Gullans, letter II; English poems, 23; Latin poems, 13 and 15.
[2] Maid of Honour to Queen Henrietta Maria, at court from about 1632 until her marriage in 1636. See 'Fie Platonicks, fie for shame...Tis a pure court frippery': anonymous song with music by Colman.

been written not long before the poet's death. For a parallel to these among the life-records we turn to Sir Robert's will.[1] He was a bachelor without children and left substantial dowries to his nieces and his 'French bed with appurtenances' to Mistress Whorewood. To his friend and fellow-poet, William Murray, he left 'my hat-band sett with diamonds'.

His last piece of courtly poetry written directly to a monarch is perhaps his finest, where heart and imagination are deeply moved at the bereavement of the young King Charles of his baby son. The loss of the first-born prince is grieved for in terms of royal state, human fatherhood and Christian consolation, 'on the Princes death, to the King'. The baby was born and died on the thirteenth of May, 1629. The tree of state and the fall of new-formed fruit in May, comfort for the husbandman, the rendering of first-fruits to God and the angel-nature of the babe that dies in infancy are blended in the gentle voice of the old royal servitor speaking in love and wisdom to his Stewart master.

1   Did you ever see the day
When Blossomes fell in middst of May?
Rather did you ever see
all the blossomes on the Tree
grow to ripe fruit? some must fall,
Nature says so, though not all.
   Though one be fallen, we have store,
   The Tree is fresh and may have more.

2   And for our comfort this we know,
the soyle is good, and you may sowe.
What would we more? more seed cast on,
for so have thriving husbands done.
And though the first Cropp fayle, they find
a fruitfull earth will still be kind;
   And, sir, your patience is but Iust,
   For live we may but dye we must.

3   But this was the first? tis true
God should be first serv'd, then you.
He that made the Sun to shine
said, the first fruit shal be mine.
And thinke it not a heavy doome,
for he that gives all, may take some.
   Godes will be done, and yet to you
   his will ordaynes a Blessing too.

4   A man begettes a man, the king
did more, begatt a holy thing;

[1] See Ayton/Gullans, pp. 102–3.

An Angell, that nere knew offence,
such priviledge hath Innocence.
The king then cannot make Complaynt
when the kinges first borne is a Saint;
    Nay more, an Angell, heavenly blesst,
    so let our heavenly Angell rest.

We have seen the poet Robert Ayton progress from 'late Castalian' to Cavalier, from 'dier' or learned sonnet on a general theme to verses of *propyne* elegantly devised to please in Jacobean court circles, from northern vigour that would sound uncouth to lines of delicacy or dignity, silk of court lady or the very stuff of royalty.

How did the other 'late Castalians' fare? Could a phase of *Scottis Poesie* dependent from a court culture in Scotland continue to exist after the departure of King and court from their northern seat? If so, on what terms? Literary contact of the late Castalians with one another? Residence in Scotland or keeping company with the King in England? Continuing to please the monarch's pride in the Castalian poetry he had helped to create? Continuing to write in literary Scots or amending northern poetic language to meet the taste of court and wider public in England?

Alexander Craig came to London where he published two volumes of verses. He won recognition from the King but only briefly. He soon returned to Scotland, where he published more verse. His books of poetry declared their solidarity with the King's Castalian tradition by echoing in their titles those of earlier royal volumes—but a bid for favour through poetry could fail.[1] William Alexander fared better. The King took a personal interest in his poetry, at one point chiding him for his 'harsh verses' made after the English fashion and not in smooth Castalian style.[2] He came to hold high position of state as Earl of Stirling. His first printed drama *Darius* (1603) retained much that was Scottish in its language, but it was Englished before being included with his *Monarchick Tragedies*. These chamber dramas were written according to the best Continental critical tenets and won much admiration in their generation, but they made little impact on a London that knew the dark splendours of the Jacobean stage.

Alexander, friend of the older poet Hume, kept in touch with Drummond who was writing fine poetry in Scotland in self-made isolation from the language spoken around him. It was Alexander who wrote home to Drummond in Scotland the news of John Murray's death, 'Albion's sweetest swain'. Trace of contact between Alexander and Ayton, however, has proved hard to come by, though Ayton saluted with a sonnet the *Monarchick Tragedies*.

[1] *The Poeticall Essayes* (1604), *Poeticall Recreations* (1609).
[2] Westcott, p. 37 and p. 96. The 'harshness' I take to mean metrical roughness as found in Donne's satires.

All these poets came to conform in their writing to the English usage. But—strange though this may sound to some modern partisans of the Scottish character in literature—northernness of language was not at that time felt to be the sole hallmark of a national poetic heritage. These poets tried, like their English contemporaries, to be citizens of Europe as well as patriots.[1] Yet a consciousness did exist of a continuing tradition and style that could be called Castalian. The King's continuing approbation helped.

That consciousness can be read in other places. William Lithgow 'the traveller' prefaced his tale of his journeys with an 'Elegie' that contains a tally of the makars of Scotland:

> Amongst these long Goodnightes, farewell yee Poets deare
> Grave Menstrie true Castalian fire, quicke Drummond in his spheare
> Brave Murray ah is dead, Aiton supplies his place
> And Alen's high Pernassian veine rare poems doth embrace.
> There's manie moe well knowne, whome I cannot explaine
> And Gordon, Semple, Maxwell too have the Pernassian veine.[2]

The Scottish tradition with its 'Castalian fire' is seen from the outside too, in lines by Sir Walter Raleigh from prison greeting Lithgow's volume. (The traveller he sincerely admired but his word for the poetaster is mocking.)

> And now thy second pilgrimage I see
> At London thou resolvst to put in light...
> Meane while this Worke affordes a three-folde gaine
> In furie of thy fierce CASTALIAN veine...

Paradoxically enough, a consciousness of a national tradition in poetry is found also in the Latin verse of the time. In the great series of *Delitiae* printed in the Low Countries the *Delitiae Poetarum Scotorum* holds distinguished place. The Latin poets of Scotland knew one another and Ayton was honoured among them. Robert Farley, too, bears witness to his quality.[3]

> Grande Caledonii decus orbis et inclyta fama
> Vatum, Laurigeri, gloria prima chori...

The character of the poet Ayton comes through the adulation, his celebration of chaste love—'castae virginis ignes', his integrity—'Pagina te castum probat integra vita poetae', his songs—'Musa tua sed voce melos sibi temperat'. Ayton's muse reigned where lyre was struck and the manners of the times were portrayed. Lighthearted youth will keep his memory green.

To the songs of Sir Robert Ayton we must now turn.

[1] The comment is John Stevens'.
[2] *The Pilgrimes Farewell to his Native Country of Scotland* (Edinburgh 1618). Alen—Scots cavalier poet, several of whose pieces are recorded in manuscripts; Gordon—unknown: Maxwell—possibly James Maxwell, Gentleman of the Bedchamber, to whom some Cavalier lyrics are attributed; Semple—possibly 'of Beltrees'.
[3] *Naulogia*, 1635?: see Ayton/Gullans, pp. 88–90.

AYTON AS SONG-WRITER: A NORTHERN TRADITION?

Talia dulcisono moderaris carmina plectro
Fundis et ad citherae murmura blanda mélos.   Robert Farley, 1635

Sir Robert Ayton was renowned in his own lifetime for his songs. Do any of his lyrics belong to a northern musical tradition distinct from the song-making of the Jacobean court?

First, Robert Ayton had no direct contact with the courtly song-making in Scotland under King James VI. Though he early knew Montgomerie's work there is nothing to suggest that he knew poems of his as art-song. 'Will thou remorsles fair', an early piece of his present in the 'Semple' manuscript, is marked elsewhere as having had music—but that is in the verse anthology of a Scots cavalier of the mid-seventeenth century, where its inscription is marked with a musical sharp.[1] Such music has not come to light. A piece with the title 'Amyntas on a Symmers day' is among those for cittern in Robert Edwards' Music Book. This is undoubtedly the music for Ayton's early pastoral 'Amintas on a summer day'. Neither of these poems was current as song in Jacobean or Caroline England.

A third lyric not found at all with music in English song-books, manuscript or printed, was yet a favourite in musical circles in Scotland for over sixty years. It is the 'depairt' we spoke of above, 'Then will thou goe and leave me heir'; a version of the poem in English opening thus appears in the Ayton manuscripts. Northern record, however, preserves it in a different version, in current Scots of the seventeenth century and always with music. Early in the century it was engrossed in the extensive playing-book for the lute belonging to the Skenes of Hallyards, entitled 'Then will thou goe and leave me her'. There it keeps company with native airs and dances of Scottish provenance as well as with lute-songs and dances of King James' court in England. The same music was written out for cittern in Robert Edwards' Music Book as 'Vilte thou be gone'; again the repertory for this section of cittern music embraces native airs and tunes from furth of Scotland, though native airs predominate. In the song-book of William Stirling of Ardoe dated 1639—a cantus part-book only survives—the same tune appears together with the words, six stanzas that are near to the version in the Ayton manuscripts but not identical with it. The vocal line with the first stanza underlaid was among the pieces included at the end of a manuscript copy of Forbes' *Songs and Fancies* (1662), that was made probably not long after that first issue of the printed book. A comparison of the copies of the tune shows a gentle change coming over it: between the versions in Skene and Stirling and the record of 1662 it takes on something of the native air in rhythm and presentation.[2]

---

[1] In MS. Laing III, 436; such marking appears to mean 'there is music for this piece'.
[2] *Music of Scotland*, no. 68; Ayton/Elliott, no. 11.

9. (a) *THOU WILT NOT GOE*[1]

William Stirling's Cantus Part-Book

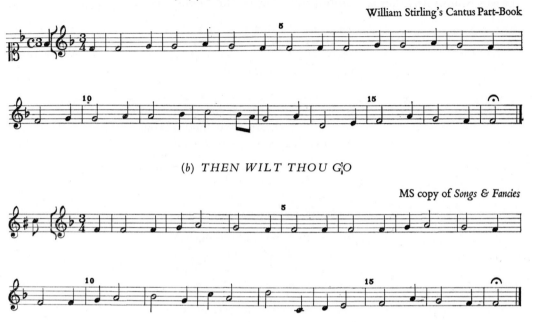

(b) *THEN WILT THOU GO*

MS copy of *Songs & Fancies*

A monophonic song, though it might originate in courtly circles as tuneful air or continuo song, could by its nature move into oral currency and the world of 'folk-song' in a way that was well-nigh impossible for the polyphonic part-song of the sixteenth century. Movement in the contrary direction is likely to have occurred also, but proof of this is difficult to come by. A native air, in all probability already provided with words from 'folk' or popular currency, could enter courtly circles as a piece for lute or cittern. Such an air can be envisaged as sung there to its 'old' words, but of this phase no complete evidence in writing has survived. Such an air with a fresh set of verses made to match it could be arranged as continuo song (song for voice and keyboard instrument) in which process changes in melody are more likely to occur than in 'straight' transcription of native air for lute-playing. Whether the tune of Ayton's 'depairt' came in from 'folk' or popular currency—as 'Vilte thou be gone'?—to be arranged for voice and instrument or whether it was composed in the first place by a 'courtly' musician we cannot tell. A wide currency in Scottish musical circles from about 1610 to 1665 is beyond doubt.

'Then wilt thou goe', presented in *Music of Scotland* as a continuo song, has the words as William Stirling knew them lightly emended with other versions in mind.

[1] Music: (a) William Stirling's Cantus Part-Book (1639), fo. 171; (b) MS. copy of *Songs & Fancies* (1662–1682), fo. 64v. (K.E.)

This text from Scotland is not known to Dr Gullans though Dauney had printed it in *Ancient Scotish Melodies* as a note to no. LXI of the Skene Manuscript.

1 Thow wilt not goe and leave me heir
O do not so, my dearest deir;
The sune's depairting clouds the sky
Bot thy depairting maks me die.

2 Thow canst not goe, my deirest heart
Bot I must quyt my choisest pairt;
For with two hearts thow must be gone
And I sall stay at home with none.

3 Meane whill, my pairt sall be to murne,
Telling the houres whill thow returne;
My eyes sall be but eyes to weip
And nether eyes to sie nor sleipe.

4 Prevent the hazard of this ill,
Goe not at all, stay with me still;
I'lle bath thy lips with kisses then
And look for mor ease back againe.

5 Since thou will needs goe, weill away!
Leave, leave one hart with me to stay;
Take mine, lett thine in pane remaine,
That quicklie thou may come againe.

6 Fairweill, deir heart, since it must be,
That thow wilt not remain with me;
My greatest greife it still sall be,
I love a love that loves not me.

Comparison with the words in the Ayton manuscript is interesting. What 'Englishing' had to be done—by Ayton or by his editing nephew—is slight. An alternative form of a word or a near equivalent had to be found: 'depairting' becomes 'departure', 'hazard' becomes 'danger' and 'in pane' (in pound) becomes in Sir John's version 'pawne'. One difference *may* be due to a miscopying, the Scots version's 'mor ease' against 'increase'.

Along with the 'Englishing' but not caused here by its exigencies, further modification was put in hand. In the second stanza the Scottish 'bot' for 'without that' disappears. The whole has been polished to become something more accomplished, perhaps, but less direct and less tender.

Thou canst not goe but with my heart
Even that which is my cheifest part
Then with two hearts thou sall be gone
And I shal rest behinde with none.

The progress of thought in the Scottish version may be indicated thus in shorthand: dearest deir, depairting as the sun's/deirest heart, depairting means loss of heart/ mourning—eyes/Go not—lips/Go then, but leave one heart/Farewell dearest heart, I am unloved.

In the Ayton manuscript version the thought has been refashioned. The stanzas have been rearranged. The second stanza has been pointed up in conceit but has lost the lead-in of 'dearest heart'. Then follows 'go not—lips', then 'And if thou needs must go, leave a heart, that thou may return'. ('And' makes blurred sense here; it is probably 'An', a strong 'if'.) Then comes 'meantime I weep—eyes', which thought is extended into a sophisticated conclusion: 'If I do close may eyes I shall dream of you.' It is possible that a rehandling of the song was done to suit a different amorous occasion! I suggest that both versions are 'good' versions; in neither case are the stanzas out of order by mistake.

It was the earlier version that passed into currency as song. The slight variations in title or first line, found among the pieces for cittern or lute and those with words underlaid to music, make it likely that the tune 'existed before' and that Ayton wrote his 'depairt' to match its music, giving a new direction to the sentiment inherent in the title or old first line—'Vilte thou be gone?' It was the earlier version in literary Scots that remained in Scotland to become a favourite song there. It was the lyric Englished and refashioned that Sir John collected after the poet's death.

A version of the poem sixteen lines long was recorded as 'Lines by King James on Queen Anne's death'.[1] The song, then, must have been a favourite in royal circles in 1619. Perhaps the King quoted 'And will thou goe and leave me heir' on that sad occasion. Indeed it may have been in wider use as a 'depairt': an adaptation of these lines provides the outset of satirical verses in broadside currency—the 'King's fare-well' to the Duke of Buckingham on his departure overseas.[2]

Three points are of interest here, and relevant to the whole course of these studies: the use of song on a ceremonial occasion, the making of a new piece on a well-known opening phrase and the currency persisting in circles about the Stewart monarch of Scottish song.

Other songs of Ayton may have had a divergence of currency into north and south.

[1] MSS. belonging to Matthew Wilson of Eshton Hall, Yorkshire vol. XXXIV: *Historical MSS. Commission Report,* III (1872), 299.

[2] 'And wilt thou goe, great duke, and leave us heere/Lamenting thee and eke thy pupill deere' and 'And wilt thou go brave duke and leave us here/That we may thinkt a happy victory'; printed in *Poems and Songs relating to the Duke of Buckingham,* ed. F. W. Fairholt, Percy Society, XXIX. Rubrics attach satiric verses opening thus to one of two departures, for Spain with Prince Charles in 1622 and for La Rochelle (Ile de Rhé) after the death of King James—that ill-fated expedition in which so many Scots perished. A cittern piece called 'The isle of Rea' is found in the same collection that has music for 'And wilt thou goe' as 'Vilte thou be gone' (Robert Edwards' Music-Book).

The Scots Cavalier anthologist caught some lyrics in an earlier form. For two more there are versions in Scots elsewhere than in the Ayton manuscripts; of 'Thou sent to me ane heart' in the song-book of McAlmain of Dunollich and Edward Millar and of 'Wrong not sweet empress' the version subscribed 'quod sumbodie' in B.M. MS. Add. 24707 which, as Dr Gullans puts it, 'is in Scottish orthography' and 'shows almost complete independence when it diverges'.

Is any general conclusion possible on songs of Ayton as written in a Scots tradition? Ayton writing as a young Castalian was not in touch with music of the court. A link with the Scots native air is, however, probable. A continuing currency in Scots for some of the songs is certain. An origin in a northern tradition for these is likely. Two pieces written in the English court to royal Stewart ladies survive in Scots; they are in courtly English as they stand in the Ayton manuscripts and as they reached wide popularity with their English settings. But did Robert Ayton address his queen in 1603 and his princess later in impeccable English or in the Scots tongue they shared? Both the royal pieces could have reverted to Scots, I admit, at a later date, borne home by a Scottish cavalier and enjoyed in Scottish company. I think no neat conclusion is possible here. If these pieces of loyal love the language of poetry is very near indeed to the language of ceremonious address. We are at the point of divergence for *Scottis Poesie*. Not for much longer was it to be written in a literary language related closely to the personal speech of the monarch. Already its language was uncouth to the majority of the company at court.

SONGS OF THE JACOBEAN AND CAROLINE COURT

When Ayton approached the new British court of King James he came into a re-nowned world of song. The English lute-ayre was already flourishing, marked by Dowland's first collection of solo-ayres printed in 1597, while the 'tuneful airs' of Campion had been collected and printed with ayres of Rosseter. This new fashion of solo song was spreading outwards and could have reached Ayton in Paris or in Fife before he came to London. However that may be, Ayton's meeting with solo art-song was significant for his development as a poet. With the new mode of song a new way of lyric-writing was established: lyrics were to be short and well seasoned, witty yet not too involved in their argument, composed in matching stanzas and in rhythms that moved lightly and featly. They were to be gracious words to wed to music, 'the two coupled lovingly together'.

Ayton's practice in song-writing was linked with the work of Campion. His lyric 'There is none, no, none but I' is, in the wording of opening phrase as in metrical pattern, patently an answer to Campion's song 'There is none, O, none but you'.

While the link between the original set of words and the answering lyric could be purely literary, it has been borne home by musical scholars how often in this epoch the connection between two such lyrics was locked in the music that matched both. Certainly Ayton's verses sing perfectly to Campion's air.

10. THERE IS NONE, NO NONE BUT I[1]

AYTON   CAMPION

There— is— none, no, none but I, None— but I so full of woe

That— I— can - not—choose— but— die Or— else beg phy - sic— from— my foe.

(Ayton's own 'There is none' was later to be set by Dr John Wilson, as we shall see.)

Campion's song reached print in his *Second Book of Airs* which bears no definite date of publication. The year 1610 has been suggested; but some of Campion's songs had been in currency since the opening years of the century. Ayton and Campion were near contemporaries. Both were early known as poets in Latin epigram and in vernacular lyric. Both were about the court between 1612 and 1620, the year of Campion's death. Indeed there is a strong likelihood of acquaintance between the two as early as 1607, when Campion devised the masque for Lord Hay, a Scots royal favourite whose interest had been fruitfully courted by Ayton. Certainly by the year 1613, which saw Campion devising the masque for Queen Anne at Caversham House and Ayton in personal attendance on the Queen as her Secretary, Sir Robert would know at first hand the delightful words and music of the court masques and the poet musician who devised them.

Ayton's verses of this time are patently of the court courtly and frequently celebrate a royal occasion; but personal presentation or ceremony was the milieu of his muse rather than entertainment or pastime organised and mounted for the court. At a later point, Ayton's pastoral and platonic or anti-platonic pieces are notably consonant with current fashion at the Caroline court—the pastoral or 'platonick' pose of the ladies—but again they voice the play or 'feigning' of social converse rather than the matter of any staged mimesis.

[1] Music: Thomas Campion, *Second Book of Ayres* (1613?) (ed. Fellowes, London 1926) no. 13. John Wilson's singing version reads 'There is none O none but I'; this may show a running together by that time of the first lines of Campion's song and Ayton's, but the alteration may be Wilson's own. (K.E.)

The 'tuneful air' of the kind that Campion wrote so masterly is found matched with other light and nimble lyrics of Ayton. Indeed the music for 'Dear, why do you say you love' may well be one of Campion's unnumbered offspring.[1] Again, Ayton's 'There is no worldly pleasure here below', whose wittily argued verses were widely popular over many years, is likely to have met its lively tune early in the century, although the words were not printed until the 1660s.[2] This song paid the price of its widespread oral and manuscript currency in the large number of variant verbal texts in which it survives. The lyric, complete in the Ayton manuscripts, is ten verses long and conducts, stanza by stanza, a light-hearted but cogent 'reasoning about love'. The poet's case is for moderation.

> I like a milde and luke-warm zeale in love
> Although I doe not like it in devotion

This provoked a rejoinder: at some point in the verses' currency an answer must have been made, meeting the turns of the argument stanza by stanza. (A version was printed in 1671 entitled 'The Answer to Love's fiery passions'.) In time stanzas of the answer mingled with stanzas of the original and confusion resulted. It looks as if the two poems were recited or sung by two performers, with an alternation, stanza by answering stanza, of Ayton's words with the other's. All the versions recorded, 'good' or 'corrupt', 'original' or 'answering' go happily to the easy swinging tune.

11. THERE IS NO WORLDLY PLEASURE HERE BELOW[3]

AYTON   ANON

There is no world-ly plea-sure here be-low Which by ex-pe-rience doth not fol-ly prove

But a-mongst all the fol-lyes that I know The sweet-est fol - ly in the world is love.

In one instance the 'tuneful air' was a dance-tune and both 'original' and 'answer' were written by the poet himself. Ayton's pair of songs 'I lov'd thee once, I'le

---

[1] Ayton/Elliott, no. 3; text from the John Gamble Song-Book: New York Public Library MS. Drexel 4257. It belonged to the court musician of that name and is inscribed partly in his hand, partly in a later one. It contains eight poems by Ayton but is not used by Dr Gullans. It has been studied by Dr Vincent Duckles (unpublished dissertation) and an edition is hoped for from his pen.

[2] Texts, variants and sources in Ayton/Gullans. Music from Bodleian MS. Ashmole 36–7: 'Love's fiery passions...'.

[3] Music: Bodleian Library MS. Ashmole 36–7, no. 192. Bar 5, note 3: B natural. (K.E.)

love thee no more' and 'Thou that lov'd once now loves no more' were entitled, when they reached print, 'On a Woman's Inconstancy and the Answer' and 'The Answer, by the author, at the King's majesty's Command'.[1] Both are found underlaid to a tune of a simple country-dance type in a Jacobean-Caroline manu-script song-book. The same tune, with no text but with the title 'I lov'd thee but once' is in Playford's *English Dancing Master* of 1652. His Majesty who liked the song is likely to have been King Charles. We know that country-dances were in vogue at this monarch's court rather than 'the graver measures danced in his father's time.[2]

This seems a clear case of a dance-tune being 'the tune in the poet's head' for a pair of poems, the old opening phrase of the favourite tune being given a new direction in his lyrics. The dance-tune has a vigorous rhythmic pattern of its own that informs the poet's words. When the songs are sung, the verve generated by the tune tosses off the defiant lines of the first poem and marks the match-points in the countering argument of the reply.

So far we have seen Ayton's words written 'to an ayre that was made before' or set by a musician simply to a tuneful air. In either case the rhythmic pattern of the tune fits the metrical pattern of the words, the first created—whichever of the two it was—moulding the second. The distribution of points of emphasis in the first stanza is conditioned by the tune or conditions the tuneful setting. This patterning is repro-duced in subsequent stanzas; variations, if any, are unobtrusive and few. Iteration of the simple melodic line serves the onward course of the poem's argument, stanza by stanza, its unsurprising flow displaying the turns of the poets' wit and bearing his thought onwards to his conluding paradox. Association with a tune or a tuneful setting encouraged 'smoothness' in a poet, ease of syllabic succession and explicit-ness of expression. The nature of the Cavalier lyric, its tone of social address, en-couraged a nearness to natural phrasing of polite discourse and the 'language of the heart'.

An adept at setting such Cavalier lyric in the simple tuneful style was Henry Lawes, musician of the Caroline court; examples of his settings of Ayton in this style will come under review later. One of his best in this mode is the song for voice and lute 'I doe confess th'art smooth and fair'.[3] The words are by an unknown author who is, however, '*aut Ayton aut diabolus*'. The poet speaks with dignity yet with charity of heart to the girl who has won success as a fashionable beauty but is now a bruised flower in a handled nosegay, no longer worthy the single devotion of a sincere love.

[1] James Watson, *A Choice Collection*, III (Edinburgh, 1711); in the Gamble MS. nos. 149 and 167, and in B.M. MS. Add. 25707; Aytont/Elliott, no. 9.
[2] *Table Talk of John Selden*, ed. Sir Frederick Pollock, p. 64.
[3] Text, variants and sources in Ayton/Gullans. Music in Ayton/Elliott, no. 8.

The temper is Ayton's as is, too, the deftness with which the tone and rhythms of courtly speech are caught. Lawes' setting is eloquent in its simplicity.

Henry Lawes was master, too, of the newer style of song-writing that by this time had come into prominence. Here, by a change in musical thought operant at this time, emphasis passed in song-setting from the music to the words. The musician's art in this style lay in catching the rhythms of speech and the fall of phrase and expressing these in musical terms, setting the words in what came to be called 'the declamatory style'.[1]

Henry Lawes was employed at court over a period of years when Sir Robert Ayton was also in royal service.[2] In a sense he takes over after the death of Campion in 1620 as the musician most likely through day-by-day proximity to be in friendly touch with Ayton and to come by copies of his lyrics for setting. He entered the King's musical service in 1625 and—with the interruption of the Civil War—he was still in it when he died in 1662. We may see the court service of King Charles and Queen Henrietta Maria as background, then, to a second happy conjunction of poet and musician, the older Scots writer of favourite lyrics and the well-known and well-loved singer, musician and setter of songs.

The setting of an Ayton lyric to a tuneful air characteristically preserved intact the poet's text and did not of itself precipitate verbal corruption, though a consequent popular currency might produce a crop of variants. With setting in the declamatory style, however, matters were different as we shall see. Ayton's lyric 'I lov'd thee once' that had been written to the lively rhythmic pattern of the country-dance tune was chosen by Henry Lawes for setting. His music is for the first stanza of the poem and has something of declamatory in its style. No further verses of the poem nor any text of the 'answer' are recorded with the music. Though both poems were made in stanzas matching as to points of emphasis, the speech-rhythms and the fall of phrases are not identical, stanza by stanza, throughout the poems. We do not know if subsequent stanzas of poem or of answer were intended to be sung to the music by Lawes; if so, it would presumably be left to the singer to make in the singing what modifications proved necessary, this being a matter for the taste and artistry of the performer.[3]

The case of this song goes to the root of some of the verbal mutation found in the

[1] In this change of musical thought many forces were at work in France and Italy first—humanism, the Academies, the desire for monody—see Frances Yates, *French Academies of the Sixteenth Century;* also M. Lefkowitz, *William Lawes,* chapter VII.

[2] See Willa McClung Evans: *Henry Lawes, Musician and Friend of Poets.*

[3] Ayton/Elliott, no. 10. Text, variants and sources in Ayton/Gullans. It is not possible to *prove* that the fitting of subsequent verses to the 'declamatory air' was left to the singer. Perhaps the composer envisaged the singing of no words other than those he provided in the text. See Duckles, 'The Gamble Manuscript as a Source of Continuo Song in England.

texts of Ayton's pieces as we gather them from manuscript sources. The song was made by Ayton at latest during the first decade of King Charles' reign. The setting by Lawes was composed, most credibly, close to the time of the song's first popularity. It was not printed until 1669 (Playford) and then only the first stanza with Lawes' setting. Both poems were printed in *Le Prince d'Amour or The Prince of Love* of 1660, but nowhere was the whole poem or the answer to be found in print with either of the musics. Whoever wished to sing the song or have it in his music-book had to assemble it himself, draw on another manuscript music-book or on the repertory of a musical friend. Scribal variants and the vagaries of oral currency both enter into it. With the Lawes setting, the licence left to the singer to render in his own way the rest of the verses if he wished to sing them was in itself an invitation to individual variation of the text in subsequent stanzas.

Another lyric of Ayton's set by Lawes belongs in all probability to the early years of the Caroline court. His pastoral 'Cloris since thou art fled away' was written in the 1630s, for the words are found in Margaret Robertson's Commonplace-book of that date.[1] The setting by Henry Lawes may well have been made about this time though the song did not reach print until 1658. In Lawes' holograph manuscript of his songs as well as in print the song is entitled 'Amintor's Welladay'; elsewhere it is 'Amyntas' Welladay' or 'Cloris and Amyntas'. Chloris or Cloris as a personal name was closely associated with the person of Queen Henrietta Maria as is testified by the many 'Cloris' or 'Cloridiae' poems or songs written for her and the attendant nymphs of her court. Amyntas, as we saw, had been used by Robert Ayton in an early pastoral and—if this is not to take the game too far—Amintor is an anagram for Mr Aiton, M. R[obert] AITON. The pastoral 'Welladay' proved a great favourite. The words of the song were translated into Latin by Henry Jacob and a setting for three voices was composed deriving from the music by Lawes. This three-part music differs in rhythm from the song as Lawes composed it; indeed the adaptation may have been made in order to suit both the Latin verses and Ayton's poem.[2]

Another musician of the Caroline court, John Gamble, recorded in his manuscript music-book a number of songs of Ayton, among them two that are apparently not known elsewhere to have had music. 'O that my tongue had been as dumb' occurs early in the book and its music is possibly the work of John Gamble himself.[3] As to the words, the stanza pattern is more varied in outline than is usual with Ayton. Developing from a four-line four-foot stanza, it has the second line broken into two

[1] In transcript only, by Buchan: B.M. MS. Add. 29408. This source is not noted by Gullans (his no. 14). Music in Lawes, *Ayres and Dialogues*, third book. Henry Lawes' version reads 'Cloris now thou', possibly because 'Cloris since thou' is difficult to sing.

[2] This music in B.M. MS. Add. 29396 fol. 46v–47, misprinted as 29296 in Gullans.

[3] Ayton/Elliott, no. 4. Gamble MS. text noted in Ayton/Shire.

rhyming half-lines while with the fourth rhymes a fifth. The music is a setting that tends towards the declamatory in style. The composer does not use the rhyme to make a point musically; indeed for effect he 'throws away' the chiming of the closely following rhyme-sounds in a way characteristic of declamatory song-writing. He may have done so nonchalantly, being concerned with the sense of the words and not with the metrical pattern of the poem. It is possible, however, that at this point in changing song-style the composer's rendering of the speech-rhythm and the run of meaning is done 'against' a background consciousness of the significant sound-pattern made by stanzaic form and rhyme. Later in the Gamble song-book comes 'Why should I wronge my judgment so'; a full text of the words is engrossed but the music was never copied in nor has it so far come to light elsewhere. This is a pity, as the verses are among the wisest and wittiest that Ayton wrote.

We have seen musicians of the later Jacobean and the early Caroline court finding Ayton's lyrics '*amoene* to music', apt for setting in styles that ranged from the tuneful air through transitional pieces to song in the declamatory style. In this type of song-making the vocal line might not only embody the speech-rhythms inherent in the poet's words but even underline them musically. It might go farther and override the metrical shape and the stanzaic form, voicing the meaning of the poem anew in the double medium of words-and-music in what was nearly an *aria parlante*. Such setting has been called 'the dramatic song'.

The songs of Ayton's were set in this style by Dr John Wilson, singer and musician under King James and King Charles. John Wilson was born in the same year as Henry Lawes; before he was twenty he may have contributed music for a court masque of the year 1613/14. He was well known in London under King James for he was a 'Servant of the City for Music and Voice' in 1622. By 1635 he was one of the King's musicians and was evidently a favourite with King Charles.[1] Again we have conjunction in court service over a number of years of Sir Robert Ayton and a musician who set his verses.

The chronology of Wilson's compositions is by no means settled. It is generally held that the bulk of his song-writing was done during his years of retirement after the defeat of the Royalist cause. It is impossible to tell meantime whether his settings of Ayton's poems were done then or at some earlier point, within the poet's lifetime. If the latter is true there is a possibility, indeed a likelihood, of consultation between poet and musician as the words were set and the song born.

We are lucky in having for this composer an authoritative book of his songs in manuscript, not a holograph manuscript but one bearing detailed corrections in his

---

[1] I take the biography of Wilson from Grove's *Dictionary of Music and Musicians;* see also W. M. Evans, *Henry Lawes...*

hand.[1] This volume lets us form a good idea of his way with lyrics he chose for setting in declamatory style as dramatic song. Of Ayton's verses he chose 'There is none, no, none but I' and 'Shall feare to seeme untrue'. The first we have seen already associated with a tuneful air of Campion's, where the iteration of the simple music stanza by stanza carried the thread of the poet's argument through to its witty and paradoxical conclusion. The heart of the song, of the words sung to an unobtrusive accompaniment on lute or keyboard, lay in the follow-through of the poem's sense, delightfully purveyed. Wilson read Ayton's verses understandingly but envisaged a song of quite a different character. For setting he has taken stanza one and the concluding stanzas five and six. Three steps of the poet's argument are thus omitted and as a result some slight modifications in wording are made to establish a new coherence. In the original poem a question had been raised in stanza four,

> Lovely eyes and loveless heart
> Why doe you soe disagree?

which was answered in stanza five by the protestation 'Noe, fair eyes, noe, noe more soe'. This line becomes in Wilson's song not an answer but an appeal or invocation, 'O fair eyes, O no more so'. By the same token the phrase in Ayton's last verse which was part of the whole argument, 'Though you should be still unkinde' has become 'Though to me you are unkind', which directs the attention not to the argument but to the 'I' of the song. One other alteration, 'must I' for 'I must' is made for reasons touching both sense and musical style: a strong musical emphasis was due on whichever of these words came first and Wilson's song emphasises 'must' more naturally than 'I'.

Wilson's 'There is none' is through-composed. In the first stanza a descending curve of music renders 'full of woe'. The change of attitude from 'O fair eyes' to 'O, no more so' is marked by a break in rhythm like that of distressed speech and 'Cruel eyes and full of guile' again descends as if in despair while the next two lines about 'fair semblance' are easy and pleasant in movement. The close is a dramatic protestation. To have set the whole poem with such strong delineation of emotion at each and every turn of Ayton's argument would have been to produce an overdone and over-coloured piece. How wise of the musician to choose, to penetrate and to render in depth aspects of feeling in the Cavalier lyric that had touched his imagination.[2]

In 'Shall feare to seeme untrue' we have again a 'Wilson' version of the words, the text as found with the music in his manuscript. This version passed into circulation, no doubt along with knowledge of his music. Wilson here sets the whole poem

---

[1] Bodleian Library MS. Music b.1, fol. 118; discussed by Margaret Crum, 'A Manuscript of John Wilson's Songs', pp. 55–7.
[2] Song fully edited in Ayton/Elliott, no. 7.

12. SHALL FEARE TO SEEME UNTRUE[1]

AYTON

JOHN WILSON

Shall feare to seeme un-true to vowes of con-stant du-ty make me dis-

-gest dis-daines un-due from an un-con-stant beau-ty? No, I doe not af-

-fect in vowes to seeme so ho-ly that I would have the world to check my constancy with

[1] Music and text: Bodleian Library MS. Mus. b.1, fos. 53 v–54 r. Tune and bass only in original. All B-naturals in tune and bass are editorial, consequent on change of key-signature; ornaments are editorial. Bar 3, bass, note 3: A. Bar 13, bass: semibreve. Bar 30, bass: G-natural is editorial. (K.E.)

fol-ly, Let hir call breach of vow, what I call Just re-pent-ance,

I thinke it bace and fool-ish too, to doate on coy____ Ac-quaint-ance.

Thus yf out of hir snare I doe at last un-fould me, Ac-cuse hir-self that caught me

there and Knew not how to hould me, and yf I Re-bell proove a-gainst my Will, I doe it,

for I can hate, as well as love, yf rea - son binde me to it

and the changes of wording are slight but significant. 'I count him base and braine-sick to That dotes on coy acquaintance' becomes 'I think it bace and foolish too To doate on coy acquaintance'. This rejection of a point of view in love's philosophy is thus made more personal to the 'I' of the song. It is likely also that 'braine-sick' was difficult to sing. 'At last I doe' has been changed to 'I doe at last' so that the strong musical accent may fall on 'last'. The turn of the argument has been altered in the final stanza: the conclusion of Ayton's 'arguing' verses was

> And if I Rebell prove
> Against my will I doe it
> Yet can I heate as well as love
> When reason binds me to it.

In the lyric as Wilson set it the edges of the argument have been somewhat softened. The result is less of a laughing philosopher's 'reasoning about love' and more of a deeply felt participation in the feeling. The song is through-composed and the

244

musician has realised in musical terms the emotional 'shape' in each of the stanzas. Instead of progress through the poem's thought step by step the musician has built a mounting curve of excitement. 'Thus if out of her snare' runs rapidly upwards and 'I do at last unfould me' is a climax of escape.

It is interesting to find in these verses the 'poulters' measure' of Ayton's early poems that in these shorter lyrics developed in his hands into a flexible medium for song-writing. The strict iambics of 'Will thou remorsles fair' have given way to a resilient variety of stress. There is a rhyme at the 'half-line' and rhyming is often feminine or rich. The phrasing is now very near to that of courtly speech.

When the poem was set by John Wilson such speech-rhythms, attained by Ayton within the deft control of the Cavalier-lyric medium, are accentuated in the new-style declamatory music. In Wilson's song we are not conscious of the metrical shape of the stanza; he uses for emphasis the strong rhymes that fall at the ends of the 'long-lines' of poulters' measure but likes to 'throw away' the intervening rhymes at the half-line. We may see here a history in the relationship of metrical pattern to music that runs parallel to the history of the 'Helicon' stanza—as it passed from stanzaic dance-song to Italianate and decorated setting—that was traced in an earlier chapter.

After the interesting and sensitive reading of the poetry evinced by John Wilson in his settings it is disappointing to find a quite different state of affairs with the music for one of Ayton's most famous pieces, 'Wrong not sweet empress of my heart'. This has long been understood as an address to a royal personage, either Queen Anne or the Princess Elizabeth, 'Elizabeth of Bohemia'. The textual complications are extensive but they repay attention. Among the twenty-seven versions cited by Dr Gullans seven are classed by him as 'fragmentary'. Three of these are short only of the final stanza and are apparently close to one another. The other four show mutation that is, I believe, connected with musical setting. One is headed 'A Song' and is a shortened version giving stanzas 1,3,4, a variant of 2 and 7 of the text as found in the Ayton manuscripts; another, headed 'Cant 5'—for 'Cantus, five stanzas'?—has the same verses. The only music known for this lyric is to be found in the Gamble song-book, as no 211. It is in the second handwriting of the manuscript, which suggests engrossing during the later decades of the century. The Gamble version consists of stanzas 1, 7, 6 and a variant of 5 and has 'deare empress' in the first line, as have all the 'fragmentary' texts. The Gamble version is set in a style of the mid century as two eight-line stanzas and its last four lines have been shaped into a climax that is quite different from the ending of the original poem. Two other of the fragmentary texts, though they are longer, end in the same way with the climactic version of stanza 5.

By bringing musical setting into the discussion of the poem and its mutations some sense is made of the dissemination of a 'fragmentary' version. It is clear that at some point a musician reshaped the poem for setting; the shortened version of the words, however, falls far below the original. Late in the day, possibly after the death of the poet, this piece found music and not particularly impressive music at that. It is a pity that the fine words were not coupled lovingly with a tuneful air earlier in the century, or, later, powerfully set as a dramatic song.

In another instance, however, 'When thou didst think I did not love', a composer, again anonymous, has set a selection of verses from an Ayton lyric and set them simply and feelingly, rendering the poet's tone of rueful charity. Nevertheless violence has been done to the argument of the song by the omission of the penultimate stanza. In the printed text of words and music (1652) a coarser phrase displaces a finer and the syntax at one point appears to have been misunderstood. The words were recorded in a manuscript from the earlier half of the century, entitled 'Constancy: A Song' and the Scots cavalier anthologist marked the piece as having music. It is possible, of course, that the text that came to the musician's hand was already corrupted—and misprinting is only too frequent in song-books of the time.[1]

We have seen Ayton's verses as sung or set in four or five of the styles of 'solo' song of the seventeenth century and once as part-song. Two of his lyrics were so much loved that at least three musics survive for each. These afford an interesting opportunity for comparison of song-styles as music and also as vehicles for the lyric's meaning. One is a royal piece written 'Upone a ringe Queen Anne sent to Sir Robert Aytoune. A diamond in forme of a hearte'...'set with a crowne above and a bloody dart pearceing it, sent in a New Yeares gift'. This exchange at New Year of gifts in jewel or verse we have met before as an antique mode of 'hansel' between servitor and monarch. The first music found for this piece 'Thou sentst to me a heart was crowned' is old-style also; as recorded in the Ballett Lute-book it resembles an *air-de-cour* such as Ayton might have known in France; in fact the words may have been 'writ to an ayre that was before'.[2] It would bear a somewhat old-world mien in the world of Jacobean song. Both words and music, then, may well come from the early years of Ayton's secretaryship to the Queen. 'The wayward rhythm moves from twos to threes in alternate lines of the verse and the progression, unforeseen by the musically amateur, makes the song poignant and melancholy.' The aspect of the poem's meaning that is brought out is the suffering of the lover, no matter that the love-grief was 'courtly', a delicate feigning.

[1] Texts and sources in Ayton/Gullans. In Ayton/Elliott, no. 6 from *Select Musicall Ayres and Dialogues* (1652), in which the airs are by Wilson, C. Coleman, H. Lawes and Webb. Dr Elliott suggest this setting may be by Wilson.

[2] Ayton/Elliott, no. 1, from William Ballett's Lute-Book (*c.* 1604).

246

13. *THOU SENT'ST TO ME A HEART WAS CROWN'D*[1]

AYTON

ANON

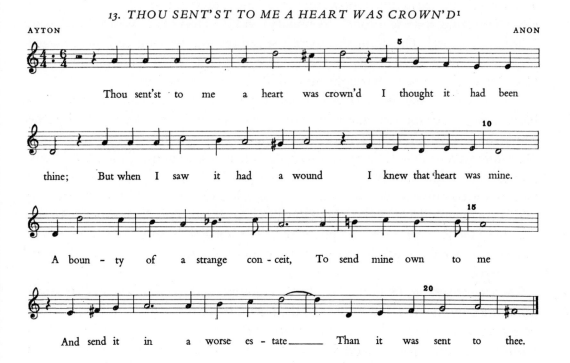

Thou sent'st to me a heart was crown'd I thought it had been thine; But when I saw it had a wound I knew that heart was mine. A boun - ty of a strange con - ceit, To send mine own to me And send it in a worse es - tate_____ Than it was sent to thee.

The three musics for this lyric have been delightfully studied by Dr Vincent Duckles.[2] Praising the first—in words that include the sentence quoted above—he finds the second, a setting in mid-seventeenth-century style from the Gamble song-book, 'somewhat commonplace'. He suggests that several features it shares with the earlier tune may consciously or unconsciously have been derived from it—the minor third at 'But when I saw' and the octave leap at 'bounty'. These are actually the most interesting points in this setting as far as rendering the meaning of the words is concerned. The octave leap and the minor third throw great emphasis on the syllable that takes the second note and in the *air-de-cour* this emphasis alighted on key-phrases of the poem's progressing thought. In the later and perhaps imitative setting these features have been elaborated each into two parallel phrases—'A bounty', 'a strange conceit', 'I saw', 'I knew'. In performance it is no longer the moving sequence of thought that is brought out but rather the balanced turns of wit that declare themselves and ask to be admired. This setting is edited as illustration to Dr Duckles' dissertation.

A declamatory setting by John Playford does not reveal anthing new in the meaning of the poem. The setting uses four eight-line stanzas and in this instance the

[1] See Elliott, *Musa Jocosa Mihi*, no. 1. (K.E.)   [2] Dissertation, unpublished.

verbal text is printed in full. It shows minor variations in stress to exist between the first eight-line stanza and the second: 'A bounty' and 'O Heavens', 'Worse estate' and 'Him with a dart'. The dramatic aspect is seized on and the song becomes a staged protestation. But both drama and eloquence of phrase were there, latent in the Cavalier poet's art, to be wrought upon farther by the musician.[1]

The piece as written in the Ayton manuscripts is thirty-six lines long, nine four-line stanzas; a text thus long but with some differences of stanza-order is found in the Music Book of McAlmain of Dunollich, a manuscript song-book of Scots provenance. No music accompanies it there, and with the lute tablature in the Ballett Lute-book no text was included. So we are at a loss to know how precisely the thirty-six-line piece was accommodated to the eight-line music. In all likelihood the four concluding lines were sung to the second strain of the music, repeated. This discrepancy between the nine four-line stanzas of the poem and the eight-line length of the music may well account for the way the later stanzas got out of order, four lines by four lines, in some texts.

The second setting, from the Gamble manuscript, and the third, from Playford's print, use only the first sixteen lines of the poem, twice through the music. If more verses were sung they had to be supplied from elsewhere—and the way was open to mistake and corruption. But it is clear that in both these cases the musician has brought his song to a conclusion with the text he provides—pressing into service a line from Ben Jonson in order to do so: 'Since thou hast slain me with a dart That soe much honoured thee.' Instead of revealing the course of the poet's thought as did the *air-de-cour*, we find the setting foreshortening the poet's argument into a few impressive attitudes that are highlighted by the musical phrasing. Although the resultant song is goodish declamatory song we cannot but resent the violation of the Ayton lyric. Here again we find that the latitude in varying the rhythm between one stanza and the next obtaining in the declamatory style of song obviously opened another way for mutation in verbal phrase.

Three musics are again found for Ayton's favourite lyric 'What meanes this strangeness now of late'. It was widely disseminated in manuscript and print both as a poem and as a song. A delightful piece, light-hearted yet moving, it is no wonder that it took the musicians' fancy. In the Ayton manuscripts and in five others the lyric is five stanzas long and reads 'niceness' in the opening line; one of these, MS. Add. 29396 in the British Museum, has music with the words, a tuneful air. The tune is brisk, almost truculent, and lets the argumentative aspect of the song be clearly heard. In these verses the poet-philosopher is taking the girl to task for 'niceness'—coyness or scrupulosity. (We recall the 'Aye so nyce' of Alexander Scott's song.)

[1] Ayton/Elliott, no. 2.

14. WHAT MEANES THIS NICENESSE[1]

AYTON

ANON

What méanes this nice - nesse now of _ late   Since time doth truth _ ap -

- prove?   Such   dis - tance may con - sist   with state, it   can - not stand   with Love

'tis   Ei - ther Cun - ninge or   dis - trust, that _ doth such waies   al - low,   the

[1] Music and text: B.M. Add. 29396, fo. 91. Tune and bass only in MS. Ornaments are editorial. Bar 1, bass: rest is editorial. Bar 7, melody: G sharp. Bar 9, double bar: repeat marks for both sections. (K.E.)

The song was also set by Dr John Wilson, but though the words appear in the 'Wilson' manuscript the music was never copied in. His text has 'niceness' in the first line, but it is unlikely that the missing 'Wilson' music was the somewhat commonplace tune quoted above.

When the words are found with the other musics the first line has been altered to 'strangeness', where the word has something of the old force of the 'straungeness' of courtly love along with the effect of 'estrangedness'. It may be that the alteration was made because the vowel-quality of 'niceness' was difficult to sing on a long note. The beautiful and moving setting by Thomas Blagrave certainly dwells on 'strangeness' with great effect. In his hands the words are wistful, meditative and pleading and the conclusion is a sad relinquishing of a love-affair rather than a witty casting-up of emotional accounts.[1]

15. *WHAT MEANS THIS STRANGENESS*

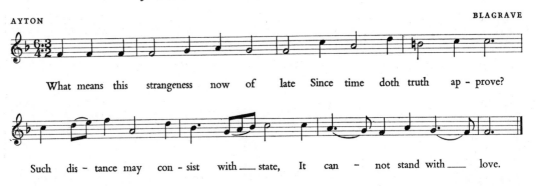

This lyric was chosen for setting by Henry Lawes; entitled 'Coyness in Love' it was printed in 1661.[2]

[1] Ayton/Elliott, no. 5. [2] H. Lawes in *Select Ayres and Dialogues* (1659) and *Treasury of Music* (1661).

16. WHAT MEANS THIS STRANGENESSE[1]

AYTON   HENRY LAWES

What means this Strange - nesse now of late? since Time doth Truth ___ ap -

- prove: this dis -tance may   con - sist   with State;   it can - not stand   with Love.

For Lawes the song is again a remonstrance by the estranged lover made more in sorrow and retreat than in truculent attack or upbraiding. This simple setting is an air poised between tune and declamation, perhaps the zone in which Henry Lawes' best songs were born.

The variants of this poem are manifold, and even when methodically tabulated they are bemusing. When the evidence of the music is introduced, however, group-variants begin to tell us something about the practice of the poet and about the interaction of poetic and musical style. This last example allows us to draw together a number of issues raised in earlier pages, the matter of Englishing and of the poet's own revising hand as well as that of mutation related to musical association.

Where this piece is recorded with music the stanzas observe a considerable uni-formity in rhythmic pattern and distribution of points of emphasis. The exception is

---

[1] Music and text: *Select Ayres and Dialogues* (1669), p. 48. Tune and bass only in source. All flats editorial except bar 3, bass, note 4. (K.E.)

the opening word of stanza 4, 'Speake but the word', and the very divergence here makes the imperative verb stand out—as indeed it should, being a turning-point in the poem's argument. (The Lawes setting could double the length of the first note and halve that of the next two to meet it.) A slightly different version of the lyric is written down in several manuscript sources, in all cases without associated music. This version contains six lines of which four, a stanza, are not found in the 'Ayton manuscripts' text and two vary widely from it. These lines are difficult to accommodate to the settings of Blagrave or Lawes and will not even sing to the anonymous 'tuneful air'.

> Express by uncontroulled lookes
>> The ridles of your mynde.
> Your eyes are cupids fortoun books
>> Where love himselfe can finde
>
> If kyndness cross your wished content
>> Dismiss me with a frowne
> I'le give you...

Dr Gullans describes this version as having 'a stanza interpolated between lines 12 and 13 and a recension of lines 13 and 14'. I suggest the converse process is more likely in face of the musical evidence: the early version had the stanza with the 'Uncontroulled lookes' and 'fortoun books' and the unsingable 'If kindness cross your wished content'. A later version has met the anonymous tune with its four-square pattern or has come in contact with the discriminating ear of Blagrave or Lawes. The words have been modified; the awkward four lines have been dropped and in their place the poet has found simplicity and concentration:

> Speake but the word or doe but cast
>> A looke which seemes to frown,
> I'le give you all the love that's past
>> The rest shall be my owne.

Grooming has been carried out by an accomplished hand that is surely the poet's own.

Of Englishing there is only a trace; one significant word is altered. The song continues—and concludes

> And such a faire and efald way
>> On both sides none can blame
> Since every one is bound to play
>> The fairest of his game.

'Efald' is Scots, meaning 'one-fold', uncomplicated, open, sincere. In all versions but one—an Ayton manuscript—it has been dropped, doubtless as incomprehensible in England, and 'equal' has been substituted. But 'equal' adds little to 'faire', whereas 'efald' lay at the heart of the Scots poet's meaning.

In this study of Sir Robert Ayton's lyrics as song no over-all casting-up of accounts is possible. Profit here and loss there have been noted in the contact of lyric-writer or his poems with song-style or with court musician. *Musa jocosa*, Ayton's merry muse, learning perhaps to sing through acquaintance with the native air of Scotland, was singularly attuned to the genius of solo song and fortunate in finding solo art-song in a variety of styles flourishing in King James' English court. Ayton's lyric of elegance, simplicity and *adresse* or of light-hearted and witty reasoning about love was characteristically cast in easily matching stanzas, the distribution of points of emphasis in the opening stanza echoed in subsequent verses. The argument of the poem ran lucidly, stanza by stanza, pointed by paradox. Such lyric was not un-influenced by being made on occasion 'to an ayre that was before'. Such writing was made for the tuneful air and the tuneful air for such writing. Intercourse between the poet's art and the musician's here was immediate and fruitful. It drew the poet towards explicitness of verbal phrase, directness of expression in phrases close to natural speech and the careful shaping of the course of his thought. In the case of our poet we may call this the Ayton–Campion conjunction.

This movement, however, coincided in time and place in the Jacobean court with a phenomenon of European musical history, the shift in song-writing from focus on the music to focus on the words. In verbal lyric style an approximation to speech-rhythms of polite converse and 'the language of the heart' that went forward under the light rein of the tuneful air now proved most congenial to setting in the new declamatory style seen in the work of such men as Henry Lawes. Verses of Ayton's in the Cavalier style proved a point of growth also in the further musical develop-ment towards dramatic song such as John Wilson's.

In our review of Ayton's words matched with music in the changing styles of song it has been demonstrated that such association with music is an important factor to be borne in mind throughout when 'the' text of a lyric or a song is to be established or when textual variation of the words is discussed. A singing version may be more accomplished, more flowing, by reason of association with a tuneful air. A fine lyric may be violated in form and sense when it is shortened and redirected to make a declamatory song; but it may also be modified to a new elegance to meet the taste of a distinguished musician; or it may be interpreted afresh in the new medium of dramatic song. Before an editor blacklists all variants as corruptions due to informa-lity of scribal transmission or oral currency he should allow for changes incidental to adaption for song-setting. The poet may have given an early version for setting and may subsequently have worked further on his own lines. He may have consulted with the musician in altering a text or have acquiesced in the musician's request for modification. Indeed a Cavalier lyric may have been launched on more than one occasion, once as words *amoene* to music—nubile as it were to the other art—and again as a song, the match of its poetry with music now accomplished.

A degree of acquaintance and of consultation between poet and musician that recalls the days of the Castalian band has been adumbrated here between Sir Robert Ayton and musicians in the Jacobean or Caroline court. This is in keeping with what is known of other poets and musicians of this epoch. With the songs of Robert Herrick for instance it has elsewhere been established that it was early versions that reached the musician's hands, their wording differing considerably from later texts that were eventually prepared for printing. The poet of this epoch has been envisaged hasting hot-foot to the musician with a new lyric, impatient to hear his words sung. Thereafter, apparently, he felt in no way committed to the early version. Thus, I submit, Ayton's first version of his 'depairt' was written in literary Scots and devised to a northern air or set to music in Scottish circles to continue in currency there; it differs substantially in plan and slightly in language from the version that reached Sir John Ayton. In the case of other fine songs of Ayton's however, it is a revised version that is found set to music, the revision being such as to suggest strongly that the poet himself was in touch with the musician.

Sir Robert Ayton was the last Castalian. In his youth a late Castalian poet of Scotland writing in literary Scots in a style influenced by royal precedent, he embodied in himself a transfer of that tradition from the northern to the southern court. Like Montgomerie he was a royal servitor close to the King—a king still conscious of the Castalian style and still speaking Scots—though, with Ayton, the court for whose pleasure his verses were made now spoke English. Montgomerie had been master in poetry to the King; Montgomerie's younger disciple was John Murray; when Murray died, Ayton 'supplied his place'. Like the early master of the Castalian band Ayton was in everyday touch with musicians of the court in which he served. Like Montgomerie he was a maker of songs when he wrote to music 'that was made before', but for Ayton solo song had taken the place of part-writing. Again like Montgomerie he was a maker of court-song when he wrote words in which the art of the poet looked out to greet the art of the musician.

IO

EPILOGUE: COURTLY SONG IN SEVENTEENTH-CENTURY SCOTLAND

THE REPERTORY of courtly part-song born in royal circles in Scotland during the reign of King James VI, or naturalised and cherished there, continued to be enjoyed in Scotland as long as the skill of singing 'to four voices' was taught and practised, that is until the later years of the seventeenth century. The best-known song of all, 'O lustie May', known as a part-song to George Bannatyne and perhaps springing in the first place from some late medieval 'Maying' in royal style, survives for us written down in all its parts in 1604 by David Melvill, bookseller of Aberdeen, at the end of his 'Book of Roundells'. David Melvill was brother to the master of the song-school of St Nicholas, the Burgh Kirk of Aberdeen, and he made manuscript part-books for the musical amateurs of neighbouring castle and university. The song was known in other regions of Scotland, engrossed in his music-book by Robert Edwards minister of Murroes Parish in Fife, who was in touch with the aristocratic music-making at Panmure House. The same song was among the additional items written into one of the sets of Thomas Wode's Part-Books. Descending probably in the repertory of the song-school of Aberdeen it reached print there in the cantus part-book of John Forbes in 1662, 1666 and 1682, his *Songs and Fancies*. Chief among a score of beautiful songs, courtly Scots in language and courtly part-writing in music, it was taught to his pupils by Robert Taitt, precentor and schoolmaster at Lauder in southern Scotland as late as 1676. The corpus of songs that were its companions shared a like history. Several of these were recorded in his music-book by one John Squyer in 1701. For part-writing indigenous to the Scottish court that is the end of the story.

We see in this the musical expression of a court-culture pass to culture of castle and college. Burgh song-schools owing their survival to a royal edict preserved part-song of the sixteenth century through the severities of Puritan dominance to a fresh lease of life at the Restoration. Part-writing in a style that had been outmoded in England for a century lingered in the northern realm that had no creative centre in which court song in newer styles could be developed.

In the later years of King James' reign in Scotland monophonic song took over from part-song as music for the courtly lyric in Scots. 'Where art thou, hope' is a distinguished example made in the style of an *air-de-cour* (*Music of Scotland*, no. 61). The story of 'Helicon' shows the dance-song stanza long known in Blackhall's four-part setting set anew for single voice and instrument in the up-to-date Italianate decorated style but we cannot claim the music as of Scottish provenance (*Music of Scotland*, no. 65). The only example in anything approaching the declamatory style made in Scotland is the undistinguished piece 'When chill cold age' perhaps from the pen of Melvill of the song-school (*Music of Scotland*, no. 66).

Monophonic song as enjoyed in musically cultured circles of seventeenth-century Scotland was various in style and in origin. The 'Irish Ho-hone', famous as a tune and as instrumental music in Elizabethan England, has words in Scottish sources only —'Yee Gods of love look down in pity', printed by Forbes in 1662 (*Music of Scotland*, no. 70). 'Balu' may be as old as the '*Gude and Godlie Ballatis*' of 1568, where words first appear for its tune. It is recorded more than once as a continuo song early in the seventeenth century in versions differing in musical detail (*Music of Scotland*, no. 69). The beautiful words were known as 'Lady Bothwell's lament' and were fashioned and refashioned by more than one Scottish Cavalier poet: we have 'Alen's Balu' and 'Palmer's Balu'.[1] On the other side of the political and religious strife that rent Scotland we have the young Covenanter poet William Cleland writing one set of verses while still at college to the 'broadside' tune 'Hullo my fancy' (*Music of Scotland*, no. 71), and another—to solace himself from melancholy thoughts, perhaps while an exile in the Low Countries—to the tune of 'Fancy free' (*Music of Scotland*, no. 72). The second tune is in the style of a native air and was probably indigenous music already widely known. Both tunes come down to us 'set by Mr Beck' in the lute book of one of the Lindsays of Balcarres, a rich and extensive collection.

Easy to point to are verses written in cultured Scots and sung to tunes that are by every token 'native airs'; finest perhaps is the lament of Chisholm of Cromlix celebrating a tragic love-song of the early years of the century.[2] 'Lady Lothian's Lilt' is a wonderful soaring tune, pentatonic, suggesting Scottish authorship in style and title; its words, by a woman, have been plausibly attributed to Lady Lothian

---

[1] 'The Balou: Allane' and 'Palmer's Balou' are titles of two sets of verses on this theme and matching this tune in MS. Laing III, 436, nos. L and LI (Edinburgh University Library). 'Allane' is the 'Alen' of Lithgow's 'Elegie'.

[2] 'Cromlet's Lilt': *The Songs of Scotland prior to Burns*, ed. Robert Chambers, p. 260. '*Cromleck's Lilt*' ed. Kenneth Elliott, The Kelvin Series of Scots Songs.

herself (*Music of Scotland*, no. 73).[1] We have glimpsed with Mure of Rowallan words by a cultured poet linked to music patently in a Scottish style, to judge by its title, 'Puirt Jean'. Indeed it is more than likely that as tuneful airs or country-dance tunes in the English court stimulated Sir Robert Ayton to write words for them, so the native air of Scotland, indigenous tunes or music of the regional dance, moved educated poets in the north to match them with verses in a Scots language still vigorous as cultured speech. To many such a tune 'old words' clung closely, giving the piece its name and continuing in vigorous currency alongside the elegant or 'cultured' lyrics.

When in the year 1707 Scotland lost its parliament a spontaneous movement towards indignant national self-expression arose in the northern capital. It seized on *Scottis Poesie* as a golden token of greatness in Scotland's past. Watson made his *Choice Collection* of comic and serious verse, including court pieces by Sir Robert Ayton and Montgomerie's 'Flyting'. Montgomerie's *Cherrie* was still in printed currency though his songs lay unknown in manuscript—the few in Forbes' printed volumes being anonymous and the books themselves rare. Allan Ramsay, as Bannatyne had done before him, collected older Scottish poetry in his *Evergreen*, significantly titled; his national-poetic piety was as great as Bannatyne's though his anxiety was differently directed. He felt it important, now, to bring the language of many pieces into touch again with Scots as spoken about him in Scotland. *The Cherrie and the Slae*, then, in its descent in manuscript and print shows us, in succession, literary Scots of the late sixteenth century in the versions of 1597, a language considerably modified towards English in the 'completion' from seventeenthcentury print, and language that makes a reassertion of its Scottish character in Ramsay's version with his modifications of phrase, grammar and spelling. It was probably through Ramsay's interest that *The Cherrie* with its now ancient stanza renewed its popularity and reached Robert Burns, who used its rhythms with delight and may have known its 'Helicon' tune.

As for the songs, the courtly pieces in part-music printed incompletely in Forbes' *Songs and Fancies* were overlooked by the enthusiasts of the *risorgimento*, perhaps because copies of this publication were not easy to come by, perhaps because the Scottish pieces were so mingled there with English madrigals and lute-songs that the volumes lacked national flavour, perhaps because the kind of music with which they were matched was not now practised in the north. The part-songs of the sixteenth

---

[1] 'Lady Lothian's Lilt', *Music of Scotland* (1964) no. 73; in an earlier edition entitled by the editors 'William Stirling's Air', from its source-book. Text of words in MS. Laing III, 436 entitled 'Lady Laudian's Lilt'; this was probably Lady Ann Ker, who may have written the words. Another 'My Ladie Laudian's Lilt' in the Skene MS. no. XV, is a different tune and the title would refer to an earlier Lady, Arabella Lothian; see Dauney, p. 222 and p. 264.

century played little part in Ramsay's other collection *The Teatable Miscellany*.[1] This volume, prepared for current musical consumption, included many monophonic songs, some with their music. These were presented as native airs of Scotland; the words were usually literary verses from the seventeenth century or they were 'old words' rendered in a now regional Scots.

The urgent need felt by the men of the *risorgimento* to honour the Scottishness of songs from their country's store was continued in the great musical collections of the eighteenth century, *Orpheus Caledonius* and Johnson's *Musical Museum*. A lyric like 'I do confess thou'rt smooth and fair', for instance, the words perhaps by Sir Robert Ayton, was felt to be relevant. New music was found for it in a vigorous Scottish dance-tune and the phrases of Cavalier dignity and regret were refashioned in a spirit of regional-national reassertion, courtly silk into good hodden-grey.

> I do confess thou art sae fair
> I had been ower the lugs in love...

One hopes the refashioning hand was not that of Robert Burns.[2]

Yet it is between Ayton, the last Castalian and Robert Burns, national poet of eighteenth-century Scotland that the thread of continuity can be traced. Monophonic song of courtly origin could by the nature of its music join the stream of the native air, as we have seen. The pattern made familiar throughout these studies, a chain of words and music, music and words, obtains without interruption. At some point in the Cavalier epoch a tune called 'Old long syne' was matched with words that have been most credibly attributed to Sir Robert Ayton. An 'answer' accrued in a way we have learned to expect. The two sets of words are in Watson's collection. The tune has been transcribed by Kenneth Elliott from a seventeenth-century manuscript and the song is in his volume. It was to the 'old' tune, in a version somewhat modified towards current taste, that Robert Burns wrote his famous song, 'Should auld acquaintance be forgot', though that song in later years came to be sung to a different Scottish air.[3] It passed thence to be to this day an international 'depairt', the song of ceremony for parting or reunion, a worldwide testimony to song of Scotland.

The vanishing-point of courtly part-song from live currency was the year 1701; the vanishing point of monophonic song to its courtly music came somewhat later.

---

[1] E.g. vol. IV has a group of six poems, 'took out of a very old MS. collection wrote by a gentleman in Aberdeen'. They are *Music of Scotland*, nos. 28, 60 and 64 and 'You meaner beauties', all songs that had been printed by Forbes, and two others which may also have been songs, one possibly a Scots courtly part-song.

[2] 'I do confess thou'rt smooth and fair' set by Henry Lawes, *Select Ayres* (1659), in Ayton/Elliott. The Scottish air and Ayton's words in Chambers, p. 270. The Scottish air, 'The Cuckoo', and revised words in *The Songs of Robert Burns* ed. James C. Dick no. 132, from *Scots Musical Museum* (1792) no. 321.

[3] 'Old lang syne': in Ayton/Elliott; this tune in a later version, *Scots Musical Museum* (1796), no. 413 and the other tune in Thomson's *Scottish Airs* (1799), no. 68, both reproduced in Dick, *Songs of Burns*, no. 233 and 234 and notes. Both tunes and their words in Chambers, pp. 274–80.

When interest turned in the nineteenth century to music of the Scottish past no courtly tradition of song was envisaged. Dauney's *Ancient Scotish Melodies* of 1838 put the repertory of the Skene lute-book into the hands of the interested public and gave us, along with a wealth of native airs in early form, the words and the music of Ayton's 'depairt'. For Dauney, song of earlier Scotland was solely monophonic song. When interest turned to finding precedent in earlier tradition for Burns' song-making *Songs of Scotland Prior to Burns* was presented by Robert Chambers. Here courtly part-song as we know it was touched upon, for 'Declair ye banks of Helicon' appears with its 'tune'—but only to be dismissed, the fine lyric as 'tedious verses' and the music as 'a fair specimen of the formal, well-bred, but not very engaging chamber minstrelsy of the reign of the Sixth James'.

It was with the second *risorgimento* of *Scottis Poesie*, the movement in the twentieth century that called itself proudly 'The Scottish Renaissance' that the music of Renaissance Scotland was at last revived. This was, however, more a case of coincidence in time than of cause and effect. The careful work of earlier antiquaries now bore fruit in live performance and earlier court-songs were given back to a Scottish audience in the radio broadcasts of 'Foundations of Scottish Music'. These were prepared by the musicologist Dr Harry M. Willsher, and the musical enthusiast Ian Whyte. An outline history of music in Scotland, based on this work for the relevant chapters, was written during the second World War by Dr Henry G. Farmer.

After the war had ended the grand project of *Musica Britannica* began to give the great music of the past to a public now hungry for polyphony, for part-writing vocal and instrumental, for music for lute or harpsichord or early song composed for voice and instrument. The moment came in 1957 when for volume xv of that series the phrasing of the manifesto was altered: '*Musica Britannica* is an authoritative national collection of the classics of British Music.' *Music of Scotland 1500–1700* was presented with the vernacular songs in the literary Scots in which they had been written. Here along with Latin church music and music of the reformed church was once more the courtly part-writing of the sixteenth century, a repertory of 'old Scotch musick'. Once more it ranked in its way with 'all sorts of English, French, Dutch, Spaynish, Latin, Italian' music, vocal and instrumental, as it had for the Master of the King's Musick in Scotland when in 1635 he described the state of his Majesty's Chapel Royal in the north, and the music of its library. After several hundred years of abeyance music of courtly Scotland was rededicated 'in *propyne*' to the monarch as a northern aspect of her nation's music, *Musica Britannica*.

APPENDIX I

John Fethy the musician 'was a Popish priest' (Wode)

1498   John Fethy, priest, went abroad to study (Arbroath) *Reg. de Aberbrothes*, II, 297 (20 July 1496) and 298 (12 December 1496). (McQuaid)

1521   Walter Fethy, chorister in Church of St Nicholas, Aberdeen. John Fethy, the same, some years later. (McQuaid)

1536   Dominus John Fathe, testator in Elgin, named after D. John Patersoun, vicar of Forres. *Register of the Great Seal*, vol. 1513–46, no. 1580. (? Pluscardine Priory or Elgin Cathedral.)

1543   John Fethy, capellanus at Elgin. 20 March 1543/4, testator. *Register of the Great Seal*, vol. 1513–46, no. 3001.

c. 1540   Vicar of Cramond, had a natural son. *Register of the Secret Seal*, vol. 1529–42, p. 524.

1545   John Fethy, Precentor of the Chapel Royal at Stirling. (McQuaid)

1546   Dominus John Fethy, a third part of the lands of Cukstoun, Forfarshire. Lord High Treasurer's Accounts, VIII, 196.

1544   John Fethy presented to a prebendcy in St Nicholas choir (Aberdeen) 'and that was to have the organs and sang school for instructing the bairns'.

1546   Reappointed.

1558   Black replaced Fethy, who was absent.
(Work-book of Professor Terry on 'song-schools in Scotland,' Aberdeen University Library.)

1554–5   John Fethy paid for tuning the organs of St Giles, Edinburgh. *Dean of Guilds Accounts, Edinburgh.*

1568   Confirmation of John Fethy's resignation of the office of master of the song-school of Edinburgh (13 September). (McQuaid)

There are frequent entries after the Reformation among the 'tierds of benefices' to a John Fethy.

APPENDIX II

A. James Lauder or Lawder, styled Sir (priestly) or Mr (M.A.)

1514   'Sir James Lawder, one of the chaplains of *Abernyte* (Abernethy) is a modest and honourable young man, a good musician, honouring his mother. He is an advocate of the consistorial court, kind and trustworthy and highly beloved for his gentle ways and his deference to his seniors.' Translation of Myln's *Vitae Episcoporum Dunkeldensium* in *Rentale Dunkeldense 1505-1517*, Scottish Historical Society, Second Series, x, ed. R. K. Hannay (Edinburgh 1915), p. 330.

1547   Mr John Sinclair, musician and Dean of Restalrig, and James Lauder 'his sistersone': permission to the latter to purchase the deanery at papal court, also permission to both to travel abroad to effect this business without 'scaith' to their benefices. *Register of the Secret Seal*, vol. II, no. 2237, 5 April.
(? Does 'Mr' stand for 'Masters'.)

1569   Mr James Lauder, exhorter and prebendary of Fardinschaw...within the cathedral kirk of Dunkeld...*Register of the Secret Seal*, vol. III, no. 611. 9 May. [Two other references are noted by McQuaid.]

1573   Licence to Mr James Lawder, Dean of Restalrig, to pass furth of this realm to parts of Flanders, Sweden or any part beyond sea on his lawful errands and business with protection of his lands and benefices, provided he does nothing against true religion or the sovereign's authority. *Register of the Secret Seal*, vol. VI, no. 2126. 14 September.

1573   Mr James Lauder demitted the deanery of Restalrig. *Register of the Secret Seal*, vol. VI, no. 2197. November.

A priest, an 'advocate' and therefore probably a University graduate, gifted in music, holding office at the College of Restalrig near Edinburgh, one of the King's 'chantorie' colleges.

B. James Lauder or Lawder, professional 'musician' of church and court; born *c.* 1534,

1547 (*under* A)   Nephew of Mr John Sinclair, old enough to go abroad and to have the Deanery purchased for him, aged thirteen. (No longer a minor. But he had already a benefice.)

1552   26 January. 'Chaplain of the Collegiate Church of St Giles.' (McQuaid)

1552   'item to James Lauder that day xxiii s.' 24 December. *Dean of Guilds Accounts, Edinburgh.*

1552   The quhilk day [26 January 1552/3] the provost, baillies, counsale and dekynnis sittand in jugement anent the supplicatioun gevin in be James Lauder, prebender of thair queir, grantis licence to the said James to pass furthe of the realme to the pairtis of England and France thair to remane for the space of ane yeir next eftir the dait heerof to the effect that he may have and get better eruditioun in musick and playing nor he hes. *Extracts from the Records of the Burgh of Edinburgh*, vol. 1528–1557, p. 176.

1562   The expensis debursit be the Quenis grace preceptis and speciale command in this inst moneth of November... item the viii day of November be the Quenis grace precept to James Lauder as the said precept togidder with his acquittance schawin...xx li[vres]. Exchequer Rolls 1563, no. 214.

1566 James Lauder, 'sone to Gilbert Lawder Burgess of Edinburght' named chaplain of St Nicholas altar in St Giles, when the chaplainry shall fall vacant by resignation or decease of Sir William Maxwell. *Register of the Secret Seal*, no. 3028. 11 August.

1569 'List of the attendants on the Queen of Scots at Tutbury Castel' according to the Index. 'Valletz de Chambre Jaques Loder.' *Calendar of State Papers, Scotland*, vol. 1563–9, no. 1194, p. 696.

1570 *c.* 1570, married Jean Hay.

1576 'To James Lauder, vallet de chambre, according to the office where he is employed: 200 livres. 19th May.' *Protocol Books.* (McQuaid)

1579 or 1580 Item by the kingis majesteis precept to his servitor James Lauder ii c merkis as for the dew price of two pair of virginallis coft be the said James in London be his hienes direction and command and deliverit to his majestie. Togidder with ane hundreth merkis for his travell and expensis to London and carreing and transporting the said two pair of virginellis thairfrom ll c livres. *Exchequer Rolls*, XXI, 162.

1580 Household List: 'ane musiciane'.
Letter from James Lauder in Edinburgh to his son John Lauder at Sheffield, dated October 1583. Summarised in *Calender of State Papers, Scotland*, vol. VI, no. 187. (Reproduced in part in Shire, *Music and Letters*, vol. XL, no. 1.) This mentions an earlier journey south made 'solely to fetch his pension'; if that is not the journey to fetch the virginals, it could have taken place in 1581.

1582 30 November. Scheme for the Ordering and Provision of the King's Household: proposed by the Privy Council, Ruthven among the signatories, and approved by the King. 'The violeris table'...the Hudsons. List of persons to be paid in money (original fol. 4) includes 'To James Lawder, musician, be his fee and ordinair 1c £'.

1583 Named by de la Mothe Fénelon in Edinburgh among those 'very affectionate to Queen Mary', James Lauder. *Lord High Treasurer's Accounts*, February 1582/3.

1584 'Fontenay à Nau [brother of Queen Mary's Secretary?].' 'Je suis logé chez le père de Jehan Laudre, que joublioys à vous recommander. Il désire par vostre moyen que la Royne lui face avoir chez le Roy son filz un office de vallet de chambre.' Edinburgh, 15 August. *Calendar of MSS Hatfield*, part III, p. 61.

1586 James Lauder gone to France (1585/6). McQuaid.

1588 Item to James Lauder, musiciane, in contentatioune of his meit and drink £160. *Exchequer Rolls*, vol. XXI, 413.

1590 Named in order of the Household, reorganised after the King's marriage.

1591 Mair allowit to the comptar be speciall command and delyverance of the kingis majestie... to James Lauder musician in part payment of thre hundreth thre scoir pundis for his intertinement of thir thrie yeiris bigane: the sowme of £180. *Register of the Secret Seal*. (This appears to cover 1588/9, 1589/90 and 1590/1.)

1593 James Lawder, among other musicians, appointed by the Burgh Council of Edinburgh to examine Mr Jhoun Chalmers in his knowledge 'in playing upon the virginalls'. *Burgh Records of Edinburgh*, vol. 1589–1603 (ed. 1927), p. 103.

1614 His widow, Jean Hay, died, a woman of substance. Edinburgh Testaments, 15 July (McQuaid)

APPENDIX III

DOCUMENTS ON ALEXANDER MONTGOMERIE

1 Alexander Montgomerie, eques Montanus vulgo vocatus, nobilissimo sanguine, Pindarus Scoticus, ingenii elegantia et carminis venustate nulli veterum secundus, regi charissimus Jacobo, qui poeticen mirifice eo aevo amplexabatur, quique poetas claros sodales suos vulgo vocari voluit, multis ingenii sui monimentis patriam Linguam ditavit et exornavit: ad me, qui impubes patriam reliqui, paucorum notitia pervenit...

In his Cerasus et Vaccinium, Lib 1, poema divinum, quo amores suos descripserat; per cerasum amicae sublimis dignitatem, per vaccinium contemnendos inferioris et fastiditae amasiae amplexus intelligens...

Obiit magno regis dolore, qui ingenii ipsius festiva comitate non vulgariter oblectabatur, anno MDXCI.

Dempster, *Historia Ecclesiastica Gentis Scotorum*

2
Epigramma
Dum moritur fidei vates Montgomrius ardens
    Romanae et sanctae Relligionis Amor
Dira Picarditas invaserat ira latrantes
    Nec tolerant sacris hunc tumulare locis.
Nobilitas favet affines dant munera, cives
    Hortantur, studio Rex favet ipse, pio.
Nulla tamen rabidos Calvini jura catellos
    Flectunt, o scelerum, monstra odiosa Deo!
Donec regali comitatu satellite vatem
    Arma et vis tumulant, dum cecidere preces.

'Thomas Duff'
Arctaunum, *c.* 1616

263

APPENDIX IV

'THE NINE MUSES' DANCE

The way of dancing 'The Nine Muses' was as follows:

> A duble forward and single backe al
> IX togeather/then the first iii pase
> forwards with ii singles and a duble and to
> torne backe to theire companie and so the
> next etc. and then the last to honour
> to the middell and imbrace and the
> middel to torne to the first and honour
> and imbrace/then one of eithyr there to
> pass rond about the midell into his
> owne place and so the othyr with a soft
> pace/And then so after with a galliard
> pace

This description seems to me clearly to indicate a dance-pair: 'obeisance'/first and second trace/ third trace/the three traces repeated to the tune now in triple time.

I imagine 'The Nine Muses' as danced in a 'square of three' formation. The first phrase of the instruction covers the 'obeisance', which by custom preceded the figured dance and its tune; for it the musicians played chords or introductory phrases of music.

$$
\begin{array}{ccc}
1 & 2 & 3 \\
4 & 5 & 6 \\
7 & 8 & 9
\end{array}
\quad \uparrow \qquad \text{all dancers facing this way}
$$

Trace I (bars 1–7 of the tune, played three times through): dancers 1, 2 and 3 execute two singles and a double forwards (8 beats) and turn back to face the others (4 beats); then dancers 4, 5 and 6 do likewise; then dancers 7, 8 and 9 likewise, ending however facing outwards.

Trace II (bars 7–11 played twice through): dancers 7, 8 and 9 turn to face 4, 5 and 6, and each honours and embraces the dancer opposite him, returning to his place; then dancers 4, 5 and 6 do likewise with 1, 2 and 3.

Trace III (bars 11–15 played twice through): dancers 1, 4 and 7 step round dancers 2, 5 and 8 respectively and return each to his own place; then dancers 3, 6 and 9 do likewise with dancers 2, 5 and 8.

The three traces are then repeated to the tune, played now in triple time and slightly more quickly—'in galliard pace'.

The first of the dance-pair is after the fashion of a pavan—a pavan being based on 'two singles and a double' 'in duple time' (Thoinot Arbeau). Instructions for performing 'obeisance', 'single' and 'double' will be found in *Dances of England and France from 1450 to 1600* by Mabel Dolmetsch (Routledge and Kegan Paul, London, 1949), chapter v, 'The Pavan'.

264

APPENDIX V

Check-list of source-books of early Scottish court-song (reproduced by kind permission of The Royal Musical Association)

AFC   Cantus part-book marked 'A.F.1611' [= Alexander Forbes of Tolquhon,] called 'The Tolquhon Cantus': the Library of the Fitzwilliam Museum, Cambridge.

AM   'The Art of Music collecit out of all ancient doctouris of music' *c.* [1580]. Second volume only survives: BM. Add. 4911.

B   Balcarres Lute-Book [*c.* 1690]: in the library of the Earl of Crawford and Balcarres.

DB   Duncan Burnett's music-book [*c.* 1610] (Master of the song-school in Glasgow). In the library of the Earl of Dalhousie: Panmure MS. 10.

DF   Dowglas-Fische[ar] part-books [*c.* 1550] (called the 'Dunkeld' part-books): Edinburgh University Library MS. 64.

DVB   Dublin Virginal Book [*c.* 1570]: Library of Trinity College, Dublin, D. 3. 30. Edited by John Ward for *The Wellesley Edition* (no. 3; 1954).

ERVB   Elizabeth Rogers' Virginal Book, 1656: BM. Add. 10337.

fi   Manuscript copy of John Forbes, Cantus, *Songs and Fancies* first edition with additional music [*c.* 1662]: The Ruggles-Brise Collection, Sandeman Library, Perth.

Ga   John Gamble's Commonplace Book [*c.* 1660]: New York Public Library. Described by Vincent Duckles in *Journal of American Musicological Society* (Summer 1948). An edition of the manuscript is promised by Dr Duckles.

Gr   David Gregory MS. [*c.* 1690]: Edinburgh University Library MS. DC. 1. 75.

Gu   James Guthrie MS. [*c.* 1650]: Edinburgh University Library MS. Laing III. 111.

LAK   Lady Ann Ker's music book [*c.* 1625–1635]: National Library of Scotland MS. 5448.

LF   Louis de France's music-book [*c.* 1680]: Edinburgh University Library MS. Laing III. 491. (Louis de France was Master of the song-school in Aberdeen, then in Edinburgh.)

MacA   Alexander MacAlman's music-book [*c.* 1650]. In the possession of Miss Gregorson of Edinburgh.

MB   David Melvill's bassus part-book, 1604: BM. Add. 36484.

MR   David Melvill's 'Ane buik of roundells, 1612'. In the Library of Congress, Washington, D.C. Edited by G. Bantock and H. O. Anderton as *The Melvill Book of Roundels* (Roxburghe Club, 1916).

RC   William Mure of Rowallan's cantus part-book [*c.* 1627–37]: Edinburgh University Library MS. Laing III. 488.

RE   Robert Edwards' commonplace-book *c.* [1630–65]. In the library of the Earl of Dalhousie: Panmure MS. 11.

RL   William Mure of Rowallan's lute-book [*c.* 1615]: Edinburgh University Library MS. Laing III. 487.

[Ru]   Russell MS., known to John Leyden, who noted variant readings from it against items in WSC.

Sk   John Skene of Hallyards' lute-book [*c.* 1625[: National Library of Scotland Adv. MS.

5.2.15. Incomplete transcription published in *Ancient Scotish Melodies*, edited by William Dauney (Edinburgh, 1838).

Sq   John Squyer's music-book, 1699–1701: Edinburgh University Library MS. Laing III. 490.

Str   Robert Gordon of Straloch's lute-book, 1627–9. Incomplete transcription (Graham, 1847): National Library of Scotland Adv. MS. 5.2.18. For title-list of contents of original see W. Dauney, *Ancient Scotish Melodies* (Edinburgh, 1838), p. 368.

TW   Thomas Wode's part-books, 1562–*c.* 1592 (with later additions by other hands, after 1606 and *c.* 1620.)

TWCi   Cantus: Edinburgh University Library MS. Laing III. 483.

TWCii   Cantus (second copy): Edinburgh University Library MS. Dk. 5. 14.

TWQ   Quintus: Library of Trinity College, Dublin, F. 5.13.

TWA   Altus: BM. Add. 33933.

TWT   Tenor: Edinburgh University Library MS. Laing III. 483.

TWBi   Bassus: Edinburgh University Library MS. Laing III. 483.

TWBii   Bassus (second copy): Edinburgh University Library MS. Dk. 5.15.

[WK]   William Ker's lute-book: See David Laing's list of contents transcribed from the original: Edinburgh University Library, manuscript note.

WSC   William Stirling's cantus part-book, 1639 ['John Leyden's vocal MS.']: National Library of Scotland Adv. MS. 5.2.14.

X   Lyra-viol MS. *c.* 1690 ['John Leyden's lyra-viol MS.']: National Library of Scotland Adv. MS. 5.2.19 (transcript).   (K.E.)

The 'Leyden Lyra-viol MS.' was not available for study at first hand as it is inaccessible in private hands. It was apparently made by or for a Scottish nobleman in the 1670s.

The Robert Taitt Music-book, made in 1676 by Robert Taitt, Master of the song-school in Lauder, is now in the William Andrews Clark Memorial Library, Los Angeles. It was described and discussed by W. H. Rubsamen in 'Scottish and English Music of the Renaissance in a newly discovered Manuscript', *Festschrift Heinrich Besseler* (Leipzig, 1962). His concordances are, however, incomplete and at several points it is difficult to agree with his findings. First-hand study of this manuscript was not possible nor was request made for words-and-music, as Dr Rubsamen hopes to publish the manuscript. Three stanzas of verbal text were kindly supplied to me in his transcription by Dr Rubsamen on request.

The 'Panmure' music manuscripts from the library of the Earl of Dalhousie are deposited with the National Library of Scotland.

Sources for Jacobean songs are given in the footnotes when the songs are mentioned.

The Pendlebury Music Library of Cambridge University has a microfilm of the Dissertation of Vincent Duckles.

BIBLIOGRAPHY

Introductory Note

The following works discuss music in earlier Scotland or earlier Scottish music in a European context:

H. G. Farmer, 'Music in Mediaeval Scotland' and *A History of Music in Scotland.* Pioneer research was done by Dr Harry M. Willsher in an unpublished doctoral dissertation, University of St Andrews 1945. Studies concerned with 'the native air' or Scottish 'Eigengut' of folk-song are William Dauney, *Ancient Scotish Melodies* (from the Skene MS.) with a dissertation, and Nelly Diem, *Beiträge zur Geschichte der Schottischen Musik im XVII. Jahrhundert*, which is inaccurate and unsystematic in entitling of MSS.

Paul H. Lang in *Music in Western Civilisation* includes Scotland in discussion of cultural relations in western Europe, drawing on Farmer. Gustave Reese, in *Music in the Middle Ages*, discusses MS. Wolfenbüttel 677 'written in the fourteenth century very likely at St Andrews, in which some of the compositions may be insular'; in his *Music in the Renaissance* he mentions work of the Scottish musicians Robert Carver (sacred music) and Robert Johnson. Donald Jay Grout in *A History of Western Music* mentions the *Scottish Psalter* of 1564. Nan Cooke Carpenter in *Music in the Mediaeval and Renaissance Universities* treats of musical culture in the Scottish Universities of St Andrews, Glasgow and Aberdeen.

F. L. Harrison in *Music in Medieval Britain* discusses extant music of Scotland in its earliest phase.

General Bibliography

Aldis H. G. *A list of books printed in Scotland before 1700.* Edinburgh Bibliographical Society Publications, Edinburgh 1904.

Alexander, Sir William. *See* Kastner, L. E.

Allen, D. C. *Francis Meres's Treatise 'Poetrie': A Critical Edition.* University of Illinois Studies in Language and Literature 1933.

Arbeau, Thoinot (pseudonym for Jean Tabouret). *Orchésographie* Lengres 1588 and 1596: English version *Orchesography*, translated by C. W. Beaumont, London 1925.

Arber, E. (ed.) *Hekatompathia or Passionate Centurie of Love* by T. Watson (1582). London 1870.

Aston, T. H. (ed.) *Crisis in Europe 1560–1660.* London 1965.

Ault, N. (ed.) *Elizabethan Lyrics.* New York 1960.

Ayton, Sir Robert, *See* Gullans, C. B. and Shire, H. M.

Balfour Paul Sir J. *The Scots Peerage.* 9 vols. Edinburgh 1904.

Bennett, J. A. W. (ed) *Devotional Pieces in Verse and Prose.* Scottish Text Society, Edinburgh, 1948–9.

Beveridge, J. 'Two Scottish Thirteenth-century Songs', *Proceedings of the Society of Antiquaries of Scotland* 1938–9.

Block, K. S. (ed.) *Ludus Coventriae or The Play called Corpus Christi.* Early English Text Society 1922.

Borland, L. 'Montgomerie and the French Poets of the early sixteenth century,' *Modern Philology,* XI (1913).

Bossy, J. 'The character of Elizabethan Catholicism' in *Crisis in Europe 1560-1660*, edited by T. H. Aston, London 1965.

Brett, P. 'The English Consort Song 1570–1625.' *Proceedings of the Royal Musical Association*, LXXXVIII (1961–2). *See also* Fellowes.

Brotanek, R. 'Philotus: Ein Beitrag zur Geschichte des Dramas in Schottland', *Festschrift zum VIII Allgemeinen Deutschen Neuphilologenlage in Wien*, 1898.

Brown, A. (ed.) *Tisdale's Virginal Book* London 1966.

Buchanan, G. *Opera Omnia*. Edinburgh 1715.

Buchanan, G. *Georgii Buchanani Scoti Poemata*. Edinburgh 1615. *See also* Gatherer, W. A.

Burel, J. '*Ane Passage of ane Pilger*.' Unique copy, BM. C. 21, b. 39.

Byrd, William. *See* Fellowes, E. H.

Calderwood, D. *See* Thomson, T.

Carpenter, N. C. *Music in Mediaeval and Renaissance Universities*. Oklahoma 1958.

Cawley, A. C. *The Wakefield Pageants in the Towneley Cycle*. Manchester 1963.

Chambers, R. (ed.). *The Songs of Scotland prior to Burns*. Edinburgh n.d. (nineteenth century)

Chappell, W. *Popular Music of the Olden Time*. 2 vols. London 1853–9.

Chappell, W. *Old English Popular Music*. Revised by H. E. Wooldridge. 2 vols. London 1893.

Charlton, H. B. *See* Kastner, L. E.

Child, F. J. *The English and Scottish Popular Ballads*. Boston 1857–9. 5 vols. Reprinted in 3 vols, New York 1957.

Coates, W. *See* Dart, Thurston.

Cohen, G. (ed.) *Œuvres complètes de P. de Ronsard*. Mayonne 1950.

Constable, Henry, *See* Grundy, J.

Corkery, D. *The Hidden Ireland*. Dublin 1956.

Craigie, W. A. (ed.) *Maitland Quarto Manuscript*, Scottish Text Society, Edinburgh 1915.

Craigie, W. A. (ed.) *The Maitland Folio Manuscript*. 2 vols. Scottish Text Society, Edinburgh 1919–27.

Craigie, W. A. (ed.) *The Historie of Judith, 1584* by Thomas Hudson, Scottish Text Society, Edinburgh 1941.

Cranstoun, J. (ed.) *The Poems of Alexander Montgomerie*. Scottish Text Society, Edinburgh, 1886–7.

Cranstoun, J. (ed.) *Satirical Poems of the Time of the Reformation*. 3 vols. Edinburgh 1889–93.

Crockett, T. (ed.) *The Poems of John Stewart of Baldynneis*. Scottish Text Society, Edinburgh 1913.

Crum, M. 'A Manuscript of John Wilson's Songs', *The Library*, Fifth Series, March 1955.

Cunningham, J. P. *Dancing in the Inns of Court*. London 1965.

Dart, Thurston and Coates, W. (eds.) *Jacobean Consort Music*, Musica Britannica, IX. London. 1955.

Dart, Thurston. 'New Sources of Virginal Music', *Music and Letters*, XXXV, no. 2 (1954).

Dauney, W. *Ancient Scotish Melodies* from a manuscript of the reign of King James VI with an introductory enquiry illustrative of the History of the Music of Scotland. Maitland Club, Edinburgh 1838.

Dempster, T. *See* Irving D.

Dick, J. C. *The Songs of Robert Burns*. London 1903.

Dickinson, W. C. (ed.) *History of the Reformation in Scotland*, by J. Knox. 2 vols. London 1949.

Diem, Nelly. *Beiträge zur Geschichte der Schottischen Musik im XVII. Jahrhundert*. Zürich and Leipzig n.d.

Dilworth, M. 'New Light on Alexander Montgomerie', *The Bibliotheck*, IV, no. 6 (1965).

Dilworth, M. 'The Latin Translator of *The Cherrie and the Slae*', *Studies in Scottish Literature*, v, no. 2 (1967).

Donald, A. K. (ed.) *Poems of Alexander Scott*. Early English Text Society, London 1902.

Douen, Orentin. *Clément Marot et le Psautier Huguenot*. 2 vols. Paris 1878–9.

Drummond, W. of Hawthornden. See Kastner, L. E.

Duckles, V. H. 'The Gamble Manuscript as a Source of Continuo Song in England', *Journal of American Musicological Society* (1948).

Duckles, V. H. 'John Gamble's Commonplace Book: a Critical Edition of Drexel MS. 4257 in New York Public Library.' Unpublished doctoral dissertation, University of California 1953.

Dunbar, John. *Epigrammaton*. London 1616.

Dunbar, William. *See* Mackenzie, W. M.

Dunlop, G. A. 'John Stewart of Baldynneis…the Scottish Desportes', *Scottish Historical Review*, XII (1915).

Durkan, J. 'Cultural Background in sixteenth-century Scotland', *The Innes Review*, no. 2 (1959).

Elliott, K. 'Music of Scotland 1500–1700.' Doctoral dissertation at the University of Cambridge 1959. Vol. I. unpublished, vol. II published as Elliott and Shire, *Music of Scotland 1500-1700*.

Elliott, K. 'Robert Edwards' Commonplace-Book and Scots Musical History', *Scottish Studies*, v (1961).

Elliott, K. and Shire, H. M. (eds.) *Music of Scotland 1500-1700*, Musica Britannica, XV. Second edition, London 1964. *Music of Scotland 1500-1700*, Selections: *see* p. 273.

Elliott, K. 'Church Music at Dunkell', *Music and Letters*, XLV (July 1964).

Elliott, K. *Cromleck's Lilt*. Glasgow and London 1964.

Elliott, K. (ed.) *Musa Jocosa Mihi*. Twelve songs for voice and keyboard by Lawes, Wilson, Blagrave, Playford and anon. to poems by Sir Robert Ayton. London 1965.

Evans, W. *Henry Lawes Musician and Friend of Poets*. Modern Language Association of America. New York 1941.

Expert, H. *Monuments de la Musique Française au temps de la Renaissance*, v, no. 26. Paris 1926.

Fairholt, F. W. (ed.) *Poems and Songs relating to the Duke of Buckingham*. Percy Society XXIX. London 1850.

Farley, Robert. *Naologia, sive Inventa Navis*, n.p. n.d. (? 1635). Copy in the Houghton Library, Harvard University. *See* C. Gullans, *The Works of Sir Robert Ayton*, pp. 88–9.

Farmer, H. G. *A History of Music in Scotland*. London, n.d.

Farmer, H. G. 'Music in Mediaeval Scotland', *Proceedings of the Royal Philosophical Society of Glasgow* (1926–7).

Fellowes, E. H. (ed.) 'The English Madrigalists', *Psalms, Sonnets and Songs*, XIV (1588). Revised by P. Brett. London 1963.

Fellowes, E. H. (ed.) *The Collected Works of William Byrd*. Revised by P. Brett. London 1964.

Fergusson, Sir J. (ed.) *The Green Garden*. London 1946.

Les Fêtes de la Renaissance (symposium). *See* Jacquot, J.

Feuillerat, A. G. *Documents Relating to the Office of the Revels in the time of Queen Elizabeth*. Louvain 1908.

Fleming, Motherwell, W. and Smith, J. (eds.). *Rob Stene's Dreame*, attributed to A. Montgomerie. Glasgow 1836.

Fowler, William. *See* Meikle, H. W.

Friedman, A. B. *The Ballad Revival*. Chicago 1964.

Friedmann, H. *The Symbolical Goldfinch*. Bollingen Series VII. Washington, D.C. 1946.

Furnivall, F. J. (ed.) *Works of William Lander*. Early English Text Society 1864–70.

Gatherer, W. A. (ed.) *The Tyrannous Reign of Mary Stewart*, by G. Buchanan. Edinburgh 1958. *See also* Buchanan, G.

Greenlaw, E., Osgood, C. G., Padelford, F. M., and Heffner, R. (eds.) *Works of Edmund Spenser*. 9 vols. Baltimore, 1943.

Grenier, Abel (ed.). *Œuvres Complètes de C. Marot*. Only vol. 1 published. Paris, n.d.

Grosart, A. B. (ed.) *The Arbor of Amitie* (1568), *Neue Sonets and poetic Pamphlets* (1568) and *Howell his Devises* (1581) by Thomas Howell. Occasional issues, Blackburn 1879.

Grout, D. J. *A History of Western Music*. London 1960.

Grove, G. *Dictionary of Music and Musicians*. London 1940.

Grundy, J. (ed.) *Poems of Henry Constable*. Liverpool 1960.

Gullans, C. B. (ed.) *The Works of Sir Robert Ayton* (*The English and Latin Poems*). Scottish Text Society, Edinburgh 1963.

Hamer, D. (ed.) *The Works of Sir David Lindsay*. 4 vols. Scottish Text Society, Edinburgh, 1929–36.

Hannay, R. K. *See* Hay, D.

Harrison, F. L. *Music in Medieval Britain*. London 1958.

Hay, D. and Hannay, R. K. (eds.) *Letters of James V, 1513–42*. Edinburgh 1954.

Heffner, R. *See* Greenlaw, E.

Henderson, G. D. *The Burning Bush*. Edinburgh 1957.

Henderson, T. F. *Scottish Vernacular Literature: a History*. Edinburgh 1910.

Hendy, A. von. 'The Free Thrall: a Study of *The Kingis Quair*', *Studies in Scottish Literature*, II, no. 3, University of South Carolina, 1965.

Heseltine, G. C. (ed.) *The Kalendar and Compost of Shepherds*, translated by R. Copland in 1518 from *Le Compost et Kalendrier des bons Bergiers* by G. Marchand (Paris 1493). First translated into Scots as *The Kalendar of Shyppars*, Paris 1503, and into English, London 1506.

Hill, G. *See* Montgomerie, W.

The Historie and Life of King James the Sext. (Anon. *c.* 1584.) Bannatyne Club, no. 13. Edinburgh 1825.

Howell, Thomas. *See* Grosart, A. B., Raleigh, Sir W.

Hudson, Thomas. *See* Craigie, W. A.

Hume, Alexander. *See* Lawson, A.

Huizinga, J. *Homo Ludens: A Study of the Play-Element in Culture*. Translated by R. F. C. Hull, London 1949.

Hutchison, H. S. P. 'The St Andrews Psalter: transcription and critical study of Thomas Wode's Psalter.' Unpublished thesis for Mus. Doc. University of Edinburgh 1957.

Irving, D. (ed.) *Historia Ecclesiastica Gentis Scotorum* by T. Dempster (1627). 2 vols. Edinburgh 1829.

Jack, R. D. S. 'Montgomerie and the Pirates', *Studies in Scottish Literature*, V, no. 2 (1968).

Jack, R. D. S. 'Scottish Sonneteer and Welsh Metaphysical', *Studies in Scottish Literature*, III, no. 4 (1967).

Jacquot, J. (ed.) *Les Fêtes de la Renaissance* (Symposium). Centre National de la Recherche Scientifique, Paris 1961.

Johnston, G. H. *The Heraldry of the Murrays*. Edinburgh and London 1910.

Kastner, L. E. (ed.) *Poetical Works of W. Drummond of Hawthornden*. 2 vols. Manchester 1913.

Kastner, L. E. and Charlton, H. B. (eds.) *Poetical Works of Sir William Alexander*. Scottish Text Society, Edinburgh 1927.

Kinnear, T. (ed.) *Poetical Works* by Sir David Murray of Gorthy, Edinburgh 1823.

Kinsley, J. (ed.) *Scottish Poetry: A Critical Survey*. London 1955.

Knox, J. *See* Dickinson, W. C.

Laing, D. (ed.) *Poems of Alexander Scott*. Edinburgh 1821.

Lang, P. H. *Music in Western Civilisation*. London 1941.

Lauder, William. *See* Furnivall.

Laumonier, P. (ed.) *Œuvres complètes de P. de Ronsard*. Paris 1925.

Laumonier, P. (ed.) *Les Œuvres de P. de Ronsard*. Paris 1914-19.

Lawson, A. (ed.) *Works of Alexander Hume*. Scottish Text Society, Edinburgh 1901-2.

Lefkowitz, M. *William Lawes*. London 1960.

Lesure, F. 'Autour de Clément Marot et de ses Musiciens', *Revue de Musicologie* XXXVIII (1950).

Lesure, F. and Thibault, G. *Bibliographie des Editions d'Adrian le Roy et Robert Ballard (1551-1598)*. C.N.R.S. Société Française de Musicologie, Paris 1955.

Lewis, C. S. *Spenser's Images of Life*. Cambridge 1967.

Lilly, Joseph (ed.) *A Collection of 79 black-letter ballads and broadsides*. London 1867.

Lindsay, Sir David. *See* Hamer, D.

Lithgow, W. *Poetical Remains 1618-1660*. Edinburgh 1863.

Lumsden, D. *An Anthology of English Lute Music*. London 1954.

Lyndsay. *See* Lindsay.

McDiarmid, M. P. 'Notes on the Poems of John Stewart of Baldynneis', *Review of English Studies*, XXIV (1948).

McDiarmid, M. P. 'John Stewart of Baldynneis', *Scottish Historical Review*, XXIX (1950).

McDiarmid, M. P. 'Some Versions of Poems by Sir Robert Aytoun and Sir William Alexander', *Notes and Queries*, n.s. IV (1957).

McDiarmid, M. P. 'Philotus: a play of the Scottish Renaissance', *Forum for Modern Language Studies*, III, no. 3 (1967).

McGrail, T. H. *The Life and Works of Sir William Alexander, first Earl of Stirling*: Edinburgh 1940.

Mackenzie, A. M. 'The Renaissance Poets (1) Scots and English' in *Scottish Poetry: A Critical Survey*, ed. J. Kinsley. London 1955.

Mackenzie, A. M. *An Historical Survey of Scottish Literature to 1714*. London 1933.

Mackenzie, W. M. (ed.) *The Poems of William Dunbar*. London 1932.

McQuaid, J. 'Musicians of the Scottish Reformation'. Unpublished doctoral dissertation, University of Edinburgh, 1949.

MacQueen, J. 'Two Versions of Henryson's Fabillis', *The Innes Review*, XIV (1963).

Maitland, J. A. Fuller, and Squire, W. Barclay (eds.) *The Fitzwilliam Virginal Book*. 2 vols. New York 1963.

Mâle, E. *L'art réligieux du troisième siècle en France*. Paris 1898. Translated by Dora Nussey as *The Gothic Image*. London 1961.

Manuscripts of the Earl of Mar and Kellie. Historical Manuscripts Commission 1904.

Marchand, G. *See* Heseltine, G. C.

Marot, C. *See* Grenier, Abel.

Meikle, H. W. (ed.) *The Works of William Fowler*. 3 vols. Third volume edited by Meikle, Craigie, and J. Purves. Scottish Text Society, Edinburgh, 1914-39.

Mitchell, A. F. (ed.) *The Gude and Godlie Ballatis*. Scottish Text Society, Edinburgh 1897.

Montgomerie, Alexander. *See* Cranstoun, J. Fleming, Shire, H. M., Stevenson, A. and Wood, H. H.

Montgomerie, W. *The Montgomerie Manuscripts 1603-1706.* Belfast 1830, re-edited by G. Hill, 1869.

Montgomery, B. de. *Origin and History of the Montgomerys.* Edinburgh 1948.

Motherwell, W. *See* Fleming.

Mure, W. of Rowallan, *See* Tough, W.

Murray, Sir David. *See* Kinnear, T.

Napier, M. *See* Russell, M.

Naylor, E. W. *An Elizabethan Virginal Book.* London 1905.

Osgood, C. G. *See* Greenlaw, E.

Padelford, M. *See* Greenlaw, E.

Pollock, Sir F. (ed.) *Table Talk of John Selden.* London 1927.

Prunières, H. *Le Ballet de Cour en France.* Paris 1913.

Raby, F. J. E. 'Philomena praevia temporis amoeni' in *Mélanges Joseph de Ghellinck.* 2 vols. Gembloux 1951.

Raleigh, Sir W. (ed.) *Devises* by Thomas Howell (1581). Oxford 1906.

Reese, G. *Music in the Middle Ages.* London 1940.

Reese, G. *Music in the Renaissance.* London 1954.

Ritchie, W. Tod (ed.) *The Bannatyne Manuscript.* 4 vols. Scottish Text Society, Edinburgh 1927–32.

Rogers, C. *The History of the Chapel Royal of Scotland.* Edinburgh 1882.

Ronsard, P. de. *See* Cohen, G., Laumonier, P.

Root, M. E. *Inchmahome Priory.* H.M.S.O. 1947.

Ross, I. 'The Form and Matter of *The Cherrie and the Slae'. University of Texas Studies in English,* XXXVIII (1958).

Rubsamen, W. H. 'Scottish and English Music of the Renaissance in a newly discovered Manuscript'. *Festschrift Heinrich Besseler.* Leipzig 1962.

Russell, M. and Napier, M. (eds.) *History of the Church of Scotland* by J. Spottiswoode. 3 vols. Spottiswoode Society, Edinburgh 1847–51.

Scott, Alexander. *See* Donald, A. K., Laing, D. and Scott, Alexander.

Scott, Alexander (ed.) *The Poems of Alexander Scott* (c. *1530*-c. *1584*). Edinburgh 1952.

Shafer, R. *The English Ode to 1660.* Princeton 1918.

Shire, H. M. 'Scottish Song-book, 1611', *Saltire Review,* I, no. 2 (1954).

Shire, H. M. 'Musical Servitors to Queen Mary Stuart', *Music and Letters,* XI, no. 1 (1959).

Shire, H. M. (ed.) *Alexander Montgomerie: Selected Songs and Poems.* Edinburgh 1960.

Shire, H. M. *Poems and Songs of Sir Robert Ayton.* Ninth of May II. Cambridge 1961.

Shire, H. M. 'Robert Edwards' Commonplace-Book and Scots Literary History, *Scottish Studies,* V (1961).

Shire, H. M. *The Thrissil, the Rois and the Flour-de-lys.* Ninth of May III. Cambridge 1962.

Shire, H. M. 'Alexander Montgomerie. The oppositione of the court to conscience...' *Studies in Scottish Literature,* III, no. 3 (1966).

Shire, H. M. *See* Elliott, K.

Smith, J. *See* Fleming.

Spenser, Edmund. *See* Greenlaw, E.

Spottiswoode, J. *See* Russell, M.

Squire, W. Barclay. *See* Maitland, J. A. Fuller.

Stafford, H. G. *King James VI of Scotland and the throne of England.* New York 1940.

Stampfer, J. L. 'The Cantos of Mutability', *University of Toronto Quarterly,* XXI, no. 2 (1952).

Sternfeld, F. W. 'Vautrollier's Printing of Lasso's *Recueil du Mellange*, London 1570', *Annales Musicologiques*, v (1957).

Stevens, J. *Music and Poetry in the Early Tudor Court*. London 1961.

Stevenson, A. (ed.) *Poems of Alexander Montgomerie; Supplementary Volume*. Scottish Text Society, Edinburgh 1910.

Stevenson, J. (ed.) *The Correspondence of Robert Bowes...ambassador of Queen Elizabeth in the court of Scotland*. Surtees Society Publications, xiv, London 1842.

Stewart, John of Baldynneis. *See* Crockett, T.

Thomson, T. (ed.) *The History of the Kirk of Scotland*, by D. Calderwood. 8 vols. Woodrow Society, Edinburgh 1842–9. Originally printed (1678) as *The true history of the Church of Scotland*.

Tough, W. (ed.) *Works of W. Mure of Rowallan*. 2 vols. Scottish Text Society, Edinburgh 1892.

Ward, J. 'Music for *A Handefull of Pleasant Delites*', *Journal of the American Musicological Society*, (1957).

Ward, J. (ed.) *The Dublin Virginal Manuscript*. Wellesley Edition no. 3. 1954.

Warner, W. *Albion's England*. London 1592.

Watson, T. *See* Arber, E.

Westcott, A. F. *New Poems of James I of England*. New York 1911.

Whitney, G. *A Choice of Emblemes*. Leyden 1586.

Willsher, H. M. 'Music in Scotland during three centuries, (1450–1750)', Dissertation for Ph.D., St Andrews University 1945.

Willson, D. H. *King James VI and I*. London 1956.

Wood, H. H. (ed.) *The Cherrie and the Slae*, by A. Montgomerie. London 1937.

Yates, F. A. *The French Academies of the Sixteenth Century*. London 1947.

Selections from 'Music of Scotland 1500–1700'

1 *Seven songs for S.A.T.B.:* nos. 40–42, 48–50, 53.
2 *Six songs for S.A.T.B.:* nos. 35, 39, 45, 54, 55, 56.
4 *Eleven solo songs:* nos. 57–62, 64, 68–9, 72–3.
5 *Three solo songs:* nos. 65, 67, 70.

Music on gramophone record

Musik fyne: songs and dances of the Scottish Court: Scottish Records, no. 33 SR 133.

INDEX OF NAMES

(including personal names, places, buildings and battles). Numbers in bold indicate main entries

INDEX OF SUBJECTS

Numbers in bold indicate main entries

acting, action-song, 9, 66, 172, 178–9 (*see also* Bacon, 'Essay')

Anglo–Scottish relations, *see* England.

'answer' to poem or song, 4, 20, 29–31, 60, 62, 87, 90, 161
  as '*imitatio*' or 'overgoing', 54, 64–6, 216, 236–8, 258
  translation/imitation, 40–1, 158

Apollo, Royal (Phoebus), 91–2, 94–7, 98, 101–4, 111, 128–9, 132, 182, 201–2, 209, 219, 225 (*see also* Cupid, Venus)

ballad (ballade, ballat) 10–23, 12–14, 25–37 (*see also* currency);
  of tradition, 15, 173, 194–5, 231 (folk-song)

broadsides (tunes or texts), 12–14, 28–9, 32–7, 163–4, 166, 169–72, 179, 189, 214, 233, 256

carol, 20, 27, 28

Castalian poetry
  the band, 85, 90–106, 115
  smoothness, 97, 115, 228
  stanzas invented, 142–4, 164–8, 173–4, 179
  song, *see* song
  sonnet, *see* sonnet, France
  the King's second volume, 110, 221, 228
  poulter's measure, 188, 221
  Castalians, younger, 181–204; late, 207–12, 215–23, 228–9;
  last Castalian, *see* Ayton, Sir Robert
  see also James VI, France, England, Italy, named poets and musicians

Catholic church in Scotland before Reformation, 38, 49–51, 57; music, 1–5, 70; musicians, *see* Carver, Robert Johnson, Fethy, Blackehall, Scott; poetry, 1–5: partly preserved by Bannatyne, 12, 21–3 (*see also* Popes)

Catholicism
  policy: European, 67–8, 77–8, 82–3, 85–6, 110–11; in Scotland, 78, 93, 203
  conspiracy, 104, 111; agents, 107, 111
  partisans, 93, 112–13
  'Catholic earls', 114
  Catholics in England, 82, 136
  devotions, 148
  poets, *see* Constable, Southwell, Montgomerie

cavalier(s), 204, 214, 223–9
  lyric, 191, 194, 204–6 (*see also* Ayton, Sir Robert)
  Cavalier, MS anthology of Scots, 230, 234, 246

Celtic culture, 6, 82, 90, 127 (*see also* Ireland)

ceremony, 6, 81, 89, 93, 98, 101, 157, 179, 225–6, 233, 235, 255, 258
  baptism, 178, 180
  coronation, 180
  espousal to Christ, 148
  wedding, 2, 151–6, 158, 191–2
  wedding psalm, 7, 70, 116
  welcome, 2, 47
  (*See also* farewell, funeral song, gifts, 'joyous entry', 'mynd'

chansonniers and *chansons* cited from them, 39, 40–3, 46, 63–5, 141, 144, 151–60, 162–3, 214
  Bibliographie, 151

Chapel Royal of Scotland
  refounded, 3, 4, 57–8, 73
  at Stirling, 49, 51–3, 70
  musicians supported, 8
  transmission and preservation of part-music through, 33
  old Scots and other part-music in library of, 1, 259
  (*see also* Fethy, Scott, Blackehall, the Hudsons)

Cherrie and the Slae, The, subjects in
  allegory a language for poet and audience, 117–20
  genre as meaningful pattern, 121–3, 124, 126
  matters of love, of state, of religion, 117–38
  allegorical figures, 126, 134
  landscape, 120–3, 127–9, 134–5
  symbols, correspondences: trees, 124–6; fruits, 125–6, 128; birds, 131; beasts, 132

cittern, 1, 230–1, 233 (*see also* Robert Edwards MS)

conceit (pun), 188–93 (*see also* Greek, Renaissance)

conceit, name, 125, 193; Ayton, 218–19, 239; Craig, 219, 224; Dyer, 223; Lauder, 77; Murray, 220; Raleigh, 90; Scott, 47
  (*see also* Apollo, Cupid, Renaisance pun)

'conceit, dark', 77, 105, 117–38

contest
  of arms, 6, 31, 83, 148–9
  horse-race, 87
  bardic, 4, 80, 120, 209, 257
  (*see also* 'flyting', answer (or overgoing), *débat*)

costume, 83, 172, 178 (*see also* acting)

counter-Reformation
  France, 67–9
  Spain, 82–6, 112–16